WITHDRAWN

Garland Studies
in Medieval Literature

Editors

Christopher Kleinhenz
University of Wisconsin–Madison

Paul E. Szarmach
State University of New York at Binghamton

Garland Studies
in Medieval Literature

HENRYSON
AND THE MEDIEVAL ARTS
OF RHETORIC

ROBERT L. KINDRICK

Volume 8
GARLAND STUDIES IN MEDIEVAL LITERATURE

Garland Publishing, Inc.
New York & London
1993

Library of Congress Cataloging-in-Publication Data

Kindrick, Robert L.
   Henryson and the medieval arts of rhetoric / by Robert L.
Kindrick.
      p.   cm. — (Garland reference library of the humanities ;
vol. 1681) (Garland studies in medieval literature ; vol. 8)
   Includes bibliographical references.
   ISBN 0–8153–1246–6 (alk. paper)
   1. Henryson, Robert, 1430?–1506?—Technique.   2. Scottish
poetry—To 1700—History and criticism—Theory, etc.   3. Rhetoric,
Medieval.   I. Title.   II. Series.   III. Series: Garland studies in
medieval literature ; v. 8.
PR1990.H4Z677   1993
821'.2—dc20   92–44717
                                                           CIP

Printed on acid-free, 250-year-life paper
Manufactured in the United States of America

For

George and Gladys Lobdell

Preface of the General Editors

Garland Studies in Medieval Literature (GSML) is a series of interpretative and analytic studies of the Western European literatures of the Middle Ages. It includes both outstanding recent dissertations and book-length studies, giving junior scholars and their senior colleagues the opportunity to publish their research.

The editors welcome submissions representing any of the various schools of criticism and interpretation. Western medieval literature, with its broad historical span, multiplicity and complexity of language and literary tradition, and special problems of textual transmission and preservation as well as varying historical contexts, is both forbidding and inviting to scholars. It continues to offer rich materials for virtually every kind of literary approach that maintains a historical dimension. In establishing a series in an eclectic literature, the editors acknowledge and respect the variety of texts and textual possibilities and the "resisting reality" that confronts medievalists in several forms: on parchment, in mortar, or through icon. It is no mere imitative fallacy to be eclectic, empirical, and pragmatic in the face of this varied literary tradition that has so far defied easy formulation. The cultural landscape of the twentieth century is littered with the debris of broken monomyths predicated on the Middle Ages, the autocratic Church and the Dark Ages, for example, or conversely, the romanticized versions of love and chivalry.

The openness of the series means in turn that scholars, and particularly beginning scholars, need not pass an *a priori* test of "correctness" in their ideology, method, or critical position. The studies published in GSML must be true to their premises, complete within their articulated limits, and accessible to a multiple readership. Each study will advance the knowledge of the literature under discussion, opening it up for further consideration and creating intellectual value. It is also hoped that each volume, while bridging the gap between contemporary perspective and past reality, will make old texts new again. In this way the literature will remain primary, the method secondary.

For this eighth volume in the series the editors welcome Robert Kindrick's study of Robert Henryson and the tradition of the three *artes* of medieval rhetoric: *ars praedicandi, ars poetriae, ars dictaminis.* Kindrick fulfills one of the aims of GSML, viz., extending the canon of works to be read and studied by providing a new framework for understanding that will inspire students and scholars to look anew at Henryson's poetry. It is certainly one of the remarkable defects of literary scholarship in this century that Henryson does not receive the attention he so richly deserves. All too often the medievalist knows only the stunning *The Testament of Cresseid,* and often that excellent work only as an appendage to Chaucer's *Book of Trolius.* Henryson's other writing typically receives no better than anthology coverage with the result that the MLA bibliography, over time, seems very scant indeed. Kindrick moves beyond the hitherto standard general-introductory treatment by seeking to link Henryson to the well-developed rhetorical traditions that produced in the later medieval period a well-grounded literature. The scholarship of the second half of the twentieth century, which has defined and described the origins and growth of the three *artes,* makes this book possible, but it is Kindrick's perception of the connection that makes it actual. Kindrick is straightforward in calling attention to the problematical relations between Henryson and the rhetorical tradition, most notably the importance of Quintilian, and he grants that some of his conclusions are suggestive rather than definitive. It is therefore clear that Kindrick is writing one of the first open "thesis" books on Henryson. As with any deep study, the reader will find it rewarding to read the mainline exposition but will also find a second reward in the knowledge accumulated to support that exposition. Thus, the chapter on the *ars praedicandi* provides, secondarily, a useful overview of that *ars.*

Christopher Kleinhenz   Paul E. Szarmach
Univ. of Wisconsin-Madison   SUNY-Binghamton

Contents

In significantly abridged versions, portions of this study have appeared in *Scottish Language and Literature, Medieval and Renaissance,* ed. Dietrich Strauss and Horst W. Drescher; *Bryght Lanternis,* ed. J. Derrick McClure and Michael R. G. Spiller; and *Studies in Scottish Literature,* 26, ed. G. Ross Roy.

The Nature of the Study

The study of medieval rhetoric has made great advances during the last fifty years, but few of those advances have been applied to the study of Middle Scots literature. For the most part, there has been increased sensitivity to the importance of the *ars praedicandi* in later Middle Scots, but little attention to the *ars poetriae* or *dictamen*. Robert Henryson is an exceptional example of the influences of medieval tradition. His poems reflect the didacticism of the *ars praedicandi*, the political interests of the *ars dictaminis*, and the practical aesthetics of the *ars poetriae*. He also shares the common concerns of all three rhetorical traditions in his interest in the relationship between speech and writing, his use of figures, and his attention to the interdependence of form and function in his poetry. His approaches to invention, style, and organization show the impact of all three major medieval traditions. It is also quite likely that his verse shows the influence of the outburst of interest in Quintilian following 1416 and, thereby, reflects Renaissance ideas about rhetoric as well.

The goal of this book is to apply the knowledge gained about the nature of Medieval rhetoric during the recent flowering of rhetorical studies (led by James J. Murphy) to the poetry of Robert Henryson. The monograph is intended primarily as a contribution to Middle Scots studies and only incidentally, if at all, as a contribution to the study of medieval rhetoric. The first chapter provides basic background information about Henryson along with an overview of medieval rhetorical traditions. For those familiar with both subjects, this chapter may be omitted except for pp. 27-30. Even though there was continuing independent study of classical rhetoricians, their most important role in this study is through their influence on the three distinctly medieval traditions. Chapters two, three, and four deal respectively with Henryson's possible use of the *ars poetriae, ars dictaminis* and *ars notaria*, and *ars praedicandi*. These chapters reveal that in some cases Henryson could have found multiple sources for his use of rhetorical devices, while in others evidence is clearly restricted to a single rhetorical school. The fifth chapter is designed to suggest some of the possible impact of Quintilian on Henryson's rhetoric. While extending the study beyond the scope of medieval rhetoric proper, it may help to enhance our knowledge of Henryson's synthetic genius.

This is not a traditional book on Robert Henryson. Since 1949, seven book-length critical studies of Henryson have appeared. Six of them (including my own) were entitled *Robert Henryson* and were comprehensive introductory studies. Even though each of these volumes served an important purpose, the time for such general approaches to Henryson scholarship has long passed. Henryson is worthy of the kind of research that has been done on Chaucer. Individual aspects of his art must receive more intense study. Such intensive attention to a restricted focus on his verse is the approach in this monograph. As a result, there is limited information on his biography and social and political *milieu*. In addition, there is minimal comment on other aspects of his poetry which do not relate to his use of specifically medieval rhetorical traditions. Readers who need such general background in approaching this volume should seek it in one of the many good comprehensive studies of Henryson's work now available. The richness of Henryson's art will, however, demand additional focused criticism through the coming years.

The entire study is designed to be suggestive rather than definitive. Many fascinating problems in Henryson's use of rhetoric remain to be explored. Two of the most complex are the possible direct influence of the *Rhetorica ad Herrenium* on his verse and a more complete analysis of the use he might have made of Quintilian. One of the most severe limitations on such studies is the current lack of information about the poet and his educational background. Given the diversity among rhetorical studies in medieval curricula, new biographical information will make it possible to speak with more assurance about the poet's use of specific works or traditions. In the meantime, his poems are the only witnesses available, and they reveal a man likely widely schooled in rhetorical traditions and eclectic in his use of rhetorical devices. Indeed, one of the fascinating aspects of speculation about Henryson's use of Quintilian is the comprehensiveness the two writers share in their approaches to the use of rhetoric. It would therefore be foolish to repeat the mistake of John Matthews Manly in his study of Chaucer and to assert that Henryson was directly influenced by Geoffrey of Vinsauf, the author of the *Rationes dictandi*, Thomas Chobham, or any other single master of Medieval rhetoric. It is instead more profitable to look at the influence of Medieval traditions in which these rhetoricians wrote, with an understanding that Henryson might have consulted their works, commentaries on their works, or different works altogether. All we can reasonably measure now is the influence of the traditions on his verse, but even that broad framework provides some interesting new perspectives on the nature of his creativity.

A few brief notes are in order about some methodological principles in this study. Because of the international nature of medieval rhetoric, examples illustrating rhetorical techniques are not confined to Britain. In quoted material, both the original language and an English translation are provided except in the case of Greek where English translations only are provided due to the intricacies of transcription. In the single instance of a document unpublished in the original language form, the published modern English transcription has been provided. Middle English and Middle Scots have not been glossed or translated, on the assumption that a reader of this monograph would have sufficient proficiency to deal with them.

My obligations for assistance in this study are particularly widespread, since it has been seven years in gestation. Ruth Hamilton and Judy Hample read the manuscript at each stage of preparation and made many helpful comments. My other readers who saw the manuscript at various stages in its development and provided guidance and wisdom to help improve it are Dale Hample, James J. Murphy, and Charles Switzer. I must make the usual disclaimer that while my readers have greatly improved the study, I alone take responsibility for whatever flaws remain. I must also express my gratitude to the staff members of the British Library, the National Library of Scotland, the University of Kansas, and the University of Illinois. Special assistance was provided by Henry Stewart and the staff of William Allen White Library at Emporia State University; Ruth Hamilton, Richard Brown and the staff of the Newberry Library; Wilson Luquire, Jane Lasky and the staff of Booth Library at Eastern Illinois University and Karen Hatcher and the staff of the Mansfield Library at the University of Montana. I also wish to recognize the dedication of Judy Sherman, Marcy Heminger, Donna Nay, and Sue Koehn in dealing with the sometimes frustrating task of preparing the manuscript. I must express my thanks to Paul Szarmach who served as a most able editor and whose comments helped me to sharpen my approach to the subject. To my many other friends and professional colleagues who have traded ideas in a spirit of critical objectivity on these subjects over the years, I offer my deepest gratitude.

Robert L. Kindrick
The University of Montana
Missoula, Montana
February, 1992

Henryson and the Medieval Arts of Rhetoric

I
Henryson and the History of Rhetoric

The many uses of rhetoric in the Middle Ages offer penetrating insights into the creative process. As recent studies have demonstrated, medieval rhetorical approaches elucidate not only what was being taught in the schools and used for exegetical commentary but also what rules and guidelines shaped the greatest poetry and prose of the period.[1] Throughout the later Middle Ages, there was an interplay among the various medieval rhetorical traditions even as each developed more highly specialized types of discourse. By the fifteenth century, medieval rhetorical theories were being blended into a multifaceted approach to stylistics and subject matter which extensively influenced secular poetry. The works of Robert Henryson, a fifteenth-century Middle Scots poet, illustrate how one educated individual dealt with the major traditions of medieval rhetoric, personalized them in his work, and adapted them to his own social and artistic needs. The lack of biographical information on Henryson makes it impossible to establish precise relationships with specific rhetorics, but medieval rhetoric shapes the *sens* and *matière* of his verse. He might have inherited his knowledge of rhetoric from the Ricardian tradition, Chaucer, or his predecessors in Scotland, and he likely might have studied rhetorical treatises directly. Even without precise attributions, such as those available in Chaucer and Wynton, Henryson demonstrates his debt to medieval rhetorical traditions through his art.

HENRYSON'S LIFE AND EDUCATION

Robert Henryson is one of the many authors of the Middle Ages whose name and works we know but whose life remains a mystery.[2] We know that Henryson lived in the latter part of the fifteenth century; that he was the author of *The Morall Fabillis*, *The Testament of Cresseid*, *Orpheus and Eurydice*, and a number of shorter poems. His poetry reveals a humanitarian and relatively learned author. Other information about his life, education, rhetorical training, and career must be speculative. Based on a reference in Dunbar's "Lament for the Makars" (1500–1506) it is likely that Henryson died no later than 1506.

Dunbar states "In Dumfermelyne he [death] has done roune with
Maister Robert Henrisoun" (ll. 81–82). There is a tradition, supported
by Henryson's verse, that he was an old man at the time of his death.
In addition to the poet's comments on his age in the prologue of the
Testament of Cresseid, perhaps the major source of this tradition is Sir
Francis Kinaston. By 1639, Kinaston had completed a Latin translation
of the *Testament* which he associated with Chaucer's *Troilus*. In his
manuscript, he included a likely spurious story about Henryson's death
which implies the decrepitude of "ane man of age":

> For this Mr Robert Henderson he was questionles
> a learned & a witty man, & it is pitty we haue no
> more of his works being very old he dyed of a
> diarrhea or fluxe, of whome there goes this merry,
> though somewhat unsauory tale, that all phisitians
> hauing giuen him ouer & he lying drawing his last
> breath there came an old woman vnto him, who was
> held a witch & asked him whether he would be cured,
> to whome he sayed very willingly. then quod she
> there is a whikey tree in the lower end of your
> orchard & if you will goe and walke but thrice about
> it, & thrice repeate theis wordes whikey tree whikey
> tree take away this fluxe from me you shall be
> presently cured, he told her that beside he was
> extreme faint & weake it was extreme frost & snow
> & that it was impossible for him to go: She told him
> that vnles he did so it was impossible he should
> recouer. Mr Henderson then lifting upp himselfe, &
> pointing to an Oken table that was in the roome,
> asked her & seid gude dame I pray ye tell me, if it
> would not do as well if I repeated thrice theis words
> oken burd oken burd garre me shit a hard turde, the
> woman seeing herselfe derided & scorned ran out of
> the house in a great passion & Mr Henderson within
> halfe a quarter of an houre departed this life.[3]

Considering the shorter life span of people in the fifteenth and sixteenth
century, this story may provide little help in determining Henryson's
birth date. Current information suggests the need for a wide range,
spanning perhaps 1420 to 1435.

Because the curricula of medieval schools were so diverse, facts about his education would be especially valuable. Unfortunately, few now exist.[4] It would be likely that Henryson attended one of the grammar schools established in Scotland prior to 1400. In any of those schools, he would have dedicated his time to the *trivium*, beginning with grammar (which likely included basic literary criticism) and working later with rhetoric and logic. Henryson would have studied a basically Ciceronian rhetoric, as modified through the years by the *ars praedicandi* and possibly the *ars dictaminis*. The poet would probably have begun his rhetorical training with a summary recitation of Aesop's *Fables*, perhaps the earliest stage in the composition of what some critics consider to be his greatest work, *The Morall Fabillis*.

Henryson is called the "Scholemaister of Dunfermling" on the title page of the 1570 edition of *The Morall Fabillis*. The appellation has remained, and it seems appropriate. Henryson's learning, the nature of his art, and the possible mention of Dunfermline abbey in "The Abbey Walk" all reinforce his role as an educator of some position. David Laing suggests that he is the "Magister Robertus Henrisone in Artibus Lieentiatus et in Decretis Bachalarius" who had legal training and was incorporated into the University of Glasgow in 1452.[5] Laing's speculation is attractive, especially since the degree would have entitled Henryson to practice law. It is, however, generally considered to be only surmise at present. The *Registrum de Dunfermelyn* also records that "Magister Robertus Henrison notarius publicus" witnessed three deeds. Henryson's possible role as a notary, given the vitality of the *ars notaria* in the later Middle Ages, would also be an important consideration in his education and in the nature of the rhetoric he might have studied. In fact, his use of notarial rhetoric in his verse reinforces the argument that he is the individual identified in the *Registrum de Dunfermelyn*, even if it does not substantiate the theory that he received a complete legal education.

Even with such speculation about his adult career, Henryson's university education remains obscure. Because of the troubled relations between Scotland and England, it is unlikely that he would have gone to a university in England. In Scotland, the most likely alternatives would have included St. Andrew's, founded in 1411, or the University of Glasgow, founded in 1451. His enrollment can be absolutely verified in neither institution, but recently, Roderick Lyall has speculated that he might have attended the University of Glasgow while possibly registered under another name, a practice that persists to the present.[6] It is also

possible that he attended a continental University. Since well before
Henryson's birth, Scots had attended the University of Paris. Charles
Elliott suggests that he might have attended the University of Louvain
or the University of Cologne, but no firm proof exists.[7] R.D.S. Jack has
argued that Henryson attended the University of Bologna.[8] While there
is no proof of Jack's assertion, it seems to be a reasonable alternative,
based on Henryson's career and poetry. John MacQueen has
demonstrated Henryson's knowledge and use of the Neoplatonism of the
Quattrocento.[9] In addition, Henryson's works and legal training show
the influence of the *ars notaria*, a special type of legal rhetoric which
developed from the *ars dictaminis*. Pavia played a major role in the
development of notarial skills, and only the University of Bologna is
known to have had faculty designated as professors of the *ars notaria*,
making it a logical choice for a young man interested in this kind of
career.[10]

Until Henryson's university is identified with certainty, we will
know only what his poetry might reveal about his university
curriculum. University instruction in rhetoric was not uniform during the
Middle Ages. Then, as now, each university had its own areas of
excellence. While the University of Bologna excelled in the *ars
dictaminis* and especially the *ars notaria*, the University of Paris (from
1215 until 1366), had limited formal requirements in rhetoric.[11]
Universities also had major differences in curricula based upon the texts
available. As P. Osmond Lewry observes, at Oxford, for instance, there
are no records of the use of Aristotle's *Rhetorica* until 1431.[12] While the
source of Henryson's university education remains unidentified, the
curriculum and emphasis of the University of Bologna have reflexes in
the rhetoric of his poetry and may help to elucidate his career. Other
aspects of Henryson's life are even more clouded. A few facts seem to
emerge from his verse. In *Orpheus and Eurydice* he asserts that he
cannot sing. He shows an acquaintance with the technology of the flax
industry in "The Preaching of the Swallow." His knowledge of medicine
in the *The Testament of Cresseid* led to early speculation that he was a
physician. But even these scant insights could be the result of authorial
posturing or research by the poet into subjects for his poems. There is
no record of Henryson's marital status or any clear reference to his
family. His politics and religious beliefs must be inferred from his verse
and contemporaneous historical sources. Such biographical uncertainty
makes the testimony of Henryson's poetry vital. Although his poems are

sometimes ambiguous witnesses, they offer the best evidence available
about the man, his learning, and his times.

MEDIEVAL RHETORIC

Even a brief review of the curricular diversity in rhetorical studies
at medieval universities will illustrate the importance of Henryson's
choice of a university to his poetry. Typically the medieval arts of
rhetoric are divided into three major schools: the *ars poetriae*
(developed from the *ars grammatica*), *ars dictaminis*, and *ars
praedicandi*.[13] While each approach to rhetoric was distinctive with its
own advocates, practitioners, and theorists, all three schools of medieval
rhetoric were often coalesced in the work of any given writer.[14]

All medieval rhetoric was also influenced by the survival of the
classical tradition. Foremost among the greatest influences in the period
of transition and into the Middle Ages was Cicero.[15] The most important
of Cicero's works which influenced medieval rhetoric was *De
inventione*. Written during his youth, this work does not reflect the
mature wisdom of *De oratore*, which had to await the high Middle
Ages for its reintroduction to the world. Cicero's *Topica* was largely
known through Boethius' *De differentus topicis*. In part because of their
political and secular emphasis, Cicero's *Epistolae* were also popular, but
James J. Murphy argues that they did not specifically become models
in the *ars dictaminis*, even though the Ciceronian pattern of organization
influenced this rhetorical school.[16] In addition, the *Rhetorica ad
Herennium* was attributed throughout the period to Cicero. The political
and social nature of Cicero's rhetoric was felt in the development of the
ars dictaminis. For St. Augustine, Cicero provided the background for
the basic argument to adapt secular rhetoric to ecclesiastical needs. In
part, Augustine's determination to establish the respectability of rhetoric
as a subject of study for the religious laid the groundwork for the later
development of the *ars praedicandi*. In his assertion of a pragmatic
approach to the importance of belief—that the preacher should use all
methods possible to bring people to salvation—Augustine argued that
"pagan" rhetoric could be of value to the clergymen. In so doing, he
used Ciceronian principles and redeemed the study of rhetoric for
clerical generations to come.[17]

Aristotle too played an important role.[18] His *Rhetorica* was likely
reintroduced into Western Europe during the thirteenth century through

translations of Arabic commentaries. Perhaps foremost among these is
that of Hermannus Allemanus who translated al-Farabi's commentary
in the middle of the thirteenth century. Of two Latin translations, by far
the most influential is that of William of Moerbecke, completed around
1270, which survives in 96 manuscripts.[19] Essentially a word-by-word
translation, Moerbecke's work had an uneven impact on medieval
education. As previously noted, there appears to be no evidence of the
book's existence at Oxford prior to 1431. Murphy's thorough analysis
of curricula and medieval rhetorical works suggests "there seems to be
little or no trace of the book in such medieval derivatives of ancient
rhetorical theory as the *ars dictaminis, ars praedicandi*, and those parts
of the *ars grammatica* which deal with poetic composition."[20] His
conclusion is that the book came to be known as a supplement to the
study of Aristotle's works on ethics and politics. Yet because of its
survival in a significant number of manuscripts, the work apparently had
an impact on the thinking of the Middle Ages.

Ancient grammatical and sophistic works influenced the Middle
Ages in ways now often hard to trace. Donatus' *Ars grammaticus* and
Priscian's *Institutio grammatica* were major influences on the teaching
of the *ars grammatica*. "Donet" (a modified form of Donatus' name)
became synonymous with the word "primer."[21] Geoffrey of Vinsauf
might have used the title of Horace's *Ars poetica* as a basis for his own
Poetria nova. Sophistic works exercised an influence through the
Declamations of Seneca the Elder. Their acquisition of *moralitates*
during the fourteenth century would certainly have helped to develop
acceptance for Henryson's use of the *moralitas*, given the widespread
popularity of Seneca's work. Priscian's *Preexerutamentia* appears only
once, in an eleventh-century catalogue of Amplonius. While these works
apparently had a significant influence on the development of both the
ars grammatica and the arts of rhetoric in the Middle Ages, much work
remains to be done in evaluating their impact.

Potentially, one of the most important classical influences on
Henryson is Quintilian. While the first two books of the *Institutio
oratoria* were widely circulated after the eleventh century, the complete
text had been lost. The sections that survived included Quintilian's
precepts on pedagogy, but the missing sections provided specifics on
organization and style, along with much of the legal emphasis of the
work. The rediscovery of the complete text by Poggio Bracciolini in
1416 is often taken as a watershed marking the beginning of the
Renaissance in rhetorical studies.[22] The text Bracciolini discovered

provided a comprehensive overview of all aspects of classical rhetoric and demonstrated the legal utility of Quintilian's work as well as its pedagogical value. How much was Henryson influenced by this rediscovery and how much is he therefore more specifically a child of the Renaissance instead of the Middle Ages? There is adequate evidence in his life and works as we know them to suggest that Quintilian was a major force. Yet this impact could also have developed from those portions of the first two books of the *Institutio oratoria* which survived through the Middle Ages. The question will be explored in Chapter Five in the light of Henryson's use of the three major medieval traditions.

It must be remembered that medieval rhetorical schools differed substantially from classical traditions. In the first place there was, at least in some sense, what Brian Vickers has called "medieval fragmentation"[23] of the more comprehensive classical approach to rhetorical studies. While it is true that there were disputes about definitional boundaries in the study of classical rhetoric (involving questions such as the relationship among philosophy, rhetoric, and grammar), there was a more general sense of the cohesiveness of the subject matter of rhetoric itself. Thomas M. Conley argues, in fact, that all three of the medieval *artes* show pervasive Ciceronian influence.[24] That medieval rhetoricians found their own focuses on rhetoric more narrowly restricted to one of the major *artes* or took special note of their shift in emphasis from one genre to another (as does John of Garland) signals a major shift in the approach to rhetorical studies.[25] By the date of Henryson's artistic maturity, however, it appears that medieval traditions were being reintegrated into a more comprehensive and synthetic study.[26] Another major difference results from the emphasis on spoken discourse in classical rhetoric which aimed at producing an excellent *orator*, a person prepared to deal with a variety of situations (many of them political) involving such discourse. The education of the orator was largely considered to be training for "public life." In medieval approaches to rhetoric there is sometimes undifferentiated emphasis on written and spoken discourse with the goal of producing an effective writer *or* speaker. Richard McKeon contends, for instance, that many current discussions of medieval rhetorical history focus not on the classical discipline but upon its medieval misinterpretations.[27] For purposes of this study, the question of "misinterpretation" makes little difference, since the goal is to show how Henryson was influenced by the study known as "rhetoric" in the Middle

Ages. However it is important to be aware that medieval rhetoricians modified and sometimes displaced the goals and techniques of classical rhetoric in their efforts to educate the perfect "rethor."

THE *ARS POETRIAE*

One of the medieval rhetorics with deepest roots in the classics is the *ars poetriae*. Its precise definition is sometimes clouded because of its early association with the *ars grammatica*.[28] The latter was carefully differentiated from the art of rhetoric and often included not only grammar but the study of literary models. The roots of this approach to the *ars grammatica* are buried deep in classical traditions. Donatus, Priscian, and Quintilian could be adduced as authorities to support this more comprehensive approach to "grammatical" studies.

Earlier studies of grammar focused on two major subjects, syntax and figures, both subsumed under later studies of stylistics and rhetoric. In these earlier works, however, there was an emphasis on studying the subjects as ends in themselves, based perhaps upon the assumption that an understanding of these subjects would prepare the student for subsequent learning in rhetoric proper. The relationship between the linguistic study of the *ars grammatica* and the study of models is perhaps best explained by Hugh of St. Victor:

> . . . duo sunt, agere de arte, et agere per artem. verbi gratia, agere de arte, ut est agere de grammatica, agere per artem, ut est agere grammatice. distingue haec duo, agere de grammatica, et agere grammatice. de grammatica agit, qui regulas de vocibus data et praecepta ad hanc artem pertinentia tractat. grammatice agit omnis qui regulariter loquitur vel scribit. agere igitur de grammatica quibusdam tantummodo scripturis, ut Prisciano, Donato, Servio convenit, agere vero grammatice, omnibus.

> [. . . Two separate concerns, then, are to be recognized and distinguished in every art: first, how one ought to treat of the art itself; and second, how one ought to apply the principles of that art in all other matters whatever. Two distinct things are

involved here: treating of the art and then treating by
means of the art. Treating of an art is, for instance,
treating of grammar; but treating by means of that art
is treating some matter grammatically. Note the
difference between these two—treating of grammar
and treating some matter grammatically. We treat of
grammar when we set forth the rules given for words
and the various precepts proper to this art; we treat
grammatically when we speak or write according to
rule. To treat of grammar, then, belongs only to
certain books, like Priscian, Donatus, or Servius; but
to treat grammatically belongs to all books.][29]

Hugh specifically defines grammar based on divisions into "the letter,
the syllable, the phrase, and the clause,"[30] thereby strictly limiting its
scope. The emergence of *ars poetriae* as a rhetorical mode more
explicitly directed to the composition of poetry is best exemplified by
a series of works written between about 1175 and 1280. The basic
modification of classical approaches was developed in two crucial early
works, Alexander de Villa Dei's *Doctrinale* and Evrard of Bethune's
Graecismus, both of which included the study of figures in their scope.
They were followed by other major texts.[31] These preceptive grammars
provide codifications of approaches to composition. Charles Sears
Baldwin notes the following characteristics of twelfth-and-thirteenth-
century works in contrast with Bede's:

> . . . first in being less a reference book for the
> study of meters than an exercise book for the actual
> writing of Latin verse, and secondly in giving less
> space to prosody than to poetic diction.[32]

Yet other elements of contrast between the *ars grammatica* and the
medieval *ars poetriae* are evident.

While continuing to emphasize syntax and figures, these works
expand the scope of the *ars grammatica* to include invention,
organization, memory[33], and general discussions of the nature of poetry
and the poet's task. In some discussions of rhetorical figures (especially
amplification and abbreviation) they sometimes make remarkably
modern assumptions about the authorial role and the nature of a poet's
use of *auctoritates*. Charles Sears Baldwin cites four crucial works:

Matthew of Vendôme's *Ars versificatoria* (c. 1175); Geoffrey of Vinsauf's *Poetria nova* (1208–13); Eberhard's *Laborintus* (c. 1213); and John of Garland's *Poetria* (after 1229).[34] Murphy adds two other works to the list of crucial texts: Geoffrey's *Documentum de modo et arte dictandi et versificandi* (after 1213) and Gervase of Melkey's *Ars versificaria* (c. 1215).[35] Of special interest for the study of Henryson is C. S. Baldwin's insight that John of Garland attempts to blend concerns of the *ars poetriae* and the *ars dictaminis*.

All of these texts have inherent interest, but probably the best known of these works is Geoffrey of Vinsauf's *Poetria nova* (written in the first decade of the thirteenth century) which J. W. H. Atkins calls "practically a treatise on rhetoric as applied to poetry."[36] Geoffrey was apparently English and was educated in Paris. He also travelled widely, having been in Rome and, very likely, Bologna. He is specifically cited as an influence by Chaucer and Wynton. Given Geoffrey's likely influence on medieval education and, more specifically, Henryson's knowledge of Chaucer, Geoffrey might well have had an influence (direct or indirect) on Henryson's work. Ernest Gallo has shown that Geoffrey was probably familiar with the *Rhetorica ad Herrenium* and Horace's *Ars poetica*.[37] Several sections of Geoffrey's work have important implications for the study of Henryson, especially his sections on Disposition, Amplification and Abbreviation, and Ornaments of Style.[38] These aspects of Geoffrey's approach will be treated in greater detail later as will his stylistic precepts.

Other aspects of the *ars grammatica* had less discernible influence on Henryson's verse.[39] Speculative grammar, for instance, raises some of the most interesting and vexing questions in linguistic philosophy but appears to have had little direct influence on Henryson's work. Exploring questions about the basic signification and use of words as "signs," it provided the impetus for the nominalist-realist debate and the search for a universally applicable theory of grammar. As in recent grammatical studies, debates arose about the importance of "correctness" and traditional standards of usage versus creativity and poetic innovation. Attempts to define clearly the functions and studies of the fields of grammar, rhetoric, and dialectic persisted. In brief, the *ars grammatica* was a far more complex field than the more narrowly defined modern study of grammar. Richard Schoeck has argued that it is important for us to modify and expand our limited notions of grammar in approaching the *ars grammatica*, and Baldwin comments on "the shifting boundaries between *grammatica* and *rhetorica*."[40] For the purpose of evaluating Henryson's use of medieval rhetoric the *ars poetriae* is a singularly important facet of this complex area of study.

THE *ARS DICTAMINIS*

The *ars dictaminis* is, as Murphy has argued, one of the most truly medieval forms of rhetoric.[41] The title of this school of rhetoric is often translated as "the art of letter writing." In many ways this translation is misleading. Indeed, the *ars dictaminis* was concerned with proper rhetorical approaches for correspondence. Yet at the outset such correspondence was very often political in nature, having likely developed from the traditional *nuntius* as a means of communication among spiritual or temporal leaders. The *ars notaria*, which developed from the *ars dictaminis* and also achieved pre-eminence at Bologna, was more specifically dedicated to legal correspondence. The legal and political nature of the *ars dictaminis* reflects the overall emphasis of Ciceronian rhetoric which dominated medieval approaches to the study well into the fifteenth century.

Because of its origins in the necessities of political and theological protocol, the *ars dictaminis* has a firm grounding in the oral tradition. As a substitute for oral communication, it introduces an emphasis on written discourse and its potential auricular appeal. One of the earliest exponents of the "art of letter writing" is C. Julius Victor, who in the fourth century A.D. associated epistolary writing with the *sermo* (informal discourse). Such informal discourse seems to be marked by a generally conversational tone. Victor differentiates between official and unofficial epistles and explores how writing differs from spoken discourse, particularly with regard to the lack of immediate audience response.[42]

A practical explanation of this school of rhetoric is provided in the work of the sixth-century orator Cassiodorus Senator. Having had extensive, first-hand political experience, Cassiodorus was well-postured to base his observations on immediate political needs. His model of the formula for the *quaestor* in the *Variae* likely reflects his personal experience with the illiterate Theodoric:

> . . . nullus ita iudicum potest esse gloriosus quam
> ille qui est in cogitationum nostrarum participatione
> susceptus. . . . Haec nostris cogitationibus necessario
> familiariter applicatur, ut proprie dicere possit quod

nos sentire cognoscit. . . . paratus semper ad subitum
et ut ait Tullius magister eloquentiae. . . . quanto
facundior debet esse, qui ore principis populos
noscitur ammonere, ut recta diligant, perversa
contemnant . . . nam si nos, ut assolet, causam gestis
audire contingat, quae auctoritas erit linguae, quae sub
oculis regalem genium possit implere?

[. . . No Minister has more reason to glory in his
office than the Quaestor, since it brings him into
constant and intimate communication with
Ourselves. The Quaestor has to learn our inmost
thoughts, that he may utter them to our subjects. . . .
[He] has to be always ready for a sudden call, and
must exercise the wonderful powers which, as Cicero
has pointed out, are inherent in the art of an orator.
. . . He should so paint the delights of virtue and the
terrors of vice that his eloquence should almost make
the sword of the magistrate needless. . . . [He] has to
speak the king's words in the king's own presence
. . . with suitable embellishment.][43]

As an important political official, the *quaestor* faced a dilemma
common to executive aides or secretaries to this day: how to take the
thoughts and language of an unlearned executive and translate them to
paper in a form which would be effective with the ultimate recipient.
As a "verbal minister" the *quaestor* was to translate and transmogrify
the ideas of his superior and get results. Because such individuals
occupied political positions, the *ars dictaminis* had a political and
practical emphasis from its outset. The consolidation of learning
(including rhetoric) in the Church and the increasing illiteracy among
monarchs during the earlier Middle Ages brought both this position and
this school of rhetoric greater importance and prestige.
    Around the seventh century collections of model letters
evolved. They provided paradigms of address (for superiors, equals, and
inferiors), along with *formulae* for private discourse, public decrees, and
royal acts. The sheer number of such examples to survive prior to the
tenth century indicates significant influence. A. Giry has catalogued
several hundred letters in formulaic collections, and Karl Zeumer has

collected most of them. There are at least eight major collections from the earlier Middle Ages.[44]

The systematic study of the medieval *ars dictaminis* is closely tied to Alberic of Monte Cassino.[45] His *Dictamen radii* and *Breviarum de dictamine* helped to provide a theoretical framework for the study of this rhetorical form. Alberic emphasizes written discourse by his use of the term *scriptor* in his description of the rhetorical task. He also emphasizes systematic approaches to organization and style (especially figures) in his approach to the subjects. He gives particular attention to those parts of discourse (the *salutatio* and *exordium*) most appropriate to the goal of adapting Ciceronian principles to writing. In the *Breviarum*, he also gives attention to the auricular devices of *rithmus* and *metrum*, a continuing interest in the *ars dictaminis*.

Many of the major concerns of this rhetorical school are exemplified in these earlier works: the emphasis on political discourse with a strong interest in practical results, the attention to written discourse with the twin goals of auricular and intellectual appeal, the formulaic adaptation of traditional Ciceronian principles of style and organization to the needs of epistolary discourse. The essence of all of these techniques can be summed up in the definition of epistle in the *Summa dictaminis aurelianensis*:

> *De epistola.* Epistola sic diffinitur. Epistola est oracio congrua suis e partibus convenienter conposita affectum mentis plene significans. Oracio congrua dixi ad exclusionem earum que non sunt oraciones. Suis e partibus dixi, quia quinque sunt partes dictaminis: salutacio, exordium, narracio, peticio, et conclusio. Convenienter conposita dixi, quia quod primum est in dictamine non debet fieri medium vel ultimum, vel e converso. Affectum mentis plene significans, quia ille qui mittit illi cui mittitur animum suum debet declarare.

> [Concerning the epistle. An epistle is defined thus: An epistle is a coherent discourse, by its parts, suitably arranged, signifying fully a state of mind. I said "coherent discourse" to the exclusion of those which are not discourses. I said "its parts" because there are five parts of dictamen: salutation, exordium,

narration, petition, and conclusion. I said "suitably
arranged" because that which is first in dictamen
should not be middle or last, or the opposite. I said
"signifying fully a state of mind" because it ought to
declare the mind of him who sends it to the mind of
the one to whom it is sent.][46]

Hugh of Bologna, Baldwin, Bernard de Meung, and Brunetto Latini
are among the distinguished rhetoricians who contributed to the further
development of this school of rhetoric. Refinements developed in the
study of organization, the use of proverbs, the adaptation of the *ars
grammatica*, the use of allegory, and the *cursus*. As already noted,
Bologna became the seat of such studies (with some competition from
Orleans) under the triad of Hugh, Boncompagno, and Guido Faba. One
specific development of this school, the *ars notaria*, deserves special
attention. The position of notary in the Middle Ages in certain ways has
no modern counterpart. The notary assumed some of the functions of
Cassiodorus' *quaestor*, often holding positions in the most sensitive
areas of government. The notary bore some of the responsibilities of a
modern attorney, having responsibility for drafting laws and legally
binding contracts. In addition, medieval notarial education prepared the
student to function as an executive secretary, sometimes emphasizing
the ability to deal with shorthand notation as a means of taking dictation
rapidly and continuing the attention of the *ars dictaminis* to formulaic
models of letters.[47] This mixture of functions is reflected in the *artes
notariae*, especially those produced in Italy where the *ars notaria*
flourished.

That there was special attention to the *ars notaria* in Bologna is
hardly surprising, given the city's association with the *ars
dictaminis*. Indeed, all of the functions of this more specialized
rhetorical art are derivative of or closely related to those of the *ars
dictaminis*. The attention of notarial training to civil and legal material,
dictation (and the relationship between oral and written discourse), and
the potential for broader political service and discretion all echo
Cassiodorus and other earlier students of the *ars dictaminis*. Yet one of
the earliest existing studies, perhaps a precursor of Italian models, is
that of John of Tilbury, an Englishman of the late twelfth century.
John's study deals with the *ars notaria* at the lowest level. He gives
most of his attention to a system of shorthand designed to enable the
notary to transcribe dictation.[48] This skill had likely existed for

centuries, since we know that Cicero's secretary had developed such a system for transcription. John's implicit emphasis throughout on the necessity of transcribing official conversations, commands, or legal pronouncements also provides an early basis for the development of more specialized legal skills which ultimately bring the *ars notaria* to dominate the *ars dictaminis* in Italy. Janet Coleman argues that by the middle of the fourteenth century, many students went to Oxford "only to learn the techniques of writing formal letters and for drawing up documents pertaining to the business of agriculture."[49]

Hermann Kantorowicz asserts that Irnerius of Bologna spearheaded the development of this more specialized branch of rhetoric in the late eleventh or early twelfth century.[50] Unfortunately, no organized version of his writings survives and his influence is subject to the interpretation of later glosses. Rainerius of Perugia is also identified with this school. His *Ars notariae* of the early thirteenth century reflects the same kind of legal emphasis to be found in the earlier anonymous *Formularium tabellionum*. Rainerius divides his work into three parts dealing with contracts and covenants, legal judgments, and wills. His treatise shows the emphasis on elements of formulaic diction and organization, which especially influenced some of Henryson's fables.[51] The legalistic tone and direction of his work reinforce the function of the notary as attorney. In this respect, Rainerius and his colleagues helped to shape profoundly the development of the emerging legal profession.

The Ciceronian emphasis which dominated political rhetoric of the Middle Ages clearly helped this rhetorical school to sharpen its approaches to issues of state. While the focus of rhetoric seemed to narrow in scope in the *ars notaria* as it vied with the *ars dictaminis* in Bologna, this rhetorical school continued to provide excellent training for those who wished to pursue careers reaching to the highest levels of government and civil service. Indeed, the growing popularity of this study is marked by the emergence of a faculty of *notaria* at the University of Bologna after 1250 and the organization of notaries into a guild or protective association in the same city.[52]

Murphy suggests that the *ars dictaminis* was displaced because of "certain failures" which led to the development of the *ars notaria*.[53] Very likely these "failures" were the result of social change rather than inherent defects in the earlier school of rhetoric. The emergence of nation-states, greater emphasis on written records as a means of maintaining communal memory and establishing justice in the Middle

Ages, development of specialized governmental functions, and concomitant refinement of legal and governmental protocol must all have played a role in demonstrating needs for the increasingly legalistic habit of mind which the *ars notaria* reflects. Henryson's *Fabillis* vividly illustrate the frustrations of not knowing how to deal with governmental bureaucracies or going to court without adequate legal representation. His study of the *ars notaria* is reflected not only in one of his professional roles but in the focus of a significant portion of his poetry.

THE *ARS PRAEDICANDI*

The *ars praedicandi* has received considerable attention recently in terms of its influence on medieval literary production. Chaucer, Henryson, Langland, and the Pearl-Poet have all been evaluated in terms of their potential debt to this rhetorical school. It is hardly surprising that the *ars praedicandi* would attract so much attention. Its influence in medieval life was pervasive in both popular oral and written discourse through the influence on the sermon, which in turn had a major impact on secular poetry and speech.

In many ways, the *ars praedicandi* is not necessarily a medieval development in rhetoric. It had a long tradition in Judaic and early Christian thought on which medieval theories built. St. Augustine was one of the earliest Christian commentators to explore the art of preaching and its importance. It has already been observed that he was especially influential in legitimizing the study of pagan rhetoric for Christians with his assertion that all available means should be used to save souls. St. Augustine argued that even hypocrites should preach if they could do so effectively and benefit others through their hollow admonitions to salvation.[54] The study received even greater attention as the Church expanded.

Several major principles marked the later development of the *ars praedicandi*. One involved a basic difference in the goals of proof between classical argument and Christian logic. Aristotle, Cicero, and Quintilian all asserted that the proper end of rhetoric was to provide likely and probable conclusions in a world where absolute truth was hard to find. Note, for instance, Aristotle's comment on logic in the *Rhetorica*:

The function of Rhetoric, then, is to deal with things about which we deliberate, but for which we have no systematic rules; and in the presence of such hearers as are unable to take a general view of many stages, or to follow a lengthy chain of argument. But since few of the propositions of the rhetorical syllogism are necessary, for most of the things which we judge and examine can be other than they are, human actions, which are the subject of our deliberation and examination, being all of such a character and, generally speaking, none of them necessary; since, further, facts which only generally happen or are merely possible can only be demonstrated by other facts of the same kind, and necessary facts by necessary propositions (and that this is so is clear from the Analytics), it is evident that the materials from which enthymemes are derived will be sometimes necessary, but for the most part only generally true.[55]

Christian preaching, on the other hand, asserted the goal of rhetoric was to lead humankind to absolute truth, predicated on the Old Testament and the teachings of Christ. Murphy summarizes the Christian approach as follows:

Christ was therefore able to use the Testament as absolute, apodeictic proof. Other Jews were already accustomed to this, but his reinforcement transmitted the methodology to the newly conceived world-wide missionary effort which we have come to call Christianity. And of course his own statements and his own history, recounted by the Gospel writers, became themselves a "New" Testament ranking in "apodeicticity" with that known to the earlier Jews; thus Paul, Peter, and all other later preachers could quote him afterwards in absolute proof.[56]

Thus the fundamental tenets of logic became subject to indisputable authority in theory, if not always in practice.[57] The importance of this shift in the role of logic and authority had implications for organization as well. Yet A.J. Minnis argues that this authoritative bent in the *ars praedicandi* was subject to a reversal in thinking during the Middle Ages, especially in Abelard's approach to the interpretation of the Fathers.[58]

Another vital rhetorical development was an increasing awareness of different levels of audience ability. In some ways classical rhetoric was based on both elitist and democratic assumptions. It was elitist in that it was class-based. One would attempt to persuade only citizens or nobles (of one's own station or above). Despite Aristotle's comments on the need for broad applications of argument, one generally did not need to persuade slaves or others who were completely uneducated. Within that framework, there tended to be an assumption on the part of many classical rhetoricians that all auditors would possess roughly the same abilities in logic and understanding and would generally respond in similar ways to appeals through *logos*, *ethos*, and *pathos*. Even Quintilian, who shows sensitivity to audience abilities in his *Institutio oratoria*, assumes overall homogeneity in social standing, education, and other elements in the audiences he describes. Medieval exponents of the *ars praedicandi* could make no such assumptions.

The marriage of Ciceronian rhetorical principles with the extended appeal of Christianity to members of all social classes and all levels of understanding created a need for heightened awareness of audience ability. Pope Gregory notes this major problem when he states:

> . . . non una eademque cunctis exhortatio congruit, quia non cunctos par morum qualitas astringit. . . . Pro qualitate igitur audientium formari debet sermo Doctorum ut et sua singulis congruant et tamen a communis ædificationis arte nunquam recedat. . . . Unde et Doctorum quisque ut in una cunctos virtute charitatis ædificet, ex una doctrina non una eademque exhortatione corda tanqere audentium debet. . . .

> [one and the same exhortation does not suit all, inasmuch as neither are all bound together by similarity of character. . . . Therefore, according to the quality of hearers ought the discourse of teachers be fashioned, so as to suit all and each in their several needs, and yet never deviate from the art of common

edification . . . Whence every teacher also, that he
may edify all in the one virtue of charity, ought to
touch the hearts of his hearers out of one doctrine, but
not with one and the same exhortation.][59]

In its most sophisticated form, this awareness appeared in admonitions
to employ multiple levels of meaning in every piece of discourse. An
audience could thereby interpret the discourse, based on individual
ability to fathom the speaker's message. All interpretations could be
"correct" at a certain threshold of understanding and intelligence. The
intellectual nature of these levels of interpretation also meant they were
hierarchically arranged. Insights into higher and more abstract meanings
showed a more sophisticated view of the world than a grasp of only
literal meanings. Ultimately, four hierarchically-structured levels of
interpretation evolved. Harry Caplan has provided a helpful overview
of the structure of this system:

Senses are multiplied in four ways: (1) according
to the *sensus historicus* or *literalis*, by a simple
explanation of the words; (2) according to the *sensus
tropologicus*, which looks to instruction or to the
correction of morals. It is well to introduce the ways
of the world, in order to dissuade the hearers from
vice. This sense may be used either mystically or
openly. Openly; "Just as David conquered Goliath, so
ought humility to conquer pride," Mystically: "Let thy
garments be always white" (Eccles. 9:8) is explained:
"At all times let thy deeds be clean"; (3) according to
the *sensus allegoricus*. Exposition by this sense is
exposition by a "sense other than the literal." "David
rules in Jerusalem," which according to the literal
sense is to be interpreted exactly as the words sound,
by the allegorical sense signifies that "Christ reigns in
the Church Militant." The *sensus allegoricus* uses
exemplification by simile, as when the life of Christ,
or lives of the Saints, are introduced, with an
injunction that the hearer follow in their
footsteps. With (4) the *sensus anagogicus*, used
mystically or openly, "the minds of the listeners are
to be stirred and exhorted to the contemplation of

> heavenly things." So, "Blessed are they that wash
> their robes in the blood of the Lambe that they may
> have right to the tree of life" (Vulg. Rev. 22:14), in
> the mystic use of this sense, means "Blessed are they
> who purify their thoughts that they may see Jesus
> Christ, who says: 'I am the way, the truth, and the
> life'" (John 14:6). Openly, explain it as "Blessed are
> the pure in heart, for they shall see God" (Matt.
> 5:8).[60]

These levels of meaning have been used by modern critics as a basis for
convenient (and sometimes controversial) interpretation of literary
works.[61] As with many such rhetorical devices their definitions are
sufficiently vague that their interpretation in a literary work may be
subject to debate. Judson B. Allen argues that there are special problems
in "late medieval poetry because of the existence of the great referential
systems of allegory, both literal and spiritual, and because the languages
which these systems produced are not always used in the same way."[62]
Such complications must be considered in any application of these
techniques to Henryson's verse. Yet in the later Middle Ages, this
system was ubiquitously employed as a solution to a central rhetorical
problem of medieval Christian preaching.

Figures were critical in reaching the diverse audiences targeted by
preachers. Two major figures of the *ars praedicandi* which had an
influence on Henryson were the *exemplum* and the beast fable.[63] The
basic nature of the *exemplum* makes it an effective figure in appealing
to multiple levels of understanding. Coleman argues that the widespread
appeal of the *exemplum* was an unintended development from homiletic
formularies:

> By including vast quantities of pagan *exempla*
> side by side with excerpts from the church fathers, the
> preaching handbooks integrated pastoral theology into
> current attitudes to morality, employing homely
> stories which were amusing but had some didactic
> message, and could be shown to be universally and
> eternally true and relevant to the Christian dilemma.[64]

The beast fable, so prominent in Henryson's work, is based on
rhetorical goals similar to those of the *exemplum*, while expanding the

general uses of metaphor and allegory through personification to teach a moral lesson. Robert of Basevorn's section on winning over the audience lists six possible methods, most of which can be accomplished by the *exemplum* or the beast fable. G. R. Owst demonstrates that the *exemplum* and the beast fable sprang from the same roots—the desire to illustrate a sin or virtue with "subtlety in sermons."[65] Owst argues that this emphasis on subtlety was widely appreciated among medieval preachers, as illustrated by Basevorn. They were well aware of the need to mix "delight with instruction" in order to bring their congregations to an understanding of God's will. Because the various levels of audience abilities sometimes made their task difficult, they often appended a "moral" to insure that the audience would get the doctrinal point. Throughout the Middle Ages, the relative appropriateness of the moral to its tale presented interesting rhetorical problems in comparison and contrast. The *Gesta Romanorum*, for instance, without its *moralitates* could be considered simply a collection of immoral, pagan tales. Yet, with the *moralitates* appended, it was a model and handbook for preachers of the fourteenth and fifteenth centuries who found such tales an effective means of reaching their audiences. Because the original tales had often been created with artistic goals very different from those of the medieval author, the marriage between tale and *moralitas* might seem troubled to any but the most credulous reader. Henryson too found the *moralitas* to be a valuable rhetorical tool and wrestled with concerns about apparent discrepancies between the story and the moral interpretation.

The organizational devices of the *ars praedicandi* evolved in formulaic fashion. Robert of Basevorn, for instance, provides a list of vital sermon elements:

> Sciendum igitur quod in sermonibus curiosissimis viginti duo maxime observantur, quae sunt: thematis inventio, auditus allectio, oratio, introductio, divisio, partium declaratio, partium confirmatio, dilatatio, digressio, quae magis proprie posset vocari transitus, correspondentia, correspondentiae congruentia, circulatio, convolutio, unitio, clausio, coloratio, vocis discretio, gestus convenientia, opportuna jocatio, allusio, inculcatio, rei dicendae ponderatio. Horum prima quindecim locis suis semel ponuntur, vel saltem in paucis locis; residua tria in multis locis, et

communiter allusio et inculcatio in omni fere loco
poni possunt.

[It must be realized that in the most carefully
contrived sermons twenty-two ornaments are
especially employed. These are: Invention of the
Theme, Winning-over of the Audience, Prayer,
Introduction, Division, Statement of the Parts, Proof
of the Parts, Amplification, Digression, which is
properly called 'Transition,' Correspondence,
Agreement of Correspondence, Circuitous
Development, Convolution, Unification, Conclusion,
Coloration, Modulation of Voice, Appropriate
Gesture, Timely Humor, Allusion, Firm Impression,
Weighing of Subject Matter. The first fifteen of these
are inserted into their proper places once, or at any
rate into a few places; the remaining three, and
generally Allusion and Firm Impression, can be
placed almost anywhere.][66]

The arrangement of these elements could be predicated on the occasion,
the nature of the audience, and the rhetorical situation. They illustrate
how the basic use of authority, *exempla*, and multiple meaning could be
organized to lead a diverse audience to God. While the *formulae* of the
ars praedicandi were initially developed to help preachers reach their
diverse audiences, some students of the school neglected the potential
flexibility they offered. In the later Middle Ages, the *formulae* and some
hackneyed books of models became easy "trots" for lazy clergy who
needed a quick sermon. Yet the continuing vitality of the *formulae* is
illustrated by Henryson himself in "The Preaching of the Swallow." In
this tale he demonstrates how to use formulaic organization without
becoming a slave to it, as will be shown in Chapter Four.

All of these techniques show a basic shift from classical approaches
in this school of rhetoric. The major goal was still *effective* discourse,
and the ultimate test remained pragmatic. Yet the focus had shifted from
speaker to auditor. Whereas the classical orator was interested in
influencing the thoughts or will of others to cultivate his own image or
enhance his power, the basic goal of the *ars praedicandi* was to secure
the ultimate spiritual welfare of the listener (the speaker was likely
already on the road to salvation). In practice, of course, this goal was

imperfectly implemented, but the shift itself has significant implications for the Middle Ages. However, as a means of solving what Jerrold E. Seigel calls the central dilemma of medieval rhetoric—how to join eloquence with wisdom[67]—the *ars praedicandi* was nonpareil.

AUTHORIAL ROLE

From all of the major schools of rhetoric (but most especially the *ars praedicandi*) a basically four-part concept of authorial role emerged. Writers could assume the role of *scriptor, compilator, commentator,* or *auctor.*[68] Based in good part on the four functions of scriptural transmission and commentary, these roles provided the medieval writer a framework for choosing an authorial *persona.*

As *scriptor,* the medieval writer was merely a transcriber, conveying intact material which had been transmitted to him. St. Bonaventure sees this role as involving no authorial intrusion; the writer conveys the text *nihil mutando* with an eye to precise preservation of what has been transmitted to him. This role reflects the most basic transcribing function and makes no provision (if properly executed) for independent authorial comment. While vital in all rhetorical schools, the function was ostensibly essential to the *ars dictaminis.* As previously noted, the function of the *quaestor* or *dictator* initially was to reflect the wishes and thoughts of his superior, had the superior been literate and sensitive to rhetorical effects, as precisely as possible. In fact, the role of the *dictator* was such that his personal intrusion into the substance and *forma tractandi* of the communication expanded his role beyond the early bounds of the *scriptor*'s role.

The second major role is that of *compilator.* The *compilator* differs from the *scriptor* in having substantial responsibilities in the arrangement of material. Like the *scriptor,* he is bound to transmit what he selects, *nihil mutando.* Unlike the *scriptor,* he has a great deal of freedom in organization. He may choose entire works or only selections for a compilation. He may (within stringent limitations for Scripture) arrange or rearrange as he sees fit to help a reader understand the author's intention. While he still is not permitted the luxury of an authorial voice in the selections themselves, his greater discretion in the arrangement of materials provides a considerable amount of rhetorical control. This role assumed a great deal of significance in the later Middle Ages when it became a defensive posture for writers (including

Chaucer) [69] who apparently wished to be held blameless for their subject matter. There appears to be a fascinating interaction between this role and the role of *auctor*.

The *commentator* is certainly permitted his own voice but with some restrictions. His function requires that he use an authoritative text (written by an established *auctoritas*—in the earlier Middle Ages, usually a scriptural source) as a basis for his comments. The basic goal of the comments should be to elucidate the intention of the *auctoritas*, often through the four-fold exegetical techniques. As Rita Copeland has demonstrated,[70] the interpretive role of the *commentator* provided extensive latitude for insertion of authorial voice and personal prejudice. Yet, at least in the most ideal version of his function, the *commentator* was obliged to follow precisely the course of the *auctoritas* on whom he was commenting. Both Chaucer and Henryson seem to assume this role in the prologues of their works, often citing not scriptural but secular *auctoritates* as the basis for their commentary.

Finally, there is the role of the *auctor*, who presents his own ideas (or, earlier, the ideas of Divine Mind speaking through him), sometimes using other works as sources of enlightenment or subject matter. Yet the authorial voice is clearly present and distinctive. Minnis carefully traces the development of the *auctor* in the Middle Ages, emerging from a role much like that of the *scriptor* to its final status as *auctoritas*.[71] In the earlier Middle Ages, scriptural studies tended to view the human writer as an instrument for the voice of God. Particularly during the twelfth and thirteenth centuries, more interest evolved in the human writer, as a general acceptance developed that *all* writing proceeds from God for the edification (if not emulation) of humankind (Romans, 15:4). As greater awareness of and interest in the human *auctor* evolved, Pagan *auctoritates* also achieved gradually greater preeminence. Thus, by the fifteenth century, it was possible for Henryson to use Aesop or even Chaucer as an "authority" on which to build a "commentary" or sequel. The interplay among the roles of *compilator*, *commentator*, and *auctor* is one of the most interesting aspects of the poetry of both late medieval authors.

While these four roles are firmly grounded in scriptural interpretation and the *ars praedicandi*, clearly they also had implications for the *ars dictaminis* and for the use of elements in the *ars poetriae*. The interactive concept of authorial voice illustrates the comprehensive nature of medieval rhetoric. The synthesis (sometimes systematic, sometimes muddled) of medieval rhetorical techniques and the reassertion of traditional classical models influenced every serious writer of the fifteenth century. Henryson was no exception.

HENRYSON AND RHETORICAL TRADITIONS

How would Henryson have known and used these rhetorical traditions? There can be no doubt that he studied at least some of the major works with conscious attention to the rhetoric itself. As previously noted, his university education would have required the study of logic, grammar, and rhetoric, no matter which institution he attended.[72] Precisely which works he would have studied, however, would have depended on the curriculum of the specific university in which he matriculated. The range of possibilities is a broad one, but it seems almost certain that he would have been exposed to the *ars poetriae* and elements of the *ars praedicandi* wherever he studied. If indeed he was a schoolmaster, his study of rhetoric would have been intensified by his responsibilities for the education of children entrusted to his care. He would certainly have taught grammar along with rudiments of literary criticism involving works such as Aesop's fables, a staple of the late medieval curriculum.[73] The mixture of classical and Christian elements in the curriculum would have demanded that he also maintain a certain continuing awareness of the major developments in rhetoric as well. If he were an attorney or, more likely a notary, he would have studied the *ars dictaminis* and the *ars notaria*, perhaps in even greater detail and with more self-awareness than any of the other forms. Especially if his notarial training were provided in one of the studios at Bologna, Henryson would have been required to give close and precise attention to language and the legal *formulae* of these rhetorical schools. Since the generation of such language would have been at the heart of his notarial career, Henryson would have had to maintain an awareness of changes in legal structure and terminology. There were other avenues through which he would have been exposed to such rhetorical traditions. As a man with religious and moral interests, he would have been witnessed the practice of the *ars praedicandi* in church, listening to sermons (there is now no evidence that he himself preached, although it is a possibility). In his role as a professional educator, he would have found works on education to be filled with discussions of rhetoric. It is this role which likely could have led him to study Quintilian.

Given all of these sources of potential influence, it seems certain that Henryson possessed a relatively high degree of self-awareness in his use of rhetoric. He had studied rhetoric, he made his living in part through the use of rhetoric, and he taught it. In some poems, such as *Orpheus*, "Ane Prayer for the Pest," and "Sum Practysis of Medecyne," his rhetorical self-awareness is indisputable. However, it is also to be found in some of the less "artful" verse, most notably *The Morall Fabillis*. Henryson's sense of invention, organization, and style reflects the deliberate and conscious choices made by a skilled rhetorician. As Douglas Gray argues, Henryson "seems effortlessly to achieve an eloquence which eludes all his contemporaries."[74]

That does not always mean, however, at every moment he was conscious of either the particular school of medieval rhetoric or the specific work from which he drew a rhetorical device. In certain instances, his rhetorical sources seem as clear to modern critics as they must have seemed to him. "The Preaching of the Swallow," by virtue of its style and its very organizational structure is clearly based on the rhetorical principles of the *ars praedicandi*. So, too, "The Sheep and the Dog" has a definite debt to the *ars notaria*. Yet in other instances, such as *The Testament of Cresseid* or the *Orpheus*, some of the distinctions cannot be so clearly made. Part of Henryson's genius is his ability, by design or intuition, to mix rhetorical techniques in a single work. Just as many of the basic elements of the classical tradition were adapted by all three major rhetorical traditions of the Middle Ages, Henryson might well have learned and taught rhetorical techniques without the clear taxonomy and sharp distinctions modern scholarly hindsight has provided. Allegory, for instance, is a figure that Henryson would have studied in virtually any of the rhetorics which he used. It is particularly important in the *ars praedicandi* as a central basis for understanding Scripture, but it had applications in the *ars dictaminis* and the *ars poetriae*. While it is virtually certain that Henryson learned his specific applications of this figure from the rhetoric of preaching, it is important to be aware that he could likely have refined his use of it through techniques from the other two rhetorical schools. In other instances where the source of influence is less evident, such as his sensitivity to the relationship between speech and writing, the three schools of medieval rhetoric demonstrate common concerns which could have influenced Henryson simultaneously.

There are major questions about the nature of Henryson's audience. Gregory Kratzmann argues that at least the *Orpheus* and *The*

Testament of Cresseid were written for a court audience,[75] and certainly there are elements such as the setting, style, and characterization of both poems which support his hypothesis. In particular, the *Orpheus* would suggest that Henryson was using a classical tale in a fashion which would delight courtly audiences, at least on one level of interpretation. Yet there are also reasons to challenge Kratzmann's hypothesis about even these two works. Cresseid's wretched fate is hardly a traditional ending for a tale of courtly love. Henryson's choice of sources for the *Orpheus* demonstrates his strong commitment to moral and essentially theological commentaries. The elements of some of Henryson's other works certainly suggest that, if he wrote for a courtly audience, it was not his only audience. For instance, despite his assertion that he was working at the request of "ane lord," the ethical tenor of *The Morall Fabillis* suggests the use of forms of the beast fable more typical of pedagogy than courtly amusement, and the work champions the lower classes, often at the expense of the nobility. In view of all the evidence, John MacQueen believes that Henryson's verse would have shocked the court,[76] while W.S. Ramson suggests that if Henryson wrote for a courtly audience, he did so without sympathy.[77] Perhaps a more likely solution to the problem is to recognize that Henryson might well have written for a variety of audiences. The records of early Scottish printing demonstrate, somewhat like Caxton's records, that works were published which appealed to both the nobility and a rapidly-developing literate middle class composed of members drawn from all strata of society.[78] Henryson's synthesis of medieval rhetorical traditions in his verse might indeed be a recognition of the greater heterogeneity of his audience.

It is important to keep in mind that Henryson's age was a period of major cultural and social transition, not only in Britain but throughout Europe. In rhetoric, not only were there changes in the stasis of the three major medieval traditions, but new elements, some introduced by the "rediscovery" of Quintilian, continued to infuse the study of rhetoric and education in general. The full range of Henryson's rhetorical accomplishment can only be understood by viewing his verse through the prism of medieval traditions with an awareness of developing Renaissance ideas.

CONCLUSIONS

There is a great deal of evidence about the nature of medieval rhetoric. Based on information available, it is possible to categorize in retrospect the major medieval schools and identify their practitioners. There is also evidence, varying in quality, about the impact of rhetoricians on authors of the Middle Ages. For instance, Chaucer seems to acknowledge his debt to Geoffrey of Vinsauf in "The Nun's Priest's Tale." Geoffrey is also cited by Andrew of Wynton in his *Original Chronicle*. In the instance of Quintilian, the works of Lorenzo Valla, a dedicated student of Quintilian's work, were transmitted to Scotland and are to be found in Aberdeen University MS. 222. G. R. Owst has documented numerous parallels between the literature of the Middle Ages and the *ars praedicandi*. Even with such evidence of direct citation of authority and analogues, many questions must remain about Henryson's use of specific sources. So little direct evidence about his education and rhetorical training is available that more is to be derived from analogues than sources.

Uncertainty in rhetorical studies is not a new problem. In *The Nichomachean Ethics*, Aristotle commented on the relative validity of rhetorical studies: ". . . it is evidently equally foolish to accept probable reasoning from a mathematician and to demand from a rhetorician scientific proofs."[79] Probable reasoning has now become commonplace among mathematicians and physicists, and rhetorical studies yet remain uncertain. So must it be with any understanding of Henryson's use of rhetoric. Yet, the major traditions of medieval rhetoric undoubtedly influenced Henryson's works, even without leaving direct and specific references in his poetry. Examining the analogues and potential influences of these traditions on Henryson's verse can provide insights into his creative thinking.

Notes
Chapter I

1. See, for an example of an early study, Marburg B. Ogle, "Some Aspects of Medieval Latin Style," *Speculum*, 1 (1926), 170–89. Ernst R. Curtius greatly expanded the field of study in *European Literature and the Latin Middle Ages*, trans. Willard Trask, (New York, 1953). Other crucial works are cited below. See also James J. Murphy, *Medieval Rhetoric: A Select Bibliography* 2nd ed. (Toronto, 1989), *passim*.

2. For general information on the little that is known about Henryson's life, see Douglas Gray, *Robert Henryson* (Leiden, 1979), pp. 1–30; John MacQueen, *Robert Henryson* (Oxford, 1967), pp. 1–23; Marshall Stearns, *Robert Henryson* (New York, 1949), pp. 3–13; and Robert L. Kindrick, *Robert Henryson* (Boston, 1979), pp. 15–27.

3. The *Kinaston Manuscript* as reproduced by G. Gregory Smith in *The Poems of Robert Henryson*, Scottish Text Society, 64, 55, 58 (Edinburgh, 1914, 1906, 1908), pp. ciii-civ.

4. However, for valuable speculation see MacQueen, pp. 4–23 and R.D.S. Jack, *The Italian Influence on Scottish Literature* (Edinburgh, 1972), pp. 8–9.

5. David Laing, ed., *The Poems and Fables of Robert Henryson* (Edinburgh, 1865), pp. xiii–xiv.

6. Roderick Lyall, "Glasgow's First Poet: In Search of Robert Henryson," *College Courant*, 72 (1984), 13–16.

7. Charles Elliott, ed., *Robert Henryson, Poems*, 2nd ed. (Oxford, 1975), p. xxiv.

8. Jack, p. 8.

9. John MacQueen, "Neoplatonism and Orphism in Fifteenth-Century Scotland," *Scottish Studies*, 20 (1976), 69–89.

10. On Pavia, see Charles M. Radding, *The Origins of Medieval Jurisprudence* (New Haven, 1988), pp. 37–67. See also James J. Murphy, *Rhetoric in the Middle Ages* (Berkeley, 1974), pp. 263–66; Herman Kantorowicz, *Studies in the Glossators of the Roman Laws* (Cambridge, 1938), especially pp. 33–37.

11. See P. Osmund Lewry, "Rhetoric at Paris and Oxford in the Mid-Thirteenth Century," *Rhetorica*, 1, no. 1 (1983), 45–63; Murphy, p. 94 and Ruth Morse, *Truth and Convention in the Middle Ages* (Cambridge, 1991), pp. 16–22. For additional comments on curricular diversity, see A.B. Cobban, *The Medieval Universities* (London, 1970); Curtius, pp. 145–66; Hastings Rashdall, *The Universities of Europe in the Middle Ages*, ed. F. M. Powicke and A. B. Emden (London, 1936); and Douglas Kelly, *The Arts of Poetry and Prose* (Turnhout, 1991), pp. 131-32.

12. Lewry, p. 58; see also James J. Murphy, "The Earliest Teaching of Rhetoric at Oxford," *Speech Monographs*, 27 (1960), 345–47, and "Rhetoric in Fourteenth-Century Oxford," *Medium Aevum*, 34 (1965), 1–20.

13. See Charles Sears Baldwin, *Medieval Rhetoric and Poetic* (New York, 1928); J.W.H. Atkins, *English Literary Criticism: The Medieval Phase* (Cambridge, 1934), Brian Vickers *In Defense of Rhetoric* (Oxford, 1988), pp. 214–53; and most especially Murphy, *Rhetoric in the Middle Ages*, now the standard in the history of this period. See also Martin Camargo, "Rhetoric," in *The Seven Liberal Arts in the Middle Ages*, ed. David Wagner (Bloomington, 1983), pp. 96–124. The summary that follows is indebted to Baldwin and most especially to Murphy.

14. See Camargo, p. 97, and Murphy, *Rhetoric in the Middle Ages*, pp. 362–63.

15. See John O. Ward, "From Antiquity to the Renaissance: Glosses and Commentaries on Cicero's *Rhetorica*" in *Medieval Eloquence*, ed, James J. Murphy (Berkeley, 1978), pp. 25–67, and

Thomas M. Conley, *Rhetoric in the European Tradition* (New York, 1990), pp. 90–100.

16. Murphy, *Rhetoric in the Middle Ages*, p. 109.

17. S. Aureli Augustini, *De doctrina christiana*, ed. William M. Green (Vienna, 1963), IV, 151–53; for a translation, see St. Augustine, *On Christian Doctrine*, trans, D. W. Robertson, Jr. (New York, 1958), pp. 164–65. See also Baldwin, *Medieval Rhetoric and Poetic*, pp. 51–55; Murphy, *Rhetoric in the Middle Ages*, pp. 47–64; Ward, pp. 27–8; and Erich Auerbach, *Literary Language and Its Public in Late Latin Antiquity and in the Middle Ages*, trans. Ralph Manheim (New York, 1965), pp. 33–53. A longer version of Murphy's comments will be found in "Saint Augustine and the Debate about a Christian Rhetoric," *Quarterly Journal of Speech*, 46 (1960), 400–10. Comment on both Augustine's general contribution to rhetoric and his reflections on the sinful nature of those who use rhetoric to lie will be found in C. Jan Sweavingen, *Rhetoric and Irony* (New York, 1991), pp. 175-214.

18. For comment on the influence of Aristotle and his commentators, see *Medieval Literary, Theory and Criticism*, ed. A.J. Minnis and A.B. Scott with David Wallace (Oxford, 1988) pp. 277–79; see also Judson B. Allen, "Hermann the German's Averroistic Aristotle and Medieval Poetic Theory," *Mosaic*, 9 (1976), 67–81.

19. The index of manuscripts is to be found in George Lacombe, *Aristoteles Latinus*, II (Cambridge, 1955), p. 1348.

20. Murphy, *Rhetoric in the Middle Ages*, p. 96.

21. See Jeffrey F. Huntsman, "Grammar," in Wagner, *The Seven Liberal Arts in the Middle Ages*, pp. 71–72; see also Murphy, ed., *Three Medieval Rhetorical Arts* (Berkeley, 1971), p. x.

22. For commentary of the "rediscovery" of Quintilian and the dissemination of the complete text of the *Institutio oratoria* after 1416, see M. Fabii Quintiliani, *Institutionis oratoriae*, ed. F.H. Colson (Cambridge, 1924), vol. I, pp. lxiv–lxxxix. Other recent attention is discussed in chapter five.

23. See Vickers, pp. 214–53; John Monfasani, *George of Trebizand* (Leiden, 1976), pp. 245–46. For a slightly contrasting opinion, see Renato Barilli, *Rhetoric*, trans. Giuliana Menozzi (Minneapolis, 1989), p. 45.

24. Conley, pp. 93–100.

25. For interesting comment on Geoffrey of Vinsauf's possible interest in effecting a synthesis, see Martin Camargo, "Toward a Comprehensive Art of Written Discourse: Geoffrey of Vinsauf and the *Ars Dictaminis*," *Rhetorica*, 6, no. 2 (1988), 167–94; on some additional problems with regard to definition, see William A. Wallace, "Aristotelian Science and Rhetoric in Transition: The Middle Ages and the Renaissance," *Rhetorica*, 7, no. 1 (1989), 7–21.

26. See Charles Sears Baldwin, *Renaissance Literary Theory and Practice*, ed. D. L. Clark (New York, 1939); James J. Murphy, ed. *Renaissance Eloquence*, (Berkeley, 1983); and Vickers, 254–93. For comments on another form of integration which might have particular importance for *The Testament of Cresseid* and the *Orpheus*, see Mark D. Johnston, "The Treatment of Speech in Medieval Ethical and Courtesy Literature," *Rhetorica*, 4, no. 1 (1986), 21–46.

27. Richard McKeon, "Rhetoric in the Middle Ages," *Speculum*, 17 (1942), 2; see also Ward, pp. 28–29, and Jerrold E. Seigel, *Rhetoric and Philosophy in Renaissance Humanism* (Princeton, 1968), pp. 178–80. See also, however, Murphy's comments on the pragmatism of medieval rhetoric and his candid assertion that medieval rhetoric has goals different from those of classical rhetoric, *Three Medieval Rhetorical Arts*, pp. xiv and xxiii.

28. Seigel, pp. 178–79; Baldwin, *Medieval Rhetoric and Poetic*, 184–85, and Ward, pp. 105–06.

29. Hugh of St. Victor, *Didascalicon*, ed. C. H. Buttimer (Washington, 1939), III, 5, p. 56; translation by Jerome Taylor (New York, 1961), pp. 89–90.

30. *Ibid.*, II, 28; Taylor, p. 80.

31. *Three Medieval Rhetorical Arts*, p. xx.

32. Baldwin, *Medieval Rhetoric and Poetic*, p. 185.

33. See Mary Carruthers, *The Book of Memory* (Cambridge, 1990), p. 42.

34. *Ibid.*, pp. 184–95.

35. Murphy, *Rhetoric in the Middle Ages*, p. 135.

36. Atkins, p. 97.

37. Ernest Gallo, *The Poetria Nova and Its Sources in Early Rhetorical Doctrine* (The Hague, 1971), pp. 133–40.

38. In addition to Gallo's text, the original text of Geoffrey will be found in *Les arts poetiques du XIIᵉ et du XIIIᵉ siècle*, ed. Edmond Faral (Paris, 1923). A convenient and useful translation is Geoffrey of Vinsauf, "The New Poetics," trans. Jane Baltzell Kopp, in *Three Medieval Rhetorical Arts*, ed. Murphy, pp. 27–108.

39. See Huntsman, pp. 58–95. Some of the origins of these discussions may be found in Augustine, *Concerning the Teacher and On the Immortality of the Soul*, trans. George G. Leckie (New York, 1938), pp. 8–56.

40. Richard J. Schoeck, "On Rhetoric in Fourteenth-Century Oxford," *Medieval Studies*, 30 (1968), 214–25; Baldwin, *Medieval Rhetoric and Poetic*, p. 185.

41. Murphy, *Rhetoric in the Middle Ages*, p. 184. However, see Ward, pp. 28–29 for a summary of objections to the *ars dictaminis* as a true form of rhetoric.

42. C. Iulius Victor, *Ars rhetorica*, in *Rhetores Latini Minores*, ed. Carolus Halm (Leipzig, 1863), pp. 371–448; see especially pp. 447–48, 384, and 429–31.

43. Cassiodorus Senator, *Variae*, ed. T. Mommsen, Monumenta Germaniae Historica, Auctorum Antiquissimorum XIII (Berlin, 1894), p. 178; translation from *The Letters of Cassiodorus*, trans. Thomas Hodgkin (London, 1886), pp. 300–01.

44. See A. Giry, *Manuel de diplomatique* (Paris, 1925), pp. 482–84, and Karl Zeumer, *Formulae merowingici et karolini aevi*, Monumenta Germania Historica, Legum V (Hanover, 1886). Other formularies survive. This list is established in Murphy, *Rhetoric in the Middle Ages*, p. 200.

45. For particular comment on Alberic's contribution, see Murphy *Rhetoric in the Middle Ages*, p. 203.

46. Ludwig Rockinger, *Briefsteller und Formelbucher des eilften bis vierzehnten Jahrhunderts* (Munich, 1863; rpt. New York, 1961), I, p. 103. Translation is from Murphy, *Rhetoric in the Middle Ages* p. 228.

47. For examples of such formularies, see Zeumer.

48. John of Tilbury, *Ars notaria* in *"Ars Notaria*: Tironische Noten und Stenographie im 12. Jahrhundert,"* ed. Valentin Rose, *Hermes*, 8 (1874), 303–26.

49. Janet Coleman, *Medieval Readers and Writers 1350–1400* (New York, 1981), p. 29. See also Henry Gerald Richardson, "Business Training in Medieval Oxford," *American Historical Review*, 46 (1941), 259–80.

50. Kantorowicz, p. 33.

51. See Rainerius, *Ars notariae*, ed. Ludwig Wahrmund (Innsbruck, 1917).

52. Murphy, *Rhetoric in the Middle Ages*, p. 265.

53. *Ibid.*, pp. 265–66.

54. *De doctrina christiana*, ed. Green, IV, 151; Robertson, trans., p. 164.

55. Aristotle, *The "Art" of Rhetoric*, trans. John Henry Freese, (Cambridge, MA, 1926), I, ii, 12–13; pp. 23 and 25.

56. Murphy, *Rhetoric in the Middle Ages*, p. 277; see also Baldwin, *Medieval Rhetoric and Poetic*, pp. 151–82 and A.J. Minnis, *Medieval Theory of Authorship* (Philadelphia, 1984, rev. ed., 1988) pp. 73–90.

57. However, see Baldwin, *Medieval Rhetoric and Poetic*, p. 3 for an opposing view of Aristotle's notion of truth. See also Aristotle's own comments ". . . Rhetoric is useful, because the true and the just are naturally superior to their opposites. . . ." *The "Art" of Rhetoric*, I, i, 12; p. 11.

58. Minnis, p. 63.

59. S. Gregorii. *De cura pastorali* (Brussels, 1685), pp. 110-11; translation from Saint Gregory, *Pastoral Rule* (New York, 1895), Part Three, Prologue, p. 24.

60. Harry Caplan, "The Four Senses of Scriptural Interpretation and the Medieval Theory of Preaching," *Speculum*, 4 (1929), 282. For a contemporaneous point of view, see Guibert de Nogent, "Liber quo ordine sermo fieri debeat," *PL*, ed. J. P. Migne (Paris, 1853), 156, 21–32; a useful translation is "The Way a Sermon Ought to be Given," in *Readings in Medieval Rhetoric*, ed. Joseph M. Miller, Michael H. Prosser, and Thomas W. Benson (Bloomington, 1973), pp. 170–71. For a comment on how this approach to writing may be viewed as part of a larger concept of medieval aesthetics, see Umberto Eco, *Art and Beauty in the Middle Ages*, trans. Hugh Bredin (New Haven, 1986), especially pp. 52–64.

61. For a perspective on this controversy see D.W. Robertson, *A Preface to Chaucer* (Princeton, 1962), and *Critical Approaches to Medieval Literature*, ed. Dorothy Bethurum (New York, 1960), pp. 1–82.

62. Judson Boyce Allen, *The Friar as Critic* (Nashville, 1971), p. 150.

63. See Minnis, pp. 103–06 for a discussion of the *exemplum*.

64. Coleman, p. 180.

65. G.R. Owst, *Literature and Pulpit in Medieval England*, 2nd ed. (Oxford, 1966), pp. 195–209.

66. Robert of Basevorn, "Forma Praedicandi," in Th. M. Charland, *Artes Praedicandi* (Paris, 1936), p. 249; translation from "The Form of Preaching," trans. Leopold Krul, in *Three Medieval Rhetorical Arts*, ed. Murphy, pp. 132–33.

67. Seigel, pp. 173–80.

68. For a discussion of these *personae* and authorial roles, see Minnis, pp. 73–159, especially, pp. 94–95.

69. *Ibid.*, pp. 198–200.

70. Rita Copeland, *Rhetoric, Hermeneutics, and Translation in the Middle Ages* (Cambridge, 1991), pp. 63–86.

71. *Ibid.*, pp. 73–159.

72. For additional discussion of Henryson's university curriculum, see MacQueen, *Robert Henryson*, pp. 4-15; and William J. Courtenay, *Schools and Scholars in Fourteenth-Century England* (Princeton, 1987), pp. 20–55.

73. On the curriculum Henryson would have taught, see Courtenay, pp. 15–20; and A. F. Leach, *The Schools of Medieval England* (London, 1915).

74. Douglas Gray, "'The' Ende is Every Tales Strengthe': Henryson's *Fables*," *Proceedings of the Third International Conference on Scottish Language and Literature*, ed. Roderick J. Lyall and Felicity Riddy (Stirling/Glasgow, 1981), p. 226.

75. Gregory Kratzmann, *Anglo-Scottish Literary Relations 1430–1550* (Cambridge, 1980), p. 30.

76. John MacQueen, "The Literature of Fifteeth-Century Scotland," in *Scottish Society in the Fifteenth Century,* ed. Jennifer M. Brown (London, 1977), p. 206.

77. W. S. Ramson, "A Reading of Henryson's *Testament* or 'Quha falsit Cresseid?" *Parergon,* 17 (1977), 27.

78. See Harry G. Aldis, *A List of Books Printed in Scotland before 1700* (Edinburgh, 1904), p. 1; see also Ian Jamieson "Some Attitudes to Poetry in Late Fifteenth-Century Scotland, *Studies in Scottish Literature,* 15 (1980), pp. 28–42.

79. *The Nichomachean Ethics of Aristotle,* trans. and intro., Sir David Ross (London, 1961), p. 3.

II
Henryson and the *Ars poetriae*

BACKGROUND

In part because of its debt to the *ars grammatica*, the *ars poetriae* illustrates both the survival of classical traditions and the adaptation of those traditions in the Middle Ages.[1] Initially conceived as the study of grammar in the fashion of Donatus and Priscian, the *ars grammatica* also assumed the study of literature into its scope. The assumption was, perhaps, a logical development; literary models have always been essential to the study of a coherent and basically static model of grammar. The emphasis of later Roman grammarians and tenth- and eleventh-century commentators on "correctness" made it essential that language usage be standardized and regularized through reference to the best written authorities.[2] The further development of a more comprehensive *ars poetriae* would seem to be a natural synthesis of these two interests in the *ars grammatica*.

That this "extension" of the *ars grammatica* caused some controversy is a matter of record.[3] The debate was an ancient one. Even in the *Institutio oratoria*, Quintilian observed that it was an issue in need of resolution:

> Nos suum cuique professioni modum demus. Et grammatice (quam in Latinum transferentes litteraturam vocaverunt) fines suos norit, praesertim tantum ab hac appellationis suae paupertate, intra quam primi illi constitere, provecta; nam tenuis a fonte assumptis historicorum criticorumque viribus pleno iam satis alveo fluit, cum praeter rationem recte loquendi non parum alioqui copiosam prope omnium maximarum artium scientiam amplexa sit. . . .

> [The two professions must each be assigned their proper sphere. *Grammatice*, which we translate as the science of letters, must learn to know its own limits,

especially as it has encroached so far beyond the
boundaries to which its unpretentious name should
restrict it and to which its earlier professors actually
confined themselves. Springing from a tiny fountain-
head, it has gathered strength from the historians and
critics and has swollen to the dimensions of a
brimming river, since, not content with the theory of
correct speech, no inconsiderable subject, it has
usurped the study of practically all the highest
departments of knowledge.][4]

Grammarians and rhetoricians both continued to redefine the boundaries
of their subjects of study in the Middle Ages, with the grammarians
ultimately expanding their subject into structure, stylistics, and other
elements. John of Salisbury reflects some of the consternation about
proper classification of the study of poetry in his comment:

> Adeo quidem assidet poetica rebus naturalibus, ut
> eam plerique negauerint gramatice speciem esse,
> asserentes eam esse artem per se, nec magis ad
> gramaticam quam ad rethoricam pertinere, affinem
> tamen utrique, eo quod cum his habeat precepta
> communia.

> [Suffice it to say that all of these are products
> from nature's workshop. Indeed, so closely does it
> cleave to the things of nature that several have denied
> that poetry is a subdivision of grammar, and would
> have it be a separate art. They maintain that poetry no
> more belongs to grammar than it does to rhetoric,
> although it is related to both, inasmuch as it has rules
> in common with each.][5]

Other authorities, following the lead of Averroes and Greek
commentators on Aristotle, placed the arts of poetry in the general study
of logic.[6] In retrospect, there is much to support Paul E. Prill's thesis
that "those who stood on the cusp between the classical and medieval
periods likewise understood that poetry was best understood from the
precepts of rhetoric rather than those of grammar."[7] This perspective is
reflected in the development of the theory of the *ars grammatica*. A

crucial stage in the evolution of the *ars grammatica* into the *ars poetriae* occurred between 1175 and 1300, the period during which the basic preceptive grammars were written. By extending the field of their study not only to stylistics but also to invention, organization, memory, delivery, and audience analysis (in at least a crude sense), the writers of these grammars—Geoffrey of Vinsauf, Matthew of Vendôme, John of Garland, Gervase of Melkley and Eberhard—established the study of "poetics" as one of the major approaches to medieval rhetoric.[8]

Several major issues appear in all of the preceptive grammars. First their general emphasis is the transposition of theory into practice. They attempt to help the reader actually compose verse. This practical bent is sometimes related to a more general emphasis on pedagogy. They also share, most often implicitly, a special interest in the relationship between speech and writing. Since people in the Middle Ages generally possessed a greater awareness than moderns of the basically oral nature of poetry, this school of rhetoric reflects the need to preserve and translate auricular appeal. While I have chosen to treat Henryson's use of some of these devices in Chapter Three to show how they may be related to the *ars dictaminis,* there is no doubt that the *ars poetriae* was the major vehicle for discussions of such figures as meter and rhyme. This interest was closely related to an emphasis on use of the appropriate level of style. In general, these works insist on the use of stylistic variation to match both the audience and the subject matter. Finally the organization of the plot is also a subject of general interest, sometimes treated briefly, sometimes (as in Geoffrey) treated at length.

Which of these major "preceptive grammars" would Henryson most likely have studied? Two of them seem to offer the most specific points of contact, but without precise information about his education, the choice of sources must remain speculative. The question is also complicated by our lack of knowledge about the history of the *artes poetriae* themselves. Much recent work has been done by James Murphy, A. J. Minnis, Marjorie Curry Woods, Douglas Kelly, and others to help us understand the history of these works, their influence, and the role of their *commentatores.*[9] Such current research has revealed a complex web of relationships, transmission, and interpretation. Based on what is now known, any speculation about Henryson's use of one or another of the central works must be prefaced by the *caveat* that he might have used the text itself, a commentary on the text, a plagiarized version of the text, another text influenced specifically by the work in question, or a work generally influenced by this tradition in the Middle Ages.[10]

There seem to be no distinctive elements from Matthew of Vendôme's *Ars versificatoria* (which Helen Waddell calls "the dullest Art of Poetry that has ever been written"[11]) in Henryson's verse. Henryson might well have found solace in the comments about the difficulties of teachers in Eberhard's *Laborintus*,[12] but most of the other elements in Eberhard he could have learned from Quintilian or from the *Rhetorica ad Herrenium*, erroneously attributed to Cicero and quite popular during the Middle Ages. Gervase of Melkley cites Geoffrey of Vinsauf along with both the *Poetria nova* and the *Documentum* in his *Ars versificaria* and clearly accepts him as a master. Even Gervase's attention to *dictamen* shows little to suggest a direct influence on Henryson. Without additional proof these three masters of the *ars poetriae* must be considered unlikely to have influenced Henryson directly.

HENRYSON AND JOHN OF GARLAND

There remain two of the masters of the *ars poetriae* whose work might show more specific influence on Henryson. The potential source I wish to examine in greatest detail is Geoffrey of Vinsauf's *Poetria nova*, but John of Garland's *De arte prosayca, metrica, et rithmica* deserves preliminary comment. It should be noted that Atkins comments about both that ". . . it is somewhat disappointing to find that the main body of theorising set forth by both Geoffrey and John of Garland deals primarily with formal and superficial considerations that have little to do with the essence of the poetic art."[13] Certainly their contemporaries did not share this view, for their influence is well attested.[14] It should also be observed that both bring the study of poetry within the framework of rhetoric, providing sections not only on invention, style, and organization, but also, for instance, on memory—the handmaid of both composition and delivery.[15] John's successful career insured the widespread influence of his work. Having studied at Oxford some time during the first two decades of the thirteenth century, he immigrated to the University of Paris. In 1229, he was appointed one of the first two masters of grammar at the newly established University of Toulouse. John's work was comprehensive in its scope and helped to establish his intellectual reputation on an international scale.[16]

There is no case for John's direct influence on Henryson, but parallels do exist. First it is worth noting that John gives concerted attention to the *ars dictaminis*, reviewing it as a form of prose writing.[17] While such attention need prove nothing (as noted in the case of Gervase of Melkley above), Henryson's interest in the *ars dictaminis* and the more specialized *ars notaria* would have been stimulated by his notarial career, possibly providing a secondary reason for him to investigate the work. John's comments on invention and the selection of material are also of interest, especially given Henryson's attention to the fabulist's art. In dividing the types of discourse, John observes:

> *De Causa Eligendi.* Notandum ergo quod eligere debemus materiam triplici de causa; uel quia protendit nobis iocundum uel delectabile uel proficuum: iocundum in mente, quadam amenitate; delectabile in uisu, pulchritudine; proficuum ex rei utilitate.

> [*On the Principle of Selection.* Note then that we should select subject matter from a threefold principle; because it offers to us what is either entertaining, or attractive, or profitable: the entertaining appeals to the mind, by reason of a certain pleasantness; the attractive appeals to the eye, by reason of it beauty; the profitable appeals by reason of its utility.][18]

The basic principle invoked in these lines is in one sense a commonplace in medieval rhetorical studies. Yet, in a broad way, there are interesting reflections in Henryson's general Prologue to *The Morall Fabillis*:

> Sa springis thair ane morall sweit sentence
> Oute of the subtell dyte of poetry,
> To gude purpois, quha culd it weill apply

> The nuttis schell, thocht it be hard and teuch,
> Haldis the kirnell, sueit and delectabill;
> Sa lyis thair ane doctrine wyse aneuch
> And full of frute, vnder ane fen₃eit fabill;
> And clerkis sayis, it is richt profitabill

> Amangis ernist to ming ane merie sport,
> To blyth the spreit and gar the tyme be schort.
>
> For as we se, ane bow that ay is bent
> Worthis vnsmart and dullis on the string;
> Sa dois the mynd that is ay diligent
> In ernistfull thochtis and in studying.
> With sad materis sum merines to ming
> Accordis weill; thus Esope said, I wis,
> *Dulcius arrident seria picta iocis.*[19]

The emphasis on mixing instruction and delight in both passages, while hardly unique, is illustrative of how both John and Henryson were generally influenced by the survival of classical goals in the Middle Ages. For Henryson, the *ars dictaminis*, the *ars praedicandi* or Quintilian could also possibly have been a source for this doctrine. Umberto Eco observes that this mixture of instruction with delight was a basic principle of medieval aesthetics, noting that medieval arguments about the relationship between beauty (delight) and the good (instruction) may be based in part on Aristotle's *Rhetorica*.[20] The same emphasis is to be found in the *ars praedicandi*, reflecting the need to capture the attention of as many converts as possible to insure that the message of salvation would be heard. Ian Jamieson has shown that by the fifteenth century the emphasis on mixing instruction with delight is a pervasive concern of poetic art in Scotland.[21]

Of greatest interest is John's reference to Virgilian levels of style, dependent on the audience:

> Item sunt tres stili secundum tres status hominum.
> Pastorali uite conuenit stilus humilis, agricolis
> mediocris, grauis grauibus presonis, que presunt
> pastoribus et agricolis. Pastores diuicias inueniunt in
> animalibus, agricole illas adaugent terram excolendo,
> principes uero possident eas inferioribus donando.
> Secundum has tres personas Virgilius tria composuit
> opera: Bucolica, Georgica, Eneyda. Potest grauis
> materia humiliari exemplo Virgilii, qui uocat Cesarem
> Titirum—uel seipsum, Romam fagum; potest et
> humilis materia exaltari, ut in graui materia coli
> muliebres uotantur ''inbelles haste.''

[There are, again, three styles, corresponding to
the three estates of men. The low style suits the
pastoral life; the middle style, farmers; the high style,
eminent personages, who are set over shepherds and
farmers. Shepherds find riches in animals; farmers
accumulate them by cultivating the earth; but princes
possess them by giving them away to inferiors. Virgil
composed three works to correspond to these three
types, the *Eclogues*, the *Georgics*, and the
Aeneid. High matter can be lowered, in imitation of
Virgil, who calls Caesar—or himself—Tityrus and
Rome a beech; and low matter can be exalted, as
when in a treatment of a high subject women's
distaffs are called "the spears of peace."][22]

These comments are also echoed by Geoffrey in the *Poetria nova*.
Geoffrey begins with a brief discussion of propriety, particularly in
figures. While his remarks are especially pointed about maintaining
"dignity," they illustrate his sense of stylistic decorum:

. . . Ergo memento
Ne sis praeproperus; sed in his quae dixeris esto
Argus et argutis oculis circumspice verba
In re proposita. Sententia si sit honesta,
Ejus ei servetur honos: ignobile verbum
Non inhonestet eam, sed, ut omnia lege regantur,
Dives honoretur sententia divite verbo,
Ne rubeat matrona potens in paupere panno.

[. . .Therefore remember: be not hasty; but in those
things that you intend to say, be an Argus and spy out
words for your proposed subject with sharp eyes. If
your meaning be dignified, let its dignity be preserved
to it: let no ignoble word dishonor it. But in order
that all things may be governed by rule, let rich
content be dignified by rich expression; do not let a
wealthy matron blush in a pauper's gown.][23]

At the conclusion of his section on "Ornaments of Style," he makes the
same case for stylistic variation that John does, expanding his comments

on stylistic variation in the context of potential influences of character, setting, and circumstances:

> Si bene dicta notes et rebus verba coaptes,
> Sic proprie dices. Si mentio namque sit orta
> Forte rei, sexus, aetatis, conditionis,
> Eventus, si forte loci vel temporis: haec est
> Debita proprietas, quam vult res, sexus, aetas,
> Conditio, eventus, tempus, locus.

> [If you mark well these remarks and accurately fit words to concepts, in so doing you will speak suitably. If perchance mention of something is raised, whether of sex, of age, or station, of circumstance, or perhaps of place or of time, that propriety is due which the thing, the sex, the age, the station, the circumstance, the time or the place demands.][24]

While Geoffrey's commentator notes that this section deals especially with diction, its implications extend to syntax and figures. Geoffrey's comments that comic discourse is marked by "animi levitatus" [lightness of heart] while for serious discourse "maturus animus maturaque verba" [your speech and attitude should be serious][25] cannot be confined to word choice alone but also refer to an overall tone that of necessity involves sentence structure and figurative phrases.

One of the most significant aspects of Geoffrey's treatment of figures is definitional. In the rhetoric of preaching, the discussion of *figura* was often directed to allegory, metaphor, and other devices relating to exegetical interpretation. John of Salisbury, St. Thomas Aquinas, and a host of other commentators devote their attention to how figures foreshadow or stand for other events, divine and human. Like other authors of preceptive grammars, Geoffrey did not allow himself to be limited by such definitions. He used a classical approach to the discussion of figures which encompassed a variety of tropes and schemes. In addition to figures included in his discussions of organization and amplification and abbreviation, he enumerates a full range of rhetorical devices including meter, repetition, metaphor, the *exemplum*, hyperbole, and the varieties of functional shift.

All of these devices have implications for Henryson's ability to develop a range of artistic voices. In addition to their central role in his use of the three major levels of style, their relative emphasis in the other schools of medieval rhetoric provides insight into Henryson's rhetorical sources. Metaphor, simile, personification, and allegory tend to dominate the *ars praedicandi*, even though they are not the only figures treated in the rhetoric of the pulpit. The *ars dictaminis* treats figurative devices with special emphasis on properly conveying authorial intent through the metamorphosis of speech into writing. One of the major contributions of the *ars poetriae* is its continuing emphasis on the broader classical definition of figures. This more comprehensive approach to the subject kept a wide array of techniques affecting every level of discourse before the medieval author or student of literature. Henryson's use of special techniques from other rhetorics will also provide a key to his borrowings from *dictamen* and the pulpit.

As is the case with other medieval vernacular poets, Henryson's use of metric patterns to reflect speech must be considered in a speculative manner. Nonetheless, his poems demonstrate a clear concern to reflect either conversational or more ornate and formal patterns of speaking, based on our present knowledge of the language. First, Henryson's metric and stanzaic forms owe a debt to Chaucerian or Ricardian influence. In his landmark edition of the poems, G. Gregory Smith (in assessing Henryson's contribution as a "Scottish Chaucerian") suggests that Henryson might have followed Chaucer so slavishly that his use of Chaucer's metric and stanzaic patterns actually introduced a formalism unnatural to the Scots dialects. Smith asserts that Henryson "is one of the forerunners of the band of poets who broke with the older habits of Northern verse and established that more or less artificial style, which expressed in a language modified to its own purposes, ruled for over a century."[26] Smith's stance must be evaluated in terms of his general thesis about Henryson's contribution to the Scottish tradition primarily as a follower of Chaucer, a thesis which is now generally discredited.[27] His evaluation also suggests artificiality in Chaucer's language, a subject open to wide debate.[28] As will be evident in Henryson's use of alliteration, he never abandoned the Northern traditions so much as Smith indicates. Yet it is clear that he did borrow metric and stanzaic forms from Chaucer and the South. For instance, his use of rhyme royal in *The Testament of Cresseid* may reflect part of his general debt to *Troilus and Criseyde*, as the following lines illustrate:

> Quha wait gif all that Chauceir wrait was trew?
> Nor I wait nocht gif this narratioun

> Be authoreist, or fen₃eit of the new
> Be sum poeit, throw his inuentioun
> Maid to report the lamentatioun
> And wofull end of this lustie Creisseid,
> And quhat distres scho thoillit, and quhat deid.
>
> (ll. 64-70)

To what extent is rhyme royal an "artificial" form, as Smith suggests?
The answer is hard to determine, especially in languages which may
have modern reflexes but no current native speakers. Certainly
Chaucer's role in adapting rhyme royal to English was vital and even
his use of the form has been criticized as showing a type of artificiality,
most especially in his rhyme structure.[29] Yet the association between
rhyme royal and the poetry of King James I in Scotland may have
suggested by Henryson's day that it could be more "native" than
"foreign." Henryson's use of this stanzaic and metric form shows
concerted attention to the interrelation between speech and writing,
whether he was struggling with a foreign form or believed he was
adapting a well-established one to his purposes. Similar cases may be
made about his use of other forms. Cresseid's complaint and that of
Orpheus are written in the six-line stanza that Chaucer used in "Anelida
and Arcite." The "natural" aspect of this rhythmic form is also subject
to controversy,[30] but it illustrates Henryson's eclecticism in selecting
metric forms and other auricular devices to deal with presentation of his
poetry in a written form which conveys a linguistic structure for final
interpretation by the auditor or reader.

Henryson's use of another major figure, alliteration, from a very
different tradition reinforces the notion that his artistic habits were
eclectic as he attempted to wrestle with the problems of converting oral
material into writing. Probably one of the major aspects of Henryson's
heritage of the Scots tradition is an interest in alliteration, a basically
oral device which serves as an ornament to enhance memory and
auricular appeal. Felicity Riddy has noted that, while portions of the
alliterative tradition in Scotland remain obscure, its presence is attested
as early as 1285–6 in a passage quoted by Wynton.[31] Despite the
presence of French elements, the Wynton passage shows strong
alliterative influence. Ironically, perhaps, this figure is one that Guido
Faba specifically eschews. At least in part, his admonition to avoid
alliteration and other repetitive figures seems to be related to the strong
admonition "to be brief," which appears throughout the *artes*

dictamini.[32] Indeed in much modern English composition, alliteration is often perceived as an error. Yet given the Northern tradition, and its influence on Henryson, it was an excellent device to reflect the highly structured oral traditions of Middle Scots. It could also have been inherited in part from Chaucer.[33] However, Henryson shares elements with other Scottish poets who participated in the alliterative revival of the fifteenth century. *The Buke of the Howlat*, *The Awntyrs of Arthur*, and *Rauf Coilyear* are among central works which reflect this tradition. The following lines from *Rauf Coilyear* (1450–1500) demonstrate some traditional elements of the alliterative revival.

> In the cheiftyme of Charlis, that chosin Chiftane,
> Thair fell ane ferlyfull flan within thay fellis wide,
> Quhair Empreouris and Erlis and vther mony ane
> Turnit fra Sanct Thomas befoir the ȝule tyde.
> Thay past vnto Paris, thay proudest in pane,
> With mony Prelatis & Princis, that was of mekle pryde;
> All that went with the king to his worthy wane,
> Ouir the feildis sa fair thay fure be his syde.
> All the worthiest went in the morning;
> Baith Dukis and Duchepeiris,
>
> Barrounis and Bacheleiris,
> Mony stout man steiris
> Of town with the King.[34]

As suggested in these lines, alliteration is often used in conjunction with formulaic diction. The very nature of the figure limits the appropriate number of synonyms which can maintain the basic phonetic pattern. As a result, phrases such as "feildis sa fair" recur as set phrases in numerous alliterative poems. The relationship between alliteration and oral-formulaic techniques may also suggest a habit of mind which would lead to a natural association with the formulaic elements of the *ars dictaminis* and the *ars notaria.*[35] As Riddy observes, in Henryson's use of this figure he is both an innovator and a traditionalist; not only does he bring "new forms into the alliterative tradition, but he also uses old ones."[36] Even in an "ornate" and possibly youthful work such as *Orpheus and Eurydice*, alliteration is part of the substratum of his verse structure. While Henryson shows Chaucerian influence in *The Testament of Cresseid*, likely a later and more mature work, the influence of the alliterative tradition remains strong, as the following lines illustrate:

'Quhair is thy garding with thir greissis gay
And fresche flowris, quhilk the quene Floray
Had paintit plesandly in euerie pane,
Quhair thou was wont full merilye in May
To walk and tak the dew be it was day,
And heir the merle and mawis mony ane,
with ladyis fair in carrolling to gane
And se the royall rinkis in thair ray,
In garmetnis gay garnischit on euerie grane?

(ll. 425-33)

The alliterative tradition is strongest perhaps in "Sum Practysis of Medecyne," in which Henryson uses it as a basic ornament to hold the entire poem together:

Guk guk, gud day, schir: gaip quhill ȝe get it.
Sic greting may gane weill; gud laik in ȝour hude.
ȝe wald deir me I trow, becaus I am dottit,
To ruffill me with a ryme–na, schir, be the rude.
ȝour saying I haif sene and on syd set it,
As geir of all gaddering, glaikit nocht gude;
Als ȝour medicyne by mesour I haif meit met it,
The quhilk I stand ford ȝe nocht vnderstude,
Bot wrett on as ȝe culd to gar folk wene
For feir my longis wes flaft,
Or I wes dottit or daft:

Gife I can ocht of the craft,
Heir be it sene.

(ll. 1–13)

"Sum Practysis" also shows Henryson's attention to spoken language in other ways. The neologisms likely reflect his sensitivity to spoken discourse of the period.[37] The word "guk" may reflect Henryson's attempt to imitate the sound made by a person being dosed with medicine.

Finally, Henryson's use of apostrophes also reflects his sensitivity to realistic speech. Lines such as the following from "The Scheip and the Doig" illustrate Henryson's debt to the oral tradition:

> . . . O lord, quhy sleipis thow sa lang?
> Walk, and discerne my cause groundit on richt;
> Se how I am be fraud, maistrie, and slicht
> Peillit full bair, and so is mony one
> Now in this warld richt wonder wo begone.
> 'Se how this cursit syn of couetice
> Exylit hes baith lufe, lawtie, and law.
> Now few or nane will execute iustice . . .
>
> (ll. 1295–1302)

This use of apostrophe is marked by a casual, conversational tone which differentiates the passage from more formal and highly-structured prayers. The tone of exasperation and frustration in the sheep's remarks almost constitute a reproach to the Almighty. The theological directness of this passage is also remarkable. There is no invocation of the saints or other intermediaries. All in all, the lines constitute an expression in the vein of "Oh God, aren't you going to do something about this?" reflecting the same colloquial language and tone.

Henryson's sensitive ear and his awareness of the intricate relationship between speech and writing enabled him to use the continuing classical emphasis on figurative language as the basis for establishing the appropriateness of style to subject and account for much of the dramatic success of his work. Note, for instance his use of plain style in "The Two Mice" from *The Morall Fabillis*:

> This maid thay merie, quhill thay micht na mair,
> And 'Haill, ȝule, haill!' cryit vpon hie.
> ȝit efter ioy oftymes cummis cair,
> And troubill efter grit prosperitie.
> Thus as thay sat in all thair iolitie,
> The spenser come with keyis in his hand,
> Oppinnit the dure, and thame at denner fand.
>
> Thay taryit not to wesche, as I suppose,
> Bot on to ga, quha micht formest win.
> The burges had ane hole, and in scho gois;
> Hir sister had na hole to hyde hir in.
> To se that selie mous, it wes grit sin;

So desolate and will off ane gude reid;
For verray dreid scho fell in swoun neir deid.

(ll. 288–301)

The syntactic structure, figures, and diction all show this passage provides a basic level of discourse associated with the plain style. While the sentences themselves are not necessarily brief, the syntactic units tend toward simplification, using active voice and traditional subject-verb-complement order. The figures are also generally common figures of everyday speech. He employs periphrasis by including well-known proverbs such as "efter ioy oftymes cummis cair," a conversational figure which will receive further treatment in the discussion of the *ars praedicandi.* He uses what might be termed typically Scottish litotes in "Thay taryit not to wesche, as I suppose," certainly not a figure associated with high style in Middle Scots. His metaphors, such as "thay sat in all thair iolitie," reflect common syntactical constructions of Middle Scots. His use of alliteration would not have been considered an attempt to achieve high or middle style during the period. As will be shown later, this figure enjoyed a revival during Henryson's lifetime, and, perhaps because of its auricular appeal, it was often associated with "folk verse." While his diction contains some romance elements,[38] they are generally unobtrusive, including words such as "prosperitie" and "desolate" which were widely attested by the date of the composition of this tale. His use of "denner" instead of "supper" might provide some interesting fodder for discussions about the early use of French derivatives, but the most important point is that these lines, like much of the frame of Henryson's composition in *The Morall Fabillis,* are basically in plain style. In fact, as Lois Ebin has observed, Henryson even shows distrust of eloquence by using it for the voice of the frog in "The Paddock and the Mouse" and warning in the *moralitas* about the "fals intent vnder ane fair pretence" (l. 70). While the poet demonstrates his remarkable ability to vary the language styles of his animal characters, plain style is the basic vehicle of the narrative frame for Henryson's fables.

At the other extreme of John's stylistic spectrum is the "high" style, as illustrated by the following passage from "Ane Prayer for the Pest":

Superne lucerne, guberne this pestilens,
Preserue and serue that we nocht sterf thairin,
Declyne that pyne be thy devyne prudens,

> For trewth, haif rewth, lat nocht our slewth ws twyn;
> Our syte, full tyte, wer we contryt, wald blin;
> Dissiuir did nevir, quha euir the besocht
> But grace, with space, for to arrace fra sin;
> Lat nocht be tint that thow sa deir hes bocht!
>
> (ll. 65–72)

These lines illustrate Henryson at his most "aureate," and they will later be considered in conjunction with his use of the *ars praedicandi*. The syntax of these lines is complicated, using a form of apostrophe. The compound verb phrases are in the imperative mode associated with such an invocation, but they contribute to the complexity of the syntax because of their necessary ellipsis of the subject. The interruption of the sequence of verb phrases with implied subjects by a unit with more regular subject-verb-complement order (l. 69) adds yet another dimension to their syntactic complexity. They become even more obscure because of the diction and figures. The use of Latin derivatives such as "Superne," "lucerne," and "guberne" is made even more complicated by their arrangement in a series which produces a triple rhyme in the first three words of the stanza. The use of internal rhyme coupled with a high proportion of romance derivatives establishes a level of style which is reinforced by the syntactic complexity of these lines. To cite only one other example, the further use of ellipsis complicates the lines even more. While omitting the subject is traditional in imperative forms, Henryson also uses artistic ellipsis as in the omission of the direct object in line 66 ("Preserue and serue [us]"). The net result is an aureate stanza which demonstrates that Henryson could easily have held his own with Dunbar, had he chosen to follow this poetic tradition exclusively. This use of aureation in a religious poem such as the "Prayer" reinforces Janel M. Mueller's concept of the relationship between aureation and the *ars praedicandi*,[39] a subject to be explored at greater length in Chapter Four.

Perhaps a more commonplace example of Henryson's high style is to be found in the following lines from *Orpheus and Eurydice*:

> The nobilnes and grete magnificence
> Off prince or lord, quha list to magnify,
> His grete ancester and linyall descense
> Suld first extoll, and his genology,
> So that his hert he mycht enclyne thare by

The more to vertu and to worthynes,
Herand reherse his eldirs gentilnes.

It is contrair the lawis of nature
A gentill man to be degenerate,
Noucht folowing of his progenitoure
The worthy reule and the lordly estate;
A ryall renk for to be rusticate
Is bot a monster in comparison,
Had in despyte and foule derision.

I say this be the grete lordis of Grewe,
Quhilk sett thair hert and all thair hale curage
Thair fadirs steppis iustly to persewe,
Eking the worschip of thair hye lynage;
The ancient and sad wyse-men of age
War tendouris to the yong and insolent
To mak thame in all vertu excellent.

(ll. 1–21)

While these lines do not match the resplendence of those in "Ane Prayer for the Pest," they show Henryson's ability to match the standards of the high style at a level below the extremes of aureation, even though this high style is not sustained throughout the poem. Like the passage from the "Prayer," the sentence structure is complex, using a number of dependent clauses. The ultimate result is a preponderance of compound-complex syntactic forms, the most sophisticated types in the language and benchmarks of florid style. The syntactic complexity is enhanced by the use of less common figures such as anastrophe (ll. 1–2), personification (l. 4), abbreviation (l. 11), hyperbole (l. 13), and direct address (l. 15), among others. Despite the difficulties in tracing the history and definition of these figures in the Middle Ages,[40] it is clear that Henryson is selecting figures appropriate to high style, even using only his own canon as a standard for judgment. The diction also shows a higher number of Latin and French cognates in comparison with the lines cited from "The Two Mice." Words such as "nobilnes," "magnificence," "contrair" show that Henryson was displaying his knowledge of ornate diction in this passage.[41] His stylistic level also is reflected in his reduced use of the common and more traditional figure of alliteration in this passage. The sentence structure is more complex, marked by obtrusive syntactic figures such as inversion and anastrophe, and Henryson states that he is writing with the edification of men of high birth in mind. Even without the extreme aureation of the "Prayer," these lines show that Henryson was quite capable of using the sophisticated level of florid style commonly attributed to the Makars.[42]

Henryson's repertory includes the full range of stylistic levels. An example of his "middle style"[43] is found in the following lines from *The Testament of Cresseid*:

> Thocht lufe be hait, ₃it in ane man of age
> It kendillis nocht sa sone as in ₃outheid,
> Of quhome the blude is flowing in ane rage;
> And in the auld the curage doif and deid
> Of quhilk the fyre outward is best remeid:
> To help be phisike quhair that nature faillit
> I am expert, for baith I haue assaillit.
>
> I mend the fyre and beikit me about,
> Than tuik ane drink, my spreitis to comfort,
> And armit me weill fra the cauld thairout.
> To cut the winter nicht and mak it schort
> I tuik ane quair—and left all vther sport—
> Writtin be worthe Chaucer glorious
> Of fair Cresseid and worthie Troylus.

(ll. 29–42)

Granted that "middle style" is a concept harder to define and that this poem is likely not directed to "farmers"[44] (as John suggests it should be), the diction, figures, and sentence structure of the lines establish a middle ground between the plainer style of the frame of *The Morall Fabillis* and the more florid, perhaps youthful, style of *Orpheus and Eurydice*. These lines from the prologue show a continuing use of longer sentences, but their syntactic elements are less complicated by the use of inversion, abbreviation, and other syntactic figures than those in the opening of *Orpheus*. The units marked in Denton Fox's text by semicolons make up complete syntactic elements, and there is less use of periodic sentence structure. Subject-verb-complement word order is dominant. There is use of a mixture of figures (both common and less common) such as metaphor, personification, parallelism, and hyperbole.

The diction also shows a range of elements similar to that in the language as a whole. Romance elements appear, but the words are commonly attested and do not seem so ostentatious as those in the *Orpheus*. At the other extreme, Henryson has generally avoided Scots colloquialisms. When compared with some of Henryson's other works, the vocabulary of *The Testament of Cresseid* likely presents fewer barriers to the modern reader than any of his other works (with the possible exception of *The Morall Fabillis*, which has the complication of colloquial constructions). This middle style may represent Henryson's most successful effort to write in "Inglis," the language the Makars designated as their idiom.

One more example of Henryson's stylistic variation will help to show both his control and innovation and, at the same time, to illustrate the complexity of his work. The following lines from "Sum Practysis of Medecyne" have a complicated and confusing linguistic history:

> Guk guk, gud day, schir: gaip quhill ₃e get it.
> Sic greting may gane weill; gud laik in ₃our hude.
> ₃e wald deir me I trow, becaus I am dottit,
> To ruffill me with a ryme–na, schir, be the rude.
>
> ₃our saying I haif sene and on syd set it,
> As geir of all gaddering, glaikit nocht gude;
>
> (ll. 1–6)

Students of Henryson's language are often uncertain how to deal with this poem.[45] The first problematic aspect appears in the diction. As previously noted, "Guk, guk," may actually be an example of onomatopoeia, a less sophisticated (perhaps even immature) figure being used to convey the meaning "open wide" or echoing the sound of a person taking medicine. The use of direct address in line one coupled with the imperative mode provides some of the same syntactic complications as those in "Ane Prayer for the Pest." The use of colloquial diction such as "gape," "deir," and "dottit" suggests a lower level of style. The lower stylistic level is reinforced by alliteration. A simple analysis of a few lines might suggest that the poem is one of most conversational in Henryson's canon. Yet other elements may belie that suggestion. For one thing, the poem is barely intelligible to many modern readers who know Middle English or even Middle Scots. Syntactic complications such as those in lines five and six (which are generated at least in part by the alliterative pattern) are hardly marks of plain style. The use of Latin medical borrowings such as "Dia longum" and "Dia culkakit" later in the poem certainly suggests a more florid level of diction as well. The very use of colloquial terms in conjunction with the alliterative pattern may be a mark of stylistic complexity and an attempt at humor. Elements of the poem's style combine to produce a bathetic contrast among words, figures, and sentence structure in the portrayal of medieval medical practice. The playfulness of Henryson's stylistic variation in the poem results in a comic bronx cheer to the medical profession. The poem also shows that Henryson is capable of mixing stylistic levels in a most complicated manner for purposes of humor.

GEOFFREY OF VINSAUF

The elements of stylistic variation were widely understood in the Middle Ages. Henryson might have learned them from a number of works in the *ars poetriae* tradition, including John and Geoffrey. Other aspects of his rhetoric, however, appear to be more directly indebted to the tradition of Geoffrey of Vinsauf. Unfortunately, little is known of Geoffrey's life. He was likely of English descent and studied in Paris. His reputation has also been clouded by the lack of information about his personal history.[46] The rationale for choosing him as a model for Henryson is more certain. He apparently was well-known in fourteenth-century England, as studies of Chaucer illustrate.[47] Even if Chaucer was not directly influenced by Geoffrey, as Murphy contends,[48] it is still evident that he was influenced by the traditions embodied in Geoffrey's work. Given that Henryson views himself as a student of Chaucer, at least in *The Testament of Cresseid*, it is likely that he felt Geoffrey's influence, even if indirectly. It is also of interest that Geoffrey might well have been a guest lecturer in Bologna,[49] an area which, as already noted, suggests special interest for Henryson because of his notarial training. Martin Camargo has shown that Geoffrey, like John, had an influence on the *ars dictaminis*. Camargo's observation that Geoffrey's attempt at a synthesis of rhetorical schools was impeded by the fact "that *dictamen* was never as widely used in England as it was elsewhere"[50] may also suggest additional reasons for Henryson to have pursued his education in Italy. Finally, the popularity of Geoffrey's work, as cited by Gervase and as widely translated as late as the

fifteenth century, indicates another possible connection.[51] Insofar as
Geoffrey's *Poetria nova* embodies basic thinking on the *ars poetriae* in
the later Middle Ages, it can help shed light on Henryson's rhetoric
whether he actually knew the text or not. For all of these reasons,
Geoffrey has been chosen as the basic model for Henryson's use of the
ars poetriae.

Geoffrey's *Documentum de mode et arte dictandi et versificandi* is
in many respects a reorganization of his more widely popular *Poetria
nova*[52] so the *Poetria* will be used as the basic source for evaluating
Henryson's poems. The work was likely completed between 1208 and
1213, a date relatively early in the history of the *ars
poetriae*. Geoffrey's treatise clearly owes a debt to the *Rhetorica ad
Herrenium* and the general Ciceronian tradition, but it is also indebted
to Horace's *Ars poetica*, as his title suggests. Geoffrey's work was the
subject of over a dozen commentaries, one of which has been edited
and translated by Marjorie Curry Woods. The work has been entitled *In
principio huius libri* because it is anonymous and no title is provided by
the author.[53] The commentary is instructive in showing how the
medieval mind would have interpreted Geoffrey's admonitions.

I. Invention

The *Poetria nova* begins with a dedication to "Papa Nocenti" and
some general remarks on poetry. Perhaps the most interesting of his
comments involve invention and the need for preconception and creative
leisure. In this section, he also asserts the need for appropriate
decorum:[54]

> Non manus ad calamum praeceps, non lingua sit ardens Ad
> verbum: neutram manibus committe regendam
> Fortunae; sed mens discreta praeambula facti,
> Ut melius fortunet opus, suspendat earum
> Officium, tractetque diu de themate secum.
> Circinus interior mentis praecircinet omne
> Materiae spatium. Certus praelimitet ordo
> Unde praearripiat cursum stylus, aut ubi Gades
> Figat. Opus totum prudens in pectoris areem
> Contrahe, sitque prius in pectore quam sit in ore.

> [. . . let not the hand be in a rush toward the pen, nor
> the tongue be on fire to utter a word; commit not the
> management of either pen or tongue to the hands of
> chance, but let prudent thought (preceding action, in
> order that the work may fare better) suspend the
> offices of pen and tongue and discuss long with itself
> about the theme.
>
> Let the mind's inner compass circumscribe the whole
> area of the subject matter in advance. Let a definite plan
> predetermine the area in which the pen will make its way
> or where it will fix its Gibraltar.
>
> Ever circumspect, assemble the whole work in the
> stronghold of your mind, and let it be first in the mind
> before it is in words.][55]

Geoffrey's commentator observes that "Locus iste principaliter assignatur inuentioni et secondario narrationi" [This section is assigned first to Invention and second to the Narration].[56] Remaining ambiguous, he then goes on to state "conuenit enim descriptioni utriusque . . ." [it fits the description of either. . .]. The commentator also argues by negative contrast for the need to "think something through" and to be prepared to undertake a project in an organized way. Geoffrey's emphasis on deliberation and planning encourages a more intellectual approach to invention, suggesting the need for *prudentia* and attention to *divisio*. Yet he does not elaborate on *topoi* or attempt to help a writer find ways to explore a subject. He seems to take it for granted that the writer has something to say. Most modern rhetoricians would observe that these remarks are hardly to be considered an organized treatment of invention when compared with the work of Aristotle or Cicero. Because Geoffrey's comments are so general and because he mixes his discussions of *topoi* and figures, it is hard to assess their potential impact on Henryson. His stylistic and organizational devices clearly reflect an overall "plan" for his poetry and perhaps even an unbecoming scholarly habit of mind. However, possibly the most important point in Geoffrey's comments is his very extension of "grammatical" precepts into the area of invention, which also illustrates a crucial step in the development of the *ars poetriae*. It appears that Henryson was also familiar with Boccaccio's *De genealogia deorum*, another potential source of influence of the *ars poetriae* on his work. MacQueen feels that in his portrayal of the nine muses "it is almost certain" that Henryson used the work as a source.[57] If Henryson had used Boccaccio, he might well have profited from the Italian poet's comments on invention. In fairness, however, it should be remembered that many aspects of invention were to some extent predetermined in medieval theological-aesthetic viewpoints. Eco has shown how philosophers such as Aquinas expounded a far-reaching theory of aesthetics, which would have had special implications for invention.[58]

2. Organization

Geoffrey next proceeds to *divisio*, reinforcing the argument about the importance of planning and organization to his theory of invention. He draws a distinction between nature and art, pointing out, however, that the two paths are indiscernible when the skillful artist practices his craft. Like John,[59] he comments that nature itself has only one form—natural chronology—but that the ordering of material through art may take at least eight additional forms. Using the beginning of the narrative as his focal point (a perspective common in classical rhetoric) he asserts that an artistically organized narrative may begin at the end of a chronological sequence, in the middle, or with a proverb or an *exemplum* drawn from the beginning, middle, or end. Given the multiple possibilities for the use of proverbs or *exempla*, Geoffrey considers the above list to include all eight of the forms of organization based on artifice. For purposes of this analysis they may be conveniently classified as follows:

    I.   Beginning with the end.
    II.   Beginning with the middle.
   III.   Beginning with a proverb drawn from the beginning.
   IV.   Beginning with a proverb drawn from the middle.
    V.   Beginning with a proverb drawn from the end.
   VI.   Beginning with an *exemplum* drawn from the beginning.
  VII.   Beginning with an *exemplum* drawn from the middle.
 VIII.   Beginning with an *exemplum* drawn from the end.

After briefly contrasting these patterns of organization with natural order (which always begins with the first element in the chronology of the narrative), he returns to the patterns for more detailed analyses, explaining the role of proverbs and *exempla*.

Geoffrey's comments on organization certainly strike many rhetoricians as quite limited, providing little or no attention to the traditional patterns of discourse to be found in Aristotle.[60] Yet, for his purposes, they provide sufficient detail to help a poet order his work. In his analysis of the beginning of a discourse, Geoffrey is primarily interested in two basic aspects of discourse: chronology and *sentence*. Both are of vital concern to the poet, who might have little use for concepts of expository or argumentative discourse such as *amplificatio* or *refutatio*. In fact, the chronology and *sentence* of Henryson's major works are the two most interesting elements of his organization. Yet Henryson's verse suggests another type for Geoffrey's format, a type perhaps covered (but not explicitly so) in Geoffrey's discussion of *exempla* and proverbs. Henryson's use of the allusive introduction deserves special comment. While the *sentence* of such allusive introductions may show affinitives with the *exemplum* or the proverb, I believe that Henryson's use of allusion shows a more pronounced influence of the *ars praedicandi*.[61] Having noted that point, I wish to provide a tentative analysis of Henryson's use of Geoffrey's patterns, along with separate rubrics for natural order and the allusive introduction:

Henryson's Introductions

Geoffrey's Types	I.	II. *(Testament of Cresseid)*	III. *Orpheus*	IV.	V. "Garmont of Gud Ladeis"	VI. *(Orpheus)*	VII.	VIII. "Preaching of the Swallow"	*Natural*	*Allusive*
									"Cock & Jasp"	Prologue, *(Morall Fabillis)*
					"Annunciation"	"Aganis Haisty Credence"		"Cock & the Fox"	"Fox & Wolf"	Prologue, "Lion & the Mouse"
					(Testament of Cresseid)				"Parlement of the Beistis"	*(Testament of Cresseid)*
									"Lion and Mouse" (Tale)	"Two Mice"
									"Wolf and Lamb"	"Sheep and Doig"
									"Robene & Makyne"	"Fox, Wolf & Cadger"
									"Bludy Serk"	"Fox, Wolf & Husbandman"
									"Sum Practysis of Medecyne"	"Wolf and Wether"
									"Ane Prayer for the Pest"	"Paddock and Mouse"
									"Aige"	("Bludy Serk"?)
									"Want of Wyse Men"	
									"Abbey Walk"	
									"Deth and Man"	
									"Three Deid Pollis"	

Given the structure of Henryson's works and especially his extensive use of prologues and epilogues, the classification of any single work may be debated, but, even allowing for a significant margin of error, this profile illustrates some interesting aspects of Henryson's art. In this analysis, he never uses the Type I introduction (beginning with the end). He uses the Type II introduction (beginning with the middle) only if the prologue to *The Testament of Cresseid* is omitted: if it is included in the total work (as I believe it should be), the work is either a Type V (beginning with a proverb drawn from the end) or an Allusive work. It is a Type V work if one accepts only the initial line as the beginning ("Ane doolie sessoun to ane cairfull dyte . . ."); this proverb is drawn from the fate which befalls Cresseid at the end of the tale. Yet, if Henryson's attention to Chaucer's *Troilus*, explicit and extensive throughout the prologue, is considered his actual "beginning," then the poem falls into the Allusive type. Types III-VIII (using proverbs and *exempla*) all have in common a tendency to emphasize the *sentence* of the work. Henryson makes use of them in varying degrees but seems to show a clear preference for the Natural and Allusive beginnings. One conclusion must emerge from this analysis. These patterns of organization or other similar patterns would suggest possible distortion of chronology or emphasis on *sentence* as a means of artistically varying the pattern of organization. Insofar as Henryson was aware of these principles of *divisio*, he shows an interest in the emphasis on *sentence* to virtual exclusion of chronological distortion.

This tendency undoubtedly develops in part from the nature of his sources and *genres*. For instance, beast fables usually do not lend themselves to *in medias res* techniques as well as do epics. It may also be argued that his best known work, *The Testament of Cresseid*, is simply derivative from Chaucer in that it begins "in the middle" of Cresseid's history, following her from her desertion of Troilus to her wretched death.[62] The perspective will depend upon how much artistic integrity one wishes to give to a "sequel." If such a work is to be viewed *only* as an appendage to the original, it is clear that Henryson's poem could reflect Geoffrey's Type II or Type V structure. Yet, if the work is granted artistic integrity in its own right and is considered in view of its allusive introduction (current tendencies among Henryson scholars[63]), it should be classified elsewhere. However, even if the *Testament* is considered as an exception, there is no question that Henryson generally tends to use straightforward chronology. He interrupts chronological order to effect his desire to reinforce his *moralitas* through the use of a proverb or *exemplum*.[64] The use of allusion serves a similar function.

As noted, Henryson frequently often uses a beginning which alludes to other works or authors. Mary Carruthers has shown how such allusive patterns are often influenced by the emphasis of medieval rhetoricians on memory, a subject Geoffrey[65] also treats. Henryson's most frequent exercise of this faculty and greatest number of concentrated allusions involve Aesop. "The Two Mice," for instance, begins with the line "Esope, myne Author, makis mentioun . . ." (l. 1). While several of the tales in *The Morall Fabillis* begin with such brief allusions, Henryson's allusive style reaches its full force in his prologues. The prologue to "The Lion and the Mouse" begins with a dialogue between Henryson and Aesop. Henryson falls asleep and then awakens within a dream to meet Aesop. He acknowledges his debt to his master and finally persuades him to tell the fable. In some regards the incident itself could be considered an *exemplum* in Geoffrey's scheme of organization, but it seems to have a broader function. As Minnis has shown, an introduction citing authority was commonplace during the Middle Ages.[66] However, typically such allusion or citation of authority used Scripture as the only source in the earlier Middle Ages. It is relatively later in the Middle Ages that secular (classical or even near contemporary) authors gain sufficient status to be cited as *auctoritates*. In *The Morall Fabillis*, Henryson clearly accepts Aesop as his *auctoritas* and his "gude maister," expecting that the reader will share his reverence. Henryson's use of another secular authority as a source is illustrated by the prologue to *The Testament of Cresseid* where Henryson shows his adulation of Chaucer:

> I mend the fyre and beikit me about,
> Than tuik ane drink, my spreitis to comfort,
> And armit me weill fra the cauld thairout.
> To cut the winter nicht and mak it schort
> I tuik ane quair—and left all vther sport—
> Writtin be worthie Chaucer glorious
> Of fair Cresseid and worthie Troylus.

(ll. 36–42)

Henryson's citation of Chaucer (even if he later says "Quha wait gif all that Chauceir wrait was trew?") demonstrates both the reverence in which Chaucer was held and the shifting nature of literary "authority" in the fifteenth century. Instances such as these could be multiplied. Henryson's use of this type of beginning serves much the same function as his use of proverbs and *exempla*. Proverbs and *exempla* are figures commonly used to reinforce the authority of a poet's narrative. Insofar as they are related to Scripture, traditional wisdom, and common sense, they were used in the Middle Ages to help persuade an audience that the author had something useful to say.[67] In the same fashion, Henryson's allusive introductions are designed to illustrate his use of *auctoritates*, revered authors whose works and reputations would provide moral authority for Henryson himself. This use of secular *auctoritates* is an interesting development from the use of scriptural *auctoritates* in the *ars praedicandi*, and, it will merit more attention later.[68] For the time being, suffice it to observe that Henryson's use of allusive introductions strengthens the argument that his organizational devices took reinforcement of *sentence*, not artistic distortion of chronology, as their overwhelming goal.

After his discussion of introductions, Geoffrey gives special attention to two rhetorical approaches involving both invention and the use of figures. Geoffrey's section on Amplification and Abbreviation is nothing less than a short course in the use of source material, even though he elucidates the techniques for general plot principles, not strictly for evaluating and using sources:

> Principio varium dedit ars praescripta tenorem:
> Te vocat ulterior progressus. Dirige gressum
> Ulterius cursumque viae, premente figura.
>   Curritur in bivio: via namque vel ampla vel arta,
> Vel fluvius vel rivus crit; vel tractius ibis,
> Vel cursim salies; vel rem brevitate notabis,
> Vel longo sermone trahes. Non absque labore
> Sunt passus utriusque viae: si vis bene duci,
> Te certo committe. . . .

> [As aforesaid, art has given a varied purport to the beginning of the poem. Now progress beckons you farther. Direct your step and your course farther along the path, overall structure being now the consideration stressed.

The path is pursued in one of two ways. For
either your path will be broad or narrow, either a
river or a rivulet; either you will proceed discursively,
or you may skip along hastily; either you will note a
thing briefly, or draw it out in an extended
treatment. Not without toil is either path pursued; if
you wish to be well guided, commit yourself to a
dependable guide.][69]

His commentator observes:

Huc usque docuit quomodo diuersis modis
sumendum sit principium. Nunc transeundum est ad
alia que fiunt duobus modis: uel dilatando materiam
uel coartando.

[Up to this point he has taught how the beginning
ought to be undertaken in various ways. Now he must
turn to the other parts, which are developed in one of
two ways: either by expanding the material or by
compressing it.][70]

If this is a continuation of his discussion of *divisio*, it clearly extends
beyond the classical tradition, even incorporating specific techniques
Matthew of Vendôme generally assigns to invention.[71] Geoffrey's larger
perspectives must not be ignored. Yet determining to follow the "broad"
or "narrow" path is so much a part of the central question in using
sources that his remarks would have had immediate and obvious
implications for the poet plying the synthetic and often derivative craft
of medieval authorship.

The Testament of Cresseid offers numerous possible approaches to
Henryson's use of the methods of Amplification in working from
Chaucer.[72] However, I consider *The Testament* to be largely an
independent work, based on Chaucer in only the most general way with
critical differences in characterization, *sentence*, and tone. The situation
with regard to "The Fox, the Wolf, and the Cadger" in *The Morall
Fabillis* offers many of the same possibilities with regard to a
"suggestion" for the tale that Henryson might have found in
Caxton.[73] Henryson's use of Nicholas of Trivet in *Orpheus and
Eurydice* is based on a similar kind of Amplification, if indeed Trivet

was his major source. Two examples of Henryson's work will help to illustrate his specific use of Amplification and Abbreviation.[74] An example of his use of the first technique may be found in his adaptation of a fable from Odo of Cheriton. An example of the second may be found in his use of Chaucer's "Nun's Priest's Tale" in *The Morall Fabillis*. These tales illustrate possible extremes in Henryson's use of Geoffrey's rhetorical techniques, even though such analysis is always subject to the objection voiced best by Fox[75] that Henryson might well, in either case, have been working from more general traditions of the beast fable.

3. Amplification and "The Two Mice"

Henryson's use of Amplification is illustrated by his modification of Odo of Cheriton's "The House Mouse and the Field Mouse." Jamieson contends that certain elements of this fable show that it is the likely source for Henryson's "The Two Mice."[76] Odo's version is sufficiently brief to merit complete quotation:

Contra symaniacos et usurarios

Quedam Mus domestica querebat a campestri Mure quid co(m)mederet. Que respondit : Duras fabas, quandoque sicca grana tritici uel [h]ordei. Et ait Mus domestica : Arida sunt cibaria tua. Mirum est quod fame non peris. Quesiuit siluestris : Et quid comedis tu? Certe comedo pingues morsellos, quandoque album panem. Iterum adiecit : Venias ad prandium meum et optime comedes. Placuit campestri et iuit ad domum alterius Muris. Homines sedentes ad prandium micas et morsellos proiecerunt. Mus domestica dixit siluestri : Exeas de foramine; ecce quot bona proiciuntur. Exiuit campestris et cepit unum morsellum, et saltauit Catus post Murem, et vix euasit in foramen. Ait Mus domesticus: Ecce, frater, quam bonos morsellos frequenter comedo; maneas mecum per aliquot dies. Respondit Mus siluestris : Boni sunt morselli; sed habes singulis diebus talem socium? Et quesiuit domestica qualem. Et ait siluestris : Vnum magnum Murilegum qui fere me totum deuorauit.

Respondit Mus domestica : Certe ita est, quoniam
patrem meum et matrem interfecit, et ego multociens
uix euasi. Et ait campestris : Certe nollem habere
totum mundum cum tali periculo; remaneas cum
morsellis tuis. Melius uolo uiuere cum pane et aqua
in securitate quam habere omnes delicias cum tali
socio:

Rodere malo fabam quam cura perpete rodi.

Sic plerique, si intelligerent rectores ecclesiarum
qui sunt indigni et symoniaci et usurarii cum quanto
periculo comedunt, quoniam super morsellum iniuste
adquisitum sedet Diabolus, sedet Catus qui animas
deuorat, mallent comedere panem [h]ordeaceum cum
bona consciencia quam omnes delicias cum tali socio.

[The House Mouse and the Field Mouse

Against simoniacs and usurers

The house mouse asked the field mouse what he
usually had to eat. The field mouse replied: "Wild
beans and, sometimes, dried wheat or barley
grains." "Those are quite meagre rations," answered
the house mouse. "It's a wonder you don't waste
away from hunger."

The woodland mouse then returned the
question: "And what do you eat?" "I indeed eat rich
morsels and, now and then, even have white
bread." Then he added further: "You should join me
for lunch. You'll dine on the best." Since this pleased
the field mouse, he visited the home of the house
mouse. There, men sitting at lunch tossed down
morsels and scraps. Said the house mouse to the
woodland mouse: "Don't stay standing in the entry
hole. Come on in! See how good the things are that
they're tossing aside." So the field mouse entered and
snatched a single morsel. And a cat pounced after him

and, immediately, our mouse leaped back toward the hole.

Then the house mouse said: "Ah, my brother, see what good morsels I eat regularly. You ought to stay on with me for several days." The woodland mouse replied: "They are good morsels. But do you daily have such a remarkable kind of partner?" And the house mouse asked what kind of partner he meant. "Why that monstrous mouser," said the woodland mouse, "the one who just about ate me whole." And the house mouse said in reply: "Oh of course. That's how things are. He killed both my father and mother and, often, I have barely escaped myself." The field mouse answered: "Well certainly, I would not wish to gain the whole world if it included a danger that great. You can stay with your morsels. I plan to live better, having my bread and water in security, than I would having every delicacy—while having, also, a 'partner' like that."

I'd rather gnaw a bean than be gnawed by continual fear.

Thus many men—hoping to make acquaintance with rulers of the churches, rulers who are undeserving and are simoniacs and usurers—eat their meals in the company of a danger just as great. For over the unjustly acquired morsel sits the Devil, the cat who devours souls. They might well prefer eating barley bread, accompanied by a good conscience, over dining on all sorts of delicacies while having such a "partner."][77]

There are parallels between this fable and Henryson's, some likely generic. The relative separation in social status and well-being of the two mice, the invitation to dine, the *sentence*, elements of the *moralitas*, and the appearance of the cat to interrupt the feast are all elements parallel with Henryson's poem. Jamieson emphasizes particularly the extra attention to the cat as a reason for believing Odo's fable to be Henryson's immediate source.[78] If Jamieson's hypothesis is correct, Henryson's use of this fable shows his powers as an original creative force and sheds some interesting light on his use of techniques of Amplification as described in the *Poetria nova*.

Geoffrey generally couches his approach to Amplification in terms of the use of a series of figures mixed with *topoi*. Since invention is a critical part of the creative task in "amplifying" or "drawing out" a tale, such mixture is hardly surprising. His argument for the use of multiple techniques is that "sententia cum sit/Unica, non unoveniat contenta paratu /Sed variet vestes et mutatoria sumat. . . ." [though your sententia be one single thing, let it not come content with one costume].[79] Having briefly made his point at the outset, Geoffrey then launches into a descriptive catalogue of the "varieties of apparel," including the following: repetition, periphrasis, comparison, apostrophe, personification, digression, description, and opposition. At appropriate points in the text, he also provides models of the techniques for possible imitation. While this list of techniques is not necessarily exhaustive in terms of modern approaches to expanding source material, it would have provided Henryson a useful catalogue in his approach to a tale such as Odo's.

In contrast with Odo's brief fable, Henryson's tale of "The Uponlandis Mous and the Burges Mous" runs to 202 lines with a *moralitas* of an additional 31 lines. Henryson's adaptation can be used to illustrate virtually every one of Geoffrey's techniques. The use of repetition, Geoffrey's first technique, is one of the most often noted elements of the tale. In this instance, Henryson uses repetition in close conjunction with additional description. As previously observed, Jamieson comments about the attention to the cat in Odo's tale. Henryson expands the incident even more:

> With fair tretie ʒit scho gart hir vpryse,
> And to the burde thay went and togidder sat.
> And scantlie had thay drunkin anis or twyse,
> Quhen in come Gib Hunter, our iolie cat,
> And bad God speid. The burges vp with that,
> And till hir hole scho fled as fyre of flint;
> Bawdronis the vther be the bak hes hint.
>
> Fra fute to fute he kest hir to and fra,
> Quhylis vp, quhylis doun, als tait as ony kid.

> Quhylis wald he lat hir rin vnder the stra;
> Quhylis wald he wink, and play with hir buk heid;
> Thus to be selie mous grit pane he did;
> Quhill at the last throw fair fortune and hap,
> Betwix the dosor and the wall scho crap.
>
> Syne vp in haist behind the parraling
> So hie scho clam that Gilbert micht not get hir,
> And be the clukis craftelie can hing
> Till he wes gane; hir cheir wes all the better.

(ll. 323–40)

Odo's "our mouse leaped back toward the hole" has been amplified by a description of the tossing and torment to which Gib submits her. In similar fashion, we learn additional information about her hairbreadth escape. This incident also provides an example of repetition of a scene Henryson himself introduced earlier in the tale. If Henryson found one interruption of the mice's feast to be effective in Odo, it would appear that he decided to double the artistic tension by making the cat one of two intruders on their meal. The first is a spencer, whose appearance in their world is less comic and less unsettling than that of the cat:

> Thus as thay sat in all thair iolitie,
> The spenser come with keyis in his hand
> Oppinnit the dure, and thame at denner fand.
>
> Thay taryit not to wesche, as I suppose,
> Bot on to ga, quha micht formest win.
> The burges had ane hole, and in scho gois;
> Hir sister had na hole to hyde hir in.
> To se that selie mous, it wes grit sin;
> So desolate and will off ane gude reid;
> For verray dreid scho fell in swoun neir deid.
>
> Bot, as God wald, it fell ane happie cace:
> The spenser had na laser for to byde,
> Nowther to seik nor serche, to char nor chace,
> Bot on he went, and left the dure vp wyde.
> The bald burges his passage weill hes spyde;

Out off hir hole scho come and cryit on hie,
'How fair ȝe, sister? Cry peip, quhair euer ȝe be!'
(ll. 292–308)

The spencer provides a more mundane interruption of their planned schedule. His intrusion is abrupt, since he "had na laser for to byde," and he poses no real threat to the mice, who are able to scramble for cover quickly. Henryson's use of this incident as foreshadowing heightens the drama when, later in the poem, the two mice must deal with the more serious threat posed by the cat. By using Geoffrey's precept "multiplice forma/Dissimuletur idem" [one and the same thing be disguised in multiple form],[80] Henryson has heightened his comedy by establishing a progression of two threatening experiences with the second described in somewhat more burlesque and hyperbolic terms. He has also reinforced his (and Odo's) *sentence* by showing that the world of the burgess mouse, which initially appeared comfortable and satisfying, is threatened in the narrative not just once but twice. Some commentators have even attempted to show how Henryson established contemporaneous political meanings with this use of repetition, associating the spencer with royal intrusions on the prerogatives of the burgesses of Edinburgh and the cat possibly with James III whose efforts to consolidate the kingdom of Scotland intruded on the traditional prerogatives of rural nobles and burgesses alike.[81] Henryson's goals could have been artistic, moral, or political.

Henryson's approach to these two scenes also establishes his use of another of Geoffrey's techniques. Comparison (including contrast) in fact provides the overriding framework for Henryson's Amplification of the poem. One of the major points of difference between Odo's poem and Henryson's is the greater reinforcement of the comparison and contrast between the lives of the two mice. As observed above, part of the contrast is established through repetition, but, since comparison is so important in reinforcing the *moralitas* of the tale, Henryson uses it as the basic structure for developing Geoffrey's other techniques of Amplification. With regard to comparison itself, Geoffrey cites three major linguistic signals: "more than, less than, just as. " Henryson uses the relationships established by these words in his portrayal of the two mice. Their individual characterizations are established in a comparative network, with the safe penury of the uponland mouse's life sharply contrasted with the perilous affluence of the town mouse. Words and phrases such as "eldest," "Mair to blame," "weill suffice," "better"

and the like are key fulcrums in the poem. In one form or another states
of comparison are emphasized in every aspect of Henryson's expansion
of this poem, as illustrated by the analysis below. They also underlie the
central theme of his *moralitas*.

Geoffrey's technique of periphrasis is exemplified in the use of
proverbs when the burgess mouse comments "My gude friday is better
nor your pace" (l. 248). As a form of periphrasis, the proverb expands
the number of words needed to convey the content, cloaks it in a
familiar mode of expression, and appeals to the authority of traditional
wisdom. To illustrate the context and other aspects of Henryson's use
of this device, compare his passage with Odo's Spartan "Those are quite
meagre rations . . . . It's a wonder you don't waste away from hunger":

> Quhen thay wer lugit thus, thir sely myse,
> The ȝoungest sister into hir butterie hyid,
> And brocht furth nuttis and peis, in steid off spyce;
> Giff thair wes weilfair, I do it on thame besyde.
>
> This burges mous prunȝit forth in pryde,
> And said, 'Sister, is this ȝour dayly fude?'
> 'Quhy not,' quod scho, 'think ȝe this meit nocht gude?'
>
> 'My fair sister,' quod scho, 'haue me excusit;
> This rude dyat and I can not accord.
> To tender meit my stomaok is ay vsit,
> For quhy I fair alsweill as ony lord.
> Thir wydderit peis and nuttis, or thay be bord,
> Wil brek my teith and mak my wame ful sklender,
> Quhilk vsit wes before to meitis tender.'
>
> (ll. 204–10, 218–24)

Henryson uses apposition as a means of periphrasis, modifying "they"
in line 204 with "thir sely myse," a repetition and expansion of the
pronoun. However, his use of periphrasis is also directly related to the
use of description. The meal served by the uponland mouse becomes
more vividly "This rude dyat." The effects of such fare on the city
mouse will not be simply pain and hunger, but the food "Wil brek my
teith and mak my wame ful sklender." The city mouse's stomach is a
special subject for artistic expansion since it has grown accustomed "to
meitis tender." In his use of periphrasis in these lines, Henryson

continues to implement the technique of comparison, emphasizing the differences between the customs and expectations of the two mice.

Henryson relies on description as a means of amplification throughout the poem. Geoffrey's definition of description includes what modern rhetoricians would call "description" and "narration." Generally Henryson's most distinctive use of the technique in this poem occurs in conjunction with the device of personification that he inherited in his use of the beast fable. Personification is inherent in this genre.[82] Henryson's decision to use this form committed him irrevocably to giving non-human things or creatures human characteristics. Perhaps, however, the difference between great and pedestrian fabulists is illustrated by their use of pertinent detail in the description of characters or extension of personification. One of Henryson's small masterpieces is the depiction of the country mouse. In Odo, the mouse is described simply as a "field mouse" or a "woodland mouse," stereotyped in the interests of concentrating on the moral. From the outset, Henryson provides additional description which gives the creature a personality and a place:

> Esope, myne authour, makis mentioun
> Of twa myis, and thay wer sisteris deir,
> Of quham the eldest duelt in ane borous toun;
> The vther wynnit vponland weill neir,
> Richt soliter, quhyle vnder busk and breir,
> Quhilis in the corne, in vther mennis skaith,
> As owtlawis dois, and levit on hir waith.
>
> This rurall mous in to the wynter tyde
> Had hunger, cauld, and tholit grit distres. . . .
>
> (ll. 162–70)

The country mouse lives alone and subsists on products grown by others. In winter the mouse must confront cold and hunger. In addition both mice are female, a subject of comment and speculation in Henryson criticism. This detail possibly plays on sexual stereotypes to enhance their vulnerability to the intrusions of the cat and the spencer but it also provides a framework for the depiction of character. The fact that the country mouse lives "uponland" provides a specifically Scottish sense of her origin. Perhaps one of Henryson's most striking additions is to be found in his assertion that she lives "As outlawis dois," to some scholars a further reflection that she may be closely associated with highlands outlaws of Scotland.[83] That association seems further reinforced when she is later visited by her sister. The burgess mouse arrives in pilgrim's garb, interpreted as protection against bandits who would be less likely to harm a member of clergy or someone on a religious pilgrimage. Henryson's description of their meeting reinforces the possible associations with illegal activity:

> Bairfute allone, with pykestaf in hir hand,
> As pure pylgryme, scho passit owt off town
> To seik hir sister, baith oure daill and down.
>
> Throw mony wilsum awyis can scho walk,
> Throw mosse and mure, throw bankis, busk, and breir,
> Fra fur to fur, cryand fra balk to balk,
> 'Cum furth to me, my awain sueit sister deir!
>
> Cry peip anis!' With that the mous culd heir
> And knew hir voce, as kinnisman will do
> Be verray kynd, and furth scho come hir to.
>
> (ll. 180–89).

The signal which prompts the country mouse's appearance suggests her furtive nature and less than legitimate status. This element of her character is a reflection of the harsh life in the Scottish highlands during the fifteenth century and also reinforces the use of comparison in the framework of the tale.

Henryson also extends the description of the country mouse's lodging and food, which reflect on her general character and, more specifically, her secretive nature. Odo treats the lodgings not at all and mentions only that the country mouse eats "wild beans and, sometimes, dried wheat or barley grains." Henryson, apparently not content with Odo's brevity, provides additional detail to make the scene fully dramatic:

> And in the samin thay went, but mair abaid,
> Withoutin fyre or candill birnand bricht,
> For comonly sic pykeris luffis not lycht.
> Quhen thay wer lugit thus, thir sely myse,
> The 3oungest sister into hir butterie hyid,

> And brocht furth nuttis and peis, in steid off spyce;
> Giff thair wes welfair, I do it on thame besyde.
> This burges mous prun3it forth in pryde,
> And said, 'Sister, is this 3our dayly fude?'
> 'Quhy not,' quod scho, 'think 3e this meit nocht gude?'
>
> 'Na, be my saull, I think it bot ane scorne.'
> 'Madame,' quod scho, '3e be the mair to blame.
> My mother sayd, efter that we wer borne,
> That I and 3e lay baith within ane wame;
> I keip the ryte and custome off my dame,
> And off my syre, levand in pouertie,
> For landis haue we nane in propertie.'
>
>   (ll. 201–17)

The fact that they eat "Without fyre or candill" once again calls attention to the element of secrecy in the country mouse's life. Henryson tells us that the uponland mouse has a "butterie" in which her food is stored and he relates in detail the dialogue between the two mice about the menu. All of these details enhance the drama and the effectiveness of the *moralitas* of the tale.

The appeal that the country mouse makes to their family history, not found in Odo, is an example, no matter how brief, of another of Geoffrey's techniques, digression. Geoffrey defines digression as follows:

> Si velit ulterius tractatus linea tendi,
> Materiae fines exi paulumque recede
> Et diverte stylum; sed nec divertere longe
> Unde gravet revocare gradum : modus iste modesto
> Indiget ingenio, ne sit via longior aequo.
> Est etiam quaedam digressio quando propinqua
> Transeo, quod procul est praemittens ordine verso.
> Progressurus enim medium quandoque relinquo
> Et saltu quodam quasi transvolo; deinde revertor
> Unde prius digressus eram.
>
> [If the lines of the treatise need to be stretched out still farther, step outside the confines of the subject matter and give a little ground and divert your

stylus; but do not divert it far off, to a point from
which it may be troublesome to recall your step. This
device requires a discreet talent lest it be a bypath
longer than is meet. Indeed, it is a kind of digression
when I pass over things which are near, presenting in
inverted order what is at a distance. For now and
then, being about to proceed to the middle, I leave
off, and by a leap as it were, I vault over a certain
matter; then I revert to the point whence I had before
digressed.][84]

The digression to an earlier period in time fits his model perfectly.
While the uponland mouse's remarks do move the subject of discussion
from the meal to their family history, the digression is a relatively
natural one. It constitutes a type of response to the city mouse's finicky
rejection of the meal while exploiting a natural human characteristic.
It is typical for relatives long separated to discuss family relationships
both as a means of "catching up" on news and re-establishing bonds and
common interests. In that sense, Henryson's use of this digression
follows Geoffrey's admonition not to "divert [your stylus] far off."

Another stanza in this same scene illustrates Henryson's use of
Geoffrey's technique of opposition. Geoffrey lists opposition last among
his techniques of Amplification, perhaps suggesting that he felt its
usefulness would be limited. He defines it as follows:

Quaelibet induitur duplicem sententia formam :
Altera propositam rem ponit et altera tollit
Oppositam. Duplex modus in rem consonat unam
Sieque fluunt vocum rivi duo :. . . .

[. . . any statement you please may be dressed in
twofold form. One sets out the thing proposed and the
other denies the reverse of it. A twofold mode thus
harmonizes into one statement, and the stream of
words flows in two branches.][85]

Geoffrey's examples suggest that he intends this figure to be used with
shorter syntactic and narrative units rather than for more sweeping
purposes or organizational structure. Henryson makes use of this figure
throughout his works, but one example immediately follows the lines

discussed above. After the country mouse has accused the burgess
mouse of unduly putting on airs because "landis have we nane in
propertie" (l. 217), the burgess mouse responds:

> 'My fair sister,' quod scho, 'haue me excusit;
> This rude dyat and I can not accord.
> To tender meit my stomok is ay vsit,
> For quhy I fair alsweill as ony lord.
> Thir wydderit peis and nuttis, or thay be bord,
> Wil brek my teith and mak my wame ful sklender,
> Quhilk vsit wes before to meitis tender.'
>
> (ll. 219–24)

The second two lines of this stanza, contrasting "This rude dyat" with
"tender meit" provide a classic example of the use of opposition as
defined and illustrated by Geoffrey. This figure occurs often. Elements
of opposition include "blyith curage" and "ane Kow" (l. 235), "nicht"
and "day" (l. 257), fasting and "feist" (ll. 318–22), among others. It
appears most directly in the country mouse' cry of escape from the
burgess mouse' lodging after the former has been pommeled by the cat:

> 'Thy mangerie is mingit all with cair;
> Thy guse is gude, thy gansell sour as gall;
> The subcharge off thy seruice is bot sair;
> Sa sall thow find heir-efterwart may fall.
> I thank ȝone courtyne and ȝone perpall wall
> Off my defence now fra ȝone crewell beist.
> Almichtie God keip me fra sic ane feist.
>
> (ll. 344–50)

This entire passage uses opposition for a summary statement of the
major theme of the poem. The line, "Thy guse is gude, thy gansell sour
as gall" (l. 345), especially reflects the precise figurative language
Geoffrey suggests. At the level of the phrase and the sentence, this
figure was clearly useful to Henryson in emphasizing the general
framework of the poem that he established through the more
comprehensive use of comparison.

Henryson's expansion of Odo's *moralitas* further reflects the
importance of digression, comparison, and opposition in his use of
Amplification, while also introducing a new technique. Instead of Odo's

exhortations against simoniacs and usurers, Henryson provides a more fully developed exposition of the general human condition as exemplified by this tale, leaving no doubt that the country mouse has wisdom on her side:

> Freindis, heir may ȝe find, will ȝe tak heid,
> In this fabill ane gude moralitie:
> As fitchis myngit ar with nobill seid,
> Swa intermellit is aduersitie
> With eirdlie ioy, swa that na state is frie
> Without trubill or sum vexatioun,
> And namelie thay quhilk clymmis vp maist hie,
> And not content with small possessioun.
>
> Blissed be sempill lyfe withoutin dreid;
> Blissed be sober feist in quietie.
> Quha hes aneuch, of na mair hes he neid,
> Thocht it be littill into quantatie.
> Grit aboundance and blind prosperitie
> Oftymes makis ane euill conclusioun.
> The sweitest lyfe, thairfoir, in this cuntrie,
> Is sickernes, with small possessioun.
>
> O wantoun man that vsis for to feid
> Thy wambe and makis it a god to be;
> Luke to thy self, I warne the weill on deid.
> The cat cummis and to the mous hes ee;
> Quhat is avale thy feist and royaltie,
> With dreidfull hart and tribulatioun?
> Thairfoir, best thing in eird, I say for me,
> Is merry hart with small possessioun.
>
> Thy awin fyre, freind, thocht it be bot ane gleid,
> It warmis weill, and is worth gold to the;
> And Solomon sayis, gif that thow will reid,
> 'Vnder the heuin I can not better se
> Than ay be blyith and leif in honestie.'
> Quhairfoir I may conclude be this ressoun:
> Of eirthly ioy it beiris maist degre,
> Blyithnes in hart, with small possessioun.   (ll. 365–95)

Henryson's more expository digressions in this *moralitas* (sometimes coupled with an appeal to scriptural authority as in lines 389–96) emphasize his theme while generally adhering to Geoffrey's admonitions about relevance. The overall framework of his *moralitas* remains comparison, as in the fable itself. His use of opposition is found in lines such as lines 368–72, where he discusses the intermingling of "adversitie" with "eirdlie joy." Henryson has also made use of another of Geoffrey's techniques, completing the catalogue of the rhetoric of amplification. In lines lines 381–86, he introduces the technique of apostrophe. Geoffrey defines apostrophe as follows:

> Latius ut curras, sit apostropha quarta morarum,
> Qua rem detinease et ubi spatieris ad horam.
> Delecteris ea, sine qua satis esset abundans
> Coena, sed egregiae sic crescunt fercula mensae.
> Pompa dapum veuiens numerosior et mora mensae
> Tordior est signum sollemne.

> [In order that you may run still more at large, let apostrophe be the fourth device of delay, by which you may conserve the material, and within which you may expand by the hour. You may give pleasure with this device; without it your meal may be abundant enough, but with it your mere dishes become excellent courses. A parade of courses coming more numerously, and tarrying at the banquet table that proceeds more deliberately, is a mark of distinction.][86]

Geoffrey's comment that the writer may "spatieris ad horam" [expand by the hour] is doubly interesting. First, it reflects his own interest in the figure. Apostrophe, while fourth in his list of techniques of Amplification, is provided the lengthiest treatment in the section on model exercises. His comment on the technique also provides insight into Henryson's apostrophes which are often the subject of special critical interest. The technique was one which allowed the poet an opportunity to blend his poetic powers with the full range of approaches from the *ars dictaminis* and the *ars praedicandi*.

The apostrophe above clearly reflects influences of the hortatory tone of preaching. Henryson uses the fable as an opportunity to challenge "wantoun man," whose attention to needs of the flesh results in idolatry of the belly. He expands the theme to a broader focus on human appetite by directly questioning the value of "feist and royaltie" when purchased at cost of woe and dread. The theme was common in the pulpit, and the exhortation to live more virtuously is typical of Henryson's *moralitates* in the fables. Other noted apostrophes, such as the apostrophe to the "Man of Law" in "The Wolf and the Lamb" (ll. 2721–27), the apostrophe (not prayer) to God in "The Sheep and the Dog" (ll. 1295–1320) and Cresseid's apostrophe to the gods in *The Testament of Cresseid* (ll. 126–40), have all provided stimulating subjects for critical discussion.[87] Often, Henryson uses the apostrophe to epitomize his *sentence*, as he does in "The Two Mice." He may also use it to make a point about social justice, as in "The Sheep and the Dog" or he may use it as a dramatic watershed, as in *The Testament of Cresseid*. Henryson's use of this rhetorical device shows his attraction to it, sophistication in using it, and interest in reinforcing the *sentence* of his tales. Part of the reason for his interest in this particular figure could be because apostrophe, as a form of direct address, is closely based on the same principles as dialogue. One of Henryson's greatest strengths is his dialogue, which shows he possessed an ear attuned to speech and occasion.[88] With such gifts, he might be expected to find apostrophe an attractive means of expanding a tale or making a dramatic point.

Henryson used every technique in Geoffrey's inventory in this tale, whether or not he learned them specifically from the *Poetria nova* and whether or not he knew their technical names (which he likely would have, given his position as schoolmaster). If Henryson created his tale from a variety of sources, using Odo as the basis, the argument hardly needs to be modified. His creative selectivity would still reflect his own rhetorical training and preferences.

4. *Abbreviation and "The Nun's Priest's Tale"*

The same principles hold true when considering Henryson's use of Abbreviation. In the case selected here, however, there is more widespread acceptance of his source, partly perhaps because of the tradition that Henryson is considered to be a "Scots Chaucerian."[89] It is in fact generally acknowledged that Henryson's "The Taill of Schir Chanteclair and the Foxe" borrows directly from Chaucer's "Nun's Priest's Tale." The relative length of the two fables (Henryson's by far the shorter) provides an opportunity to examine Henryson's creative powers in the process of abbreviating a longer tale to suit his purposes. Geoffrey's techniques of Abbreviation are instructive in evaluating Henryson's process of creation.

Treating Abbreviation in direct contrast with Amplification, Geoffrey makes the following observations:

> Si brevis esse velis, prius ista priora recide,
> Quae pompam faciunt; modicumque prematur in orbem
> Summula materiae, quam tali comprime lege. . . .
>
> Hac brevitate potes longum succingere thema,
> Hac cymba transire fretum. Narratio facti
> Eligit hanc formam verbi, quae facta modeste
> Non superinfundat nubem, sed nube remota
> Inducet solem.
>
> [If you wish to be brief, first cut out all the aforementioned devices, which make for conspicuousness; and let there be compressed into a modest circumference a little summary of the material . . . . By means of this brevity you can cinch in an extensive theme; in this small boat you can cross an ocean. Narration of action elects this form of expression, which, performed discreetly, does not spread a cloud, but, every such cloud being far away, ushers in the sun.][90]

Clearly one of the primary focuses of Abbreviation is to target the techniques of Amplification first. That procedure alone would constitute an inventory of eight approaches. However, Geoffrey also lists seven other techniques of Abbreviation, some of which are of marginal relevance to vernacular written discourse. The techniques are also not completely discrete in terms of his initial advice with regard to Amplification. His list is as follows:

> Plurima perstringat paucis expressa locutrix
> Emphasis; –ore brevi dispendia lata coartet
> Articulus punctim caesus; – compendia quaedam

Ablativus habet cum sit sine remige solus;
– Respuat audiri bis idem; – prudentia dicti
In dictis non dicta notet; – conjunctio ne sit
Nodus clausarum, sed eas sinat ire solutas;
– Vel manus artificis multas ita conflet in unam,
Mentis ut intuitu multae videantur in una.

[Let Dame Emphasis, acting as speaker, bind many
things straitly; let Articulus, chopped off in short
phrases, compress broad roundabout things in a brief
expression; the Ablative has certain abridged
constructions in which it may stand alone without a
"rower" [i.e., a preposition]; let the same thing disdain
to be heard twice; let the skill of your expression
signify what is not said in what is said; let no
conjunction be at the joining of clauses, but leave
them to go alone; or the hand of the artificer may so
combine many matters in one, that by the insight of
the mind many things may be apparent in a single
statement.][91]

The admonition to use "no repetition of the same word" clearly overlaps
with his attempt to build on his section on Amplification. Other
techniques in this list focus more closely on syntactic compression than
general organizational strategies, perhaps on the assumption that his
negative contrast with Amplification would include the more general
approaches. He offers only two models of Abbreviation and uses his
treatment of the subject as a model of the approach itself. With a total
inventory of fifteen techniques, Geoffrey provides a vivid example of
how to use Abbreviation in dealing with complicated material. In fact,
his commentator observes "Quos quia <de> breuitate docet sub breuitate
restringit, sicut et supra in illis septem modis quibus ampliabatur
materia, diutius est immoratus" [Since he is teaching about
Abbreviation, he does so briefly, just as above he delayed a long time
on the seven methods by which material is amplified].[92]

Henryson's "Schir Chantecleir and the Foxe" demonstrates a
distinct and obvious debt to Chaucer's "Nun's Priest's Tale." Donald
MacDonald has noted eight elements which clearly identify Chaucer's
tale as Henryson's source:

1) The names of the animals.
2) The description of the cock's owner as a poor widow.
3) The emphasis on Chantecleir's beauty.
4) The praise of Chantecleir's singing by the fox.
5) The fox's attempts to disguise his tricks.
6) The repetition of the fox's attempt to trick Chantecleir.
7) The reversal of the final speeches.
8) The structure of the digression in the animals' debate.[93]

The number of distinctive parallels provides a firmer basis for this source relationship than the one between "The Two Mice" and Odo's tale. In contrast with *The Testament of Cresseid*, this tale includes the same major narrative events as Chaucer's and therefore offers an opportunity to observe Henryson at his most "Chaucerian" moment.

Henryson's text is a total of 216 lines, including the *moralitas* and a brief prologue, as compared with Chaucer's 626 lines, not including the epilogue. In view of the fact that Henryson's *moralitas* is 27 lines, he had to compress Chaucer's actual narrative within 189 lines, "abbreviating" his source to less than one-third of its original size. For the most part, the techniques he uses involve Geoffrey's admonition to "cut out" the elements in Chaucer's tale which would have been considered in the inventory of Amplification.

Given the task that lay before him, Henryson's prologue is surprising. Instead of immediately engaging the narrative, he begins with a digression on personification in the beast fable which was ultimately drawn from Aristotle:[94]

> Thocht brutall beistis be irrationall,
> That is to say, wantand discretioun,
> ȝyt ilk ane in thair kyndis naturall
> Hes mony diuers inclinatioun:
> The bair busteous, the volff, the wylde lyoun,
> The fox fenȝeit, craftie and cawtelows,
> The dog to bark on nicht and keip the hows.
>
> Sa different thay ar in properteis
> Vnknawin vnto man and infinite,
> In kynd hauand sa fell diuersiteis,
> My cunning it excedis for to dyte.
> For thy as now, I purpose for to wryte

Ane cais I fand quhilk fell this anther ȝeir
Betwix and foxe and gentill Chantecleir.

(ll. 397–410)

This use of comparison in such a theoretical setting suggests that Henryson intended to mix Amplification with Abbreviation in this tale. Once into the narrative, however, Henryson begins his use of Abbreviation immediately. It is evident in the initial description of the poor widow. Chaucer's widow and her life are described in some detail:

A povre wydwe somdeel stape in age
Was whilom dwellyng in a narwe cotage,
Biside a grove, stondynge in a dale.
This wydwe, of which I telle yow my tale,
Syn thilke day that she was last a wyf,
In pacience ladde a ful symple lyf.
For litel was hir catel and hir rente,
By housbondrie of swich as God hire sente
She foond hirself and eek hir doghtren two.
Thre large sowes hadde she and namo,
Three keen, and eek a sheep that highte Malle.
Ful Sooty was hir bour and eek hir halle,
In which she eet ful many a sklendre meel.
Of poynaunt sauce hir neded nevere a deel—
No deyntee morsel passed thurgh hir throte.
Hir diete was accordant to hir cote.
Repleccioun ne made hire never sik;
Attempree diete was al hir phisik,
And exercise, and hertes suffisaunce.
The goute lette hire nothyng for to daunce,
N'apoplexie shente nat hir heed.
No wyn ne drank she, neither whit ne reed.
Hir bord was served moost with whit and blak—
Milk and broun breed, in which she foond no lak;
Seynd bacoun, and somtyme an ey or tweye,
For she was, as it were, a maner deye.[95]

Henryson has compressed these 25 lines into seven:

> Ane vedow dwelt in till ane drop thay dayis
> Quhilk wan hir fude off spinning on hir rok,
> And na mair had, forsuth, as the fabill sayis,
> Except off hennis scho had ane lyttill flok,
> And thame to keip scho had ane iolie cok,
> Richt curageous, that to this wedow ay
> Deuydit nicht and crew befoir the day.

(ll. 411–17)

His most obvious device has been the elimination of description. Gone are the details about her age, her two daughters, the other farm animals, along with the opposition in the description of her diet and the repetition about her poverty. Henryson instead uses implication in placing emphasis on her poverty through the phrase "na mair had" in line three of the stanza. By using these techniques of Abbreviation he has made his widow far poorer than Chaucer's.

In the same stanza, Henryson introduces Chantecleir and the hens. Once again his laconic introductions bear comparison with Chaucer's:

> With stikkes, and a drye dych withoute,
> In which she hadde a cok hight Chauntecleer.
> In al the land of crowyng nas his peer.
> His voys was murier than the murie orgon
> On messe-dayes that in the chirche gon.
> Wel sikerer was his crowyng in his logge,
> Than is a clokke or an abbey orlogge.
> By nature he knew ech ascencioun
> Of the equynoxial in thilke toun;
> For whan degrees fiftene weren ascended,
> Thanne crew he that it myghte nat been amended.
> His coomb was redder than the fyn coral,
> And batailled as it were a castel wal;
> His byle was blak, and as the jeet it shoon;
> Lyk asure were his legges and his toon;
> His nayles whitter than the lylye flour;
> And lyk the burned gold was his colour.
> This gentil cok hadde in his governaunce

> Sevene hennes for to doon al his plesaunce,
> Whiche were his sustres and his paramours,
> And wonder lyk to hym as of colours;
> Of whiche the faireste hewed on hir throte
> Was cleped faire damoysele Pertelote.
> Curteys she was, discreet, and debonaire,
> And compaignable, and bar hyrself so faire,
> Syn thilke day that she was seven nyght oold,
> That trewely she hath the herte in hoold
> Of Chauntecleer, loken in every lith.
> He loved hire so that wel was hym therwith.
> But swich a joye was it to here hem synge,
> Whan that the brighte sonne gan to sprynge,
> In sweete accord, "My lief is faren in londe"—
> For thilke tyme, as I have understonde,
> Beestes and briddes koude speke and synge.
>
> (ll. 2848–81)

In his wholesale reduction of this passage Henryson has eliminated any
mention of the cock's beautiful voice, possibly because it would repeat
information provided later in the fable. He excises all detail about the
cock's appearance along with Chaucer's brief digression on the cock's
sense of time. He has expunged as well Chaucer's use of comparison
in Chauntecleer's description and has deleted any indication that
Pertelote has a central role in the barnyard.

In all of these regards, Henryson follows Geoffrey's advice. He
omits all of the initial discourse between Chauntecleer and Pertelote,
thereby eliminating not only dialogue but the digression on
Chauntecleer's dream and a significant number of the allusions in
Chaucer's tale along with an apostrophe, all techniques of Amplification
(ll. 2889–3214). He also omits Chaucer's reintroduction of Chauntecleer
with its pastoral description and digressions. When Henryson introduces
the fox, he uses a version of Geoffrey's concept of fusion:

> Ane lyttill fra this foirsaid vedowis hows,
> Ane thornie schaw thair wes off grit defence,
> Quhairin ane foxe, craftie and cautelous,
> Maid his repair and daylie residence,

> Quhilk to this wedow did grit violence
> In pyking off pultrie baith day and nicht,
> And na way be reuengit on him scho micht.
>
> (ll. 418–24)

In Chaucer's tale, the fox, Russell, receives greatest emphasis in the
lines by being placed as the first element in the sentence:

> A col-fox ful of sly iniquitee,
> That in the grove hadde woned yeres three,
> By heigh ymaginacioun forncast,
> The same nyght thurghout the hegges brast
> Into the yerd their Chauntecleer the faire
> Was wont, and eek his wyves, to repaire,
>
> (ll. 3215–20)

Henryson's change in emphasis here allows him to move from the
description of the widow's lodging and situation to the immediate
introduction of the fox. This technique of Abbreviation permits him to
delete almost 350 lines of Chaucer's poem while maintaining the
narrative flow of his own tale. In the introduction of the fox, Henryson
eliminates many of the same types of details that he targeted in the
description of Chauntecleer along with Chaucer's apostrophe to this
"false mordrour" (ll. 3226–51), details in the description of the cock,
and a digression based on St. Augustine, Boece and Bishop Bradwardyn
on free will and predestination. Henryson substitutes for these details
and digression a brief comment on the fox's plans, thereby providing
the transition for the meeting between Chantecleir and the fox.
Henryson also eliminates initial mention of witnesses (Pertelote and the
rest of the flock) and direct reference to Chauntecleer's fear, which he
handles by implication in his dialogue:

> Dissimuland in to countenance and cheir,
> On kneis fell and simuland thus he said,
> "Gude morne, my maister, gentill Chantecleir!'
> With that the cok start bakwart in ane braid.
> 'Schir, be my saull, ꝫe neid not be effraid,
> Nor ꝫit for me to start nor fle abak;
> I come bot heir seruice to ꝫow to mak.
>
> (ll. 432–38)

The fox's initial remarks are reduced to a scant ten lines expunging allusions, detail about the family and the fox's closeness to Chauntecleer's father (some of which will subsequently appear). Henryson also introduces a response on the part of the cock to help maintain narrative continuity. He states in amazement, "Knew ȝe my father?" (l. 446). The comment would be unnecessary in Chaucer both because of the length of the fox's speech and Chaucer's depiction of the cock's reaction. Chaucer dedicates 54 lines (ll. 3282–3335) to dialogue between the fox and the cock. This passage concludes with the fox's grabbing Chantecleir "by the gargat" (l. 3335). In his shorter version, Henryson does not move immediately to the fox's seizure of the cock. Henryson reintroduces approaches from the fox's initial speech, once again omitting descriptive detail and Chaucer's allusions to Boece and *Daun Burnel the Ars*:

> 'Knew ȝe my father?' quod the cok, and leuch.
> 'ȝea, my fair sone, forsuth I held his heid
> Quhen that he deit vnder ane birkin beuch;
> Syne said the Dirigie quhen that he wes deid.
> Betuix vs twa how suld thair be ane feid?
> Quhame suld ȝe traist bot me, ȝour seruitour,
> That to ȝour father did sa grit honour?
>
> 'Quhen I behald ȝour fedderis fair and gent,
> ȝour beik, ȝour breist, ȝour hekill, and ȝour kame—
> Schir, be my saull, and the blissit sacrament,
> My hart warmys, me think I am at hame.
> ȝow for to serue, I wald creip on my wame
> In froist and snaw, in wedder wan and weit,
> And lay my lyart loikkis vnder ȝour feit.'
>
> (ll. 446–59)

However, Henryson amplifies the capture scene in some interesting ways. In Chaucer's poem the capture follows hard on the heels of the fox's lengthy address with no intervening dialogue between him and Chauntecleer. It is described in a mere four lines:

> And daun Russell the fox stirte up atones,
> And by the gargat hente Chauntecleer,
> And on his bad toward the wode hym beer,
> For yet ne was ther no man that hym sewed.
>
> (ll. 3334–37)

Chaucer then employs digression and apostrophe (including one to Geoffrey himself) to emphasize in possibly burlesque terms the nature of this great "calamity."[96] Henryson employs more variety in his dialogue and adds details to the capture not found in Chaucer. First, besides wryly noting his connection with Chantecleir's family, the fox takes special pains to challenge the cock's identity as a means of getting him to sing:

> '3e ar, me think, changit and degenerate
> Fra 3our father and his conditioun.
> Off craftie crawing he micht beir the croun,
> For he wald on his tais stand and craw.
> This is na le; I stude beside and saw.'
>
> (ll. 462–66)

The trick works, but, even after the cock demonstrates his voice, the fox continues the challenge. Having used the cock's father as basis for challenging his singing, the fox now renews his challenge on the basis of intellect. He grants that the cock is his "fatheris sone and air vpricht" but asserts that he is "slicht" of his father's "cunning":

> Quod schir Lowrence, 'Weill said, sa mot I the.
> 3e ar 3our fatheris sone and air vpricht,
> Bot off his cunning 3it 3e want ane slicht.'
>
> (ll. 469–71)

This challenge prompts additional dialogue:

> 'Quhat?" quod the cok. "He wald, and haif na dout,
> Baith wink, and craw, and turne him thryis about.'
>
> (ll. 472–73)

For details prior to the capture, Henryson seems to return directly to Chaucer's text. Chaucer provides the following description of the cock's motivation:

> This Chauntecleer his wynges gan to bete,
> As man that koude his traysoun nat espie,
> So was he ravysshed with his flaterie.
> Allas, ye lordes, many a fals flatour
> Is in youre courtes, and many a losengeour,
> That plesen yow wel moore, by my feith,
> Than he that soothfastnesse unto yow seith.
> Redeth Ecclesiaste of flaterye;
> Beth war, ye lordes, of hir trecherye.   (ll. 3322–30)

Chaucer not only shows that flattery led the cock to his folly but even inserts a brief digression. His admonition to "ye lordes" is inserted into the dialogue along with the admonition to consult Ecclesiastes for good advice. Henryson maintains the same narrative events and theme, incorporating them into one stanza in which the capture is described:

> The cok, inflate with wind and fals vane gloir,
> That mony puttis vnto confusioun,
> Traisting to win ane grit worschip thairfoir,
> Vnwarlie winkand walkit vp and doun,
> And syne to chant and craw he maid him boun—
> And suddandlie, be he had crawin ane note,
> The foxe wes war, and hint him be the throte.
>
> (ll. 474–80)

In reducing Chaucer's elaboration of this theme Henryson has eliminated both Chaucer's use of comparison (with the court) and his citation of scriptural authority. He cannot resist slightly expanding the thematic implications in line 475. The line "That mony puttis vnto confusion" introduces a generalization of his theme largely expanded in the narration of the cock's unwise actions. Yet these lines receive far less emphasis than Chaucer's. While Chaucer inserts his thematic expansion into an obtrusive apostrophe and follows his advice with a biblical citation, Henryson inserts his moral comment in a subordinate clause. Henryson tends to reserve allegorical comparisons and biblical allusions more strictly for his *moralitates*.

Henryson then omits completely Chaucer's subsequent digression
and apostrophes, perhaps because some of the irony implicit in this
passage did not fit his purpose. He turns next to Pertok, Sprutok and
Coppok, deleting Chaucer's reference to the death of Priam. He also
abbreviates the grief of the hens before the appearance of the
widow. Chaucer engenders bathos in this scene through his use of
exaggeration and the comparison established by the use of allusion:

> Certes, swich cry ne lamentacioun
> Was nevere of ladyes maad whan Ylioun
> Was wonne, and Pirrus with his streite swerd
> Whan he hadde hent Kyng Priam by the berd
> And slayn hym, as seith us *Eneydos,*
> As maden alle the hennes in the clos,
> What they had seyn of Chauntecleer the sighte.
> But sovereynly dame Pertelote shrighte
> Ful louder than dide Hasdrubales wyf
> What that hir housbonde hadde lost his lyf,
> And that the Romayns hadde brend Cartage.
> She was so ful of torment and of rage
> That wilfully into the fyr she sterte
> And brende hirselven with a stedefast herte.
> O woful hennes, right so criden ye
> As whan that Nero brende the citee
> Of Rome cryden senatoures wyves
> For that hir husbondes losten alle hir lyves—
> Withouten gilt this Nero hath hem slayn.
>
> (ll. 3355–73)

Henryson eliminates the bathos along with the comparison by simply
stating "With that Pertok, Sprutok, and Coppok cryit" (l. 483). With the
appearance of Chaucer's widow and her two daughters in lines
3375–3402, comic turmoil ensues. They cry "Out, harrow and
weylaway!" and raise such a commotion that the whole farmstead
becomes embroiled in their anguish. From their viewpoint, "It seemed
as that hevene sholde falle" (l. 3401). Henryson deletes virtually all of
Chaucer's details and comparisons at this point, summarizing the
widow's reaction as follows:

> The wedow hard, and with ane cry come out.
> Seand the cace scho sichit and gaif ane schout,
> 'How, murther, reylok!' with ane hiddeous beir,
> 'Allace, now lost is gentill Chantecleir!'
>
> As scho wer woid, with mony ȝell and cry,
> Ryuand hir hair, vpon hir breist can beit;
> Syne paill off hew, half in ane extasy,
> Fell doun for cair in swoning and in sweit.
>
> (ll. 484–91)

While there is still hyperbole in these lines, Henryson's excisions diminish the bathetic tone in Chaucer's lines. His description of the situation is more realistic, relying less on emotional exaggeration than Chaucer's description. He does not involve "Colle, oure dogge" along with Talbot and Garland in a farm scene arousing "cow and calf" (l. 3385). Certainly Henryson makes no suggestion that Heaven might fall. His widow's grief remains exaggerated, emphasizing Chantecleir's importance to the farm, but he has neatly compressed Chaucer's 28 lines into eight.

Chaucer then turns immediately to another scene involving Chauntecleer and Russell, but Henryson chooses to keep his focus in the barnyard, once again amplifying Chaucer's tale through the use of dialogue. He focuses particularly on Chantecleir's character by introducing dialogue among his now (apparently) widowed hens:

> 'Allace', quod Pertok, makand sair murning,
> With teiris grit attour hir cheikis fell,
> 'ȝone wes our drowrie and our dayis darling,
> Our nichtingall, and als our orlege bell,
> Our walkryfe watche, vs for to warne and tell
> Quhen that Aurora with hir curcheis gray
> Put vp hir heid betuix the nicht and day.
>
> 'Quha sall our lemman be? Quha sall vs leid?
> Quhen we ar sad quha sall vnto vs sing?
> With his sweit bill he walk brek vs the breid;
> In all this warld wes thair ane kynder thing?
> In paramouris he wald do vs plesing,
> At his power, as nature list him geif.
> Now efter him, allace, how sall we leif?'

Quod Sprutok than, 'Ceis, sister, off ȝour sorrow.
ȝe be to mad, for him sic murning mais.
We sall fair weill, I find Sanct Iohne to borrow;
The prouerb sayis, "Als gude lufe cummis as gais."
I will put on my haly-dayis clais
And mak me fresch agane this iolie May,
Syne chant this sang, "Wes neuer wedow sa gay!"

'He wes angry and held vs ay in aw,
And woundit with the speir off ielowsy.
Off chalmerglew, Pertok, full weill ȝe knaw
Waistit he wes, off nature cauld and dry.
Sen he is gone, thairfoir, sister, say I,
Be blyith in baill, for that is best remeid.
Let quik to quik, and deid ga to the deid.'

Than Pertok spak, that feinȝeit faith befoir,
In lust but lufe that set all hir delyte,
'Sister, ȝe wait off sic as him ane scoir
Wald not suffice to slaik our appetyte.
I hecht ȝow be my hand, sen ȝe ar quyte,
Within ane oulk, for schame and I durst speik,
To get ane berne suld better claw oure breik.'

Than Coppok lyke ane curate spak full crous:
'ȝone wes ane verray vengeance from the heuin.
He wes sa lous and sa lecherous,
Seis coud he nocht with kittokis ma than seuin,
Bot rychteous God, haldand the balandis euin,
Smytis rycht sair, thocht he be patient,
Adulteraris that list thame not repent.

'Prydefull he wes, and ioyit off his sin,
And comptit not for Goddis fauour nor feid,
Bot traistit ay to rax and sa to rin,
Quhill at the last his sinnis can him leid
To schamefull end and to ȝone suddand deid.
Thairfoir it is the verray hand off God
That causit him be werryit with the tod.'

                                              (ll. 495–543)

Only Pertok of all the hens seems to have any regrets about the loss of their "lemman", and her lament is partially self-centered with concern expressed about the hens' future. Even these feelings, however, are spurned by Sprutok and Coppok, who generally view Chantecleir as a tyrant who received his "just desserts." The supposedly deceased head of the flock is described as "ane verray vengeance from the heuin" and is accused of anger, lust, and pride among other sins. Sprutok even indicates that she will don her holiday finery to celebrate his death. She goes on to use a proverb (an example of Geoffrey's periphrasis) to indicate how little she is affected by Chantecleir's death. Given his general abbreviation of this tale, it is significant that Henryson uses most of Geoffrey's techniques of amplification, including repetition, comparison, digression, and opposition in this unflattering analysis of Chantecleir's character. In function, these lines are similar to Chaucer's dialogue on dreams between Chauntecleer and Pertelote. In both instances, we are provided revelations about the cock's character. Henryson's passage, however, seems much more severe in its portrayal of Chantecleir.[97] By introducing the scene after the cock has supposedly been killed, he makes the comments seem much harsher. Woe be to the creature who has such sentiments for his epitaph!

Some of the relative grimness of this scene is lightened when Henryson again turns his attention to the widow, who has been lying in a swoon the whole time. It is now discovered that indeed she has small hunting dogs (with alliterative names!) and she calls them into the search for Chantecleir, thus raising a Chaucerian clatter—somewhat reduced, but a clatter nonetheless:

> Quhen this wes said, this wedow fra hir swoun
> Start vp on fute, and on hir kennettis cryde,
> 'How, Birkye, Berrie, Bell, Bawsie, Broun,
> Rype Schaw, Rin Weil, Curtes, Nuttieclyde!
> Togidder all but grunching furth ȝe glyde!
> Reskew my nobill cok or he be slane,
> Or ellis to me se ȝe cum neuer agane!'

> With that, but baid, thay braidet ouer the bent;
> As fyre off flint thay ouer the feildis flaw;
> Full wichtlie thay throw wood and wateris went,
> And ceissit not, schir Lourence quhill thay saw.
>
> (ll. 544–54)

Henryson has now introduced a reduced version of the Chaucerian turmoil in lines 3375–3401. He has also resumed Chaucer's storyline and accordingly turns his attention to the cock and the fox. In Chaucer's version of the tale, it is the cock who initiates the conversation while he is lying on the fox's back. He argues that the fox should show his courage and face down his pursuers (ll. 3405–13). By contrast, Henryson begins the scene with the fox's thoughts:

> Vnto the cok in mynd he said, 'God sen
> That I and thow wer fairlie in my den.'
>
> Then spak the cok, with sum gude spirit inspyrit,
> 'Do my counsall and I sall warrand the.
> Hungrie thow art, and for grit trauell tyrit,
> Richt faint off force and may not ferther fel:
> Swyith turne agane and say that I and ȝe
> Freindis ar maid and fellowis for and ȝeir.
> Than will thay stint, I stand for it, and not steir.'
>
> (ll. 556–64)

He has omitted the detail about Chauntecleer's being on the fox's back. Chantecleir uses exactly the same number of lines as Chaucer's Chauntecleer for his appeal, but Henryson has changed the nature of his argument. Instead of appealing to the fox's own vainglory and sense of power, Henryson's Chantecleir relies on the *topos* of expediency and appeals to Lowrence's hunger and weariness. His appeal reduces the reassurance that the hounds will indeed retreat in the face of Lowrence's challenge. Chaucer's Russell responds tersely and immediately, "In feith it shal be don" (l. 3414). Henryson amplifies this response by inserting a comment on Lowrence's character:

> This tod, thocht he wes fals and friuolus,
> And had frawdis, his querrell to defend,
> Desauit wes be menis richt meruelous,

> For falset failȝeis ay at the latter end.
> He start about, and cryit as he wes kend. . . .
>
> (ll. 565–69)

In both tales the cock escapes. In this passage Henryson cannot resist
adding brief authorial comment to Chaucer's narrative:

> With that the cok he braid vnto a bewch.
> Now iuge ȝe all quhairat schir Lowrence lewch.
>
> (ll. 570–71)

In Henryson, the balance of the tale consists of only 14 lines. Chaucer
employs 19 lines for the same dialogue. Russell feigns an apology to
attempt to regain the cock's confidence. Chantecleer responds that he
will not believe the fox and adds ". . . I shewe myself both blood and
bones/If thou bigyle me any ofter than ones" (ll. 3427–28). Russell
recognizes his fault and admits his indiscretions as one who "jangleth
whan he shoulde holde his pees" (l. 3435). Henryson once again
abbreviates this scene while simultaneously slightly shifting the focus:

> Begylit thus, the tod vnder the tre
> On kneis fell, and said, 'Gude Chantecleir,
> Cum doun agane, and I but meit or fe
> Salbe ȝour man and seruand for ane ȝeir.'
> 'Na, murther, theif, and reuar, stand on reir.
> My bludy hekill and my nek sa bla
> Hes partit lowe for euer betwene vs twa.
>
> 'I wes vnwyse that winkit at thy will,
> Quhairthrow almaist I loissit had my heid.'
> 'I wes mair fule,' quod he, 'coud nocht be still,
> Bot spake to put my pray in to pleid.'
> 'Fair on, fals theif, God keip me fra thy feid.'
> With that the cok ouer the feildis tuke his flicht;
> And in at the wedowis lewer couth he licht.
>
> (ll. 572–85)

In the fox's first speech, he deletes the feigned apology and repentance,
along with the fox's offer to explain what he intended if Chantecleir is
willing to come down from the tree. Instead he substitutes the fox's

blunt and unconvincing offer to be Chantecleir's servant for a year. In the cock's response, Henryson deletes Chaucer's proverbial "I shrewe myself both blood and bones/If thou bigyle me any ofter than ones" (ll. 3427–8). Henryson's Chantecleir begins his speech with name calling and emphasizes his own bedraggled physical condition. At the end of the cock's speech, Chaucer has included another proverb echoing the foolish action which brought Chauntecleer to his current state through use of the words "wynke" and "wynketh." Henryson has retained the coherence device in "winkit" but has eliminated the proverb and made the cock's comment a much more straightforward self-indictment for his foolishness. Chaucer's Russell responds with his own self-indictment, and Henryson's Lowrence echoes the sentiment. Lowrence, however, uses comparison, a technique of Amplification, in his initial comment "I wes mair fule." With Russell's last speech, Chaucer ends his tale and moves to his moral lesson. Henryson elects to give the cock one more response and see him safely to the barnyard. Both authors append a "moralite" to this tale. Chaucer's is approximately eleven lines long and cites St. Paul. Henryson's is 35 lines long and provides an interpretation of each of the two major protagonists. The two *moralitates* are similar in theme.

Henryson's use of Abbreviation in treating Chaucer's "Nun's Priest's Tale" suggests some interesting perspectives on his view of the poet's craft. The evidence indicates that Henryson followed Geoffrey's advice to "cut out" the devices of Amplification—repetition, periphrasis (including the use of proverbs), comparison, apostrophe, personification, digression, description, and opposition—when reducing the length of a source. To a lesser extent he also used the other specific devices of Abbreviation as Geoffrey described them, perhaps especially emphasis, avoidance of repetition, and a fusion of concepts. Possibly because his deletions were so significant, there is less evidence of his use of the grammatical and stylistic techniques Geoffrey mentions. This approach seems to be typical, however, of Henryson's use of longer sources. He is most inclined to borrow a general storyline or a moral theme from his sources instead of making precise and detailed use of another author's language.[98] Given this evidence (and ignoring for the moment the arguments that all rhetoric is "only common sense" or learned by osmosis[99]), it is clear that Henryson knew the tradition embodied in Geoffrey, even if he had never studied the *Poetria nova* itself.

Another observation about Henryson's use of Abbreviation relates to his general artistry. In "The Cock and the Fox" he has not the slightest hesitation in mixing techniques of Amplification at key narrative points with his efforts to reduce the length of a work. Nor does Henryson hesitate to modify themes or sentiments while retaining approximately the equivalent length of a portion of a source he is shortening. This suggests that Henryson viewed Abbreviation and Amplification not as approaches to be slavishly followed in the treatment of sources but instead as portions of a full *repertoire* of artistic techniques in developing source materials to suit his personal taste and special rhetorical needs. Indeed, a review of his use of these two approaches in the *Fabillis* indicates that generally he favored Amplification. In his use of Odo, Caxton, the *Roman de Renart*, Gualterus' *Romulus*, Nicholas Trivet, Chaucer, and others, Henryson most often tends to expand a tale or to work from an idea or suggestion in a longer work to create his own poetry.[100] Based on what is now known about his sources, Henryson's use of them clearly suggests that he conceived his artistic role in treating sources in the broadest possible terms. While his sense of artistic freedom makes it difficult to trace his sources with precision, it also reflects the special interest of his poems and a more general attitude towards the authorial voice in fifteenth-century Scotland.

Henryson's use of any specific *ars poetriae* must remain the subject of speculation. His stylistic control, organization, and use of other poetic techniques all show the influence of this major medieval rhetorical tradition. Yet while Henryson was certainly aware of the tradition of Geoffrey of Vinsauf, he did not follow it slavishly. His use of Geoffrey's principles of organization is modified by his own interest in allusive introductions which reflect a new interest in secular *auctoritates*. His approach to Amplification and Abbreviation is tempered by his own artistic goals as he relies most heavily on Amplification (with its potential for greater scope in artistic creation) and feels free to mix the two approaches. He clearly has a debt to the tradition of Geoffrey, John of Garland, Gervase of Melkley, Eberhard, and Matthew of Vendôme, but the sophistication of his artistry shows the mastery of a student who has learned the material and adapted it to his special poetic needs.

Notes
Chapter II

1. See Martin J. Camargo, "Rhetoric," pp. 105–07; see also Schoeck, pp. 214–25; Murphy, *Rhetoric in the Middle Ages*, pp. 136–50; and James A. Schultz, "Classical Rhetoric, Medieval Poetics, and the Medieval Vernacular Prologue," *Speculum*, 59 (1984), 1–15.

2. See Huntsman, pp. 62–63; and Murphy, *Rhetoric in the Middle Ages*, p. 32.

3. See Vickers, pp. 220–21; Paolo Bagni, "Grammatica e Retorica nella Cultura Medicvale," *Rhetorica*, 2, no. 3 (1984), 267–80; Curtius, pp. 438–45; and Murphy, *Rhetoric in the Middle Ages*, pp. 174–75.

4. *The Institutio oratoria of Quintilian*, trans., H.E. Butler (Cambridge, MA, 1930), II, i, 4; pp. 206–07. There is general agreement that the translation by John Selby Watson (1856) is perhaps the best attempted; see James J. Murphy, ed., *On the Teaching of Speaking and Writing* (Carbondale, IL, 1987), p. lii. However, the more general accessibility of Butler's complete text, along with its facing Latin text, make it the best edition for current use.

5. Ioannis Saresberiensis, *Metalogicon*, ed. Clemens C. I. Webb (Oxford, 1929), I, xvii, p. 43; translation by David D. McGarry, *The Metalogicon of John of Salisbury* (Berkeley, 1955), pp. 51-52. See also Minnis, Scott, and Wallace, p. 279.

6. Minnis, Scott and Wallace, pp. 279–80. For additional comment on this problem in the ancient and medieval periods, see Wesley Trimpi, "The Quality of Fiction: The Rhetorical Transmission of Literary Theory," *Traditio*, 30 (1974), 1–118.

7. Paul E. Prill, "Rhetoric and Poetics in the Early Middle Ages," *Rhetorica*, 5 no. 2 (1987), 133.

8. For texts of these and other works, see Faral, pp. 104–380. Other texts will be cited.

9. Minnis, especially, pp. 160–210; Douglas Kelly, *Medieval Imagination: Rhetoric and the Poetry of Courtly Love* (Madison, 1978); Marjorie Curry Woods, ed. and trans., *Early Commentary on the "Poetria Nova" of Geoffrey of Vinsauf* (New York, 1985), and Murphy, *Rhetoric in the Middle Ages*, pp. 135–93.

10. For comment on the problems of attempting to establish precise influences, see James J. Murphy, "A New Look at Chaucer and The Rhetoricians," *Review of English Studies*, 15 (1964), 1–20.

11. Helen Waddell, *The Wandering Scholars* (New York, 1961), p. 136.

12. See *Laborintus* in Faral, pp. 366–70, lines 835–990; translation in *The Laborintus of Eberhard*, trans. Evelyn Carson (Unpublished thesis, Cornell University, 1930), pp. 59–66.

13. Atkins, p. 99.

14. On Geoffrey, see especially Ernest Gallo, "The *Poetria nova* of Geoffrey of Vinsauf," in *Medieval Eloquence*, pp. 68–69. See also Murphy, *Rhetoric in the Middle Ages*, pp. 169–93. For John, see Traugott Lawler, ed. and trans. *Parisiana Poetria of John of Garland* (New Haven, 1974), pp. xvii–xix.

15. See Carruthers, especially pp. 25–30 and 146, 247, and 251.

16. *Parisiana Poetria*, pp. xi–xv.

17. *Ibid.*, pp. 58–83.

18. *Ibid.*, pp. 32-33.

19. *The Poems of Robert Henryson*, ed. Denton Fox (Oxford, 1981), pp. 3–4. ll. 12–28. Hereafter, unless otherwise specified, this edition of Henryson will be used as the text for all of the poems: line numbers only will be provided. For comment on the "nuttis schell" metaphor and information on a parallel with a twelfth-century commentary on the *Thebiad*, see Philippa M. Bright, "Medieval

Concepts of the *figure* and Henryson's Figurative Technique in *The Fables*," *Studies in Scottish Literature*, 25 (1990), pp. 144–45.

20. Eco, p. 22.

21. See Jamieson, "Some Attitudes to Poetry in Late Fifteenth-Century Scotland," pp. 28–42.

22. *Parisiana Poetria*, pp. 86-87.

23. *Poetria nova*, ed. Faral, p. 220, lines 748–55; translation from "The New Poetics," p. 60. These editions will be used for all references to Geoffrey's text. For Geoffrey's original text with a facing translation, see Ernest A. Gallo, *Poetria Nova and Its Sources in Early Rhetorical Doctrine*, pp. 14–129.

24. *Poetria nova*, ed. Faral, pp. 253–54, lines 1842–47; translation from "The New Poetics," p. 99.

25. *Ibid.*, Faral, lines 1911 and 1918; translation pp. 101 and 102, respectively.

26. *The Poems of Robert Henryson*, Smith, ed., p. lxxxix.

27. See particularly Florence Ridley, "A Plea for the Middle Scots," in *The Learned and the Lewed*, ed. Larry D. Benson (Cambridge, MA, 1974) pp. 175-96, and Kindrick, *Robert Henryson*, pp. 28-56.

28. A good summary of the issues surrounding Chaucer's vocabulary and diction is provided by Norman Davis in "Chaucer and Fourteenth-century English," in *Geoffrey Chaucer*, ed. Derek Brewer (Athens, Ohio, 1975), especially pp. 71-84. See also David Wallace, "Chaucer's Continental Inheritance: The Early Poems and *Troilus and Criseyde*," in *The Cambridge Chaucer Companion*, ed. Piero Boitani and Jill Mann (Cambridge, 1986), especially pp. 25-27.

29. Michio Masui, *The Structure of Chaucer's Rime Words* (Tokyo, 1964).

30. *Ibid.*, pp. 222-26. See also A. Wigfall Green, "Meter and Rhyme in Chaucer's *Anelida and Arcite*," *University of Mississippi Studies in English*, 2 (1961), 55-63.

31. Felicity Riddy, "The Alliterative Revival" in *The History of Scottish Literature*, I, ed. R. D. S. Jack (Aberdeen, 1988), see pp. 39-40.

32. Charles B. Faulhaber, "Letter-Writer's Rhetoric: The *Summa dictaminis* of Guido Faba," in *Medieval Eloquence*, pp. 92-93.

33. For comment on Chaucer's use of alliteration see Stuart Robertson, "Old English Verse in Chaucer," *Modern Language Notes*, 42 (1928), 234-36; and Roland M. Smith, "Three Notes on the Knight's Tale," *Modern Language Notes*, 51 (1936), 320-22.

34. *The Taill of Rauf Coilyear*, ed. Sidney J.H. Herrtage, Early English Text Society, Extra Series 39 (Oxford, 1882), p. 3.

35. One central modern work on the use of oral-formulaic elements in the alliterative tradition is Ronald A. Waldron, "Oral-Formulaic Technique and Middle English Alliterative Poetry," *Speculum*, 32 (1957), 792–804.

36. Riddy, p. 42.

37. For analysis of Henryson's language in this poem see Denton Fox, "Henryson's 'Sum Practysis of Medecyne,'" *Studies in Philology*, 69 (1972) 453–60; and A.M. Kinghorn, "The Minor Poems of Robert Henryson," *Studies in Scottish Literature*, 3 (1965), pp. 30–40, especially 38–39.

38. Bengt Ellenberger *The Latin Element in the Vocabulary of the Earlier Makars: Henryson and Dunbar* (Lund, 1977), especially pp. 58-60.

39. Janel M. Mueller, *The Native Tongue and the Word* (Chicago, 1984), pp. 162–77.

40. *Three Medieval Rhetorical Arts*, p. xi.

41. Yet on the overall diction of the poem, see Ellenberger, pp. 61–62.

42. See W.S. Ramson, "The Aureate Paradox," *Parergon*, n.s.1 (1983), 93–104. For a summary of the issues, see Kindrick, *Robert Henryson*, pp. 29–31.

43. See, however, A.C. Spearing, *"The Testament of Cresseid* and the High Concise Style," in *Criticism and Medieval Poetry* (London, 1964), pp. 118–44.

44. *Parisiana Poetria*, pp. 86–87.

45. For comment, see H. Harvey Wood, ed. *Poems and Fables of Robert Henryson* (Edinburgh, 1933, rev. 1958), pp. 268–69; Kinghorn, "The Minor Poems of Robert Henryson," pp. 38–39; and Denton Fox, "Henryson's 'Sum Practysis of Medecyne,'" pp. 453–60.

46. Murphy, *Rhetoric in the Middle Ages*, p. 169.

47. See John M. Manly, "Chaucer and the Rhetoricians," *Proceedings of the British Academy*, 12 (1926), 95–113; Janette Richardson, *Blameth Nat Me: A Study of Imagery in Chaucer's Fabliaux* (The Hague, 1970); and Robert O. Payne, "Chaucer's Realization of Himself as Rhetor," in *Medieval Eloquence*, ed. Murphy, pp. 270–87.

48. Murphy, "A New Look at Chaucer and the Rhetoricians," pp. 1–20.

49. See Murphy, *Rhetoric in the Middle Ages*, p. 169.

50. Camargo, "Toward A Comprehensive Art," p. 186.

51. See Gallo, who reports a survey showing the existence of over 200 mss., "The *Poetria nova* of Geoffrey of Vinsauf," *Medieval Eloquence*, p. 68; see also Murphy, ed., *Three Medieval Rhetorical Arts*, p. xxii for comments on Geoffrey's "representative" work.

52. See Roger P. Parr, trans., *Documentum de mode et arte dictandi et versificandi* (Milwaukee, 1968) pp. 97–105.

53. Woods, *Commentary*, p. xxi.

54. See Eco, pp. 4–16.

55. *Poetria nova*, ed. Faral, pp. 198–99, 11. 50–59; translation from "The New Poetics," p. 34–35.

56. Woods *Commentary*, pp. 16–17.

57. MacQueen, *Robert Henryson*, p. 28. However, Roderick Lyall has challenged MacQueen's assertion in "Henryson and Boccaccio," *Anglia*, 99 (1981), 38–59. Ian Bishop has explained another approach to invention in Henryson in "Lapidary Formulas as Topics of Invention—From Thomas of Hales to Henryson," *Review of English Studies*, 37 (1986), 469–77.

58. Eco, pp. 92ff.

59. See *Parisiana Poetria*, pp. 52–57.

60. See Camargo, "Rhetoric," who observes that for the most part the masters of the *artes poetriae* were "grammarians rather than rhetoricians" (p. 107).

61. Minnis, pp. ix–xi.

62. See C.W. Jentoft "Henryson as Authentic 'Chaucerian': Narrator, Character, and Courtly Love in *The Testament of Cresseid*," *Studies in Scottish Literature*, 10 (1972), pp. 94–102; and Marshall W. Stearns, "Henryson and Chaucer," *Modern Language Quarterly*, 6 (1945), 271–84.

63. For a good summary of the arguments see Florence Ridley, "A Plea for the Middle Scots," pp. 175–96; see also Walter Scheps, "Chaucer and the Middle Scots Poets," *Studies in Scottish Literature*, 22 (1987), pp. 44–59.

64. For special comment see Donald MacDonald, "Chaucer's Influence on Henryson's *Fables*: The Use of Proverbs and Sententiae," *Medium Aevum*, 39 (1970), 21–27.

65. Carruthers, pp. 189–220.

66. Minnis, pp. 9–72.

67. Owst, *Literature and Pulpit*, pp. 149–209.

68. Minnis, pp. 73–117.

69. *Poetria nova*, ed. Faral, p. 203, lines 203–11; translation from "The New Poetics," p. 41.

70. Woods, *Commentary*, pp. 38–9.

71. See Matthew of Vendôme, *Ars versificatoria* in Faral, IV, 1-3, p. 180; translated in *The Art of Versification*, trans. Aubrey E. Galyon (Ames, 1980), p. 100. On the role of these techniques in medieval narrative, see Jane Baltzell, "Rhetorical Amplification and Abbreviation in the Structure of Medieval Narrative," *Pacific Coast Philology*, 2 (1966), 32–38. For comment on their classical roots, see Kelly, *The Ares of Poetry and Prose*, p. 77.

72. In addition to other works cited above, see, for instance, Stearns, *Robert Henryson*, pp. 48–67, and, for a summary of viewpoints, Gray, *Robert Henryson*, pp. 162–66.

73. Gavin Bone, "The Source of Henryson's 'Fox, Wolf, and Cadger,'" *Review of English Studies*, 10 (1934), 319–20.

74. On Henryson's sources see I.W.A. Jamieson, "A Further Source for Henryson's 'Fabillis.'" *Notes and Queries*, 14 (1967), 403–05; "Henryson's 'Fabillis': An Essay Towards a Revaluation," *Words: Wai-Te Atu Studies in Literature*, no. 2, ed. P.T. Hoffman, D. F. McKenzie, and Peter Robb, (Wellington, New Zealand, 1966) pp. 20–31; "Henryson's *Taill of the Wolf and the Wedder*." *Studies in Scottish Literature*, 6 (1969), pp. 248–57. See also Donald MacDonald, "Chaucer's Influence on Henryson's *Fables*: The Use of Proverbs and

Sententiae"; "Henryson and Chaucer: Cock and Fox." *Texas Studies in Literature and Language,* 8 (1966), 451–61; "Henryson and the *Thre Prestis of Peblis,*" *Neophilologus,* 51 (1967), 168–77 ; "Narrative Art in Henryson's *Fables,*" *Studies in Scottish Literature,* 3 (1965), pp. 101–13. See also MacQueen, *Robert Henryson,* pp. 208–21; and Evelyn S. Newlyn "Tradition and Transformation in the Poetry of Robert Henryson," *Studies in Scottish Literature,* 18 (1983), pp. 33–58. Additional sources will be cited throughout this study.

75. Denton Fox, "Henryson and Caxton," *Journal of English and Germanic Philology,* 67 (1968), 592–93.

76. Jamieson, "A Further Source for Henryson's *Fabillis,*" pp. 403–04.

77. *Les Fabulistes Latins,* ed. Leopold Hervieux (Paris, 1896), pp. 190-91; translation from *The Fables of Odo of Cheriton,* trans. John C. Jacobs (Syracuse, 1985), pp. 87–88.

78. Jamieson, "A Further Source for Henryson's Fabillis," p. 404.

79. *Poetria nova,* ed. Faral, p. 204, lines 220–22; translation from "The New Poetics," p. 41.

80. *Ibid.,* Faral, p. 204, lines 224–25; "The New Poetics," p. 42.

81. For a summary, see Kindrick, *Robert Henryson,* pp. 77–78.

82. See Gray, *Robert Henryson,* pp. 31–161.

83. See MacQueen, *Robert Henryson,* pp. 123–24.

84. *Poetria nova,* ed. Faral, p. 213, lines 527-36; translation from "The New Poetics," pp. 52–53.

85. *Ibid.,* Faral, pp. 217-18, lines 669–72; "The New Poetics," p. 57.

86. *Ibid.,* Faral, p. 205, lines 264-69; "The New Poetics," p. 43.

87. To cite only two examples, comment about his apostrophe in the "Tale of the Sheep and the Dog" will be found in Kurt Wittig, *The Scottish Tradition in Literature* (Edinburgh, 1958), p. 50; for comment on Cresseid's apostrophes, see MacQueen, *Robert Henryson*, pp. 45–93; Gray, *Robert Henryson*, pp. 162–208 and Kindrick, *Robert Henryson*, pp. 118–48.

88. For general comment, see Wittig pp. 34–37; and Kindrick, *Robert Henryson*, pp. 39–43.

89. See, for instance, Ronald Marken, "Chaucer and Henryson: A Comparison," *Discourse*, 7 (1964), 381; H. Harvey Wood, "Robert Henryson," in *Two Scots Chaucerians* (London, 1967), pp. 7–23; and Ian Robinson's *Chaucer and the English Tradition* (Cambridge, 1972), pp. 234–35, 242–44.

90. *Poetria nova*, ed. Faral, pp. 218–19, lines 690–92, 702–06; translation "The New Poetics," p. 58.

91. *Ibid.*, Faral, pp. 218–19, lines 693–701; "The New Poetics," p. 58.

92. Woods, *Commentary* pp. 60-61.

93. Donald MacDonald, "Henryson and Chaucer: Cock and Fox," pp. 454–59.

94. In his commentary on this poem, Fox observes "The ultimate source for these lines is probably the beginning of Aristotle's *Historia animalum . . .*" *Poems*, p. 212; see also Ian Carrothers, "Henryson's Use of Aristotle and Priscian in the Moral Fables," *Actes du 2ᵉ Colloque de Lanque et de Litterature Ecossaises*, ed. Jean-Jacques Blanchot and Claude Graf (Strasbourg, 1979), pp. 278–79.

95. *The Works of Geoffrey Chaucer*, ed. F. N. Robinson (Boston, 1957), p. 199, ll. 2821-46. This edition will be used for all citations from this tale.

96. See Payne, "Chaucer's Realization of Himself as Rhetor," p. 273.

97. See, for instance, Evelyn S. Newlyn, "Of Sin and Courtliness," in *Actes du 2ᵉ Colloque de Lanque et de Litterature Ecossaises*, ed. Blanchot and Graf, especially pp. 269–273.

98. See especially Carrothers, p. 285.

99. For an example of such arguments in Classical rhetoric, see *Cicero on Oratory and Orators*, John Selby Watson, trans. and ed. (Carbondale, 1986), *De oratore*, I, xviii–xix; pp. 26–8.

100. See Jamieson, "Henryson's 'Fabillis': An Essay Towards a Revaluation," pp. 20–31, and "The Minor Poems of Robert Henryson," *Studies in Scottish Literature*, 9 (1971–72), especially pp. 146–47. See also MacDonald, "Narrative Art in Henryson's Fables," pp. 101–13, and, for longer studies that reinforce this point, A.R. Diebler *Henrison's Fabeldichtungen* (Halle, 1885) and Marianne Powell, *Fabula Docet* (Odense, 1983).

III
Henryson and the *Ars dictaminis*

THE NATURE OF *THE ARS DICTAMINIS*

Just as in his use of the *ars poetriae*, Henryson incorporated the general traditions of the *ars dictaminis* into his verse. As earlier noted, Murphy has called the *ars dictaminis* the most truly medieval form of rhetoric. Richard McKeon and John O. Ward, however, have asserted that it is a substitute for the study of genuine classical rhetorical traditions during the earlier centuries of the high Middle Ages, in part because of its interest in written discourse.[1] Yet, no matter how misguided classical purists might consider this rhetorical tradition, it was a powerful social force during Henryson's life.[2] Charles B. Faulhaber succinctly captures the essence of the controversy:

> It is one of the paradoxes of the history of rhetoric that what was in Antiquity essentially an oral discipline for the pleading of law cases should have become in the Middle Ages, in one of its major aspects, a written discipline for the drawing up of quasi-legal documents.[3]

Especially given Henryson's role as a "notarius publicus" and the close association between the *ars dictaminis* and the *ars notaria*, their influence on his poetry and his life[4] seems especially pertinent.

There are three salient elements associated with the *ars dictaminis* and, subsequently, the *ars notaria*: an emphasis on politics and law, an awareness of many of the intricate relationships between speech and writing with special emphasis on written discourse, and refined formulaic structure (at least by the date Henryson would have studied the subject). The *ars dictaminis* was generally used in deliberative and forensic discourse; the *ars notaria* more specifically applied to forensic settings. The *ars notaria* differed from the *ars dictaminis* in degree instead of kind. Its emphasis on language appears in formulaic diction and set phrases that relate more directly to courts of law (either secular or ecclesiastical). Its formalism in organization reflected a close attention to appropriate legal procedures in a less centralized system of justice. The other major rhetorical schools of the period also embraced some of these elements. The *ars poetriae* was concerned with the interrelationship between speech and writing and developed its own highly codified system of rhetorical devices based upon classical models.[5] The *ars praedicandi* shared virtually all of these concerns along with the extra burden of interpreting Scripture at a series of levels from which all could profit. However, Henryson's poetry reflects the political interests and emphasis on precision in language of the *ars dictaminis*. His understanding and use of formulaic language and organization owe a debt to both the *ars dictaminis* and the *ars notaria*. The interdependence and similarity of goals of these two rhetorical traditions are reflected in Henryson's use of them in his verse.

Murphy and Giles Constable have explored the history of the *ars dictaminis* in terms of the necessity of sending messages over long distances,[6] especially when the person who originated the message might not be able to deliver it personally. While the difficulties that emerged in such rhetorical situations—involving the relationship between speech and writing in conveying authorial intent—clearly have an application to the problems of the poet, they determined the fates of nations in political discourse. It was essential that political leaders communicate, but it was also clear that such communication could not always be face-to-face. Problems involving distance and security, as well as sheer physical endurance, often made such first-hand diplomacy impossible. Other reasons for the developing emphasis on written discourse include the displacement of oral political discourse during the later Roman Empire, as outlined by Caplan.[7] The genesis of the *ars dictaminis*, then, is political. That political emphasis continued to inform the development of the rhetorical tradition throughout its history. Its political origins also involved attention to audience sensitivity, as the works of major medieval rhetoricians will attest. It is difficult to agree with Vickers that the "loss of a social role led to the atrophy, not only of the audience, but of the speaker."[8] The *ars dictaminis* and the *ars notaria* certainly dealt with more restricted rhetorical contexts than those generally found in classical approaches, but these contexts still reflected a need to anticipate audience response, especially in the more rigidly-structured format of written discourse.

The relationship between speech and writing was not exclusively the concern of the *ars dictaminis*. It was also considered in the *ars praedicandi*, as will be explored in greater depth in Chapter Four, and in the *ars poetriae*. The central problem was a vital one for the poet as well: transmission of an author's intention in a text essentially removed from the composer with no possibility for personal interaction between the writer and the audience. Geoffrey of Vinsauf cautions the poet that dealing with this issue requires a triple judgment, using critical faculties of the poet's art:

> Cum faciem verbi speculeris, an inquinet illam
> Forte latens aliquis vermis, non sola sit auris
> Nec solus judex animus : diffiniat istud
> Judicium triplex et mentis et auris et usus.

> [When you consider the appearance of a word, to see
> if perchance some lurking worm befouls it, let not the
> ear nor the mind alone be judge. Let the triple
> judgment of mind, ear, and usage decide it.][9]

While the rhetorical and linguistic approaches to the relationship varied among the medieval rhetorical schools, it was a common concern. For the poet, the issue involved his role as an *auctor*. For the *dictator*, the role involved the interplay between scriptorial and authorial roles. The authority afforded the *quaestor* often meant that he was not just a *scriptor* but also the creator of the message. John of Salisbury, for instance, apparently was given extensive authorial privileges in a letter that the Archbishop of Rheims wrote to the Pope about the exile of the Archbishop of Canterbury.[10] L.B. Dibben cites other examples of authorial latitude extended to secretaries and notes that some obtained the status of council members.[11] More recently, Malcolm Richardson has also examined the role of the "professional writing clerk," commenting on its importance in the later Middle Ages.[12] Perhaps the origins of both authorial latitude and the importance of the *scriptor* can be explained in part by the early policy of attesting to scribal responsibilities, which A. Giry notes. He cites examples from the eighth century which show the importance of "scriptum per manum" signatures. One example is as follows:

> Scriptum per manum Theodari notarii et scriniarii
> sanctae Romanae ecclesiae, in mense octobria,
> indictione quarta.

[Written by the hand of Theodore, notary and scribe
of the holy Roman church, in the month of October,
fourth indiction.][13]

The policy of dating and signing letters was essential, both as a
convenience for the recipient and an essential mechanism of
accountability for the sender. However, with this practice came an
increasingly greater level of social status for the *scriptor*, along with
enhanced individual recognition and broader authorial responsibilities.
Such latitude is also reflected in C. Julius Victor's definition of the
Quaestor. Charles M. Radding has demonstrated how notaries evolved
into *iudices* during the seventh and eight centuries and assumed ever
greater importance in the judicial system.[14] As any modern speech
writer knows, the difficulties of formulating and transmitting someone
else's thoughts add another complicating dimension to the already
problematic relationships between speech and writing. The *ars
dictaminis* ultimately sought a solution in a rigid formalism intended to
freeze discourse in intersubjectively transmissible *formulae* to reduce
ambiguity and misinterpretation.

The importance of this rhetorical tradition was recognized early in
the Christian period. In the fourth century, C. Julius Victor noted the
importance of the *epistola* and observed that its format was not
explained in traditional manuals of rhetoric.[15] Murphy suggests that
educated individuals in the Roman empire would have been expected to
master the art of letter writing without specific training.[16] Victor
specifically relates it to the *sermo* as a type of informal discourse. The
relationship is particularly interesting because it suggests an early bridge
between the *ars dictaminis* and the *ars praedicandi*.[17] Victor notes that
such informal discourse is usually not to be delivered in a high
oratorical fashion because the style of delivery might be a diversion
from the content. He comments on the importance of delivery in a
conversational tone, taking proper note of the social status of the
audience and the originator of the message, and he introduces what will
later become a continuing admonition in the *ars dictaminis* to be brief.[18]
In this sense, his rhetorical practice illustrates a very basic audience
analysis as well as a sensitivity to the relative roles of spoken and
written discourse. While he distinguishes between official and familiar
letters, his advice is more useful for official correspondence.   His
emphasis on the use of formulaic materials to arrange a satisfactory
conciliation between the audience and the writer and the demands of

speech and writing was to be a continuing theme of both the *ars dictaminis* and the *ars notaria*.

Victor's theories about rhetorical discourse suggest several specific guidelines for this rhetorical school. The term, "*ars dictaminis*," is often translated as "the art of letter writing." While I am not prepared to accept Mary Carruthers extension of the term to include all products of the post-invention stage of rhetoric,[19] I have elsewhere noted that such translation may be misleading because it may seem trivializing and too restrictive.[20] It is hardly suggestive of the many complex elements of this rhetorical school. Boncampagno, Hugh of Bologna, Guido Faba and, the earliest master of the school, Alberic of Monte Cassino,[21] all dealt with problems of political discourse, relationships between speech and writing, and the complexities of rhetorical *formulae* in establishing their doctrines. With its origins centered in Bologna, the *ars dictaminis* began to establish itself as an independent rhetorical discipline when Alberic applied basic principles of rhetoric to the task of writing official correspondence. Such correspondence was political or legal in nature, having apparently developed from the traditional *nuntius* as a means of communication among political or spiritual leaders and their subordinates. Constable comments incisively on how the political elements in the origins of letter-writing insured that the documents would indeed be "public":

> The historian using medieval letters and letter-collections must be ready to judge them by different standards than apply to letters today. Whereas intimacy, spontaneity, and privacy are now considered the essence of the epistolary genre, in the Middle Ages letters were for the most part self-conscious, quasi-public literary documents, often written with an eye to future collection and publication. In view of the way in which letters were written and sent, and also of the standards of literacy in the Middle Ages, it is doubtful whether there were any private letters in the modern sense of the term. As in Antiquity, when the earliest letters were concerned with factual rather than private affairs, medieval letters were often intended to be read by more than one person even at the time they were written.[22]

With its roots in a largely illiterate society, the *ars dictaminis* expanded the range of its techniques as literacy became more widespread. Guido Faba is perhaps representative in his efforts to combine pedagogical tradition and dictaminal materials to provide easy access for a growing number of students.[23] With the development of a class of legal *scriptores*, the role of the *ars dictaminis* became more and more entrenched not only among the clergy but also the developing middle class.

HENRYSON'S POLITICS AND THE *ARS DICTAMINIS*

As previously noted, the *ars dictaminis* has its origins in political discourse, possibly a continuing reflection of the dominant nature of Ciceronian rhetoric in the Middle Ages. Perhaps the outstanding exponent of the political importance of the *ars dictaminis* is Cassiodorus Senator. During a full political career in the sixth century, Cassiodorus served as minister of Theodoric the Ostrogoth, an illiterate king. Having the advantage of literacy, Cassiodorus served as an essential interpreter of the king's thoughts to his political publics. In his own job description, embodied in the *Variae*, Cassiodorus notes the importance of the literate minister to the functions of diplomacy. While the passage has already been cited, it is of sufficient importance to note it in greater detail again here:

> Si tantum clarae sunt dignitates quantum nostris aspectibus perfruuntur, si praesentia frequens prodit dominantis affectum, nullus ita iudicum potest esse gloriosus quam ille qui est in cogitationum nostrarum participatione susceptus. aliis enim pecuniae publicae committimus procurationem, aliis causas concedimus audiendas, aliis partrimonii nostri iura delegamus: quaesturam toto corde recipimus, quam nostrae linguae vocem esse censemus. Haec nostris cogitationibus necessario familiariter applicatur, ut proprie dicere possit quod nos sentire cognoscit: arbitrium suae voluntatis deponit et ita mentis nostrae velle suscipit, ut a nobis magis putetur exisse quod loquitur. o qam arduum est subiectum verba dominantis assumere, loqui posse quod nostrum

credatur et provecti in publicum decorem gloriosam
facere falsitatem! Considerate quid ponderis habeatis
pariter et decoris. si quid dubitamus, a quaestore
requirimus, qui est thesaurus famae publicae,
armarium legum, paratus semper ad subitum et, ut ait
Tullius magister eloquentiae, nihil praestabilius
videtur quam posse dicendo tenere hominum mentes,
allicere voluntates, impellere quo velit, unde autem
velit, deducere. nam si oratoris est proprium graviter
et ornate dicere, ut possit animos iudicum
commovere, quanto facundior debet esse, qui ore
principis populos noscitur ammonere, ut recta diligant,
perversa contemnant, bonos sine fine laudent,
pessimos vehementer assusent? ut paene feriata sit
districtio, ubi praevalet eloquentiae fortitudo. sit
imitator prudentissimus antiquorum, mores et alienos
corrigat et suos debitat integritate custodiat. Talem
denique oportet esse quaestorem, qualem portare
principis decet imaginem. nam si nos, ut assolet,
causam gestis audire contingat, quae auctoritas erit
linguae, quae sub oculis regalem genium possit
implere? adesse debet scientia iuris, cautela sermonis,
ut nemo debeat reprehendere quod principem
constiterit censuisse. opus erit praeterea firmitas
animi, ut a iustitiae tramite nullis muneribus, nullis
terroribus auferatur. Nam pro aequitate servanda et
nobis patimur contradici, cui etiam oportet oboediri.
sed vide ut tantum doctrinae deferas, quatenus
probabiliter omnia perquisitus exponas. aliae quippe
dignitates assessorum solacia quaerant: tua vero
dignitas principi consilia sumministrat.

['No Minister has more reason to glory in his
office than the Quaestor, since it brings him into
constant and intimate communication with
Ourselves. The Quaestor has to learn our inmost
thoughts, that he may utter them to our subjects.
Whenever we are in doubt as to any matter we ask
our Quaestor, who is the treasure-house of public
fame, the cupboard of laws; who has to be always

ready for a sudden call, and must exercise the
wonderful powers which, as Cicero has pointed out,
are inherent in the art of an orator. He should so paint
the delights of virtue and the terrors of vice, that his
eloquence should almost make the sword of the
magistrate needless.

'What manner of man ought the Quaestor to be,
who reflects the very image of his Sovereign? If, as
is often our custom, we chance to listen to a suit,
what authority must there be in his tongue who has to
speak the King's words in the King's own presence?
He must have knowledge of the law, wariness in
speech, firmness of purpose, that neither gifts nor
threats may cause him to swerve from justice. For in
the interests of Equity we suffer even ourselves to be
contradicted, since we too are bound to obey her. Let
your learning be such that you may set forth every
subject on which you have to treat, with suitable
embellishments.']²⁴

These lines are instructive to the historian in terms of the balance of
power in Theodoric's court and Cassiodorus' sense of his own
importance. Procopius also speaks of the importance of the *quaestor*,
even noting that, in Justinian's court, Proclus "used to decide all
measures as he himself thought fit."[25] Both passages are instructive to
the student of rhetoric in understanding the early foundations of the
political nature of the *ars dictaminis*. When political discourse became
so various and complex that it called for the creation of the legal
profession, it is easy to see why the *ars dictaminis* became the basis for
legal rhetoric as embodied in the *ars notaria*, the rhetoric of the
profession Henryson likely chose for part of his living.

The likely strength of Henryson's connection with the *ars
dictaminis* is reinforced by his political interests. Fables, by their nature,
are political documents. Annabel Patterson has shown how the fable of
necessity embodies political stances:

1. literature, in its most basic form, has always spoken to
    unequal power relations

2. those without power in those relations, if they wish to comment upon them, must encode their commentary;
3. writing is authorized by authorship, texts needing a name to cling to if they are to acquire cultural resonance;
4. wit (literary ingenuity) can emancipate;
5. basic issues require basic metaphors; when, as in the fable, the role of metaphor is to mediate between human consciousness and human survival, the mind recognizes rock bottom, the irreducibly material, by rejoining the animals, one of whom is the human body.[26]

It is hardly remarkable that Henryson's fables have been extensively evaluated in terms of their approach to politics. Since 1949, when Marshall Stearns outlined Henryson's sympathy for the "pure peple,"[27] it has been debated whether Henryson was working in the more general tradition of advice to princes or dealing with specific political situations. Both types of analysis are based on the assumption that Henryson had a deep and continuing interest in politics and legal procedures.

The argument that Henryson is working from the tradition of advice to princes has been best summarized by Roderick Lyall.[28] One classic Scottish example of this type of literature is John of Ireland's *Meroure of Wyssdome*, written about 1490 for James IV. Such works, Lyall contends, exercised a significant influence over fifteenth-century Scottish poetry. The tradition emphasizes accumulated wisdom, political philosophy, and general principles of political guidance. Examples which may appear to be specific are more likely drawn from the "conventional wisdom" of the literary and historical tradition than from close observation of contemporaneous political events. Thus, while "The Lion and the Mouse" might appear to have reference to James III and his counselors, Lyall contends that it is best read in a more general literary and political context of deliberative discourse. He believes that it is a mistake to evaluate Henryson's poetry in terms of his references to the political events of his day. Even Lyall's arguments are persuasive about the influence of the *ars dictaminis* on Henryson. The "advice to princes" tradition was very directly associated with this rhetorical tradition in its development. Its portrayal of royal vices and virtues, for instance, often seems based on the description of conduct adapted from letters and decrees. However, if additional proof of Henryson's political interests is needed, others have been even more specific.

Stearns, MacQueen, Ranald Nicholson, and I[29] have all contended that Henryson had more immediate political examples in mind. One of the most marked instances is "The Tale of the Lion and Mouse." In his portrayal of the lion, Henryson has created a royal portrait closely paralleling that of James III, and his narration may represent the events of the Lauder Rebellion. The Lauder Rebellion is a major event in a series of political crises that resulted from the Stewarts' attempts to consolidate political power into the hands of the monarchy during the fifteenth century. Later chronicles argue that, although James III himself was considered a negligent aesthete by many of the rural Scottish nobles, his counselors were bitterly resented for their arrogant use of the crown's authority, "low birth," and preferential treatment. As members of a centralized court, they were a threat to the feudal barons who felt themselves gradually being displaced. In 1482, the king and his "familiars" were seized at Lauder Kirk. The courtiers, including Thomas Cochrane, Thomas Preston, and William Roger, were robbed and hanged from the side of Lauder Bridge. The king was removed to Edinburgh. After some negotiations (and a period in which Scotland was officially ungoverned), he was released in a staged attack on the castle by the burgesses of Edinburgh under the leadership of Provost Walter Bertram. In part because the symbol of royal power in Scotland was the lion, the leader of the rebellion subsequently became known as Archibald "Bell-the Cat," Earl of Angus.

The narrative events of Henryson's fable contain significant parallels to this political crisis, and even his animal characters show a similarity to the major figures in the Lauder rebellion. The lion, for instance, seems to reflect James III. The lion's regal description shows that he is a creature of great promise, yet he is lazy:

> He lay so still, the myis wes not effeird,
> Bot to and fro out ouer him tuke thair trace;
> Sum tirlit at the campis off his beird,
> Sum spairit not to claw him on the face;
> Merie and glaid, thus dansit thay ane space,
> Till at the last the nobill lyoun woke,
> And with his pow the maister mous he tuke.

(ll. 1412-18)

The lion's cruel predatory nature may be less a reflection on James himself than on the depredations of his counselors. He is also hunted by "rurall men," and he is capable of great cruelty:

> . . . the lyoun held to hunt,
> For he had nocht, bot leuit on his pray,
> And slew baith tayme and wyld, as he wes wont,
> And in the cuntrie maid ane grit deray;
>
> (ll. 1510-13)

Suggestions about the political allegory of this tale indicate that the "rurall men" are rebellious Scottish barons. The criticism reflects the assessment by historians that James III was more interested in the arts and his mistresses than he was in ruling Scotland. The mice, like the burgesses of Edinburgh intially have no reason to believe that he will actually exercise his royal prerogatives. Were any doubt left about the political implications of this tale, Henryson notes in his *Moralitas* that the lion may be "a prince or emprior/A potestat or yet a king with crown" (ll. 254-55). The parallels between this portrait and that of James III have been thoroughly explored. As the allegory would imply, Nicholson identifies the mice who free the lion, once he is seized by the hunters, as the burgesses of Edinburgh who freed James III after his imprisonment.[30]

There appear to be other political overtones to Henryson's work. I have already commented that the "The Two Mice" illustrates Henryson's sensitivity to class differences in fifteenth-century Scottish society. The uponland mouse, visiting her city sister, is accustomed to a sense of security appropriate to the country but not to the city. The meal that the two sisters enjoy is first disturbed by the spenser. More unsettling, perhaps, is the intrusion of the cat, a more disruptive force, possibly representing the king himself.[31] Henryson's expansion of this scene, showing how the cat toys with the uponland mouse and causes her "grit pane" (l. 334), may show the unsettling consequences of the extension of royal power, as the monarchy attempted to profit from fledgling entrepreneurism through increased taxes and control of commerce. While the uponland mouse's city sister seems accustomed to such disruptions, the uponland mouse herself is frightened. She is not used to such rough treatment. She does indeed believe, "Thy mangerie is mingit all with cair" (l. 344). Whether the cat represents invasions, royal tariffs, or even compulsory royal loans, it is clear that there were

intrusions upon the lives of all Scots, especially the burgesses.
Fifteenth-century Scottish history would certainly provide a basis for the
political interpretation of this tale.[32]

Perhaps one of the most controversial tales in terms of political
implications is "The Tale of the Wolf and the Wether." The basic
argument of political critics is that the tale illustrates James' unwise use
of his counselors. Criticism of James III's counselors assumed almost
legendary proportions in later accounts of his reign. George Buchanan
and John Lesley, among other Scottish historians, indicated that James'
judgment with regard to his counselors was notoriously bad.[33] James
was not the only king to be accused of such judgments. Both veneration
for the monarchy and fear of the immediate consequences of criticizing
a reigning king or queen made the "bad counselors" approach a popular
attack for malcontents and the political opposition throughout the later
Middle Ages. This tale reflects the traditional perception that all would
be well if only the king would change his advisors. The shepherd,
whose obligation is to guard his flock, loses his faithful sheep dog. He
is in despair, when a wether offers the advice that the dog be skinned
and that the wether use the skin as a disguise in protecting the flock
against wolves. The shepherd agrees, even taking issue with proverbial
wisdom in his comment, "Quha sayis ane scheip is daft, thay lieit of it"
(l. 2492). Once the hound is skinned, the wether takes up his watch.
His first challenge is from a hungry wolf, who steals a lamb. In
pursuing the wolf, the wether loses all sight of reason. When the wolf
drops the lamb to enhance his escape, the wether states:

> 'Na,' quod the wedder, 'in faith we part not swa:
> It is not the lamb, bot the, that I desyre;
> I sall cum neir, for now I se the tyre.'

> (ll. 2534-36)

Finally, when the hound's skin is torn off in pursuit, the wether's trick
is discovered and the wolf turns upon him. Now that both are properly
positioned in the state of nature, the wolf boldly questions the sheep's
effrontery:

> 'Is this ȝour bourding in ernist than?' quod he,
> For I am verray effeirit, and on flocht:
> Cum bak agane, and I sall let ȝow se.'
> Than quhar the gait wes grimmit he him brocht:

'Quhether call ᴣe this fair play or nocht:
To set ᴣour maister in sa fell effray,
Quhill he for feiritnes hes fylit vp the way?'

(ll. 2560-66)

While the wolf's questions may seem cruel and arrogant, the wether's
humble reply seems to establish his own sense of their appropriateness
in the hierarchy of nature.

'Schir,' quod the wedder, suppois I ran in hy,
My mynd wes neuer to do ᴣour persoun ill.
Ane flear gettis ane follower commounly,
In play or ernist, preif quha sa euer will.
Sen I bot playit, be gracious me till,
And I sall gar my freindis blis ᴣour banis:
Ane full gude seruand will crab his maister anis.'

(ll. 2574-80)

His humility and the acknowledgement that the wolf is his "maister"
both show that the sheep realizes his transgression. The wolf, however,
is angered by the act and breaks the sheep's neck, a form of execution
particularly appropriate to political allegory, given the fates of
Cochrane, Preston, and Rogers.

It is possible that there are also references in this work to the
Lauder rebellion.[34] In his *Moralitas* Henryson emphasizes the
importance of having advisors who are noble in breeding and
demeanor. Since James' advisors had come from social origins that
were less than noble, the general impression in the countryside was that
their advice to the King was also "low." And Henryson, very
conservatively, emphasizes the importance of blood in the role of noble
deeds:

Heir may thow se that riches of array
Will cause pure men presumpteous for to be;
Thay think thay hald of nane, be thay als gay,
Bot counterfute ane lord in all degre.
Out of thair cais in pryde thay clym sa hie
That thay forbeir thair better in na steid,
Quhill sum man tit thair heillis ouer thair heid.

> Richt swa in seruice vther sum exceidis,
> And thay haif withgang, welth, and cherising,
> That thay will lychtlie lordis in thair deidis,
> And lukis not to thair blude nor thair ofspring.
>
> (ll. 2595-2605)

He further warns:

> Thairfoir I counsell men of euerilk stait
> To knaw thame self, and quhome thay suld forbeir,
> And fall not with thair better in debait,
> Suppois thay be als galland in thair geir:
> It settis na seruand for to vphald weir,
> Nor clym sa hie quhill he fall of the ledder:
> Bot think vpon the wolf and on the wedder.
>
> (ll. 2609-15)

These lines contain general moral advice. The admonition that such men need to "knaw thame self" is good counsel in virtually any aspect of life. Yet the emphasis on "riches of array" and the folly of "pure men" who "counterfute ane lord" and "fall of the ledder" tie this *moralitas* directly to a courtly setting. The fact that Thomas Cochrane, the major focus of much of the anger that led to the rebellion, had risen from a mason's apprentice to courtly power may make Henryson's advice even more pointed. Given the events of 1482, such specific warnings seem to indicate that Henryson has particular individuals in mind.

It does not matter in the rhetorical context whether one accepts the position espoused by Roderick Lyall or that espoused by the other critics. In either case, Henryson's rhetoric was oriented towards political events and political advice. Indeed, by this date, even the *ars praedicandi* had developed its own guidelines for the treatment of political issues—a stock subject of medieval preachers—and that tradition shows a common interest with the *ars dictaminis* in its treatment of political activities. George Gopen has observed that "It is not difficult to see why several critics have mined Henryson's works for political allegory and social commentary, but to view them only as such, or even primarily as such would be to obscure their relationship to the fable tradition, to ignore their original, innovative use of the fable form, and to limit the possibilities of interpretation and response."[35] However, to ignore Henryson's political interests is also to obscure a significant aspect of his art, an aspect related directly to the *ars dictaminis*. While Henryson's interest in politics is not the primary reason to read his verse, the reader who lacks an understanding of his political allusions loses critical insights into the poet and his craft.

HENRYSON'S POETIC CRAFT AND THE *ARS DICTAMINIS*

The *ars dictaminis* recognized several important facts about the nature of discourse, facts that seem particularly pertinent in view of the "intermediate age" of written discourse which has dominated for the last 2000 years. The *ars dictaminis* confronts a central problem in current rhetorical theory—the relationship between spoken and written discourse. The roots of ancient rhetoric are basically oral.[36] Yet the very development of the *ars dictaminis* reflects the need to find ways of dealing with the problems of written communication. Such problems had existed for generations of poets after the widespread development of written forms insured that their works would be interpreted by another rather than performed by the author.[37] The political urgency of insuring accurate communication among powerful nobles and their subordinates required that more attention be given to the problems of transforming speech into writing and back into accurate speech. The decline of a generally learned nobility and citizenry after the fall of Rome complicated the problems considerably, eliminating the assurance of a common language and cultural background as a basis for interpreting written communication. Perhaps ironically, the resurgence of literacy in the fifteenth century also made the problem a critical one for Henryson and his contemporaries. The difficulties are profound. In direct oral communication, a great deal of information is conveyed by suprasegmentals and by non-verbal signals which may accompany the speaker's presentation. In written discourse, a writer must do without such crucial resources. In political discourse, ambiguity in writing could make the difference between peace and war. The importance of this political role in the development of modern standard English has been explored in some detail by John Hurt Fisher.[38] Richardson has more specifically delineated the role of *dictamen* in establishing standard written forms in the fifteenth century.[39] The author of *Rationes dictandi* (anonymous, 1135) expresses the problem eloquently and simply when he notes that "Est igitur epistola congrua sermonum ordinatio ad

exprimendam intentionem delegantis institua" [An epistle or letter, then,
is a suitable arrangement of words set forth to express the intended
meaning of its sender].[40] Guido Faba recognizes the relationship
between this problem and the *ars dictaminis* when he defines a letter as
a *libellus*, more specifically a legal petition.[41] The idea that the *ars
dictaminis* deals with written discourse which must substitute for direct
oral discourse is also explored by Alberic of Monte Cassino, who refers
to *scriptores* rather than *oratores*.[42] Commenting on the auricular
aspects of political discourse, Hugh of Bologna noted early on that it
developed "oratio a lege merri soluta" [without accountability to
metrical law].[43] Yet, in part because of its sensitivity to speech patterns,
the *ars dictaminis* developed a special interest in the *cursus*, or rhythm,
of Latin prose. The *cursus* is highly complicated in its applications
because of its particular reference to Latin; nonetheless, it illustrates the
special emphasis that this rhetorical school (and later the *ars notaria*)
placed on delivery, perhaps a natural development in view of its
political origins. The recognition of the critical interaction between
speech and writing in the transmission of a text and intention is shared
by Henryson and the authors of the *artes dictamini*.

   Henryson's sensitivity to language problems is well attested:[44] His
sense of stylistic control illustrates his ability to vary levels of formality
and approach in different rhetorical situations. This kind of rhetorical
control likely developed from the climate of emerging literacy in
fifteenth-century Scotland. In addition to general social factors involved
in language evolution, there were more specifically Scottish elements
which had an impact on his language use.[45] First, Scotland shared
elements in its language evolution with England and continental
nations. Vernacular tongues continued their emergence as the languages
of literature, commerce, and politics. In addition, the Latin substratum
was strong in the evolution of vernacular tongues and Latin remained
as a *lingua franca* in its own right. One study suggests that as much as
40% of the enfranchised citizenry of London could have been literate
in Latin in the later fifteenth century.[46] Because of the international
nature of culture, and more specifically theology and politics, there was
extensive mutual influence among evolving vulgar tongues.

   These influences took a variety of forms in fifteenth-century
Scotland. Excluding Scots Gaelic, Middle Scots developed largely from
the language base of the Northumbrian dialect of Middle English.
While numerous phonetic and orthographic differences exist between
this language and Chaucerian Middle English,[47] the spoken language

remained very close to the speech of Northern England. The tongue existed in numerous dialects, some apparently with modern reflexes but without written records from the period. Two dialects predominated: spoken Middle Scots, which served much the same purpose that "standard spoken English" serves today, and literary Middle Scots, often incorporating Southern elements but still reflecting the spoken language of the North.[48] A great deal of work has been done by A.J. Aitken, Derrick McClure, and others[49] to explain dialectal structure.

One means of evaluating Henryson's debt to oral traditions and his ability to deal with some of the critical problems in the development of Middle Scots is through his use of figurative language. Medieval rhetorical texts list a variety of figures (sometimes not specifically so designated) which are based in orality and which have auricular appeal. The *artes dictamini* were generally more concerned with organization, as illustrated by the *Rationes dictandi*, than with specifics about stylistic ornamentation or variation. The *artes praedicandi* provided even more general guidelines about figurative language, while still emphasizing auricular appeal, as will be illustrated in Chapter Four. Probably the major attention to this problem in the *ars dictaminis* is to be found in the emphasis on the *cursus*. The relative lack of attention to specific figures may indicate either heavy reliance on the formularies or assumption of prior knowledge of figurative devices from the classical tradition or the *artes poetriae*.

One of the most important figures for Henryson is meter. The importance which the *ars dictaminis* attached to the rhythm of delivery is evident in its interest in the *cursus*. Despite the fact that the study of the *cursus* tended to be based specifically on Latin and that it has not received sufficient study, its attention to auricular appeal, metrics, and audience appeal shows a clear affinity with concerns of poetry. Bernard de Meung of Orleans establishes some basic principles underlying the study in the prologue to his *Summa dictaminis*:

> Ad doctrinam dictaminum accedentes et dantes operam, primo loco debemus cognoscere quid sit dictamen et quid sit eius species. Dictamen est litteralis editio verborum venustate eggregia, sententiarum coloribus adornate. Litteralis editio est pro genere, cetera pro differentiis.

Sciendum est quod sunt ornatus dictaminis,
ornatus verborum et ornatus sententiarum, de quibus
plenius agitur in arte rethorica. Due sunt species
dictaminis, metricum et prosaicum. metricum in quo
observatur correptio et producto sillibargum, qual est
Virgilianum, Ovidianum, etc. huius modi. Prasaicum
est ubi metri ratio non servatur, quale est Tullianum,
Salustianum, Gregorianum et aliorum prosaice
scribentium. Prosaici dictaminis multe sunt species:
decretum, preciptum, privilegium, omelia, epistole
et plures alie. Pretermissis aliis, agamus de
epistola. . . .

[In the first place, taking up the doctrine of
dictamen, and presenting this book, we ought to know
what dictamen is and what are its kinds. Dictamen is
a literary account brilliant with the beauty of words
and adorned with colors of thought. "Literary
account" is the generic term; the rest is *differentia*.

Know that there are two ornaments of *dictamen*,
ornaments of words and ornaments of thoughts,
considering which much is said in the art of rhetoric.
There are two kinds of *dictamen*, metrical and
prosaic. The metrical kind is one in which the
shortening and lengthening of syllables is observed,
such as the Virgilian, Ovidian, and others in this
mode. The prosaic kind is where the principle of
meter is not followed, such as the Ciceronian,
Sallustian, Gregorian, and others writing in prose.
There are many kinds of prosaic *dictamen*: decretals,
precepts, privileges, homilies, epistles, and many
others. Leaving aside the others, let us take up the
epistle. . . .][50]

This kind of general advice is sometimes expanded to provide a
typology of three types of discourse--*metricum*, *rithmicum*, and
prosaicum.[51] Both Alberic and Hugh of Bologna accept this typology.
Alberic does so by implication, noting that his *Breviarum de dictamine*
is about "prosaico dictamini opus,"[52] suggesting thereby that other types

exist. Hugh deals with the issue more directly, basically asserting the same categories described by Bernard.[53] Yet, this interest sets the stage for a special concentrated attention to stylistics in the study of the *cursus*, or rhythmic prose patterns associated with the *ars dictaminis*. Rhythmic Latin prose had earlier received attention from Cicero and was a natural concern in the liturgy of the early Church. Murphy traces its development in the *ars dictaminis* to John of Gaeta who used the *cursus* to alter chancery style. Murphy observes that, despite the independence of attention to the *cursus*, it became intimately involved with the *ars dictaminis*.[54] Aldo Scaglione asserts that attention to the *cursus* "indicates a subtle but far-reaching transformation in sensitivity to sentence forms."[55] Faulhaber provides an excellent summary of the nature of the *cursus* as found in Guido Faba's *Summa dictaminis*:

> There were three primary forms of the cursus--
> planus, tardus, and velox--, all of which are explained
> and illustrated by Guido, although without using those
> terms. The basic principle is simple. The clause must
> end with a word of three or four syllables. If it ends
> in a trisyllable, then the preceding word must have
> the same stress pattern (i.e., both words must be
> either paroxytones or proparoxytones). If it ends with
> a word of four syllables, then the preceding word
> must have the opposite stress pattern (i.e., a
> proparoxytone must be preceded by a paroxytone, and
> vice versa). The clause endings given by these rules
> all have two primary accents (since each type is
> composed of two words) and either two or four
> unstressed syllables between the primary stresses).[56]

Bene of Florence draws distinctions between the uses of the *cursus* in French and those in Latin.[57] Whether or not the precise linguistic principles could have been transferred from a romance language to Scots, the same interest in auricular appeal would have been conveyed in the teaching of *cursus*. Unfortunately, no documents such as Bene's have survived for Middle Scots. There was, as Faulhaber notes, the considerable danger that an uninventive writer could turn these *formulae* into doggerel. W.A. Pantin has observed that "the *cursus* makes a good servant, but a bad master."[58] Such danger was also present in the use of meter, Henryson's primary figurative device in dealing with the relationship between speech and writing. That Henryson remained the master of metric forms has already been demonstrated in Chapter Two. His ability to combine a variety of metric patterns with alliteration, assonance, rhyme, and other auricular figures shows a clear harmony of interest between his interests and the emphasis on the transmutation of speech into writing of the *ars dictaminis*.

Many of Henryson's other figures reflect points of mutual interest between the *ars dictaminis* and *ars poetriae*. Geoffrey lists a number of figures of speech related to diction[59] which have particular relevance for Henryson's efforts to wrestle with the speech-writing relationship. Another factor that complicates his use of both schools of rhetoric is that Henryson was steeped in traditional literary approaches to language and familiar with new experiments in usage. Henryson informed himself about traditional literary genres and *formulae*. His emphasis on the literary and literate tradition follows a long line of precursors, including Chaucer, Gower, and the *Pearl*-Poet. Perhaps one of the most important literary influences on Henryson was what J. A. Burrow has described as the "Ricardian tradition."[60] Burrow lists a number of characteristics which define the Ricardian writers, among whom are Langland, Gower, and the Pearl-Poet. Their attention to style and rhetorical *formulae* demonstrates a commitment to the *literary* nature of their writing and at least an intuitive grasp of the highly structured system of the *ars poetriae*. One salient characteristic of these writers is their emphasis on the use of literate and sometimes aureate diction. Dunbar, for instance, is often contrasted with Henryson as being a more "literate" poet. This same kind of emphasis on the aureate, however, appears in Henryson's works. Stephen Hawes defines aureate diction as the use of "Termes eloquent . . . Electynge wordes whiche are expedyent In Latyn or in Englysshe after the intent."[61] While aureate diction also developed through a separate line in the Scottish tradition, Henryson's conscious acknowledgement of Ricardian sources demonstrates the influence of this tradition on his verse. Perhaps most often cited with regard to his debt to this particular use of literary language is "Ane Prayer for the Pest". The attention to rhyme, assonance, alliteration, and the use of Latin derivatives in this poem demonstrate that Henryson, when he chose to, could compete with the best of the aureate poets. It might be suggested that "Ane Prayer for the Pest" is too easy a case. Yet even *Orpheus and Eurydice* contains language of the same sort, for instance in lines 1–5. Other examples could be adduced from *The Testament of Cresseid* and *The Morall Fabillis*. Henryson's use of these aureate techniques, involving the most literate and complicated diction of the rhetoric of his day, shows the complex influences of the Scottish, Ricardian, and pulpit traditions.

The *ars dictaminis* gave little attention to the trope of irony, likely because its inherent ambiguity could engender confusion and unnecessarily complicate the *scriptor's* task. It should merely be noted here that Henryson's irony also shows a debt to the Ricardian tradition.[62] However, his techniques of literary realism, another Ricardian element, may show the influence of the art of letter writing, even though it has been argued that Henryson borrowed not directly from the *ars dictaminis* or from the Ricardian tradition but instead specifically from the Chaucerian tradition.[63] The life-like character portraits of Henryson's animals are often compared with those of Chaucer in *The Canterbury Tales*. Yet realistic description was also a vital part of the *ars dictaminis* and Henryson's mastery of the technique may show the influence of this rhetorical school.[64] Because of the lack of opportunity for audience response, realistic portrayal of character and depiction of events were considered to be essential in the *ars dictaminis*. Among the "suitable embellishments" discussed by Cassiodorus Senator was the virtue of realistic narration and description to enhance the role of the *dictator* as a "verbal minister" to handle political problems.[65]

Henryson's artistic realism has been widely recognized as a major strength of his verse.[66] His use of psychological realism is illustrated by *The Testament of Cresseid* during the final meeting between Troilus and Cresseid. Marshall Stearns has shown that the subconscious recognition of Cresseid by Troilus seems to be based upon principles in Aristotle's *De anima* and *De memoria*, sources well regarded in Henryson's lifetime.[67] The major Aristotelian principle used in this scene is that of reproductive imagination. Riding through the city, Troilus encounters the begging lepers. He rides directly up to Cresseid:

> Than vpon him scho kest vp baith hir ene,
> And with ane blenk it come into his thocht
> That he sumtime hir face befoir had sene,
> Bot scho was in sic plye he knew hir nocht;

> ₃it than hir luik into his mynd it brocht
> The sweit visage and amorous blenking
> Of fair Cresseid, sumtyme his awin darling.
>
> (ll. 498–504)

Without recognizing her consciously, he is sufficiently moved to contribute generously to the lepers in honor of his lost love. Henryson not only uses the Artistotelian principle but even goes out of his way to provide a theoretical explanation for the reader:

> Na wonder was, suppois in mynd that he
> Tuik hir figure sa sone, and lo, now quhy:
> The idole of ane thing in cace may be
> Sa deip imprentit in the fantasy
> That it deludis the wittis outwardly,
> And sa appeiris in forme and lyke estait
> Within the mynd as it was figurait.
>
> (ll. 505–11)

Similar reliance on Aristotle is to be found in *Orpheus and Eurydice*[68] and *The Morall Fabillis*. The latter work also shows his realism in the depiction of social classes and grievances. Henryson's animal world includes all categories of society, from the most noble to the most poverty-stricken. He describes nobility, with all of its magnificence and glory, in the "Tale of the Lion and the Mouse," depicting the lion as "king of beistis coronate" (l. 1462). While he paints the lion in all his regal grandeur, he is not blind to the obverse side of the noble classes. In "The Tale of the Wolf and the Lamb" and "The Trial of the Fox" Henryson is able to depict the stupidity and malice which sometimes inform the actions of the upper classes. In the former tale, for instance, he portrays the wolf as "mychty men" and "men of heretege" who are, through their actions, "fals pervertaris of the lawis" (l. 100). While Henryson has idealistic attitudes towards the role of the king and the possibilities of providing for a just society, he also argues in most of his verse that noble social status itself is no guarantee of just and fair action. In other class representations, he apparently describes the urban upper-middle class in the burgess mouse in "The Two Mice." He is also able to portray lower-level clergy in the depiction of the sheep in "The Sheep and the Dog," and even extends his portrayals to rustics in "The Fox, The Wolf, and the Husbandman." It is part of his genius that he is able to capture not only human folly but human ideals, as in his depiction of the swallow in "The Preaching of the Swallow."[69]

Perhaps, however, his masterpiece of realistic description occurs in *The Testament of Cresseid*. In describing Cresseid's disease, a result of self-indulgence and venereal excess, Henryson shows his close observation of a real illness of the day. He describes the curse on Cresseid in the following terms:

> 'Thy cristall ene mingit with blude I mak,
> Thy voice sa cleir vnplesand hoir and hace,
> Thy lustie lyre ouirspred with spottis blak,
> And lumpis haw appeirand in thy face. . . .
>
> (ll. 337–40)

This description contains such detail that, in 1841, J. A. Y. Simpson was able to diagnose Cresseid's disease as elephantiasis leprosy.[70] While syphilis might appear to moderns to be a more appropriate punishment for sexual sins, leprosy in the late Middle Ages was associated with sexual excess. Given that perception and Henryson's grim and realistic description, the disease which Cresseid must endure seems particularly tailored to her sins. Realism was also a concern of the medieval pulpit, as will be illustrated in Chapter Four. The dual influences of the *ars dictaminis* and the *ars praedicandi* would have found a willing student in a young poet influenced as well by Chaucerian and Ricardian literary practices.

The trope of allegory will be explored at greater length in the discussion of the *ars praedicandi*, but it also merits brief attention in conjunction with the *ars dictaminis*. It is quite possible that Henryson could have become acquainted with allegory through his study of the *ars poetriae* or even more specifically through works such as Bede's *De schematibus et tropis*.[71] In addition, C. Julius Victor had early noted the value of using figurative language in official letters.[72] Basic emphasis on the importance of allegory is found in Alberic of Monte Cassino.[73] It becomes even more evident in the *Rationes dictandi* when it is noted that securing the goodwill of a listener or reader requires "quedam apposita uerborum ordinatio recipientis animum conpetenter alliciens" [a certain fit ordering of words effectively influencing the mind of the recipient].[74] Allegory is listed as a dictaminal figure by the author of the *Compendium rhetoricae* (1332), a manual generally treating dictaminal style.[75] However, allegory hardly attained the eminent role in the *ars dictaminis* that it was accorded in the *ars praedicandi*. The very nature of the figure allows for multiple interpretations which would suit perfectly the various audiences targeted by medieval preachers but which could result in unfortunate misunderstandings among diplomats or ministers of state. Hence, even though he often employed allegory for political purposes, Henryson's use of this figure will be explored at greater length in conjunction with the *ars praedicandi*.

Henryson's control of figurative language extends far beyond this brief catalogue and even the more group explored in Chapter Two. His use of figures incorporates elements of every literary and rhetorical tradition current in Scotland during his lifetime. The influence of the *ars dictaminis* and the *ars notaria* mixed with Ricardian, Scottish, and Chaucerian traditions to help shape his comprehensive approach to figurative language.

THE FORMULAE OF ARRANGEMENT IN THE
ARS DICTAMINIS

Just as Henryson's use of figures was influenced by the *ars dictaminis*, his sense of organization and many features of his language were influenced by the emphasis on *formulae* in both the *ars dictaminis* and the *ars notaria*. The major solution to the problems of assuring accurate transmission of text and intent of the *ars dictaminis* was to rely on form in language and text. Formulaic elements infused the language, especially the diction and organization, of this rhetorical school, as illustrated by the numerous formularies which have survived. Giry has catalogued and organized the most important of them.[76] As will later be illustrated, the formularies of the *ars dictaminis* shared common rhetorical goals with the formulaic collections of the *ars praedicandi*, the most important of which was to help the uninitiated or less skilled take advantage of greater wisdom in formulating letters and legal documents or sermons. Formulaic elements would have had a strong literary influence on a learned man such as Henryson.

Murphy traces the development of the dictaminal formula of arrangement to its Ciceronian roots:

By 1200 the great mass of popular manuals were written—most of them in Italy—by such masters as Bernard of Bologna, Bernard de Meung, Guido Faba, Boncompagno, Bene of Lucca, Lawrence of Acquilegia, Pons of Provence, and Thomas of Capua. The doctrine was simple enough: basically it depended upon an analogy to the Ciceronian parts of speech. Cicero named six major parts of a speech: *exordium*, or introduction; *narratio*, or background, *divisio*, or statement of parts; *confirmatio*, or proof; *refutatio*, or attack against an opponent's argument; and finally, *peroratio* or conclusion. The *dictamen* writers divided the Ciceronian *exordium* into two separate parts: first, the *salutatio*, or formal greeting of the addresses by his titles and praises, and second, the *captatio benevolentiae*, or introduction proper in which goodwill was sought. The *dictamen* doctrine goes on to make *narratio* the next part, explaining background. Then there is, in place of Ciceronian *confirmatio*, the petition—*petitio* and, finally, *conclusio*—but there is very little theory about conclusions in medieval dictamen treatises. So we have as a consequence the "approved format" of a five-part letter—salutation, introduction, narration, petition and conclusion.[77]

The principle of division is clear in the anonymous *Rationes dictandi*. After defining a letter, as noted above, the author goes on to state that there are five parts of a letter—the salutation, the securing of good-will, the narration, the petition, and the conclusion. He then proceeds to a description of each section, emphasizing (as Geoffrey of Vinsauf did) the beginning. In the section on the salutation, for instance, he divides salutations into three types (prescribed, subscribed, or circumscribed) and explains how even distinctions in the use of accusative case and the dative case can make the difference in success or failure by indicating "humilitatem uel certe nullam arrogantiam" [humility and certainly not pride].[78] C. Julius Victor had earlier established the critical social typology for salutations. He divided salutations on the basis of whether the recipient was a superior, equal, or inferior. Constable has shown that the attention of *dictatores* to such matters of protocol "with regard to the membership in the various orders" was so pronounced that their works provide a significant perspective on social caste in the Middle Ages.[79] In general, the author of the *Rationes dictandi* recognizes Victor's social distinctions, as the following models from his text illustrate:

Salutatio pape inuariabiliter universis destinata.

Innocentius episopus seruus seruorum dei dilecto in Christo filio N Romanorum imperatori augusto salutem et apostolicam benefictionem.

Salutatio imperatoris ad omnes.

N dei gratia Romanorum imperator augustus fauentino episcopo, uel *pictauiensi comiti,* uel *pisano populo, gratiam et bonam uoluntatem.*

Quando tamen ad imperatorem quilibet episcopus uel dux uel cuiuslibet ciuitatis populus scribit, hec vel his similia circa regium nomen debent adiungi: *inclyto excellentissimo   inuictissimo   precellentissimo triumphatori   semperque   augusto   Romanorum imperatori C N pisanus archiepiscopus licet indignus debitam in Christo subiectionem,* uel conpetentem aliquam de supradictis.

Salutationes ecclesiasticorum uirorum inter se.

N dei gratia sancte bononiensis ecclesie episcopus licet indignus perpetuam in Christo salutem, uel *salutem in Christo perpetuam, fraternam salutem et orationes in domino, fraterne salutis et caritatis augmentum, fraterne dilectionis affectum,* uel *salutem et precordiales orationes in domino.*

Euenit autem prelatos habere sub se reuerendas personas. Quibus non *benedictionem,* set *salutem et uere* uel *sincere* uel *pure religionis augmentum.*

Ad monachos precipue.

Uere in Christo religionis augmentum, sancte conuersationis meritum, eterne meritum felicitatis.

Ad monachos namque scribentes semper de religione uel de sancta conuersatione facere mentionem consueuimus.

Salutationes ecclesiasticorum prelatorum ad subditos.

N dei gratia sancte bononiensis ecclesie episcopus licet indignus P sancte Marie plebano salutem et benedictionem, salutem et benedictionis augmentum, benedictionem in domino cum salute.

[The Pope's Universal Salutation

Bishop Innocentius, servant of the servants of God in His beloved son Christ, to N—, august emperor of the Romans, sends greeting and papal blessings.

The Emperor's Salutations to All Men

"N—, august emperor of the Romans by the grace of God, expresses friendship and good wishes to the Bishop of Faventia," or "to the Earl of Pictava," or "to the people of Pisa."

But when any bishop or duke or people of any city writes to the emperor, the following things or ones like them should be added in conjunction with the name of the ruler: "To the renowned, most excellent, most invincible, most eminent conqueror and always august emperor of the Romans, C—, N—, archbishop of Pisa, though unworthy, expresses his due obedience in Christ," or something similar to the forms above.

Salutations of Ecclesiastical Among Themselves

"N—, by the grace of God bishop of the holy church of Bologna, although unworthy, sends unceasing good wishes in Christ," or "greeting in Christ eternal," "fraternal greetings and prayers in the Lord," "desires an increase of fraternal good-will and love," "expresses a feeling of brotherly affection," or "sends greetings and heartfelt prayers in the Lord."

Now, it may happen that prelates have reverend persons under their authority to whom not "blessings" but "greetings and an increase of true" or "sincere" or "Pure piety" should be written.

Principally to Monks

". . . An increase of true piety in Christ," "the reward of holy conversation," "the reward of eternal bliss."

For truly, in writing to monks we are accustomed to make mention always of "piety" or "holy conversation."

Salutations of Prelates to their Subordinates

N—, by the grace of God bishop of the holy church of Bologna, although unworthy, sends to P—, servant of the church of Holy Mary, greetings and blessings," "greetings and an increase of blessing," or "blessings in the Lord with good-wishes."][80]

To illustrate the importance that the authors of the *artes dictamini* attached to such protocol, Alberic of Monte Cassino provided a lengthy discussion of the difference between the *salutatio* and the *exordium*, and, giving more attention to the traditional *exordium*, Guido Faba authored a collection of 330 *sententiae*, in a work entitled *Exordium*, to be used in the introductions of letters.[81] Of Guido's eight major works, four are specifically dedicated to the *exordium*, a level of attention which helps to explain its prominence in the *Rationes dictandi*. After a detailed outline of the salutation, the *Rationes dictandi* deals rather more briefly with the other elements of a letter. Perhaps the comments in the section on "securing goodwill" are typical. Providing far less detail in this section, the author observes that good will of the audience requires the "fit ordering of words" to influence the minds of the audience,[82] illustrating the emphasis on diction and figures in this rhetorical school. Having touched briefly on a few *topoi* and circumstances which may affect the subject, he then observes "Est item sepe numero maxima pars captandi beniuolentiam in ipsa salutationis serie" [besides, very often the largest part of the securing of goodwill is in the course of the salutation itself].[83] The other parts of the letter receive even less comment. He divides narrations into two categories; simple and complex. He further complicates his categorization into a six-element grid when he notes that narrations may be about the past, present, or future. He comments on "nine species" of petitions: "aut enim est deprecatiua, aut preceptiua, aut conminatiua, aut exhortatiua, aut hortoria, aut ammonitoria, aut consultoria), aut correptoria, aut siquidem absoluta" [supplicatory or didactic or menacing or exhortative or hortatory or admonitory or advisory or reproving or even merely direct].[84] He also notes that petitions may be simple or complex. He then takes up the conclusion, observing that a major function is to organize the material so as to leave an impression on the recipient's memory. The conclusion then may be used for affirming or denying or even for personal comments which may have nothing to do with the letter itself. He concludes the treatise with comments on abbreviation, transition and coherence devices, grammatical construction, and possible variations in the formula. These aspects of the *formulae* became so highly organized that Lawrence of Aquilegia could produce a work such as the following:

Incipit practica sive usus dictaminis

Prima tabula

Salutaciones ad summum pontificem [85]

Sanctissimo
Clementissimo
Beatissimo

in Christo patri ac domino Clementi divina providencia sacro-
sancte romane ac universalis ecclesie summo pontifici Rodolfus ca-
dem providencia Romanorum imperator et semper augustus, vel talis

rex
dux
comes

talis loci

salutem cum omni reverencia subiectiva.
salutem et omnimodam reverenciam.
reverenciam tam debitam quam devotam.

Prelati vero vel alie minores vel equales persone scribendo pape debent tacere salutem, et debent dicere sic:

tam prompte quam debite reverencie famulatum.
debitam cum devocione reverenciam.
se ipsum ad pedum oscula beatorum.

Narraciones ad eundem

flexis genibus
manifesto,
devotissime
reseramus,
reverenciae
intimamus,

vestre insinuacione presencium

quod

talis miles iniquitatis filius et minister ecclesiam mihi commis-
sam cotidie destruit et devastat.
magistrum P de tali loco, virum utique nobilem, litterarum scien-
cia redimitum, in spiritualibus et temporalibus circumscriptum,
in nostrum elegimus episcopum et pastorem.
accincta est contra nos tocius regni Anglie fortitudo, cuius gentes
terram nostram armata manu excelso brachio et potenti hostiliter
invaserunt.

Peticiones ad predictum

Sanctitati
Clemencie
Beatitudini
Pietati
Misericordie
Apostolic gracie
Sancte paternitati

Eapropter

sanctitati
clemencie
beatitudini
pietati
misericordie
apostolice gracie
sancte paternitati

vestre

que nullum in tribulacione
despicit suam misericordiam
imploratem,
quam orbi dominus prepoouit
universo,
quam divina gracia preelegit,
quam altissimus multa
sanctitate beauit,
apud quam non est accepcio
personarum,
que aperta tenet brachia
redeunti,
que cunctum populum
christianum semper respicit
oculo pietatis,

supplica-
mus
supplico

prece humillima
et devote,
reverencia quanta
possum,
cum omni
reverencia
subiectivc,

quatenus

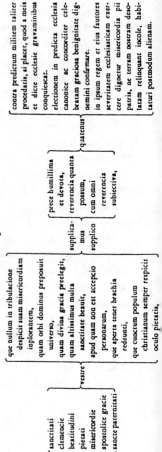

contra predictum militem taliter
procedatis, si placet, quod a meis
et dicte ecclesie gravaminibus
conquiescat.
electionem in predicta ecclesia
canonice ac concorditer cele-
bratam graciosa benignitate dig-
nemini confirmare.
in ipsum regem et eius fautores
severitatem ecclesiasticam exer-
cere dignetur misericordia pii
patris, ne terram nostram deso-
latam reliquant incole, habi-
taturi postmodum alienam.

Even Lawrence's rigid formalism demonstrates clear and interesting parallels between the *ars dictaminis* and Geoffrey's *Poetria nova*. It should be noted, in fact, that the author of the *Candelabrum* quotes Geoffrey directly when discussing stylistics.[86] Perhaps the most interesting element of the formulaic approach is an attempt to reduce the number of rhetorical responses in a given situation to a limited number of repetitive structures. The skilled rhetorician could profit from Lawrence's brief comments on possible variations in the formula. The number of formularies in existence from the period suggests that such tightly organized structural principles proved to be an important element in rhetorical training during the Middle Ages. Besides the specific *formulae* that the author of the *Rationes dictandi* cites, numerous others appear. Ludwig Rockinger has transcribed the formularies from Baumgartenberg, and Karl Zeumer has compiled the most systematic collection available.[87] The formularies generally focus most attention on the salutation and *exordium*, in the fashion of the *Rationes dictandi*, apparently sharing the assumption that all other parts will flow naturally from the beginning. Some, however, such as the *Marculfi formulae*, provide texts of complete letters, similar to modern business software or letter manuals, which would require only minor changes to be adapted by the sender.[88] The collections also show significant sensitivity to the social status of the sender and recipient, providing numerous specific examples of how to address superiors, inferiors, and equals, with subtle variations based on relative social status. In the *Dictamina rhetorica*, Guido Faba also followed this tradition by presenting hundreds of models for use in the composition of letters.

THE *ARS NOTARIA*

As varied and complex as these rhetorical elements are, it is hardly surprising if they underwent further transition as both literacy and legal rights were extended during the Middle Ages. While the origins of the *ars dictaminis* may be found early in the medieval period in the correspondence among rulers, the more general extension of formal mechanisms and forums for resolving both criminal and civil legal matters during the period called for the continuing development of a legal caste and the extension of the *ars dictaminis* into matters of more mundane nature than those generally resolved in the king's court.[89] As legal structure expanded, it maintained and enhanced its rhetorical basis, a continuing interrelationship which has led one student of modern law to conclude "we might regard law as a branch of rhetoric."[90] The expansion of access to law called for a more sharply defined legal rhetoric and a class of individuals trained to deal with that rhetoric and legal procedures. Henryson, perhaps like Chaucer,[91] was likely a member of that burgeoning class of legal experts, as evidenced by the title "notarius publicus." For him, then, the *ars notaria* would have been a familiar kind of rhetoric, both through study and daily use. What we know about the *ars notaria* suggests that it was a more highly structured and more legalistic rhetorical form of the *ars dictaminis*. Murphy asserts that it "concerned itself with the physical forms of documents" and Gianfranco Orlandelli comments on the necessity of "perfezione" in the discipline.[92] In order to insure accuracy and conform to legal procedures, there was a special emphasis on diction and "set phrases." The language of law had widespread influence on literary figures in the later Middle Ages. Julian Wasserman and Lois Roney have pointed out, for example, the emphasis that Chaucer's lawyer places on language.[93] In the midst of Custance's tribulations, the lawyer feels obliged to comment on how she communicated in a foreign country:

> A maner Latyn corrupt was hir speeke
> But algates thereby was she understoude
>
> (ll. 519–20)

The comment shows a clever touch in characterization. For obvious reasons lawyers must be sensitive to language and precision in its use. Henryson, as both a notary and a poet, was doubly susceptible to the influence of the *ars notaria* in his verse.

The origins of the *ars notaria* are to be found in the dictaminal rhetoric governing correspondence involving secular and religious decrees. Such documents used their own vocabulary to establish the relationships among correspondents and to simplify communication (at least in the minds of notarial authorities). Diction was therefore a key factor in the *ars notaria*. This rhetorical school made use of stipulative definitions and employed numerous neologisms from Latin. Its development reached its high point in the latter part of the Middle Ages, when notaries often became major forces in the administration of the state. Geoffrey Barraclough makes the following observation about the status of the *notarius publicus* in Papal curia:

> Public notaries were not indeed regarded as
> *officiales sedis apostolice*: recognition as such came
> first with the full development of the Middle
> Ages. But they were not merely private assistants of
> the higher officers of the various courts in which they
> functioned. Not only do we find duties imposed upon
> them, which could of their nature only be imposed on
> public officials—duties, that is to say, which were
> unremunerative, and which a private notary would
> have no advantage in performing; but it is clear that
> even if not appointed by, they were in the last
> analysis responsible to the Vice-chancellor himself.[94]

Barraclough goes on to comment that the "public notary was active in almost every department, legal and administrative . . .,"[95] illustrating the power and importance of this class.

The major interests of the *ars notaria* were formulated in the work of one of the earliest exponents of this school of rhetoric, Rainerius of Perugia, who wrote his *Ars notariae* between 1226 and 1233. One of the major differences between Rainerius' work and that of previous dictaminal writers is his emphasis on courts of law and judicial procedure. Perhaps because of the development of a more complex and unified legal framework, Rainerius provides a new incentive for careful attention to organization, language, and procedure. These emphases were certainly important during Henryson's lifetime; James J. Robertson observes that "By the fifteenth century, the beginnings of mature law in Scotland can be discerned."[96] Such maturity in the legal system developed earlier in other countries, notably Italy. With legal decisions made at the level below the head of state or church, there came to be a renewed emphasis on careful and standard legal diction in written agreements and opportunities for pleading in secular and religious courts. It may indeed be such extension and regularization of the legal system which gave birth to the *ars notaria* rather than, as Murphy suggests, some innate failure in the *ars dictaminis*.[97] The expansion of legal activities also called for an enhanced sensitivity to audience and setting in the *ars notaria*, as illustrated in the *Ordo iudiciarius*. Aegidius makes special mention of the human and situational factors involved in the *ars notaria*, noting the special importance of the personal factors, nature of the subject, time, and place.[98]

Henryson's fables show this kind of sensitivity to legal structure and the rhetorical setting. That both his professional affiliation and writings show an affinity for the developing middle-class access to law outside a royal court is suggestive about his education. In fact, by the date at which Henryson was educated, legal training had become a generally recognized kind of preparation for a career in government service.[99] His dual careers would likely have been seen as complementary, even as they are today.

HENRYSON AND THE POETIC FORM OF *DICTAMEN*

Henryson's use of the formulaic elements of political and legal documents is ample. One debt to this tradition also reflects a central concern of the *ars poetriae* and the *ars praedicandi* and appears in the *exordium* in *The Morall Fabillis*. In explaining the importance of the introduction, Alberic states that it should follow the basic Ciceronian objective of making the audience receptive and well-disposed, employing a proper mixture of delight and instruction.[100] Henryson conscientiously strives to fulfill these goals, as once again illustrated by the prologue to the *Fabillis* and his famous lines about the "nuttis schell" and the "bow that ay is bent." Henryson returns to the same theme in the prologue of "The Lion and the Mouse," which has created speculation about both the sequence of composition of the fables and his own extended concern about the relationship between instruction and delight. This principle is common to all medieval rhetorical schools. Yet, given his political interests in the fables, it should be observed that this general goal is in keeping with the principles of the *ars dictaminis* and the *ars notaria*.

Other aspects of his use of dictaminal rhetoric are to be found in "The Lion and the Mouse." Indeed, in many ways the poem is a structured "dictaminal dialogue" based on the rhetorical situation described by C. Julius Victor involving the interaction of subordinate and superior. The marked contrasts in this dialogue, a subject of general critical comment,[101] can be explained in part by the many elements of "dignified" dictaminal rhetoric that appear in the consideration of both deliberative and forensic issues. Because of the dramatic nature of his verse, it would have been impossible for Henryson to use precisely the five-part pattern of organization developed in this rhetorical school. Yet basic elements of this pattern are present along with the sensitivity to social status and elements of formulaic language. As previously noted, the tale is preceded by a dialogue between Henryson's authorial *persona* and Aesop, which sets the scene for the fable itself. Henryson clearly acknowledges that Aesop is his superior, calling him "'O maister Esope, poet lawriate'" (l. 1377). He further advances his own petition that Aesop "wald dedene to tell ane prettie fabill/ Concludand with ane gude moralitie" (ll. 1386–87). Aesop at first declines, commenting cynically, "For quhat is it worth to tell ane fen$_3$eit taill/ Quhen haly preiching may na thing auaill?" (ll. 1389–90). Finally persuaded by Henryson's arguments, Aesop delivers the fable. This petition-and-response format precurses the structure of the dialogue in the tale, as does the language establishing the relationship between Aesop and Henryson. The master-subordinate relationship and its structure of pleas and reactions was a common subject of the *artes dictamini* and provides the overall structure for both this prologue and the tale.

After the initial narrative describing the mice's abuse of the lion and disregard of his power, the first direct statement from a character in the fable is the maister mouse's lament about being caught by the lion. It is comparatively direct and natural:

> 'Now am I tane ane wofull presonair,
> And for my gilt traistis incontinent
> Off lyfe and deith to thoill the iugement.'
>
> (ll. 1422–25)

The lion's response to the crime of the maister mouse and his cohort—running over the lion's body while he slept—seems harsh indeed:

> Than spak the lyoun to that cairfull mous:
> 'Thow catiue wretche and vile vnworthie thing,
> Ouer malapart and eik presumpteous
> Thow wes, to mak out ouer me thy tripping.
>
> Knew thow not weill I wes baith lord and king
> Off beistis all?'
>
> (ll. 1426–31)

These lines, in a certain sense, constitute a salutation and *exordium*, albeit in a most disparaging tone. The lion reminds the mouse of his station and of the lion's position and honor. Their harshness may be more easily understandable, if the lion's language is compared with portions of a letter from Emperor Henry IV to Pope Gregory VII. The pointed recriminations and the very nature of the charge parallel Henryson's lines:

> H. non usurpative, sed pia dei ordinatione rex Hildebrando iam non apostolico, sed falso monacho.

> Hanc talem pro confusione tua salutationem promeruisti, qui nullum in ecclesia ordinem preteristi, quem confusionis, non honoris, male-dictionis, non benedictionis, participem non feceris.

> ....

> Et nos quidem hec omnia sustinuimus, dum apostolice sedis honorem servare studuimus. Sed tu humilitatem nostram timorem fore intellexisti ideoque et in ipsam regiam potestatem nobis a deo concessam exurgere non timuisti, quam te nobis auferre ausus es minari: quasi nos a te regnum acceperimus, quasi in tua et non in dei manu sit regnum vel imperium.

> [Henry, King not by usurpation, but by the pious ordination of God, to Hildebrand, now not Pope, but false monk:

> You have deserved such a salutation as this because of the confusion you have wrought; for you left untouched no order of the Church which you could make a sharer of confusion instead of honor, of malediction instead of benediction.

> ....

> And we, indeed, bore with all these abuses, since we were eager to preserve the honor of the Apostolic See. But you construed our humility as fear, and so you were emboldened to rise up even against the

royal power itself, granted to us by God. You dared
to threaten to take the kingship away from us—as
though we had received the kingship from you, as
though kingship and empire were in your hand and
not in the hand of God.][102]

The angry tone and accusation of treachery in Henry's letter are parallel
in both mood and *topoi* to the reproof by Henryson's lion. Not only
does the diction of the salutation show outrage, but, in both instances,
the recipient is reminded of his social standing and his lack of personal
virtue. Both Henryson's Noble and Henry IV also feel obliged to defend
themselves against implicit or explicit charges of inaction. The lion
takes refuge in his social status, asserting that his role as "lord and
king" should have prevented his suffering such indignities from the
mice. Henry, on the other hand, argues that his attempts to be
conciliatory have been misconstrued by Gregory whom he charges with
numerous abuses. While Henry's defense comes not in the *exordium* but
near the midpoint of his letter, both the poem and the letter demonstrate
a use of the standard *formulae* and *topoi* of the *ars dictaminis*.

The mouse's response also reflects formulaic elements. It is no less
than a petition to a superior for clemency, a variation of the section on
"securing good will" of the *Rationes dictandi*:

'ȝes,' quod the mous, 'I knaw,
Bot I misknew, because ȝe lay so law.

'Lord, I beseik thy kinglie royaltie,
Heir quhat I say, and tak in patience.
Considder first my simple pouertie,
Any syne thy mychtie hie magnyfycence;
Se als how thingis done off neglygence,
Nouther off malice nor of prodissioun,
Erer suld haue grace and remissioun.

'We wer repleit, and had grit aboundance
Off alkin thingis, sic as to vs effeird;
The sweit sesoun prouokit vs to dance
And mak sic mirth as nature to vs leird;
3e lay so still and law vpon the eird

That be my sawll we weind ʒe had bene deid;
Elles wald we not haue dancit ouer ʒour heid.'

(ll. 1431–46)

This type of appeal is illustrated by the reply of the Scots to the King
of England on his demand for overlordship in 1291:

> Sire, la bone gent d'Escoce que l'autre jour
> viendrent a Norham par vostre requeste et les autres
> q'il poent avoir dedeinz si brief temps, vous
> maundent saluz par nous, et vous mercient moult de
> la bone voluntee que vous avez envers le royaume
> d'Escoce et la bone gent de la terre et encore averez,
> si vous plest, qar il entendent q'il ne ount autre chose
> deservy ne deserviront, si Dieu plest. Et vous
> maundent, sire, q'ils ount entendu la monstraunce que
> feust l'autre jour faite en l'esglise de Norham en
> vostre presence par la bouche sir Rogier Brabazoun
> vostre chivaler laquele est icele, si come ils ont
> entendu, que vous ditez que vous estez chief seignur
> du royaume d'Escoce et que l'avantdit royaume est
> tenue de vous en chief, dont vous requistez la bone
> gent que la furent q'ils vousissent aerdre a vous come
> a chief seignour, et que vous les meyntiendrez en
> pees et en quiete solonc les loys et les usages du
> royaume d'Escoce. Et pour ce que vous ne entendez
> ne ne voulez que nul homme soit desheritez, si volez
> que les demaundantz qui droit cleiment eu royaume
> monstrent en vostre presence le droit que chescun
> quide avoir, et vous vostre droit monstrer volez et par
> vostre conseil et le conseil de la bone gent du
> roiaume resoun et droit ferrez a chescun.
>
> Sire, a ceste monstrance vous respoignent la bone
> gent que icy nous ont envoiez, q'ils ne entendent mie
> que si grante chose demandroiez si bon droit ne
> entendisez avoir, mes de vostre droit rien ne sievent
> ne par vous ne par vos auncestres unques demaundé
> et usé ne ne virent, dount ils vous respoignent, taunt
> come en eaux est, que a vostre monstrance ne ount ils
> poair a respondre saunz seignur a qui la demaunde

doit estre faite et qui poair en avera a respondre, car s'il feust ensi que ils se assentissent a vostre demaunde, rien ne acrestroit a vous de droit ne de proffit ne decrestroit a lour lyge seignour; mes bien volent la bone gent du roiaume que celuy qui roy serra en l'avantdit royaume face a vous quantque reson et droiture demaunde, car il poair en avera de respondre et faire, et nul autre. Ne lour semble que autre respounce vous purront faire. . . .

[Sir, the good people of Scotland who came to Norham the other day at your request, and the others whom they have been able to [consult] in so short a time, send you their greetings by us, and they thank you very much for the kindness which you show towards the kingdom of Scotland, and the good people of the realm, and will continue to show, if it please you; for they think that they have deserved, and will deserve, nothing less, if it please God. They inform you, Sir, that they have heard the declaration made the other day, in the church of Norham, in your presence, by Roger Brabazon, a knight of yours, which amounts to this, as they understand it: you say that you are overlord of the realm of Scotland, and that the kingdom is held of you in chief, wherefore you asked the good people there present to adhere to you, as overlord, and [you say] that you will maintain them in peace and quiet, according to the laws and customs of the realm of Scotland. And since you do not intend or desire that anyone should be disinherited, you wish that the claimants who assert that they have a right to the kingdom should exhibit, in your presence, the right which each one thinks that he has, and you [also] desire to show your own right; and by your advice and the advice of the good people of the realm, you will do to each one what reason and justice demand.

Sir, to this statement the good people who have sent us here make answer that they do not in the least believe that you would ask so great a thing if you

were not convinced of your sound right to it. But they
have no knowledge of your right, nor did they ever
see it claimed and used by you or your ancestors;
therefore they answer you, as far as in them lies, that
they have no power to reply to your statement, in
default of a lord to whom the demand ought to be
addressed, and who will have power to make answer
about it. For if it should happen that they agreed to
your demand, no right or profit would accrue to you,
nor be lost to their liege lord. But the good people of
the realm earnestly desire that he who shall be kind in
the aforesaid kingdom shall do to you whatsoever
reason and justice may demand, for he, and no other,
will have power to reply and to act in the matter. It
seems to them that they can give you no other
answer. . . .][103]

Once again the appeals are similar in content and format. In both cases
ignorance and innocence are used as excuses at the beginning of the
petition. Incorporating elements of the *narratio,* the maister mouse
pleads that the mice were deceived about the lion's power and status
because "ȝe lay so law." The Scots point out that they are baffled by
the legal circumstances involving the King's claim in the absence of a
Scottish monarch to whom they owe fealty. They thank the King for his
kindness to the realm and reassure him they understand he would not
make so great a claim if he did not honestly believe in his entitlement.
The maister mouse makes an appeal to his condition and social
circumstances, urging Noble to consider the poverty of the mice and
their joy in a season of "grit aboundance" as mitigating factors in their
negligence. The Scots similarly argue that the lack of a reigning
Scottish monarch is a critical mitigating circumstance. While the
essence of their response is "we cannot do this," they go out of their
way to reassure the King that their problem is with procedural issues in
determining where to vest their loyalties. Their concluding arguments
about the welfare of the realm even anticipate the case the maister
mouse will later make about how unwholesome he would be for the
lion's diet. The mouse's lines also follow the guidelines of the
dictaminal salutation as typified in the Scottish response. The language
of his response is both courtly in diction and properly respectful,
illustrating clear acknowledgement of his status as a subordinate. Using

standard courtly terms such as "thy Kinglie royaltie" and "thy mychtie hie magnyfycence," the mouse begs for Noble's indulgence. This same tone of humility appears in Philippe de Mezières' *Letter to King Richard II*:

> Pour empetrer de la bónte divine, la benivolence et pacience de vostre audience royale, tresdebonnaire prince, je vous suppli treshumblement et devotement qu'il vous plaise avoir en ramembrance comment le Roy des roys, le doulz Jhesu, fort traveille d'aler a pie et apres longue jeune, reposant soy sur le puys de Sicar, non tant seulement benignement ouy la pecherresse Samaritaine, / mais oultre plus il li fist un grant et lonc sermon, au sauvement de son ame et, par consequent, au salut des habitans de la cite de Samarie,. . . .

> [Most gracious Prince,
> That I may obtain, through the goodness of God, a kindly and patient hearing from your royal majesty, humble and devotedly I beg that it may please you to call to mind how the King of kings, sweet Jesus, being very tired after much journeying on foot and a long fast, stopped to rest at the well of Sicar, and not only listened kindly to the sinful woman of Samaria, but spoke to her at length for the saving of her soul and, so, for the salvation of the people of Samaria].[104]

While Henryson abbreviates such elaborate forms of address, the Maister mouse touches on the lion's "kingly royaltie" and makes the same appeal for a full and patient hearing as is found in de Mezières' letter.

The appeals of the maister mouse not only parallel those in the appeal of the Scottish magnates, but add other dictaminal dimensions as well. For instance, excusing the mice's acts on the basis of poverty and ignorance, the maister mouse introduces conditions for which the king of beasts must ultimately accept responsibility. Although not so direct, a similar kind of appeal, predicated on social necessity, is illustrated by the declaration of the clergy of Scotland of their fidelity to Robert I. The putative date of this document (1310?) and its use of dictaminal techniques are of interest to students of both Scottish history and medieval rhetoric:

> Videntes igitur populus et plebs predicti regni
> Scocie multarum tribulacionum aculeis fatigati dictum
> dominum Johannem per regem Anglie pro diversis
> causis captum incarceratum, regno et populo
> privatum, ac regnum Scocie per ipsum perditum et in
> servitutem redactum, ingenti populacione vastatum,
> crebri doloris acerbitate respersum, pro defectu recti
> regiminis desolatum, omni periculo expositum, et
> occupanti concessum, populumque bonis spoliatum,
> bellis cruciatum captivatum vinculatum et
> incarceratum, stragibus immensis innocencium et
> continuis incendiis oppressum subjectum et
> mancipatum ac perpetue ruine proximum nisi divino
> consilio circa regni sic deformati ac desolati
> reparacionem et ejus regimen celerius tractaretur,
> Summi Regis providencia sub cujus imperio reges
> regnant et principes dominantur tot et tanta dampna
> gravia morte amariora rerum et corporum sepe
> contingencia pro defectu capitanei et fidelis ducis
> diucius ferre non valentes, in dictum dominum
> Robertum regem, qui nunc est, in quem jura patris
> avique sui ad predictum regnun judicio populi adhuc
> resident et vigent incorputa [*sic*] auctore divino
> convererunt, ac de consciencia et consensu eorumdem
> assumptus est in regem ut regni deformata reformet,
> corrigendaque corrigat, et dirigat indirecta.

> [Therefore the whole people of the realm of
> Scotland, wearied with the stings of many tribulations
> (for this John was taken by the king of England, for
> various reasons, and imprisoned, and deprived of his
> realm and people, and the realm of Scotland was lost
> by him, and reduced to servitude, laid waste by great
> slaughter, and imbued with the bitterness of heavy
> sorrow, made desolate by the lack of true governance,
> exposed to every danger, and given up to the
> despoiler, the inhabitants deprived of their property,

tortured with strife, made captive, bound and
imprisoned, oppressed with untold killings of
blameless people, and with continual burnings, subject
and in bonds, and nigh to perpetual ruin unless by
divine counsel speedy provision were made for the
restoration of a realm so afflicted and desolate, and of
its government, by the providence of the King most
high, under whose authority kings rule, and princes
govern), this people, being unable any longer to
endure injuries so many and so great, and more bitter
than death, which were being continually inflicted on
their property and their persons for lack of a captain
and a faithful leader, agreed, by divine prompting, on
Lord Robert who now is king, in whom reside and
remain uncorrupted, in the general opinion, the rights
of his father and his grandfather to the kingdom; and
with their knowledge and approval he was received as
king, that he might reform the defects of the realm,
correct what had to be corrected, and direct what was
without guidance].[105]

Like the maister mouse's petition, this document is a defense against
treason. The appeal to the condition of the realm adduced by both the
maister mouse and the Scottish magnates is paramount in this
passage. While the Scottish nobles had an obvious procedural excuse,
the maister mouse and the Scottish clergy must tread more gingerly. In
Henryson's fable, there is one obvious and immediate cause of the
condition of the realm—the sloth and inattentiveness of the King. For
the Scottish clergy, John's weakness and imprisonment by the English
are the cause of the "many tribulations" the country must bear. The
extra difficulties in this kind of argument were especially problematic
in the *ars dictaminis*. In offering the excuse that he did not know
whether the lion was alive or not, the maister mouse touches on a
politically delicate *topos* (perhaps a version of "competence") used in
petitionary letters such as the following appeal from Catherine of Siena
to Pope Gregory XI (1375):

Santissimo e dolcissimo padre, la vostra indegna
e miserabile figliuola Catarina in Cristo dolce Jesú vi
si raccomanda nel prezioso sangue suo con desiderio

di vedervi uomo virile senza veruno timore, o amore
carnale proprio di voi medesimo, o di veruna creatura
congiunta a voi per carne, considerando e vedendo io
nel cospetto dolce di Dio, che veruna cosa
v'impedisce il santo buono desiderio vostro, ed è
materia d'impedire l'onore di Dio e la esaltazione e
riformazione della santa Chiesa, quanto questo. Però
desidera l'anima con inestimabile amore, che Dio per
la sua infinita misericordia vi tolga ogni passione e
tepidezza di cuore, e riformivi un altro uomo, cioè di
riformazione d'affocato ed ardentissimo desiderio, che
in altro modo non potreste adempire la volontà di
Dio, ed il desiderio de'servi suoi. Oimè, oimè, babbo
mio dolcissimo, perdonate alla mia presunzione di
quello ch'io vi ho detto, e dico : son costretta dalla
dolce prima verità di dirlo : la volontà sua, padre, è
questa, e così vi dimanda. Egli dimanda che facciate
giustizia dell' abbondanzia delle molte iniquità che si
commettono per coloro che si notricano e pascono nel
giardino della santa Chiesa, dicendo che l-animále
non si debba nutricare del cibo degli uomini; poichè
esso v'ha data l'autorità, e voi l'avete presa, dovete
usare la virtù e potenzia vostra, e non volendola
usare, meglio sarebbe a refutare quello che è preso
(B); più onore di Dio e salute dell'anima vostra
sarebbe.

[Most holy and sweet father, your unworthy,
lowly daughter Catherine in sweet Christ Jesus
implores you by His precious blood; I want to see
you a forceful man, fearless and without earthly love
for yourself or for any being related to you by
blood. When I consider [this question] I can see, in
the sweet presence of God, that nothing so hinders
your good and holy wishes or tends to tarnish the
honor of God and work against the exaltation and
reformation of the holy church more than this. Thus
my soul's desire, in inestimable love, is that God in
His infinite mercy strip you of all [worldly] passion
and all indifference of the heart and make another

man of you—that is, a man re-formed in fiery and
most ardent desire. In no other way can you fulfill
God's will and his servants' desires. Oime [alas],
oime, dearest Babbo [father], pardon me for my
presumption in what I have said to you and say to
you now: it is the sweet first truth that compels me
to speak. His will, father, is this, and this is what He
asks of you: He demands that you do away with the
enormous number of iniquities committed by those
who are pastured and fed in the garden of the holy
church. He says that animals should not feed on the
food of men. Since He has given you authority and
you have accepted it, you must use your virtue [virtu]
and your power. If you are not willing to use them,
you should have refused what you took on; it would
have been better for the honor of God and the
salvation of your soul.][106]

The diplomacy necessary in this kind of appeal hardly needs
elaboration. While it may actually constitute a friendly "call to action,"
as Catherine attempts to use it, there is always danger in telling
powerful persons that they have not been sufficiently active in their
positions of command. While the target of the Scottish clergy was in no
position to respond, Henryson's maister mouse needs all the tact and
diplomacy he can muster in bringing this message to the lion face-to-
face.

   Even with the maister mouse's efforts to be tactful, the lion's
response is again harsh, reflecting the arrogance of position deriving
from his superior power:

> 'Thy fals excuse', the lyoun said agane,
> 'Sall not auaill ane myte, I vnderta.
> I put the cace, I had bene deid or slane,
> Any syne my skyn bene stoppit full off stra;
> Thocht thow had found my figure lyand swa,
> Because it bare the prent off my peroun,
> Thow suld for feir on kneis haue fallin doun.
>
> 'For thy trespas thow can mak na defence,
> My nobill persoun thus to vilipend;

Off thy feiris, nor thy awin negligence,
For to excuse thow can na cause pretend;
Thairfoir thow suffer sall ane schamefull end

And deith, sic as to tressoun is decreit—
Onto the gallous harlit be the feit.'

(ll. 1447–60)

He once again reminds the mouse of his position in the natural
hierarchy and he emphasizes the dignity of his own person. That he
clearly formulates his judgment in the political terms of the day is
indicated both by his declaration of the crime as "tressoun" and his
condemnation of the mouse to the gallows, a fate which makes no sense
when one considers the actual condition of lions and mice in the state
of nature and which is logically contradicted or ignored by the mouse
in his response. The mouse's response once again reflects the courtly
terms and petitionary mode of his earlier remarks:

'A, mercie, lord, at thy gentrice I ase,
As thow are king off beistis coronate,
Sober thy wraith, and let thi yre ouerpas,
And mak thy mynd to mercy inclynate.
I grant offence is done to thyne estate,
Quhairfoir I worthie am to suffer deid,
Bot gif thy kinglie mercie reik remeid.

(ll. 1461–67)

Having already presented a proper salutation recognizing the position of
his addressee, the balance of the maister mouse's rhetorical appeals in
this passage involve devices typical of the *exordium* in the dictaminal
arts. He begins with a direct appeal for mercy, a type of *captatio
benevolentiae* in which he solicits the goodwill of his listener. He
reinforces his previous recognition of the lion's dignity and his respect
in the phrase, "king off beistis coronate." He goes on to detail his
petition in requesting the lion to "Sober thy wraith." He takes the
diplomatic path of not questioning the lion's judgment, granting that
offense has been done to the lion's dignity and granting the justice of
the lion's verdict, "Bot gif thy kinglie mercie reik remeid."
Comparisons between his appeal and the statement of submission to
King Edward by King John of Scotland:

Johan par la grace de Dieu rey de Escoce, a touz
ceaus qui ceste lettres verront ou orront saluz. Cume
nous par mauvoys consail e faus e par nostre
simplesce eions grevousement offendu e courecé
nostre seignor Edward, par la grace de Dieu roy de
Engleterre, seignor de Hirlaunde e duc de Aquitaine
en moult des choses, ceo est a saver nous estaunt e
demoraunt a sa foy e en son homage, de fere aliaunce
au roy de Fraunce contre li qui adonk[es] estoit e
encore est son enemy, e a fere mariage ove la fielle
son frere sire Charles, e por nostre seignor grever e le
rey de Fraunce eider a tot nostre poer par gere e en
autres maners: e puis par nostre mauvoys consail
avantdit defier nostre seignor le rey d'Engleterre, e
nous metre hors de son homage e sa foy par le
homage rendre; e ausi noz gens enveer en sa tere
d'Engleterre por fere arsons, pries prendre, homicides
fere, e autres damages plusors; e la tere de Escoce,
laquele est de son fie, de genz armés e en viles,
chasteaux e aillors mettre e establir por la terre
defendre contre li e por son fie li deforcer; por
lesqueu choses e trespas desudiz nostre seignor le rey
d'Engleterre avantdit est en la terre d'Escoce entré, e
a force la ad prise e conquise, nonostant le poer que
nous avions mis contre li, laquele chose il pout fere
de droit com seignor de son fie puis que nous lui
avions le homage rendu e fet les choses avantdites.

Por laquele chose nous estant en nostre plen poer
e nostre fraunche volenté, luy avons rendu la tere de
Escoce e tote la gent ove touz leur homages.

[John, by the grace of God king of Scotland,
gives greeting to all those who shall see or hear this
letter. Seeing that we have by evil and false counsel,
and our own folly, grievously offended and angered
our lord Edward, by the grace of God king of
England, lord of Ireland, and duke of Aquitaine, in
many ways, in that while we yet owed him fealty and
homage we made alliance against him with the king
of France, who then was, and still is, his enemy,

agreeing to arrange a marriage with the daughter of
Charles, the French king's brother, and to harass our
lord, and help the king of France, with all our power,
in war and by other means; and in that by the same
evil counsel we have 'defied' our lord the king of
England, and have withdrawn ourselves from his
homage and fealty by renouncing our homage, and
also in that we have sent our men into his land of
England to burn, plunder, murder, and do many other
wrongs, and have fortified against him the land of
Scotland, whichi is his fief, by putting and
maintaining armed men in the towns, castles, and
elsewhere, to defend the land against him, and deprive
him of his fee: for all these reasons and these manyh
wrongs, our lord the king of England has entered the
realm of Scotland and taken and conquered it by
force, notwithstanding the army that we had sent
against him, a thing which he was rightly able to do
as lord of his fee, since we had renounced our
homage to him and done the things already described.

Therefore we, acting under no constraint, and of
our own free will, have surrendered to him the land
of Scotland and all its people, with the homages of all
of them].[107]

In both instances a level of humility that would be embarrassing by
modern standards is invoked in recognizing the monarch's authority.
The humble tone of the petition is clearly linked to a recognition of the
power and authority of the monarch. The maister mouse and King John
readily recognize their own faults and iniquities and throw themselves
on the mercy of the King. This type of appeal made the *captatio
benevolentiae* the perfect prelude to the petition itself.

Having now concluded the salutation and exordium (including the
captatio benevolentiae) the mouse moves to a mixture of *narratio* and
petitio. For the most part his narration is brief. Some of it has been
recited by the lion in his statement of charges, and the mouse himself
has already described the events in lines 1431-46. He therefore touches
on them very quickly and launches directly into the *petitio*:

'In euerie iuge mercy and reuth suld be
As assessouris and collaterall;
Without mercie, iustice is crueltie,
As said is in the lawis spirituall.

Quhen rigour sittis in the tribunall,
The equitie off law quha may sustene?
Richt few or nane, but mercie gang betwene.

'Alswa ȝe knaw the honour triumphall
Off all victour vopon the strenth dependis
Off his compair, quhilk manlie in battell
Throw ieopardie of weir lang defendis.
Quhat pryce or louing, quhen the battell endis,
Is said off him that ouercummis ane man
Him to defend quhilk nouther may nor can?

'Ane thowsand myis to kill and eik deuoir
Is lytill manheid to ane strang lyoun;
Full lytill worschip haue ȝwyn thairfoir,
To qwhais strenth is na compaisoun.
It will degraid sum part off ȝour renoun
To sla ane mous, quhilk may mak na defence
Bot askand mercie at ȝour excellence.

'Also it semis not ȝour celsitutde,
Quhilk vsis daylie meittis delitious,
To fyle ȝour teith or lippis with my blude,
Quhild to ȝour stomok is contagious.
Vnhailsum meit is of ane sarie mous,
And that namelie vntill ane strang lyoun,
Vont till be fed with gentill vennesoun.   (ll. 1468–95)

Because this section of discourse basically contained all forms of proof and elaborated the nature of the request, it was often the lengthiest. The maister mouse enters into general arguments based more broadly on the nature of justice and the lion's own welfare than on the merits of this particular case. In fact, the entire first stanza advances arguments about the importance of mercy in tempering justice, arguments which could have been drawn from the *topoi* of either the *ars dictaminis* or the *ars praedicandi.* Given the lion's arrogance and caprice, the mouse obviously begins with his weakest argument. He then shrewdly turns to a much stronger argument, involving the lion's honor. This appeal to self-interest was common in the dictaminal arts. It shrewdly attempted to forge a link between the petitioner's request and the welfare and reputation of the individual being petitioned. The effectiveness of this appeal might depend on a variety of political circumstances and the personality of the monarch. Henryson's maister mouse has both factors in his favor. The lion is perceived as uninterested in his realm and is surrounded by enemies. He also clearly has a healthy ego. The mouse's direct appeal to the lion's "honor triumphall" is further elaborated in ll. 1482–88, demonstrating that the lion's reputation will be little enhanced by such a victory because of his strength relative to the mouse's weakness. He finally extends the argument even more directly to the lion's sense of well-being, in the process disregarding the precise details of the lion's sentence and breaking the illusion of characterization which is essential to Henryson's use of the beast fable. Ignoring the fact that he has been condemned to be hanged, the mouse notes that he would not be good for the lion's diet! He would be "Vnhailsum" when compared with the "gentill vennesoun" which the lion should be consuming.

The mouse then enters into the *conclusio*, the final section of dictaminal organization:

> 'My lyfe is lytill worth, my deith is les,
> ʒit and I leif I may peraduenture
> Supple ʒour hienes beand in distres;
> For oft is sene, ane man off small stature
> Reskewit hes ane lord off hie honour,
> Keipit that wes, in poynt to be ouerthrawin;
> Throw misfortoun sic cace may be ʒour awin.'
>
> (ll. 1496–1502)

He concludes with a litotical appeal about his own worth and his potential value to the lion. The language of this reference to extended service and potential value is also reflected in the structure of a formula from Tours:

> Domino magnifico illo ego enim ille. Dum et
> omnibus habetur percognitum, qualiter ego minime

habeo, unde me pascere vel vestire debeam, ideo petii
pietati vestrae, et mihi decrevit voluntas, ut me in
vestrum mundoburdum tradere vel commendare
deberem; quod ita et feci; eo videlicet modo, ut me
tam de victu quam et de vestimento, iuxta quod vobis
servire et promereri potuero, adiuvare vel consolare
debeas, et dum ego in capud advixero, ingenuili
ordine tibi servicium vel obsequium inpendere
debeam et de vestra potestate vel mundoburdo
tempore vitae meae potestatem non habeam
subtrabendi, nisi sub vestra potestate vel defensione
diebus vitae meae debeam permanere.

[To my great lord (name), I, (name). Since as was
well known, I had not wherewith to feed and clothe
myself, I came to you and told you my wish, to
commend myself to you and to put myself under your
protection. I have now done so, on the condition that
you shall supply me with food and clothing as far as
I shall merit by my services, and that as long as I live
I shall perform such services for you as are becoming
to a freeman, and shall never have the right to
withdraw from your power and protection, but shall
remain under them all the days of my life].[108]

While there were fewer guidelines about the *conclusio* in *dictamen*, this
type of appeal could be very useful. In the maister mouse's case, it
serves to reinforce his argument that it would be in Noble's own best
interest to be merciful. By promising his own dedicated service in the
future, the mouse offers himself and his band as allies, allies that Noble
would clearly need in the future.

Besides using formulaic language and dictaminal *topoi*, Henryson
has organized his dialogue around the organizational framework of the
ars dictaminis. The dramatic nature of the fable would have prevented
his using a "set speech" containing all five organizational elements in
one uninterrupted utterance. However, all five are present, from
salutation to *conclusio*, in sequence in the pieces of dialogue which
comprise the maister mouse's petition. His appeal is clearly successful,
reflecting the admonition of the *Rationes dictandi* that the conclusion
should leave an impact on the reader's memory. The lion finally relents

and lets the creature go free, rewarded by the mouse's blessing "Almichty God mot ₃ow for₃eild" (l. 1509). The mouse is, of course, able to return the lion's clemency when the lion is later captured.

Elements of dictaminal rhetoric appear along with aspects of dialectic[109] in many of Henryson's works, including "The Tale of the Wolf and the Wether," *The Testament of Cresseid*, *Orpheus and Eurydice*, and shorter poems such as "The Ressoning betuix Aige and Yowth" and "The Ressoning betuix Deth and Man." In other poems, Henryson's use of dictaminal devices is directly related to courtroom situations and also illustrates his use of the techniques of the *ars notaria*. Henryson's knowledge of both legal procedures and dictaminal techniques is illustrated in "The Trial of the Fox." As contrasted with his emphasis on dictaminal principles of *divisio* in "The Lion and the Mouse," the most obvious indications of Henryson's awareness of these rhetorical traditions in this tale are to be found in his use of the diction and terminology of courtly and legal pronouncements. Insofar as his language in "The Lion and the Mouse" reflects the terminology of the royal court, he employs elements of the *ars dictaminis* with early foreshadowings of the *ars notaria*. "The Trial of the Fox" reflects a greater interest in the *ars notaria* while continuing the use of the *ars dictaminis*.

The fable even begins with a legal theme, emphasizing the fox's desire to claim his inheritance. The fox's introduction is shadowed by comment on his father's death for his crimes:

> This foirsaid foxe that deit for his misdeid
> Had not ane barne wes gottin richteouslie
> That to his airschip micht of law succeid,
> Except ane sone, the quhilk in lemanrye
> He gottin had in purches priuelie,
> And till his name was callit Father-war,
> That luifit weill with pultrie to tig and tar.

> (ll. 796–802)

After Henryson's shrewdly deceitful protagonist, Lowrence the fox, has found his father's body, rejoiced in his inheritance, and thrown his father's body into a bog with a curse, the real legal action of the court begins. He goes to rest on a small hill and sees a unicorn appear suddenly as a "pursephant"—a heraldic officer empowered to deliver legal documents. As will be demonstrated later, Henryson consciously mixes heraldic animal imagery with his use of legal structure in this tale.[110] In this fable Henryson also refines his use of the *ars notaria*. The Unicorn's opening remarks reflect legal language heard in courts of law to this day:

> Vnto ane bank, quhair he micht se about
> On euerilk syde, in haist he culd him hy,
> Schot out his voce full schyll, and gaif ane schout,
> And "Oyas! Oyas!' twyse or thryse did cry.

> (ll. 845-48)

This traditional call to order sets the scene for other judicial elements in this tale. The court assembles with much pomp and circumstance, and Henryson provides a complete catalogue of the animals attending, some derived from nature and others derived from the world of myth. When the lion (another heraldic symbol) finally convenes the court, his comments reflect dictaminal *formulae* already noted above, as illustrated by the following lines:

> 'I lat ȝow wit, my micht is merciabill
> And steiris nane that ar to me prostrait;
> Angrie, austerne, and als vnamyabill
> To all that standfray ar to myne estait.
> I rug, I reif all beistys that makis debiat
> Againis the micht off my magnyficence:
> Se nane pretend to pryde in my presence.

> 'My celsitude and my hie maiestie
> With micht and mercie myngit sall be ay.
> The lawest heir I can full sone vp hie,
> And mak him maister ouer ȝow all I may:
> The dromedarie, giff he will mak deray,
> The grit camell, thocht he wer neuer sa crous,
> I can him law als lytill as ane mous.

> (ll. 929–42)

In part, the formulaic aspects of the diction in these lines are the result of the use of alliteration, but they also reflect stock phrases and ideas of the *ars dictaminis*. The phrase "my micht is merciabill" embodies a common dictaminal element designed to emphasize the munificence of the sender. Other phrases such as "celsitude and hie maiestie" are typical dictaminal devices to emphasize the power and strength of the court. The lion's exalted self-description and reflection on his powers might well be compared with the less exalted (but still inflated) salutation of this rather mundane grant of lands to Henry Percy by Robert I (1328):

> Robertus, dei gracia rex Scottorum, omnibus
> probis hominibus tocius terre sue salutem. Sciatis nos
> de gracia nostra speciali dedisse, concessisse, et hac
> presenti carta nostra confirmasse Henrico de Percy
> militi, filio et heredi quondam Henrici de Percy
> militis, omnes terras et tenementa ac redditus que
> fuerunt dicti quondam Henrici patris sui. . . .

> [Robert, by the grace of God king of Scots, gives
> greeting to all the worthy men of the whole of his
> realm. This is to inform you that we, by our special
> grace, have given and granted, and by this our present
> charter confirmed, to Sir Henry Percy, son and heir of
> the late Sir Henry Percy, all the lands, tenements
> and rents which belonged to the late Sir Henry his
> father. . .].[111]

The extent to which dictaminal rhetoric elevated the position of the sender is illustrated by this relatively innocuous document. Even the lion does not invoke "the grace of God" albeit this was a common device. The mention of Robert's "special grace" in confirming Henry's inheritance harkens back to the theme of the lion's mercy. Interestingly enough, alliteration even appears in this document, reinforcing the formulaic nature of the language.

Perhaps, however, the most interesting direct reference to the *ars notaria* appears in a discussion of the notarial arts that occurs in the context of the lion's attempt to preserve the dignity of his court. Having taken a roll of the animals attending, the lion finds that all are present except the mare. The lion's request to her to attend court would have been extended relatively gently in a summons incorporating standard language but exhorting appearance through a firm command. Even though such documents employed formulaic language and respected the recipient's dignity, they were nonetheless backed by the weight of the crown.[112] Considering the mare's absence an affront to his person and court, the lion makes plans to send a formal command of compearance—a legal term referring to the obligation of a feudal lord to appear when summoned by the monarch or the obligation of a party to legal proceedings to appear in a court of law when summoned. This formal command establishes a clearly forensic context for much of the dialogue to follow. When the lion searches for messengers, his eye immediately alights on Lowrence. The fox pleads his unsuitability because of lameness and partial blindness (the latter an impediment to his ability to read and thereby exercise proper legal and notarial duties) and adds "The volff is better in ambassatry/ And mair cunning in clergie fer than I" (ll. 997–98). As is obvious from subsequent lines, the phrase "mair cunning in clergie" may best be interpreted as "more skillful in law."[113] The lion reacts angrily and sends both fox and wolf on the mission. When they arrive at their destination, Lowrence begins his persuasion of the mare to compear with a discussion of the wolf's craftiness as a lawyer and his expertise at notarial arts:

> 'Now,' quod the tod, 'madame, cum to the king;
> The court is callit, and ʒe ar *contumax*.'
> 'Let be, Lowrence,' quod scho, 'ʒour cowrtlie knax.'

> 'Maistres,' quod he, 'cum to the court ʒe mon;
> The lyoun hes commandit so in deid.'
> 'Schir Tod, tak ʒe the flyrdome and the fon;
> I haue respite ane ʒeir, and ʒe will reid.'
> 'I can not spell,' quod he, 'sa God me speid.
> Heir is the volff, ane nobill clerk at all,
> And of this message is maid principall.

> 'He is autentik, and ane man of age,
> And hes grit practik of the chanceliary.
> Let him ga luke, and reid ʒour priuilage,
> And I sall stand and beir witnes ʒow by.'

(ll. 1003–16)

Lowrence's argument is couched in legal terms. He notes that she is *contumax*—in "contempt of court" or negligent in her obligations to the king[114]—because of her lack of appearance before the king at his court. Her response is that Lowrence should forego his "cowrtlie knax" which one modern translator has rendered as "lawyerly tricks."[115] While the translation may be open to debate, no matter how "cowrtlie" is translated, it clearly refers to legal procedures, whether defined in courts of law or royal courts. When Lowrence reiterates his appeal, the mare's response is far more legalistic. She contends that she has a respite (a formal legal document) which relieves her from court appearances for a period of a year and offers him the opportunity to read it. She refers specifically to a type of document often granted for reasons of health or in recognition of special conditions involving the recipient's government service or financial conditions.[116] The structure of Henryson's scene, with its use of legal terminology and reference to typical legal documents suggests a superior knowledge of the law and the *ars notaria*. The average Scot of the fifteenth century would have had little opportunity for such familiarity with legal procedures and language. Henryson's poem also reflects an understanding of the contemporaneous legal system. That system is best described by W. Seagle's notion of mature law: A mature legal system is one which is "not only officialized but which is professionalized. It is the creation primarily not of court officials but of a class of professional men."[117]

Lowrence at this point defers review of the Mare's respite to the wolf, observing that he does not have skills of spelling associated with reading and writing, a clear reference to the skills intrinsic to the *ars dictaminis* and the *ars notaria*. He notes that the wolf is "ane nobill clerk," once again using the word to refer to the same body of knowledge previously referred to in the word "clergie" (l. 998)–i.e. law.[118] It has been argued that these references actually relate to religious orders and that the tale is centered on a conflict between church and state.[119] In either case the terms are used to designate an individual skilled in dictaminal and notarial arts. His argument also hinges on the fact that the wolf is "autentik" (reliable) "And hes grit practik of the chanceliary" (l. 1014). As Denton Fox appropriately notes, this reference does not refer to the chancellery hand but instead to a general knowledge of the law.[120] This association between law and skills of reading and writing indicates that the wolf is skilled in the *ars notaria*. The fact that the wolf is "ane man of age," a phrase which Henryson uses to refer to himself in the prologue of *The Testament of Cresseid* may suggest an ironic sympathy. The wolf of course deigns to examine the mare's respite and is kicked in the head for his troubles. The two return to court without the mare, where the wolf's head wound inspires the king to a "lawyer joke" of the sort still heard:

> The lyoun said, 'Be ʒone reid cap I ken
> This taill is trew, quha tent vnto it takis.
> The greitest clerkis ar not the wysest men'

(ll. 1062–64)

The action from which the tale derives its modern title transpires in about the last thirty lines of the poem. Once the two royal emissaries return to court and report on their adventures, a ewe steps forward and accuses the fox of breaking the king's peace. He is summarily sentenced to death and executed on the gallows, after having been confessed by the wolf. This tale shows clearly Henryson's knowledge of legal proceedings and, more important, legal language and rhetoric. The additional political implications—that the fable may deal with a quarrel between church and state—would certainly reinforce the tale's emphasis on legalism and the *ars notaria*. The poet did not, however, confine his use of legal rhetoric or the *ars notaria* to this tale alone.

Henryson uses the *ars notaria* throughout his work, perhaps most obviously in "The Trial of the Fox," "The Tale of the Wolf and the Lamb," and "The Tale of the Sheep and the Dog" in The *Morall Fabillis* and the trial of Cresseid in *The Testament of Cresseid*. While "The Trial of the Fox" reflects Henryson's direct knowledge of the *ars notaria* and legal procedures, it does not contain his most pronounced use of the language of *ars notaria*. Probably the best examplar of his specific use of notarial rhetoric is "The Tale of The Sheep and the Dog." Like "The Trial of the Fox" this fable illustrates Henryson's knowledge of courts and legal procedures and definitively establishes a context for forensic oratory. However, in this instance, the trial setting is moved from the royal court to a consistory court—likely a more familiar setting for Henryson and a different *milieu* for his use of the *ars notaria*. The widespread importance of such courts and a knowledge the law in Scotland is to be found in the Education Act of 1496:

> It is statute and ordanit throw all the realme that all barronis and frehaldaris that ar of substance put thair eldest sonnis and airis to the sculis fra thai be aucht or nyne yeiris of age and till remane at the grammer sculis quhill that be competentlie foundit and have perfite latyne and thereftir to remane thre yeris at the sculis of art and jure sua that thai may have knawlege and understanding of the lawis. Throw

> the quhilkis justice may reigne universalie throw all
> the realme sua that thai that ar schireffis or jegeis
> ordinaris under the kingis hienes may have knawlege
> to do justice that the pure pepill sulde have na neid to
> seik our soverane lordis principale auditouris for ilk
> small ininure.[121]

Unfortunately, there was a pressing need for such knowledge. Scottish
courts in the fifteenth century were notoriously corrupt.[122] The citizen
who went to court without some basic understanding of legal procedure
was likely to be abused. Henryson's fables suggest that even with such
understanding an unwitting person could still be duped or beguiled by
duplicitous officers of the court. The reputation of the courts and
Henryson's first-hand observations may in part account for the cynical
and pessimistic tone of this fable.

Henryson's tale opens with a masterfully abbreviated description of
the major characters and immediately establishes the court setting:

> Esope ane taill puttis in memorie
> How that ane doig, because that he wes pure,
> Callit ane scheip vnto the consistorie,
> Ane certane breid fra him for to recure.
> Ane fraudfull volff wes iuge that tyme and bure
> Authoritie and iurisdictioun,
> And on the scheip send furth ane strait summoun.
>
> (ll. 1146–52)

The nature of the dog's motive and the wolf's ability to render fair
judgment are skillfully summarized. Most important for this analysis,
however, is the legal setting of the tale. This introductory stanza
summarizes the characters involved in a law suit and the delivery of a
summons. The next stanza describes the summons itself, after the "vse
and cours and common style":

> 'I, maister Volff, partles off fraud and gyle,
> Vnder the panis off hie suspensioun,
> Off grit cursing, and interdictioun,
> Schir Scheip, I charge the straitly to compeir,
> And answer to ane doig befoir me heir.'
>
> (ll. 1155–59)

As in his references to legal documents in "The Trial of the Fox," Henryson is indeed accurate in his description of the formulation of this summons, and the procedures to be followed.[123] He then proceeds to a detailed description of the offices of the court and the specific individuals who fill them. As if the description of the wolf were not sufficiently disheartening, the other incumbents of court offices also help to assure a form of "justice" biased against the sheep:

> Schir Corbie Rauin wes maid apparitour,
> Quha pykit had full mony scheipis ee;
> The charge hes tane, and on the letteris bure;
> Summonit the scheip befoir the volff, that he
> 'Peremptourlie within the dayis thre,
> Compeir vnder the panis in this bill,
> To heir quhat Perrie Doig will say the till.'

> This summondis maid befoir witnes anew,
> The rauin, as to his office weill effeird,
> Indorsat hes the write, and on he flew.
> The selie scheip durst lay na mouth on eird
> Till he befoir the awfull iuge appeird.
> The oure off cause quhilk that the iuge vsit than,
> Quhen Hesperus to schaw his face began.

> The foxe wes clerk and noter in the cause;
> The gled, the graip vp at the bar couth stand,
> As aduocatis expert in to the lawis,
> The doggis pley togidder tuke on hand,
> Quhilk wer confidderit straitlie in ane band
> Again the scheip to procure the sentence;
> Thocht it wes fals, thay had na conscience.

> (ll. 1160–80)

All of the officers of the court are predators (or worse, scavengers) in the animal kingdom. Henryson's use of these beasts in the judicial hierarchy is intended to depict the administration of justice at its worst. Just as in "The Lion and the Mouse" Henryson's vocabulary and description of court structure seem to reflect accurately fifteenth-century legal structure, as Mary Rowlands has shown.[124] As in the case of the wolf's summons, the format and the specific language of the Raven's summons once again incorporate the actual rhetorical forms of the *ars notaria*. It is also important to note that Henryson observes other customs of law. The summons is made before witnesses, and the raven "indorsat" the writ. The fact that the sheep is described as "selie" is also of interest, since the term means "innocent" and is often used to describe saints. This is a case in which a naively trusting and basically honest defendant has been caught up in the complexities of the law.

Henryson continues his use of the *ars notaria* in the formal charge and response which follow this introduction to the court:

> The clerk callit the scheip, and he wes thair;
> The aduocatis on this wyse couth propone:
> 'Ane certane breid, worth fyue schilling or mair,
> Thow aw the doig, off quhilk the terme is gone.'
> Off his awin heid, but aduocate, allone,
> Auysitlie gaif answer in the cace:
> 'heir I declyne the iuge, the tyme, the place.
>
> 'This is my cause, in motiue and effect:
> The law sayis it is richt perrillous
> Till enter pley befoir ane iuge suspect,
> And ʒe, schir Volff, hes bene richt odious
> To me, for with ʒour tuskis rauenous
> Hes slane full mony kinnismen off myne;
> Thairfoir as iuge suspect I ʒow declyne.
>
> 'And schortlie, of this court ʒe memberis all,
> Baith assessouris, clerk, and aduocate,
> To me and myne ar ennemies mortall
> Any ay hes bene, as mony scheipheird wate.
> The place is fer, the tyme if feriate,
> Quhairfoir na iuge suld sit in consistory
> Sa laid at euin: I ʒow accuse for thy.'

> (ll. 1181–1200)

All proper procedures are followed in this passage. The clerk calls the witnesses, and, when the sheep appears, properly states the charge. The advocates are allowed to "propone"—a legal term meaning to address the court, as Fox notes.[125] The sheep "declines"—another legal term from the period—the charge and alleges bias in the court, a proper basis for a defense.[126] He bases his challenge on three elements: the judge, time, and place. The wolf, he charges, is biased and has slain many of the sheep's kin. He then expands on the predatory nature of the officers of the court, whom he argues are "ennemies mortall." While touching briefly on the difficulties in time and place, he once again emphasizes the danger he senses and the lack of fairness in the court setting. Once such an accusation had been lodged, the judge had an obligation to submit the charge to arbitration to determine its validity. Surprisingly, perhaps, the wolf abides by these procedures:

> Quhen that the iuge in this wyse wes accusit,
> He bad the parteis cheis with ane assent
> Twa arbeteris, as in the law is vsit,
> For to declair and gif arbitriment
> Quhidder the scheip suld answer in iugement
> Befoir the volff; and so thay did, but weir,
> Off quhome the namis efter ȝe sall heir.

> (ll. 1202–08)

The wolf's scrupulous adherence to the form of appropriate procedure is unanticipated. Henryson emphasizes the formality of the situation through diction permeated with legal usage of terms such as "parteis," "arbeteris," and "answer in iugement." Once the proper procedures have been implemented, the deliberations which follow are full of legal procedure and language:

> The beir, the brok, the mater tuke on hand,
> For to discyde gif this exceptioun
> Wes off na strenth, or lauchfully mycht stand;
> And thairupon as iugis thay sat doun
> And held ane lang quhyle disputatioun,
> Seikand full mony decretalis off the law,
> And glosis als, the veritie to knaw.

> Of ciuile mony volum thay reuolue,
> The codies and digestis new and ald,
> *Contra et pro*, strait argumentis thay resolue,
> Sum a doctryne and sum a nothir hald;
> For prayer nor price, trow ȝe, thay wald fald,

> Bot held the glose and text of the decreis
> As trew iugis. I schrew thame ay that leis.
>
> (ll. 1209–22)

These discussions include "full mony decretalis off the law" and involve
a review of codes and digests and all pertinent decrees. The vocabulary
in this passage is full of legal terminology. The court officers
appropriately consult references to "civile" law since the case is what
would now be called a tort and not subject to criminal action.
Henryson's abbreviation of the term "civil law" into "civile" suggests
a close familiarity with the language of attorneys. In their review, they
conduct a full legal search, examining sources "new and old" and
"contra et pro" (a set phrase from the *ars notaria*). They base their
arguments on both the "glose and text of the decreis," properly invoking
subsequent interpretations of a law or precedent-making decisions.
Clearly these animals represent individuals learned in the law and the
notarial arts of reading and writing which would allow them both to
construct and interpret legal judgments. The description of their
deliberations is infused with the legal jargon of the *ars notaria*, as is
their final decision:

> Schorlie to mak ane end off this debait,
> The arbiteris than summar and plane
> The sentence gaue, and proces fulminait:
> The scheip suld pas befoir the volff agane
> And end his pley. Than wes he nathing fane,
> For fra thair sentence couth he not appeill.
> On clerkis I do it, gif this setence wes leill.
>
> (ll. 1223–29)

Terms such as "debait," "arbiteris" "summar and plane," "proces
fulminait" "end his pley" and "appeill" all reflect terms in
contemporaneous legal usage which were the stock in trade of the *ars
notaria*.[127] This legal rhetoric continues throughout the tale, culminating
in the final judgment of the court:

> The scheip agane befoir the volff derenȝeit,
> But aduocate, abasitlie couth stand.
> Vp rais the doig, and on the scheip thus plenȝeit:
> 'Ane soume I payit haue befoir the hand

> For certane breid.' Thairto ane borrow he fand,
> That wrangouslie the scheip did hald the breid;
> Quhilk he denyit, and thair began the pleid.
>
> And quhen the scheip this stryif had contestait,
> The iustice in the cause furth can proceid.
> Lowrence the actis and the proces wrait,
> And thus the pley vnto the end thay speid.
>
> This cursit court, corruptit all for meid,
> Aganis gude faith, gude law, and conscience,
> For this fals doig pronuncit the sentence.
>
> (ll. 1230–43)

Again, the legal diction and construction are pervasive. Fox notes that "deren3eit" is used here in a formal legal sense to mean arraigned,[128] a usage which appears to be otherwise unattested. The usage of other terms such as "aduocate," plen3eit," "pleid," "contestait," "iustice in the cause furth can proceid," and "executioun," show Henryson's knowledge of legal vocabulary. While some of these terms likely might have been in general usage among the educated classes, their use in the courtroom setting and the concurrent narrowing of their definitions to the legal context both demonstrate Henryson's intimate familiarity with the rhetoric of the law. Such use of legal vocabulary and set phrases is probably the best evidence available of Henryson's understanding of the techniques of the *ars notaria*. Of his interest in its principles, especially involving its direct attention to formalism in written discourse, there can be no doubt, based on this tale and "The Trial of the Fox."

CONCLUSIONS

Henryson made extensive use of the *ars dictaminis* and the *ars notaria*. His knowledge of these rhetorics helped him to portray realistically a range of social and legal settings. In "The Lion and the Mouse" he incorporates both the formulaic language and the five-part pattern of organization of the rhetoric for royal petitions and responses. "The Trial of the Fox" enables him to display his rhetorical skill in depicting both the king's court and the actions of scoundrels skilled in the *ars notaria*. In "The Sheep and the Dog" he demonstrates his own knowledge of consistory courts and enhances the realism of the tale through the pervasive use of the diction of the *ars notaria*. Moreover, his use of dictaminal and notarial rhetoric extends through much of his verse. These three tales only provide examples of rhetorical techniques he used in other fables, *Orpheus*, and the *Testament*. His use of such rhetoric to depict royal caprice and legal injustice supports his concern about the plight of the poor, the wronged, and the powerless in Scottish society. Henryson's attention to justice, legal structure, and dictaminal and notarial rhetoric shows that he was a keen student of the law and its developing efforts to displace the ethical imperative that "might makes right" with something more akin to Kant's transcendental aesthetic.

Notes
Chapter III

1. Murphy, *Rhetoric in the Middle Ages*, p. 184; McKeon, p. 2; Ward, pp. 28-29.

2. See Giles Constable, *Letters and Letter-Collections* (Louvain, 1976); Murphy, ed., *Three Medieval Rhetorical Arts*, pp. viii and xxiii; and, more especially for Britain, Noel Denholm-Young, *"Cursus* in England," *Collected Papers of N. Denholm-Young* (Cardiff, 1969), pp. 42–73.

3. Faulhaber, p. 85.

4. Jack, pp. 8–9. See also G. Campbell H. Paton, "The Dark Age" in *An Introduction to Scottish Legal History* (Edinburgh, 1958), p. 23 for additional comment on the tendency of Scots to seek legal training in Italy.

5. Faulhaber, p. 111.

6. Murphy, *Rhetoric in the Middle Ages*, p. 194; Constable, pp. 13–14.

7. Harry Caplan, "The Decay of Eloquence at Rome in the First Century," in *Studies in Speech and Drama in Honor of Alexander M. Drummond*, ed. Herbert A. Wichelns (Ithaca, 1944), pp. 295–325; rpt. in *Of Eloquence* (Ithaca, 1970), pp. 160–95. See also Camargo, "Rhetoric," p. 101, and Vickers, pp. 214–15 and 223–27.

8. Vickers, p. 228; see also George Kennedy, *Classical Rhetoric and Its Christian and Secular Traditions from Ancient to Modern Times* (Chapel Hill, 1980), p. 24; and Conley, pp. 94–95.

9. *Poetria nova*, ed. Faral, p. 257, lines 1946–49; translation from "The New Poetics," p. 103.

10. Baldwin, *Medieval Rhetoric and Poetic*, p. 209.

11. L. B. Dibben, "Secretaries in the Thirteenth and Fourteenth Centuries," *English Historical Review*, 25 (1910), especially 430–33; see also Constable, especially pp. 49–50, and Giry, pp. 824–34; and for comment on the evolving status of the responsibilities of the *auctor* in Italy, see Helene Wieruszowski, *Ars dictaminis* in the Time of Dante," *Medievalia et Humanistica*, 1 (1943), especially 103–08.

12. See Malcolm Richardson, "The *Dictamen* and Its Influence on Fifteenth-Century Prose," *Rhetorica*, 2 no. 3 (1984), 217–18.

13. Giry, p. 670; for general comment, see pp. 670–71.

14. Radding, pp. 46–7.

15. C. Iulius Victor, *Ars rhetorica*, pp. 371–448.

16. *Three Medieval Rhetorical Arts*, p. 3; *Rhetoric in the Middle Ages*, pp. 194–95.

17. C. Iulius Victor, *Ars rhetorica*, p. 447. See Murphy, *Rhetoric in the Middle Ages*, p. 195; and McKeon, 1–32.

18. C. Iulius Victor, *Ars rhetorica*, pp. 440–46. For comment on the importance of brevity in the *ars dictaminis*, see Murphy, *Rhetoric in the Middle Ages*, p. 195, and Faulhaber, pp. 92–93. This principle has a long history in the study of Medieval rhetoric, having been recommended by Alcuin in his *Dialogus de rhetorica et virtutibus*; see *The Rhetoric of Alcuin and Charlemague* trans. Wilbur Samuel Howell (Princeton, 1941).

19. Carruthers, p. 195.

20. Kindrick, "Robert Henryson and the *Ars dictaminis*," in *Bryght Lanternis*, ed. J. Derrick McClure and Michael R. G. Spiller (Aberdeen, 1989), p. 150. See also Martin Camargo, *Ars Dictaminis, Ars Dictandi* (Turnhout, 1991), p. 20.

21. In particular, on Alberic's role as the, "father" of the *ars dictaminis* see, for a traditional view, Charles H. Haskins, "The Early *Artes Dictandi* in Italy," in *Studies in Medieval Culture* (Oxford, 1929),

pp. 171–73; see also V. Licitra, "Il mito di Alberico di Montecassino iniziatore dell' *Ars dictaminis*," *Studi Medievali*, 3a. ser. 18 (1977) fasc. 2, 609–27. Licitra challenges the traditional "myth" of Alberic's contribution.

22. Constable, p. 11.

23. Faulhaber, p. 91; for comment on the importance of pedagogical traditions in the evolution of the *ars dictaminis*, see Paul F. Gehl, "From Monastic Rhetoric to *Ars dictaminis*: Traditionalism and Innovation in the Schools of Twelfth–Century Italy," *American Benedictine Review*, 34 (1983), 33–47.

24. *Variae*, ed. Mommsen, pp. 178–79; translation from *The Letters of Cassiodorus*, pp. 300–01. While this standard translation does not include the entire text of Cassiodorus, it covers the points central to this argument.

25. Procopius, *The Secret History*, trans. G. A. Williamson (New York, 1966,) p. 69.

26. Annabel Patterson, *Fables of Power* (Durham and London, 1991), pp. 15–16.

27. Stearns, *Robert Henryson*, pp. 127–29.

28. Roderick S. Lyall, "Politics and Poetry in Fifteenth and Sixteenth Century Scotland," *Scottish Literary Journal*, 3 (1976) 5–27.

29. Stearns, *Robert Henryson*, see especially pp. 14–32; MacQueen, *Robert Henryson* pp. 1–23, 94–188; Ranald Nicholson, *Scotland: The Later Middle Ages* (New York, 1974), pp. 500–30; Kindrick, "Politics and Poetry at the Court of James III," *Studies in Scottish Literature*, 19 (1984), pp. 40–55, and "Monarchs and Monarchy in the Poetry of Henryson and Dunbar, "*Actes du 2ᵉ colloque de lanque et de litterature ecossaises*, pp. 307–25.

30. Nicholson, pp. 508–09.

31. See Kindrick, *Robert Henryson*, pp. 77–78.

32. For a summary of these perspectives, see Nicholson, pp. 397–530, and W. Croft Dickinson and Archibald A.M. Duncan, *Scotland from the Earliest Times to 1603* (Oxford, 1977), pp. 235–48. Yet, for an opposing point of view, see Norman A.T. Macdougall, "The Sources: A Reappraisal of A Legend," in *Scottish Society in the Fifteenth Century*, ed. Jennifer M. Brown, pp. 10–32.

33. See Norman Macdougall, *James III* (Edinburgh, 1982), pp. 283–85.

34. See Nicholson, pp. 500–30, and Macdougall, pp. 140–83.

35. Robert Henryson, *Moral Fables*, George D. Gopen, ed. and trans. (Notre Dame, 1987), p. 5.

36. See Caplan, "The Decay of Eloquence at Rome in the First Century," *passim.*, for additional comment on the oral nature of ancient rhetoric and its application to written discourse.

37. See Constable, pp. 11–15; Walter J. Ong, "Orality, Literacy, and Medieval Textualization," *New Literary History*, 15 (1984), 1–12, for an overview of issues; Marjorie Curry Woods, "The Teaching of Writing in Medieval Europe," in *A Short History of Writing Instruction*, ed. James J. Murphy (Davis, 1990), pp. 77–94; and Ward Parks, "The Oral-Formulaic Theory in Middle English Studies," *Oral Tradition*, 1 (1986), 636–94 for a survey of recent critical approaches. For comment on how Chaucer dealt with the same problem, see Derek Brewer, "Chaucer's Poetic Style" in *The Cambridge Chaucer Companion*, especially pp. 227–30.

38. See, for example, *An Anthology of Chancery English*, with Malcolm Richardson and Jane L. Fisher (Knoxville, 1984), and "European Chancelleries and the Rise of Standard Languages," *Proceedings of the Illinois Medieval Association*, 3 (1986), 1–33.

39. Richardson, pp. 219–26.

40. "Rationes dictandi," in Rockinger, I, iii, p. 10; translation from Anonymous of Bologna, "The Principles of Letter-Writing," trans. James J. Murphy, in *Three Medieval Rhetorical Arts*, p. 7.

41. Faulhaber, p. 94.

42. Alberic of Monte Cassino, "Albericus de dictamine" in Rockinger, I, pp. 29–46.

43. See Hugh of Bologna, "Rationes dictandi prosaice," Rockinger, I, pp. 55. This translation is Murphy's, *Rhetoric in the Middle Ages*, p. 215; see also Faulhaber, pp. 92–93.

44. See, for instance, John McNamara, "Language as Action in Henryson's *Testament of Cresseid*" in *Bards and Makars*, ed. Adam J. Aitken, Matthew P. McDiarmid, and Derick S. Thompson (Glasgow, 1977), pp. 41–51; H. Harvey Wood, "Robert Henryson," in *Edinburgh Essays on Scots Literature* (Edinburgh, 1933), pp. 1–26; and Kindrick, *Robert Henryson*, pp. 28–56.

45. See Alex Agutter, "Middle Scots as a Literary Language" in *The History of Scottish Literature*, pp. 13–25, "Standardisation in Middle Scots," *Scottish Language*, 7 (1988), 1–8; and A.J. Aitken, "Variation and Variety in Written Middle Scots," *Edinburgh Studies in English and Scots*, ed. Aitken, Angus McIntosh, and Hermann Palsson (London, 1971), pp. 177–209.

46. Paul Murray Kendall, *The Yorkist Age* (New York, 1962), p. 437. See also M.B. Parkes, "The Literacy of the Laity," in *Literature and Western Civilization: The Medieval World*, ed. David Daiches and Anthony Thorlby (London, 1973), pp. 555–77.

47. For a good summary statement on our current understanding of the orthography and phonology of Middle Scots, see Adam J. Aitken, "How to Pronounce Older Scots," in *Bards and Makars*, pp. 1–26.

48. The factors which led to the development of literary Middle Scots were much the same as those which led to literary Middle English. For a helpful analysis, see J. D. Burnley, "Sources of Standardization in Later Middle English," in *Standardizing English*, ed. Joseph B. Trahern, Jr. (Knoxville, 1989), pp. 23–41.

49. See works cited above and, for a summary, Kindrick, *Robert Henryson*, pp. 40–41.

50. Leopold Delisle, "Notice sur une 'Summa dictaminis' jadis conservé a Beauvais," *Notices et extraits*, 36 (1899), pp. 171–205: This translation is from Murphy, *Rhetoric in the Middle Ages*, p. 227.

51. Baldwin, *Medieval Rhetoric and Poetic*, p. 214.

52. "Albericus de dictamine," Rockinger, I, p. 29.

53. See "Rationes dictandi prosaice," Rockinger, I. pp. 54–55.

54. Murphy, *Rhetoric in the Middle Ages*, p. 249.

55. Aldo Scaglione, *The Classical Theory of Composition* (Chapel Hill, 1972), p. 98.

56. Faulhaber, 101–02; For a more extensive summary, see Paget Toynbee, "The Bearing of the *Cursus* on the Text of Dante's *De vulgari eloquentia*," *Proceedings of the British Academy*, 10 (1923), 360–62.

57. Ronald Witt, "On Bene of Florence's Conception of the French and Roman *Cursus*," *Rhetorica*, 3, no. 2 (1985), 77–98.

58. W.A. Pantin, "A Medieval Treatise on Letter-Writing with Examples, from the Rylands Latin MS. 304," *Bulletin of the John Rylands Library*, 13 (1929), 330.

59. See *Poetria nova*, ed. Faral, pp. 220–57, lines 737–1968; translated in "The New Poetics," pp. 60–103.

60. J. A. Burrow, *Ricardian Poetry* (New Haven, 1971), especially pp. 1–10. See also Kindrick, *Robert Henryson*, pp. 29-56, and C. David Benson, "O Moral Henryson," *Fifteenth-Century Studies* ed. Robert F. Yeager (Hamden, CT, 1984), pp. 215–35.

61. Stephen Hawes, *The Pastime of Pleasure* (London, 1865), p. 38, chap. 11, 11. 18–19.

62. See Kindrick, *Robert Henryson*, pp. 31–2.

63. C. W. Jentoft, "Henryson as Authentic 'Chaucerian': Narrator, Character, and Courtly Love in *The Testament of Cresseid*," pp. 94–102; see also Tatyana Moran, "*The Testament of Cresseid* and the *Book of Troylus*," *Litera* 6 (1959), 18–24.

64. Baldwin, *Medieval Rhetoric and Poetic*, pp. 214–15; and Faulhaber, pp. 94–95.

65. Murphy, *Rhetoric in the Middle Ages*, p. 94.

66. MacQueen, *Robert Henryson*, p. 191; Kindrick, *Robert Henryson*, pp. 32–35; Gray, *Robert Henryson*, p. 135.

67. Stearns, *Robert Henryson*, pp. 97–105.

68. See Matthew P.M. McDiarmid, *Robert Henryson* (Edinburgh, 1981), pp. 53–87.

69. See J. A. Burrow, "Henryson: *The Preaching of the Swallow*," *Essays in Criticism*, 25 (1975), 25–37.

70. J.A.Y. Simpson, "Antiquarian Notices of Leprosy, and Leper Hospitals in Scotland and England," *Edinburgh Medical and Surgical Journal*, 56 (1841), 301–30; 57 (1842), 121–56, and 294–429. In addition to Simpson, see Saul N. Brody, *The Disease of the Soul: Leprosy in Medieval Literature* (Ithaca, 1974), pp. 173–77 and John B. Friedman, "Henryson's *Testament of Cresseid* and the *Judicio Solis in Conviviis Saturni* of Simon of Couvin," *Modern Philology*, 83 (1985), 12–21.

71. See Kindrick, "Henryson and the Rhetoricians," p. 255; and Michael C. Leff, "Boethius' *De diffentiis topicis*, Book IV," in Murphy, *Medieval Eloquence*, pp. 3–24.

72. C. Iulius Victor, *Ars rhetorica*, p. 448.

73. See Alberici Casinensis, *Flores rhetorici*, ed. D. M. Inguanez and E. H. M. Willard (Monte Cassino, 1938), III, 5, p. 38; translated in "Flowers of Rhetoric," in *Readings in Medieval Rhetoric*, ed. Miller, Prosser, and Benson, pp. 138–39.

74. *Rationes dictandi*, VI, p. 18; translation from "The Principles of Letter Writing," p. 16.

75. See Murphy, *Rhetoric in the Middle Ages*, p. 237.

76. See Giry, especially pp. 482–92.

77. Murphy, *Three Medieval Rhetorical Arts*, p. xvi.

78. *Rationes dictandi*, V, p. 11; translation from "The Principles of Letter Writing," p. 8.

79. Giles Constable, "The Structure of Medieval Society According to the *Dictatores* of the Twelfth Century," in *Law, Church, and Society*, ed. Kenneth Pennington and Robert Somerville (Philadelphia, 1977), pp. 253–67.

80. *Rationes dictandi*, V, pp. 13-14; translation from "The Principles of Letter Writing," pp. 11–12.

81. Faulhaber, p. 88.

82. *Rationes dictandi*, VI, p. 18; translation from "The Principles of Letter Writing," p. 16.

83. *Ibid.*, VI, p. 19; "The Principles of Letter Writing," p. 17.

84. *Ibid.*, VIII, p. 21; "The Principles of Letter Writing, p. 18.

85. Cited by Murphy in *Rhetoric in the Middle Ages*, p. 263.

86. See Baldwin, *Medieval Rhetoric and Poetic*, p. 217.

87. Rockinger, II, pp. 715–838; Zeumer, *Formulae merowinqici et karolini aevi, passim.*

88. Zeumer, pp. 32–106.

89. For comment on this expansion of the legal structure, see Fritz Kern, *Kingship and Law in the Middle Ages* (New York, 1970),

especially pp. 145–205. For more specific detail on Scotland, see David M. Walker, *A Legal History of Scotland*, I (Edinburgh, 1988), pp. 212-45.

90. See James Boyd White, *Heracles' Bow: Essays on Rhetoric and the Poetics of the Law* (Madison, Wisc., 1985), especially, pp. 28–48.

91. See Joseph Allen Hornsby, *Chaucer and the Law* (Norman, 1988), especially pp. 7–30.

92. Murphy, *Rhetoric in the Middle Ages*, p. 264; Gianfranco Orlandelli, "Genesi dell' 'Ars notariae' nel Secolo *XIII*," *Studi Medievali* 4 (1965) fasc. 2, 363–64.

93. Julian N. Wasserman and Lois Roney, *Sign, Sentence, Discourse* (Ithaca, 1989), p. xvii.

94. Geoffrey Barraclough, *Public Notaries and the Papal Curia* (London, 1934), pp. 17–18.

95. *Ibid.*, p. 19.

96. James J. Robertson, "The Development of the Law," in *Scottish Society in the Fifteenth Century*, ed. Jennifer M. Brown, p. 139.

97. Murphy, *Rhetoric in the Middle Ages*, p. 265.

98. See *Der Ordo Iudiciarius des Aegidius de Fuscarariis*, ed. Ludwig Wahrmund (Innsbruck, 1916), p. 5.

99. See T. F. Tout, "Literature and Learning in the English Civil Service in the Fourteenth Century," *Speculum*, 4 (1929), 365–89.

100. *Flores rhetorici*, II, 5, pp. 35-36; translated in "Flowers of Rhetoric," pp. 135–36.

101. See Gray, *Robert Henryson*, pp. 74–75, and Colette Murphy, "Henryson's Mice: Three Animals of Style," *Poetica*, 23 (1986), 53–73.

102. *Die Briefe Heinrichs IV*, ed. Carl Erdmann (Leipzig, 1937), pp. 15-16; translation from *Imperial Lives and Letters of the Eleventh Century*, trans. T.E. Mommsen and K.R. Morrison, ed. R. Benson (New York, 1962), pp. 150–51.

103. "Answer rendered to the King of England by the magnates of Scotland" in *Anglo-Scottish Relations*, ed. and trans., E.L.G. Stones (Oxford, 1970), pp. 106-111.

104. Philippe de Mezières, *Letter to King Richard II*, ed. and trans. G.W. Coopland (Liverpool, 1975), pp. 75, 3.

105. Stones, ed. and trans., pp. 282-83.

106. S. Caterina da Siena, *Epistole*, ed. P. Federico Burlamacchi (Milan, 1842), pp. 78-79; translation from *Readings in Western Civilization 4: Medieval Europe*, ed. Julius Kirshner and Karl F. Morrison (Chicago, 1986), pp. 424–25.

107. Stones, ed. and trans., pp. 146-49.

108. Zeumer, *Formulae*, p. 158. Translation by Oliver Thatcher and Edgar McNeal, *A Source Book for Medieval History* (New York, 1905), pp. 342-43.

109. While it is difficult to show direct influence, James J. Murphy's assertion that Bishop Marke foreshadowed Henryson's style in *De Moderno dictamine* is quite credible. See Murphy, "A Fifteenth-Century Treatise on Prose Style," *Newberry Library Bulletin*, 6, no. 7 (1966), 205-10. For comment on the role of dialectic, see Eleonore Stump, "Dialectic" in Wagner, ed., *The Seven Liberal Arts in the Middle Ages*, pp. 125–46 and *Dialectic and Its Place in the Development of Medieval Logic* (Ithaca, 1989), *passim*.

110. MacQueen, *Robert Henryson*, pp. 149–50. For additional comment on the structure and legal procedures of such a court, see A.A.M. Duncan, "The Central Courts Before 1532," in *An Introduction to Scottish Legal History*, pp. 321–40.

111. Stones, ed., and trans. *Anglo-Scottish Relations*, pp. 342-43.

112. See, for instance, *Nobles and the Noble Life 1295-1500*, ed. Joel T. Rosenthal (London, 1976), p. 103 and *Chaucer Life Records*, ed. Martin M. Crow and Clair C. Olson (Oxford, 1966), p. 364.

113. See Gopen's translation, p. 90.

114. See *Ordo Iudiciarius*, pp. 165–67. See also, Fox, *Poems*, p. 246.

115. See Gopen's translation p. 92.

116. See, for instance, PRO, C 66/188, membrane 13; printed in Rosenthal, ed., *Nobles and the Noble Life*, p. 129.

117. W. Seagle, *The History of Law* (New York, 1946) p. xv.

118. However, for an interpretation of this tale suggesting that clerical status is the major concern, see MacQueen, *Robert Henryson*, pp. 149–53.

119. For details, see Kindrick, *Robert Henryson*, pp. 92–93.

120. Fox, *Poems*, pp. 246–47.

121. Gordon Donaldson, ed., *Scottish Historical Documents* (New York, 1970), pp. 92–93.

122. See Paton, pp. 18–24. Evidence of Paton's assertion is revealed by a review of fifteenth century statutes on legal reform. The records of the reign of James III show an especially significant number of such reform acts. See *The Lawes and Actes of Parliament* (Edinburgh, 1597), especially, 59–73.

123. See David Maxwell, "Civil Procedure," in *An Introduction to Scottish Legal History*, pp. 415–16, and Fox, *Poems*, pp. 253–54.

124. See Mary Rowlands, "Robert Henryson and the Scottish Courts of Law," *Aberdeen University Review*, 39 (1962), 219–26.

125. Fox, *Poems*, p. 256.

126. The sheep's position is based on his right to investigate "whether he who made the charge ought to make it either at that particular time, or in that way, or in that place, or in the company of those with whom he made it," *The Rhetoric of Alcuin and Charlemagne*, ed. and trans., Howell, p. 75. Norman Doe explains how this procedure was well supported by medieval legal theory in *Fundamental Authority in Late Medieval English Law* (Cambridge, 1990), pp. 87-90. This and other instances of "decline" in Middle Scots are cited by Fox, *Poems*, p. 256.

127. For more specific comment on each term, see Fox, *Poems*, p. 259.

128. Fox, *Poems*, p. 259.

IV
Henryson and
The *Ars praedicandi*

THE NATURE OF THE *ARS PRAEDICANDI*

Henryson's use of the *ars praedicandi* has received the most attention of any of his rhetorical resources,[1] in part because of his use of *moralitates* and his pronounced didactic tone. As might be expected, a great deal of attention has been given to Henryson's exegetical techniques and emphasis on moral lessons. Unfortunately, evaluations of Henryson's use of this particular element of the *ars praedicandi* have not always resulted in clarification of his verse. Controversies about his use of the *moralitas* in tales such as "The Cock and the Jasp," "The Paddock and the Mouse," and "The Sheep and the Dog" have had a major role in Henryson scholarship. At the other extreme, limited and superficial interpretations of the *moralitates* of poems such as *The Testament of Cresseid* and the *Orpheus* have sometimes resulted in simplistic readings of the works. "The Preaching of the Swallow," likely because of its title, has profited from a number of readings involving both its exegetical potential and other rhetorical devices.[2]

Part of this attention to the *ars praedicandi* in Henryson's verse is doubtless due to the nature of his art, but part of it is also likely due to the early attention which this rhetorical school received in modern criticism. Certain aspects of the *ars praedicandi* have been critical staples throughout the twentieth century. For modern criticism, Harry Caplan's seminal article in 1929, "The Four Senses of Scriptural Interpretation and the Medieval Theory of Preaching," clearly laid the groundwork for later approaches to exegetical techniques. G. R. Owst published a more comprehensive treatment of English uses of the *ars praedicandi* in 1933 in his *Literature and Pulpit in Medieval England*. While giving attention to exegetical approaches, Owst provided a more general overview of issues involving the *exemplum*, the beast fable, the use of scriptural *auctoritates*, diction, and *divisio*, among other topics. Ernst Curtius' landmark *European Literature and the Latin Middle Ages* provided a significant impetus to rhetorical studies, especially those involving the *ars praedicandi*. D.W. Robertson's

application of exegetical techniques of interpretation to Chaucer as
represented in *A Preface to Chaucer* (1962) raised a major controversy
among medievalists which continues to have implications for Chaucer
criticism.[3] Particularly because of the importance of the *ars praedicandi*
to Chaucerian studies and Henryson's notoriety as a "Scots Chaucerian"
critical studies based on the rhetoric of preaching have also extended to
Henryson. All of this attention has produced major insights into the
nature of this rhetorical school and its influence on literature.[4]

Indeed, the *ars praedicandi* was a pervasive force in the history of
medieval rhetoric. In a non-codified form, it is perhaps the oldest of the
three medieval schools. Its theoretical codification in the early thirteenth
century was preceded by the attention given earlier to the *ars
dictaminis*, but the basic groundwork for the medieval *ars praedicandi*
was laid in the fourth century, when St. Augustine provided a key
justification for adapting the pagan arts of rhetoric to Christian
preaching:

> Nam qui sapienter et eloquenter dicit, vivit autem
> nequiter, erudit quidem multos discendi studiosos,
> quamvis animae suae sit inutilis, sicut scriptum est.
> Unde ait apostolus: *Sive occasione sive veritate
> Christus adnuntietur* . . . . Multis itaque prosunt
> dicendo quae non faciunt,. . . .

> [For he who speaks wisely and eloquently, but
> lives wickedly, may benefit many students, although,
> as it is written, he "is unprofitable to his own
> soul." Whence the Apostle also said, "Whether as a
> pretext, or in truth [let] Christ be preached."
> . . . And thus they benefit many by preaching what
> they do not practice.][5]

While Augustine did not originate the application of rhetorical principles
to preaching (the phenomenon is far older than the Christian tradition[6]),
his definitive statement on the morality of using classical models to
shape the rhetoric of Christianity provided the impetus for subsequent
events. Adapting classical models and precepts for homilies became
respectable, and individuals such as John Chrysostom assumed added
importance for the medieval preacher as models of eloquence.[7]

The religious goals of Christian preaching were clear. The rhetoric was, as Murphy points out, unusual in its relationship between the speaker or writer and the audience.[8] Classical rhetoric had placed emphasis on the welfare of the speaker or writer in attempting to insure that his point of view was widely accepted and that his own goals of action were met. The goal of the Christian *ars praedicandi* was the welfare of the auditor or reader. To all intents and purposes the speaker was already saved and had greater or lesser insights into absolute truth. It was the auditor whose soul might be in peril. While the speaker wished to see his ideas and point of view prevail, it was the foolish auditor who was at risk if he did not heed the preacher's message. The basic rhetorical situation, then, involved a speaker who possessed absolute truth and, as a spiritual obligation, felt the need to share that truth with as many others as possible; the auditor was privileged to have access to what the speaker knew. Such rhetorical situations were quite different from those in the classical period, when people of roughly equal abilities came together to argue more about probabilities than about absolute truth.[9]

A major consideration which shaped the Christian rhetorical context was the ethical imperative to save as many souls as possible. This emphasis on the brotherhood of all mankind and the need to reach every segment of society also changed the rhetorical strategies. It was clear that not every individual possessed the same intellectual capabilities. Yet every individual was worthy of God's grace. How then could the preacher gain the attention of all those to be saved and insure that they would have at least a basic understanding of his vitally important message? Instruction had to be mixed with delight to gain the attention of all potential converts. Such an approach would insure the interest of an audience which might otherwise ignore the Word of God through stupidity, intellectual disdain, or commitment to another pattern of thought. Insuring that the message of Divine grace was communicated was somewhat more problematic. Medieval preachers could be expected to exercise a crude kind of audience analysis, but the heterogeneous composition of early congregations made complete differentiation of rhetorical techniques impossible. It was therefore essential that the Christian message be couched in a form which all could understand but which could appeal to even the most sophisticated level of intellect or spiritual understanding.[10] One way to approach this problem was through the fourfold level of scriptural exegesis. This exegetical approach shaped both form and substance of the *ars praedicandi*. In the later Middle Ages, as audiences became more homogeneous, another method evolved. John W. O'Malley has argued that by "the end of the Middle Ages . . . at least three distinctive styles of preaching were being practiced."[11] These styles were defined based on a more narrowly circumscribed level of audience sophistication. Only greater uniformity of education and social class in a given congregation would make such stylistic differentiation a solution to the problem of reaching all Christian audiences. A corollary factor in the history of this rhetorical tradition was its approach toward logic. As observed in Chapter One, logic in the *ars praedicandi* aimed not at approximate or tentative matters in the context of this world. Instead, it argued from irrefutable first principles to bring the audience to an understanding of absolute truth.

In view of these general considerations, what issues emerged from the study of the *ars praedicandi* that affected Henryson's verse? The emphasis on exegetical techniques has implications for virtually every aspect of Henryson's rhetoric, including invention, organization, and language. Henryson's language also reflects the specific diction of homiletics as he wrestles with the relationship between speech and writing in terms of the central problems of the arts of preaching—teaching a moral lesson and reinforcing a system of belief. His attention to particular figures, especially allegory, personification, and figures of amplification such as the beast fable, the *exemplum*, proverbs and *sententiae* also illustrates the principles of the *ars praedicandi*. His organizational practices, especially in a tale such as "The Preaching of the Swallow," demonstrate a clear influence of principles of *divisio* in the *ars praedicandi*. Moreover, his rhetorical stance shows the ability to adapt late medieval variations of authorial roles derived directly from the treatment of Scripture.

EXEGETICAL PRINCIPLES AND THE MORALITAS IN HENRYSON'S VERSE

The greatest emphasis using the *ars praedicandi* in modern criticism has been on the use of exegetical techniques to interpret secular literature. As has often been asserted, the widespread understanding and acceptance of exegesis as a means of scriptural interpretation during the period has implications for a critical understanding of medieval works.[12] It also has implications for

understanding medieval approaches to invention. Any author who begins
with the notion that his work should contain structured ambiguity which
will permit for the broadest possible audience appeal will find he makes
a predetermined commitment to certain kinds of material in addition to
a particular catalogue of figures. The sensitivity to widespread audience
appeal involved in this approach may indeed be the best refutation of
Vickers' assertion that in the Middle Ages "the interrelationship
between form and function has gone, form becoming an end in itself."[13]
Exegetical interpretations of Henryson's verse have received a great
deal of attention, particularly because of his use of the *moralitas* at the
end of many of his tales. The very notion of the appended *moralitas*
suggests that an artistic composition may be divided into two parts—one
designed to gain the reader's attention and the other structured to
reinforce the *sententia* in more explicit terms.

A pivotal concept underlying all other aspects of the *ars
praedicandi* is the need to put a substantial spiritual message in an
attractive form. While the *ars dictaminis* might have involved the most
frequent occasions of written discourse in the Middle Ages, surely, as
Robert O. Payne has noted, the art of preaching was the most public of
the rhetorical arts in the Middle Ages. For that reason, it demanded
more audience awareness (including an awareness of the nature of
irony) on the part of the speaker than the other arts.[14] Using an
approach generally drawn from classical texts, the medieval art of
preaching developed many of its own rhetorical guidelines for making
its message palatable.[15] Of particular importance in Henryson's work
were the *exemplum* and the beast fable as figures to capture audience
attention. Owst demonstrates that the *exemplum* and the beast fable
sprang from the same roots—the desire to illustrate a sin or virtue with
"subtlety in sermons."[16] This emphasis on subtlety was widely
appreciated among medieval preachers, who became aware quite early
of the need to find interesting material to bring their congregations to
an understanding of the proper way of life.[17] The theory clearly has
classical roots, and, as already shown, was a major concern in the *ars
poetriae* and the *ars dictaminis*. It is also advocated by St. Augustine,
who makes the following observations about the means which might be
used to save souls:

> Qui ergo nititur dicendo persuadere quod bonum
> est, nihil illorum trium spernens—ut scilicet doceat, ut
> delectet, ut flectat—, oret atque agat ut, quem ad

modum supra diximus, intellegenter, libenter,
oboedienter audiatur. Quod cum apte et convenienter
facit, non immerito eloquens dici potest, etsi non eum
sequatur auditoris adsensus.

[The speaker who aims at persuading people to
accept what is good should not despise any of these
three aims, that is, to teach, to give pleasure and to
move. As we have said above, he should direct his
prayer and his work to the end that he should be
heard with understanding, with pleasure, and with
ready acceptance. When he does this in an appropriate
and fitting style, he can deservedly be called eloquent,
even though he does not carry with him the assent of
his audience.][18]

Even in the most simple beast fables and *exempla* medieval preachers
could not be certain that their message would be understood. Therefore,
it was necessary to append a *moralitas* to ensure that everyone got the
point. The goal of the *exemplum* and the beast fable was to see that
common people eschewed evil and followed the good way of life. That
such stories sometimes used crude language or showed evil conduct was
of little consequence, as long as the moral was attached and clearly
explained. Henryson would have been exposed directly and indirectly
to both of these rhetorical figures in the works of Ranulph Higden,
Robert of Basevorn, and other major figures on the art of preaching.[19]
Henryson's use of them demonstrates his view of the function of poetry
and his desire to convey a moral in his writing. If such perspectives
were found only in *The Morall Fabillis*, it might be argued that
Henryson adopted this stance for a specific rhetorical *persona* and for
purposes of a single work. But such a desire to instruct extends
throughout the Henryson canon.

In order to understand the complexity of Henryson's *moralitates*,
it is vital to keep in mind these didactic goals. As already noted,
Henryson's general prologue to the *Fabillis* shows his interest in
teaching a moral lesson. The first stanza asserts the connection between
the "sweet rhethore" of "fein₃eit fables" and their purpose of bringing
mankind to virtue. The general prologue also shows his awareness of
the principle of gaining audience awareness by imbedding an important
moral message in a rhetorical form which will hold the audience's

attention. Henryson's sentiments parallel those of Ranulph Higden and John Bromyard. The sense of Henryson's lines could have been lifted directly from the *Ars componendi sermones.*[20] These sentiments are further reinforced in the prologue to "The Lion and the Mouse" where Henryson's narrator again steps into the action for a dialogue with his "master," Aesop. Henryson's dialogue with Aesop certainly reflects the traditions of the *ars poetriae* and the *ars dictaminis*, but it also has a special meaning for his use of the *ars praedicandi*. It will be recalled that he asks his master to "dedene to tell ane prettie fabill/Concludand with ane gude moralitie" (ll. 1386–87). The request itself reinforces Henryson's statements in the general prologue to the fables. However, as noted earlier, if there were any doubt about the author's intention, it is dispelled by a Aesop's response:

> 'My sone, lat be,
> For quhat is it worth to tell ane fen3eit taill,
> Quhen haly preiching may na thing auaill?
>
> 'Now in this warld me think richt few or nane
> To Goddis word that hes deuotioun . . .
>
> (ll. 1388–92)

Aesop's reluctance to tell such a tale is a purely pragmatic one, ironically contrary to the precepts of the *ars praedicandi*. He sees no point in telling a fable if men in Henryson's society will not listen to the good, direct advice that they receive from preachers and others who try to steer them on the right course. To illustrate the special relevance this passage has to the *ars praedicandi*, it might well be compared with a passage from Robert of Basevorn's "The Form of Preaching." Robert provides many details about who qualifies to be called a preacher (including specifications about the length of sermons and the frequency of preaching). While Henryson likely would not have met all the criteria, he would certainly have met Robert's initial definition of preaching: "Est autem praedicatio pluribus facta persuasio ad merendum, moderatum tempu, retinens" [Preaching is the persuasion of many, within a moderate length of time, to meritorious conduct].[21] Insofar as the beast fable is intended to move human beings to virtuous conduct, Henryson's goals certainly coincide with those implicit in Robert's definition. Interestingly enough, Henryson's Aesop even uses a version of the "past fact-future fact" *topos* on the degeneracy of modern

humans that was so popular among medieval preachers. It is the
condition of men *at this time*, enveloped in sin and possessed of evil
intentions as they are, that makes relating instructive fables such a
thankless task. This *topos* is a common one, found even in Caxton's
preface to Malory's *Morte D'Arthur* as well as collections such as the
Summa Praedicantium.[22] In brief, the dialogue between Henryson's
Aesop and his own narrative *persona* emphasizes the relationship
between improving the condition of humans lost in sin and the role of
the poet.[23] This important emphasis on the relationship between art and
morality is evidence of Henryson's comprehensive understanding of this
goal shared by the *ars poetriae*, the *ars dictaminis*, and the *ars
praedicandi*.

Even though some critics have questioned Henryson's sincerity in
his *moralitates*, his basic desire to instill a moral is genuine,[24] as a
review of even the most complex of Henryson's moral statements will
reveal.[25] A typology for the problems in the application of exegetical
techniques to the interpretation of Henryson's tales can be based on
three types of tale-moral relationships, illustrated by the following four
poems: "The Cock and the Jasp"; "The Lion and the Mouse" and the
"Wolf and the Wether"; and finally *The Testament of Cresseid*. These
poems help to elucidate the issues posed by critics who see the
moralitates as inconsistent with the tales. They also explain the
complexity of Henryson's art, as well as illustrating his special expertise
in panegyric, deliberative, and sometimes even forensic discourse.
Henryson's use of the *moralitas* in the problematic poems mentioned
above coincides with rhetorical theories underlying the *ars praedicandi*.
Even if Henryson were being ironic in these *moralitates*, his irony could
reflect his understanding of the multiple levels of audience awareness
in the *ars praedicandi*. The multiple meanings and subtle ironies of
Henryson's *Morall Fabillis* certainly suggest an awareness of different
levels of understanding in the audience and a desire to communicate
with as many members of the audience as possible.[26] In addition to
Payne, others including Caplan, Owst, and Minnis, have commented on
the importance of broad public appeal in the *ars praedicandi* in refining
the exegetical techniques of this rhetorical school.[27] Part of the reason
Henryson's *moralitates* have caused so much controversy involves the
very nature of the fourfold level of interpretation.

Guibert of Nogent established a generally contemporaneous
perspective on how Scripture (and by implication possibly other
writings) should be interpreted:

. . . Quatuor sunt regulae Scripturarum, quibus quasi quibusdam rotis volvitur omnis sacra pagina : hoc est historia, quae res gestas loquitur; allegoria, in qua ex alio aliud intelligitur; tropologia, id est moralis locutio, in qua de moribus componendis ordinandisque tractatur; anagoge, spiritualis scilicet intellectus, per quem de summis et coelestibus tractaturi ad superiora ducimur. Verbi gratia Ilierusalem, secundum historiam, civitas est quaedam; secundum allegoriam, sanctam Ecclesiam significans; secundum tropologiam, id est moralitatem, anima fidelis cujuslibet qui ad visionem pacis aeternae anhelat; secundum anagogen, coelestium civium vitam, qui Deum deorum facie revelata in Sion vident, signat. Ex his igitur quatuor modis, licet omnis fieri possit, aut certe ex singulis, tamen si quid utilius ad curam interioris hominis pensetur, magis commoda ac intelligibilis in tractando moralitas esse videtur,. . .

[. . . There are four ways of interpreting Scripture; on them, as though on so many scrolls, each sacred page is rolled. The first is History, which speaks of actual events as they occurred; the second is Allegory, in which one thing stands for something else; the third is Tropology, or moral instruction, which treats of the ordering and arranging of one's life; and the last is Anagogy, or spiritual enlightenment, through which we who are about to treat of heavenly and lofty topics are led to a higher way of life. For example, the word "Jerusalem": historically it represents a specific city; in allegory it represents the holy Church; tropologically, or morally, it is the soul of every faithful man who longs for the vision of eternal peace; and anagogically it refers to the life of the heavenly citizens, who already see the God of Gods, revealed in all his glory in Sion. Granted that all four of these methods of interpretation are valid and can be used, either together or singly, yet the most appropriate and prudent for use in matters referring to the lives of men seems to be the moral approach.][28]

The habit of mind Guibert describes became deeply ingrained. Given the importance of both preaching and scriptural interpretation, it seems likely that this same pattern of interpretation would be applied to secular texts as well. Minnis suggests that this pattern was related to the fourfold Aristotelian notion of causes.[29] Robert of Basevorn's *Forma praedicandi* reinforces Minnis' theory.[30] The potential connection between these two patterns of thinking would surely reinforce the application of exegetical techniques to secular texts. Yet this application does not mean that all four senses were to be found in every text or that all medieval authors even consciously attempted to fit their writings into one of these patterns of thought. Judson B. Allen cautions ". . . this sort of sensibility is not the only possible one . . . various sorts of sensibility, and thus various fundamental modes of literature, existed in the Middle Ages as they do now."[31] Nonetheless, Henryson's acknowledgement of the exegetical patterns in his *moralitates* shows his awareness of the exegetical habit of mind. I have contended elsewhere that this aspect of Henryson's art influences his approaches to social and political as well as moral issues.[32]

Possibly the most problematic tale-*moralitas* relationship in Henryson's verse is in "The Cock and the Jasp." Briefly, the tale is derived from Phaedrus most immediately through Gualterus and for many scholars exemplifies the most tangled of Henryson's moral conundrums. The focus of the tale is on a cock who, while scraping for food in a barnyard, finds a jewel. The cock rejects the jewel with the following comments:

> 'Thow hes na corne, and thairof I had neid;
> Thy cullour dois bot confort to the sicht,
> And that is not aneuch my wame to feid,
> For wyfis sayis that lukand werk is licht.
> I wald sum meit haue, get it geue I micht,
> For houngrie men may not weill leue on lukis:
> Had I dry breid, I compt not for na cukis.
>
> 'Quhar suld thow mak thy habitatioun?
> Quhar suld thow duell, bot in ane royall tour?
> Quhar suld thow sit, bot on ane kingis croun
> Exalt in worschip and in grit honour?

> Rise, gentill Iasp, of all stanis the flour,
> Out of this fen, and pas quhar thow suld be;
> Thow gabnis not for me, nor I for the.' (ll. 99–112)

The cock's reasoning is quite practical. Beautiful as it is, the jewel will not satisfy his basic need for food. He also observes that the jewel is out of place. It belongs on a crown in a courtly setting. The cock's logic accords, *prima facie*, with real laws of nature and society. The unwary reader may agree with the cock's assessment and even praise his wisdom, but Henryson abruptly dispels any notion that the cock's commonsensical approach is proper and appropriate in his *moralitas*:

> This gentill iasp, richt different of hew,
> Betakinnis perfite prudence and cunning,
> Ornate with mony deidis of vertew,
> Mair excellent than ony eirthly thing,
> Quhilk makis men in honour ay to ring,
> Happie, and stark to haif the victorie
> Of all vicis and spirituall enemie.
> ....
> This cok, desyrand mair the sempill corne
> Than ony iasp, may till ane fule be peir,
> Quhilk at science makis bot ane moik and scorne,
> And na gude can; als lytill will he leir—
> His hart wammillis wyse argumentis to heir,
> As dois ane sow to quhome men for the nanis
> In hir draf troich wald saw the precious stanis.
>
> Quha is enemie to science and cunning
> Bot ignorants, that vnderstandis nocht
> Quhilk is sa nobill, sa precious, and sa ding,
> That is may with na eirdlie thing be bocht?
> Weill wer that man, ouer all vther, that mocht
> All his lyfe dayis in perfite studie wair
> To get science, for him neidit na mair.
> (ll. 127–33, 141–54)

The jewel represents perfect virtue now "tynt and hid" because of the cock's ignorance. The cock is chastised for his interest in the needs of the flesh and his refusal to pursue "science." Critics have been puzzled by the vexing nature of this *moralitas*, which may seem stilted or artificial. Ruth Morse suggests that the "effect of the moral is enhanced by surprise"[33] and the surprise represents a deliberate effort to instill an allegorical habit of mind. MacQueen has noted that Henryson's discrepancies between tale and *moralitas* may reflect his broad understanding of poetic allegory,[34] Fox comments on Henryson's use of allegorical techniques, while James Kinsley and Kurt Wittig argue that Henryson's *moralitates* are sometimes artificial and "smell of the lamp."[35] Critics have sought a variety of solutions to deal with the problems. In this instance, George Gopen has suggested that the tale-*moralitas* relationship emphasizes the "high seriousness" of the fables, while Ian Bishop has argued that the influence of lapidary *formulae* in Henryson's approach to invention may help to explain the difficulty.[36] The tale and *moralitas* are compatible,[37] in part because Henryson's biblical allusions signal early in the poem that the Cock is a type of "false intellectual pride."[38] Both the narrative elements and the rhetoric of the Cock's comments argue for this interpretation. Moreover, a parallel from a Lollard sermon indicates that, at least as an *exemplum*, this theme of "safeguarding a jewel" was in general currency in the rhetoric of homiletics. The *exemplum* begins with a situation parallel to that of the Cock:

> If it were so þat a man had a precious juel which, if
> it were wel kepte, he my₃ be auaunsid foreuer, and if
> it were stolen awey, he my₃te be losten foreuer; and
> if suche a man had noon oþer house to kepe it inne
> but a feble on wiþ teerid wallis; and if so were þat a
> þefe had aspeid it, and sent to hym þat he wolde stele
> it, but þerof set no certeyn day ne houre, / a grete
> fole were he þat were in suche a case þat ne he wolde
> euer be waking, and neyþer slumur ne slepe, but
> alwey lye in awaite for þe comyng of þis þefe.[39]

The inference to be drawn from the man's lack of wisdom in guarding the precious jewel reflects Henryson's own thinking in his *moralitas*:

> But alas! it semyþ by her dedis þat þere ben many
> men in þis worlde ful recheles and taken litel hede to
> kepe þis juel and awayte þis þefe, but alwey slepen
> and slumbren in synne into þe tyme þat þis þefe come

and robbe hem of þis juel and of alle her oþer
goodis.[40]

The theory and exemplars of the *ars praedicandi* shed considerable
light on this poem. Generations of readers have been puzzled by the
contrast between the tale and *moralitas*. Without reference to the
rhetoric of preaching, the fable appears nonsensical. However, with an
understanding of the role of allusions and common symbolism in
establishing the cock's character and the tradition exemplified by the
Lollard sermon, the fable becomes not only intelligible but perhaps even
pedestrian. The rhetoric of preaching offers similar insights into other,
more complex, poems from Henryson's canon.

Another kind of difficulty, less jolting perhaps than the apparent
contradiction between tale and *moralitas* suggested by "The Cock and
the Jasp," is illustrated by the tales which involve political
commentary. While these tales have been discussed in the context of the
ars dictaminis and the *ars notaria*, they also have implications for
Henryson's use of the *ars praedicandi* and merit brief comment here.
"The Tale of the Lion and the Mouse," it will be remembered, ends
with a *moralitas* which relates the narrative directly to contemporaneous
political life. The basic interpretive problem involves Henryson's
referents for terms such as "prince," "empriour," "commountie," and
"rurall men." Henryson's direct reference to his audience (in stanza
four) may suggest a topical reading relating to the Lauder rebellion, but
the poem has also been interpreted in the general "advice to princes"
tradition. The argument for topical references is reinforced by the fact
that the *moralitates*, especially Aesop's comments, are largely
Henryson's original work. That he chose to deal with these political
themes in the *moralitas* is itself significant. In that context, his
references to the "prince" or "empriour" would likely be related to
contemporaneous figures. The parallel between the events of the fable
and the capture of James III during the Lauder rebellion provides other
insights into the signification of the major players in this drama. Such
specific political interpretations, however, have been challenged by
arguments that the poem must be read as part of a growing body of
literature that provides political advice. Works such as John of Ireland's
Meroure seem to deal less with contemporaneous political problems
than with traditional wisdom associated with political office. If
Henryson's poem is interpreted in this tradition, references to the
Lauder rebellion vanish to be replaced with general axioms such as "a

monarch must be active and visible" and "sometimes those who appear to be least powerful can provide the most help." The issues in this fable are similar to those in other fables with political *moralitates* and may best be evaluated in the context of other political tales such as the "Tale of the Wolf and the Wether."[41]

This tale, it will be recalled, deals with a foolish wether who exceeds his strength and abilities in attempting to fullfill the obligation to protect the flock. Having donned the skin of the dead watchdog, he is ultimately discovered by his (and the flock's) archenemy, the wolf. Once discovered, he is summarily executed for his presumption about his place in the hierarchy of nature. Henryson ends the tale with a *moralitas* which emphasizes a conservative political message—"blood will tell." He emphasizes that poor men who attempt to "counterfute ane lord" will come to a bad end. As previously noted, traditional interpretations suggest a direct political reference to the court of James III for both tales. Such specific political references in this fable and "The Lion and the Mouse" would find precedent in the *ars praedicandi*, as well as the *ars dictaminis*. The *ars praedicandi* had developed its own political *topoi* which dealt for the most part with contemporaneous political abuses, relating the degenerate state of contemporary society to the Seven Deadly Sins. The preaching of "Satire and Complaint" on political matters was widespread during the later Middle Ages.[42] Many examples of contemporaneous political commentary could be adduced, but perhaps one of the most direct is the following:

> This wickede pride amonge lordes and knyttes, that causeth this oppressinge of the pore peple, maketh now so gret a noyse and soun, that it is a gret clamour in al this rewme, in everi schire therof, of the extorcioneris that dwellen therinne, whiche beth as tiraunte kynges, overledynge the peple, as Pharao ladde the childern of Israel . . . . The tirauntie and wrongful overledynge on the pore peple . . . of this tirauntes is so gret and peineful to bere, that the noyse and the cri of here preyeris is herd in to the heres of god in hevene, as it was of the cheldern of Israel, for the wrongful oppressinge of Kyng Pharao in Egipte.[43]

This kind of attack on the moral bankruptcy of politicians and noble classes is a commonplace in medieval preaching. In many instances, the complaints became more specific in their attacks on particular individuals or institutions. The recent arguments by Roderick Lyall which suggest that Henryson was not dealing specifically with the court of James III in either of these fables but instead with the more general advice to princes tradition might accurately reflect the poet's purpose.[44] Yet, the fourfold method of exegesis would certainly not eliminate the possibility that he was dealing with both levels (and others) in his goals for the interpretation of the tale. Indeed, the preaching of satire and complaint makes specific provision for such multiple levels of political meaning in the interpretation of social satire. Moreover, as Owst contends, such general moral lessons were often made more effective by relying on details drawn from specific contemporaneous settings.[45] Thus, the "rurall men" described in "The Tale of the Lion and the Mouse" and the manner of death (a broken neck) described in "The Tale of the Wolf and the Wether" could have had reference to specific political events, even if more general references were part of the specific goal of Henryson's art. The fact that four levels of meaning can all be intended simultaneously provides exceptional latitude to the artist and argues for innate ambiguity in the depiction of social and political events as well as spiritual events.

"The Tale of the Lion and the Mouse" and "The Tale of the Wolf and the Wether" illustrate Henryson's political approaches to the *moralitas*. *The Testament of Cresseid* exemplifies moral and ethical ambiguities in the use of the *moralitas*, ambiguities that also fall short of the apparent direct contradictions of "The Tale of the Cock and the Jasp." Many of the problems are derived from Henryson's ambiguity in the use of the "praise and blame" *topos* common to panegyric rhetoric and the *exemplum*. The issues have direct implications for Henryson's credibility and his reputation as a "humane" author in the treatment of his subjects. There is, first, some controversy about what precisely the *moralitas* of this tale is. It may include as much as the last three stanzas of the poem:

> Quhen he had hard hir greit infirmitie,
> Hir legacie and lamentatioun,
> And how scho endit in sic pouertie,
> He swelt for wo and fell doun in ane swoun;
> For greit sorrow his hart to brist was boun;
> Siching full sadlie, said, 'I can no moir;
> Scho was vntrew and wo is me thairfoir.'

> Sum said he maid ane tomb of merbell gray,
> And wrait hir name and superscriptioun,
> And laid it on hir graue quhair that scho lay,
> In goldin letteris, conteining this ressoun:
> 'Lo, fair ladyis, Cresseid of Troy the toun,
> Sumtyme countit the flour of womanheid,
> Vnder this stane, lait lipper, lyis deid.'
>
> Now, worthie wemen, in this ballet schort,
> Maid for ȝour worschip and instructioun,
> Of cheritie, I monische and exhort,
> Ming not ȝour lufe with fals deceptioun:
> Beir in ȝour mynd this sore conclusioun
> Of fair Cresseid, as I haue said befoir.
> Sen scho is deid I speik of hir no moir.
>
> (ll. 596–616)

For the most part, the central concerns in the conclusion revolve around Cresseid's epitaph and Henryson's final moral warning.[46] To what extent does the abruptness of the epitaph suggest a harshness in Henryson's final perspective on his heroine? Does the moral warning suggest that Cresseid is to be considered an abhorrent object lesson, or is it merely a natural inference to be derived from the strictly objective evaluation of the events of her life? As in the case of other *moralitates*, the questions cannot be answered solely from the *moralitas* itself but must be resolved with reference to the ethical and symbolic structure of the entire poem. The integration of varieties of interpretation throughout the narrative of an entire text was a generally accepted exegetical principle, as illustrated by the following comments on the preacher's role by Guibert of Nogent:

> . . . ita explicet, et ut ita dicam quadam circumlocutionis mola conterendo exponat, et quod durum ac difficile etiam doctis prius videbatur, ita lucidum et apertum reddat, ut idiotis ac simplicibus perspicuum quod dicitur esse queat. Sicut enim puerulis lactis alimentum familiare est et valde necessarium, ut sine lacte non posse vivere credatur infantes, nec soli tamen eo utantur infantes, sed infroctis panum crustis etiam quibuslibet grandaevis

praestet cibum, sic plerumque cum vulgo simplex doctrina proponitur, et aliquid tamen propter intelligibiliores, ubi eorum exerceantur ingenia, ibidem interseritur, ita pascere consuevit hebetes, ut etiam solidioris additamento victus, id est interjecta ponderosiori sententia delectare soleat sapientes.

[. . . when he expounds such things by explaining them in detail, he will make clear and lucid for the peasants and common people ideas which at first seem difficult and confusing even to the very learned. For just as a diet of milk is familiar and even necessary to small children, so much so that infants cannot live without it, and not to children only, but also to men of mature age, who dip their crusts of bread in it, so also the preacher who offers simple doctrine to the people and at the same time adds something more substantial whereon the more educated can exercise their intellects, by so doing is able both to feed with his words the dull and sluggish of mind and also to inject weightier ideas as well by adding something more solid to the porridge, thus delighting the educated audience as well.][47]

In Henryson's case, the arguments about the role of the *moralitas* in establishing the theme and general symbolic structure of this poem have covered a full range of possibilities. E.M.W. Tillyard has provided an excellent example of a "conventional" interpretation of the poem.[48] Relating his analysis particularly to the parliament of the gods, he argues that Henryson approaches Cresseid's plight in terms of Christian mercy. He especially emphasizes the importance of Cresseid's recognition of her personal responsibility for her plight ("Nane but my self as now I will accuse," 1. 574), and argues that recognition is designed to stress her essential moral qualities. Her epitaph then would be tied directly to Henryson's warning in showing through terse, stark comment how even a good person can fare badly through moral immaturity that results in wantonness and excessive attachment to the things of this world. Tatyana Moran and A.C. Spearing, on the other hand, argue that Henryson treats Cresseid harshly and agree that there "is no suggestion of healing."[49] Duncan Aswell argues that the poem really does not reflect Christian values and that Cresseid and her narrator belong in a secular universe, implying also that both the epitaph and the warning are intended to reflect negatively on Henryson's heroine.[50] K.J. Harty believes that only the narrator remains disconsolate at the end of the poem.[51] If one uses Tillyard's interpretation as a basic critical touchstone, the varieties of explication offered in reaction to it do, indeed, span the critical spectrum.[52]

I have argued elsewhere that the poem should be interpreted in a Christian context.[53] On that assumption, I believe that Henryson's perspective on Cresseid is basically humane and understanding. The messages implied for the exegete then would relate to Cresseid's earlier immaturity and her spiritual growth, the use of her example as a means to establish each reader's personal salvation, and God's mercy. The variety of interpretations accorded this poem creates some critical problems with regard to the general application of exegetical techniques to medieval literature. Arguing for a single specific and consciously-forged *moralitas* presents one of the greatest difficulties. Yet one of the basic principles of both Ricardian poetry and the *ars praedicandi* is that the work reinforces its *sentence* in closure, even if the message reinforced is sometimes ironic, as in Chaucer's *Troilus and Criseyde*. Every interpretation of the *Testament* argues that the conclusion reinforces the message of the poem through serious commentary or ironic insight. For some critics the final lines reflect bitter and misogynistic censure of Cresseid's life. At the opposite extreme of critical argument, they are pervaded by the narrator's melancholy and constitute a lament for her state and the brevity of human life. The spectrum of opinion rests on poles of condemnation of and sympathy for the heroine. It has been argued that Henryson's ending for this poem is extremely harsh and reflects too much the tone of the Christian moralist, particularly given the emphasis on the redemption of Cresseid earlier in the poem. However, Cresseid's ultimate salvation and return to virtue would not necessarily deter Henryson or any practioner of the *ars praedicandi* from making her life into an object lesson. There is no contradiction between showing a hair-breadth escape by a sympathetic character and advising individuals to avoid situations which make such escapes necessary. Indeed, using stories of biblical figures who narrowly escaped losing their lives or their souls was commonplace, as exemplified in the tale of Jonah. This moral realism has major implications for determining the "final meaning" of the poem. Efforts to impose a single authoritative interpretation have plagued Chaucer studies for years, ever since exegetical techniques were first applied to the *Canterbury Tales*. Certainly, insistence on strict four-fold interpretation of every secular literary work hardly seems justified, especially in the later Middle Ages. Yet, there is no reason that a given writer could not have had more than one of the four senses in mind in creating a particular work. Sometimes the signals seem undeniable. *Piers Plowman*, for instance, seems to move effortlessly back and forth among all four levels of exegetical interpretation. The same argument would be much harder to make for the *Canterbury Tales* or *Sir Gawain and the Green Knight*. Henryson's *Testament of Cresseid* seems to be constructed basically at the level of the *sensus historicus* and the *sensus tropologicus*. It is possible to construct arguments for other levels of interpretation, but these two seem to be primary. By modern aesthetic standards, the poem is hardly vulnerable to criticism for working at both levels. In fact, it might be praised for its relative modernity. A reader who wished to pursue broader meanings could indeed use the literal and tropological levels as a foundation for interpretation. Given both levels of interpretation and the tradition of the *ars praedicandi* of showing biblical heroes or heroines engaged in immoral or unethical conduct to teach a moral lesson, the *Testament* offers less polarization in its interpretation than generally implied. The rhetorical context of the poem suggests that Henryson might well have been offering a harsh moral lesson while maintaining his sympathy for the heroine.

These issues are central *cruces* in the interpretation of the *Testament of Cresseid* but they are not unique to that poem. The same questions may arise in the analysis of Henryson's other verse, including the shorter works, *Orpheus*, and even some of the fables. They are major concerns that emerge as a result of the existence of moral ambiguities in a literary work. In that sense, the answers to these questions may require the most detailed analysis of all. Tales such as "The Cock and the Jasp" can be generally understood through specific reference to the traditions and rhetorical techniques of the *ars praedicandi*. Tales with political implications, such as "The Lion and the Mouse" and "The Wolf and the Wether," require analysis in terms of the social history along with both the *ars praedicandi* and the *ars dictaminis*. Poems such as *The Testament of Cresseid*, in which the *moralitas* permits or even encourages reflections on the moral ambiguity of the verse will often require closer textual analysis in conjunction with an understanding of social and rhetorical traditions.

The exegetical tradition also had implications for invention,[54] and it was associated with several major themes or *topoi* which appear repeatedly in both homilies and Henryson's verse. These *topoi* will receive attention throughout the discussion of the *ars praedicandi*; however, the *Testament* emphasizes an approach to invention which typifies Henryson's incorporation of exegetical and homiletic *topoi* into his verse. In one sense all of *The Testament of Cresseid* is structured around the *memento mori* theme—a common *topos* reminding mortals that neither the joys or pains of life last forever.[55] In that context, Henryson makes specific use of the *ubi sunt* motif, designed to reinforce the overall *memento mori* theme, in Cresseid's Lament. He uses five stanzas to describe her plight, drawing directly from the language of preaching as in the following example:

> 'Quhair is thy chalmer wantounlie besenc,
> With burely bed and bankouris browderit bene;
> Spycis and wyne to thy collatioun,
> The cowpis all of gold and siluer schene,
> Thy sweit meitis seruit in plaittis clene
> With saipheron sals of ane gude sessoun;
> Thy gay garmentis with mony gudely goun,
> Thy plesand lawn pinnit with goldin prene?
> All is areir, thy greit royall renoun!
>   (ll. 416–24)

The theme of this stanza is a textbook example of the homiletic tradition. Cresseid laments her loss of wealth and social status, fastening on specific images and symbols of the life she once enjoyed. Her lovely chamber with its luxuriant bed is gone, as are the exquisite wines and fine meals she once enjoyed on gold and silver dinnerware. She has also lost her luxurious garments, major symbols of her former "greit royall renoun." This stanza, the first in her "Quhair is . . ." series, primarily laments the loss of those things that satisfy the appetite, sexual, financial, or nutritional. Subsequent stanzas decry her loss of gardens, the companionship of friends and the ceremonies of rank, while revealing her keen awareness of her own physical decay. Henryson's integration of the *ubi sunt* and *memento mori* themes indicates his obligations to patterns of invention in the *ars praedicandi*. The last two stanzas of the passage integrate the two *topoi* through an apostrophe that contains the admonition to women to avoid Cresseid's example.

'O ladyis fair of Troy and Grece, attend
My miserie, quhilk nane may comprehend,
My friuoll fortoun, my infelicitie,
My greit mischeif, quhild na man can amend.
Be war in tyme, approchis neir the end,
And in ȝour mynd ane mirrour mak of me:
As I am now, peraduenture that ȝe
For all ȝour micht may cum to that same end,
Or ellis war, gif ony war may be.

'Nocht is ȝour fairnes bot ane faiding flour,
Nocht is ȝour famous laud ane hie honour
Bot wind inflat in vther mennis eiris,
ȝour roising reid to rotting sall retour;
Exempill mak of me in ȝour memour
Quhilk of sic thingis wofull witnes beiris.

All welth in eird, away as wind it weiris;
Be war thairfoir, approchis neir ȝour hour;
Fortoun is fikkill quhen scho beginnis and steiris.'

(ll. 452–69)

This admonition is repeated at the poem's conclusion. At this point, because Cresseid's redemption has not yet occurred, the warning seems harsher and more menacing. The language of the final stanza is especially imbued with elements of the pulpit. Traditional set phrases include the comparison of beauty with a "faiding flour" and the definition of renown as "wind inflat in vther mennis eiris." She virtually labels her life history as an *exemplum* from which she hopes others will profit. While medieval rhetoricians classified many of the devices in this passage as figures, they also served as stimuli to composition. The basic classical *topos* for this passage would be "past fact-future fact," which is inherent in Henryson's rhetorical devices in these lines. The interactive taxonomy of medieval rhetoric could be a means of expanding one's use and understanding of other rhetorical elements. The *topoi* that aided Henryson in the invention of this scene also led him directly to other rhetorical devices of the *ars praedicandi*. Henryson made extensive use of such homiletic *topoi* in the subjects that he treated throughout his poems, as will be shown in examples below.

SPEECH, WRITING, AND FIGURES
IN THE *ARS PRAEDICANDI*

Another major issue central, but not unique, to the *ars praedicandi* involves the interrelationship between speech and writing. Henryson's use of the *ars dictaminis* shows his sensitivity to the nuances of auricular appeal. Owst gave close attention to the importance of oral delivery to the *ars praedicandi*, and additional attention to oral elements in this rhetorical school has been provided by Mueller.[56] While Mueller is most especially interested in the development of English prose from the tradition of the *ars praedicandi*, she gives a good deal of attention to "speech-based" prose, demonstrating that early English prose style shows considerable sensitivity to the oral and auricular issues addressed in the *ars praedicandi*. The importance of this sensitivity in the *ars praedicandi* is illustrated by Robert of Basevorn's comments on eloquence:

> Omnino ideo mihi reprehensibile videtur quod quidam dicunt quod praedicatio non debet splendere falsis verborum purpuramentis colorum, cum in pluribus sermonibus Bernardi et fere semper totum sit coloratum, similiter in sermonibus aliorum sanctorum, ut patet rhetoricam scienti et sermones illos intuenti. Et Leo papa : Haec est virtus eloquentiae ut nihil sit tam exile quod non extollat, *nihil tam incredibile quod non dicendo praeornate probabile fiat, nihil tam horridum vel incultum quod non oratione splendescat*, secundum Tullium , *Paradoxis*. Quis enim haesitet quod utrumque simul, sapientia scilicet et eloquentia, plus movent quam alterum per se.

> [What some say therefore seems to me altogether reprehensible: that preaching ought not to shine with false verbal embellishments—for in very many sermons of St. Bernard the whole is almost always rich in colors. The same is true in the sermons of other saints, as is clear to one who knows rhetoric and examines those sermons. Further, Pope Leo

says: this is the virtue of eloquence, that there is nothing foreign to it that cannot be extolled, nothing so incredible that it would not become plausible by previous adornment of it, nothing so abhorrent or unrefined that it would not shine in its style. Who will hesitate to say that wisdom and eloquence together move us more than either does by itself?][57]

Robert's willingness to emphasize traditional oral eloquence illustrates a further development of the Augustinian strategy of employing pagan rhetoric to save souls. His admonition to make use of the devices of eloquence without departing from wisdom implies a union of auricular, intellectual, and spiritual appeals. It also argues for emphasizing delivery and using vocal resources to bring life to a written text. Certainly this approach to the need for an awareness of the interaction between writing and speech coincides with Henryson's interests as described earlier with regard to the *ars dictaminis*. Henryson's sensitivity to auricular figures has already been demonstrated, as has his interest in translating oral elements to written form. There are, however, certain elements, perhaps parallel with those of the *ars dictaminis* and *ars poetriae*, which demonstrate his familiarity more specifically with the art of preaching.

The interaction between homiletic rhetoric and popular and aristocratic culture has been well established.[58] Often, the direction of influence involved the assumption of common elements, proverbs, or expressions into sermons. There was also, however, another avenue of influence. Owst suggests that the poetic use of Latin vocabulary and derivatives is a result of the pervasive power of the *ars praedicandi*. Henryson's language shows the influence of *ars praedicandi* in both of these regards in addition to other borrowings and transpositions from contemporaneous sermon rhetoric. Concerns about the relationship between speech and writing have direct implications for another aspect of the *ars praedicandi*, its use of *formulae*.[59] As in the case of the *ars dictaminis*, these formulaic elements appear in both language and organization. Organizational *formulae* will be treated later but the elements of language demonstrate one way that rhetoricians attempted to deal with the relationship between oral and written discourse. The rhetoric of homilies involves "set phrases" and stipulative dictions just as does the *ars notaria*. Mueller has illustrated the syntactic importance of some of these *formulae* in terms of the modern theories of Francis

Christensen, Robin T. Lakoff, and others.[60] While Mueller's general
arguments include implications for Henryson's use of the diction and set
phrases of the *ars praedicandi*, greater insights into Henryson's use of
this rhetorical school can be achieved by looking at his specific diction
and figures. Many of the most impressive pieces of evidence for the
influence of the *ars praedicandi* on Henryson are to be found in these
language choices.

First, proverbs and *sententiae* are essentially oral formulaic
expressions. While some of them were drawn from popular or
aristocratic literature, they became a kind of stock in trade for the
medieval preacher. Others, drawn from Scripture or commentaries,
clearly reflect the background of homiletic rhetoric. Another element
in Henryson's language which shows his commitment to the language
of preaching is his use of Latin and of Latin derivatives. Owst argues
persuasively that the English pulpit had a special role in adapting the
Latin of Christianity to native English sermons.[61] B. Ellenberger's
analysis shows a significant proportion of such derivatives in
Henryson's vocabulary.[62] The extent to which they reflect strictly the
influence of *ars praedicandi*, however, is subject to debate. Henryson
also had an impetus to experiment with Latin through his developing
interest in aureation. Mueller associates aureation with the pulpit in the
late fifteenth and early sixteenth centuries.[63] Other, more traditional
scholars, however, have made the case that aureation is an early
reflection of the Renaissance spirit of word play.[64] Henryson shows
familiarity with classical tongues by quoting classical and early
Christian authors in his verse, as well as employing Latin-based
neologisms such as his description of Cresseid as the "A per se" of
Troy.

In other respects, Henryson's language shows very directly the
influence of theology and pulpit diction. It is important to have a frame
of reference for Henryson's use of homiletic diction and figures.
Sermons could be adduced at length, but perhaps one example will
provide the flavor of this element of the *ars praedicandi* as manifested
in the preacher's practice. The passage is especially interesting for its
treatment of philosophical themes in the context of God's wisdom:

> Here monye elepyde philosophres glaueron
> dyuersely; but in þis mater Godis lawe spekuþ þus, as
> dyden oolde clerkis, þat þe substaunce of a body is
> byfore þat it be seed, and now fruyt and now seed,

and now qwye and now deed. And þus monye formes
may be togydre in o þing and specially whan þe partis
of þat þing ben medled togydre; and þus þe
substaunce of o bodi is now of o kynde and now of
oþur. And so boþe þese accidentis, quantite and
qualite, may dwellon in þe same substaunce, al ₃if it
be chawnghed in kyndys, and þus þis same þing, þat
is now a whete corn, schal be deed and turne to gras,
and afturward to monye cornys. But variaunce in
workis in þis mater falluþ to clerkys, and schewyng
of equiuocacion, þe whiche is more redy in Latyn; but
it is ynow to vs to putte þat þe same substaunce is
now qwic, and now deed, and now seed and now
fruyt, and so þat substaunce, þat is now a whete corn,
mut nedis dyne byfore þat it be maad gras, and siþ be
maad an hool eer. And þus spekuþ holy wryt and no
man can disporve it. Errour of freris in þis mater is
not here to reherse, for it is ynow to telle how þei
erron in byleue.[65]

Of particular interest in this passage is the appeal to authority embodied
in phrases such as "monye elepyde philosophres," "oolde clerkis" and
"thus spekuþ holy wryt." These phases have major implications for
authorial stance in the Middle Ages, but they are also significant
examples in themselves of the principle of the diction of the *ars
praedicandi*. Other illustrations of the formulaic diction of the rhetoric
of preaching are phrases such as "Godis have spekuþ þus," and "now
qwye and now deed." The seed and fruit metaphor also results in
images traditionally associated with the pulpit. This passage hardly does
justice to the full range of *formulae* associated with the *ars praedicandi*,
but it provides examples of the pervasive nature of such standard
phrases and *topoi*. Even using only this sermon as a standard for
evaluating Henryson's use of the "stock phrases" of preaching, it is
clear that his use of such *formulae* is extensive. A review of all of
Henryson's homiletic stock phrases would be extremely lengthy, but a
few may illustrate his use of such language. "Ane Prayer for the Pest"
is, as one would imagine, full of phrases such as "God of power infinyt"
(l. 1), "Haif mercy of ws" (l. 5), and "O blissit Iesu, that wore the
thorny croun" (l. 23). Such standard phrases were as much a part of the
preacher's vocabulary as "as dyden oolde cherkis" in the sermon above.

"Ane Prayer for the Pest" also demonstrates Henryson's use of Latin-based neologisms, perhaps another major influence of pulpit rhetoric. As previously explained, this poem contains some of his most aureate language:

> Superne lucerne, guberne this pestilens,
> Preserue and serue that we nocht sterf thairin,
> Declyne that pyne be thy devyne prudens,
> For trewth, haif rewth, lat nocht our slewth ws twyn;
> Our syte, full tyte, wer we contryt, wald blin;
> Dissiuir did nevir, quha euir the besocht
>
> But grace, with space, for to arrace fra sin;
> Lat nocht be tint that thow sa deir hes bocht!
>   (ll. 65–72)

These lines add an interesting dimension to Mueller's argument about the role of the pulpit as a source of aureation. The mixture of formulaic appellations and apostrophes with aureate neologisms supports Mueller's argument that both have their basis in pulpit rhetoric. The differences between Henryson's use of aureate diction in the context of religious verse and Dunbar's extension of aureation may suggest that use of the device was being dramatically broadened in the late-fifteenth century. Indeed, Henryson's own selection of aureate terms in the *Orpheus* indicates that such extension was underway in his lifetime. "Ane Prayer" reflects the standard *formulae* found in pulpit oratory to this day. Other of the shorter poems, such as "The Annunciation" and "The Bludy Serk," follow suit, as do *The Morall Fabillis*. The most obvious example in the fables is "The Preaching of the Swallow." The opening lines suggest the extensive use of homiletic diction that is to follow:

> The hie prudence and wirking meruelous,
> The profound wit off God omnipotent,
> Is sa perfyte and sa ingenious,
> Excellent far all mannis iugement . . . .
>   (ll. 1622-25)

The themes of God's omniscience and omnipotence are introduced using traditional phrases such as "hie prudence" and "The profound wit of God omnipotent." As in subsequent stanzas, the use of direct address implies a congregation ready to hear the message of the day. Of greatest interest is that this tone appears in the rhetoric of the prologue, before Henryson even enmbarks on the tale itself. In a later stanza of the prologue, the poet becomes extremely directive:

> Luke weill the fische that swimmis in the se;
> Luke weill in eirth all kynd off bestyall;
> The foulis fair, sa forcelie thay fle,
> Scheddand the air with pennis grit and small;
> Syne luke to man, that he maid last off all,
>
> Lyke to his image and his similitude:
> Be thir we knaw that God is fair and gude.
>
> (ll. 1664–70)

The diction of the *ars praedicandi* here is reinforced by the hortatory tone which Henryson employs. In his final admonition, "Syne luke to man," Henryson's exhortation invokes the most traditional *formulae* of the creation of mankind. Phrases such as "that he maid last off all" and "Lyke to his image and his similitude" exemplify set phrases of the *ars praedicandi* that filled the language. The conjunction of these two devices continues throughout the poem. In the fable itself the Swallow's comments are filled with similar set phrases, including "For clerkis sayis . . ." (l. 1755), "prudence is ane inwart argument" (l. 1757), "full off negligence," (l. 1790), and "take gude aduertence" (l. 1792). Like the narrator of the prologue, she makes use of exhortation to impart the full impact of her pulpit language. Similar uses of homiletic diction, generally somewhat less pronounced, appear in the tales and, most especially the *moralitates*, throughout *The Morall Fabillis*. In fact, virtually none of Henryson's poems escapes this influence. *The Testament of Cresseid* contains such language, particularly in its concluding stanza, where Henryson takes a standard homiletic theme on the temptations provided by women and sheds new light on it.[66] The *Orpheus* contains stock phrases such as "this warldis vane plesance" (l. 603), "this warldis full delyte" (l. 613), and "geve us grace to stand" (l. 632) to cite only a few. Henryson's use of these elements of the language of the *ars praedicandi* shows the indelible influence of formulaic language of preaching, an influence perhaps to be expected given the moral nature of his art.

Henryson's use of the language of preaching is enhanced by his use of other figures and techniques of the *ars praedicandi*. The influences of the *ars dictaminis* and the Southern literary heritage on his realism would have been reinforced by the use made of description in the pulpit. G.R. Owst has outlined the penchant for realism on the part of medieval preaching.[67] He contends that the desire to incorporate realistic details into homiletic rhetoric has its roots in the effort both to gain the attention of the audience and to reinforce the importance of the message in the auditor's memory. He demonstrates how fourteenth–century preachers incorporated realistic details along with phrases, proverbs, and images from popular and aristocratic culture into the *ars praedicandi*. An excellent example of attention to realistic detail is to be found in "Nobilitas" from the *Summa praedicantium*:

> None multi sic laudantur nobiles moderni temporis?
> quis alique illorum laudare audiuit, uel laudare potuit,
> de strenua inimicorum expugnatoine, & patriae &
> ecclesiae defensione? sicut comendantur & laudantur
> Karolus magnus, Rolandus, & Oliuerus, & alij antiqui
> milites, sed hoc, ꝗ galeam habent deautratam precij
> ₄O. librarum & alas, & alia insignia exteriora eiusdem
> forma & maioris precij. Et ꝗ in haftilbudio grossam
> & quadratam portauit lanceam, qualem nullus alius
> portauir, vel portare potuit, & quod equum &
> ascensoreum proecit in terra. Et ꝗ cum tot equis uenit
> ad perliamentum, vel torneamentum. Et qualis est ista
> laus, nisi laus impiorum, & miserorum, & timidorum?
> de qua iob 20. Laus impij breuis. Breuis nanque est:
> quia tantum ad loca & tepora pacis, & non belli se
> extendunt, & solum ad amicos, & non ad hostes. Quid
> ualent arma, tunc deaurata. quæ hostes audaciores
> faciunt, sicut patet. A. 24. 2. Et quæ fugiendo
> hostibus læ ti prioijciunt, uel velocius fugiant, sicut
> nuper accidit. Quæ laus est contra hominem pacis
> fortissiman portare lanceam, & equum & ascensorem
> ad terram deijcere, & hostem nec cum quacunque
> tangere lancea, quia neceitatum appropinquare voluit,
> ꝗ cum longissima illum tangere potuissent. Vel quæ
> laus est, ꝗ bene equitauit & faciliter lanceam mouit,
> & agiliter se habuit cotra amicum & vicinum, &

agliter fugit inimicum regni? Vel quæ laus est, ꝙ in
factis armorum prohioitis sicut in torneameris &
huiusmodi, do quibus dictum est. L. 6. 2. & X. I. 17.
sint glorisi & appetant laudari, & in factis uirtuosis,
sicut in bellis iustis & in defesione patriæ, sint
formidolosi, & uecordes, & fugitiui, & hostes sinant
terram uastare, spoliare, & prædam auferre, & villas
comburere, & castra destruere, & capituous abducere?

[Who has been heard to praise, or could praise any of
them for strenuous battling with the enemy, or for
their defence of country and Church, as Charlemagne,
Roland, Oliver and the other knights of antiquity are
commended and praised? But rather for this—that they
have a helmet of gold worth forty pounds, *ailettes* and
other external insignia of the same style and even
greater price; that so-and-so carried into the lists a
huge square lance such as no one else carried, or
could carry, and that he flung horse and rider to the
ground; and that he rode so well and wielded that
lance of his so nimbly, as if it were of the lightest: or
again, that so-and-so came to Parliament or to the
tournament with so many horses. And what, after all,
is praise of that kind, but praise of the impious, of
wretches and of the timid? . . . For they expose
themselves in places and times of peace and not of
war; and to their friends, not to their enemies. Of
what value are arms adorned with gold, then, that
only make the enemy bolder (as is shown under *Arma*
. . .), which, too, when in flight from their foes, they
fling away, so that they may flee the faster—as
happened of late? What praise is it to bear a most
might lance against a man of peace, and to fling horse
and rider to the ground; and not touch the enemy with
any lance whatever, because one does not want to
approach him near enough to let him touch one with
the longest kind of weapon? Or what praise is it that
such a man rode so well and wielded his lance with
such ease, that he conducted himself so nimbly
against his friend and neighbour and fled so nimbly

from the enemy of the realm? What praise is it that
such are glorious and seek praise in prohibited deeds
of arms, as in tournaments and the like, while in
deeds of virtue, such as in just wars and in defence of
their own country, they are timorous, cowardly and
fugitive, allowing the enemy to devastate the land, to
plunder and to pillage, to burn the towns, destroy the
castles, and carry off captives.][68]

The realism in this passage is combined with a satirical approach to
chivalry. The comments about the armor and trappings of chivalry
illustrate the preacher's attention to the very class he is castigating.
Henryson's realism hardly needs extensive elaboration given the
analysis in Chapter Three. His medical description of Cresseid's
leprosy; his attention to the rhetoric, procedural details, and structure of
fifteenth-century courts; his precise descriptions of court life and the
abuses of the nobility, along with their grandeur; his knowledge of the
plight of the urban middle class and country peasants; and his
sympathetic understanding of the need for justice among the poorer
classes all demonstrate his keen observation of the world in which he
lived.

Henryson has the ability to mix realistic details with more abstract
ideas through his use of rhetorical figures such as personification.
Henryson's use of homiletic language is also reinforced by his use of
allegory, personification, figures of amplification such as the beast fable
and the *exemplum*, and most especially proverbs and *sententiae*. As
abbreviated embodiments of Scripture and folk wisdom, proverbs and
sententiae provide a vital link with the *ars praedicandi* both in their
direct verbal influence and as devices of invention. They demonstrate
as well the possibilities of lending both additional authority and
immediate audience identification to a work. *The Testament of Cresseid*,
as MacDonald shows,[69] is an especially good source for illustrating
Henryson's use of this figure. In addition to his extensive use of
proverbial expressions in the description of the gods (ll. 141–273),
Henryson makes use of proverbs and proverbial expressions such as the
following throughout the poem:

Perauenture all cummis for the best (l. 104)

Of man and beist, baith frute and flourishing
Tender nureis, and banischer of nicht (ll. 198–99)

All welth in eird, away as wind it weiris (l. 467)

There are also particularly rich clusters of proverbs in lines 461–80 and
540–74. While a number of these proverbial expressions have their
ultimate source in classical works such as the *Disticha catonis*, an
extremely high proportion of them relate to themes adopted by medieval
preachers. The transience of fame and riches, the uncertainties of life,
the mysterious workings of the deity, and the ultimate justice and mercy
of the divine mind are the major themes of Henryson's proverbs in this
poem, as would be expected from his theme.

MacDonald has argued that Henryson's use of such proverbs and
sententiae is derived from Chaucer. While Chaucerian influence is
likely, other evidence of his familiarity with the *ars praedicandi*
suggests that he might have learned it directly from the rhetoric of
preaching. In an effort to encourage his congregation to remember
moral precepts that he tried to instill, the   medieval preacher often
made use of simple aphorisms which would have a broad
application. The following lines from Guibert of Nogent illustrate the
general theory behind such use of proverbial material.

> Nam sicut victualia sobrie sumpta ad corporis
> nutrimentum in corpore permanent, immoderate vero
> vorata in detrimentum vergunt, et vomitum provocant;
> et qui semine legitimo et parce modesteque edito
> conjugi miscetur, prolem creat, qui vero semine fluit,
> nihil utile efficit, sed carnem foedat : ita qui nimie
> verbum profert, et id quod auditorum cordibus insitum
> erat, et proficere poterat, aufert. Cum ergo et grandis
> animi fervor prædicanti adest, et multiplex
> tractandorum materia memoriæ non deest, facundiæ
> quoque possibilitas et ornatus necessitati superest,
> penset corum qui tacite audiunt imbecillas vires,
> meliusque fore ut pauca et grate suscipiantur, quam
> innumera ex quibus nulla retineantur, finemque facere
> non differat, ut rursum eum sermonem facturus est,
> alacres eos non fastidiosos inveniat.

[We know that when food is taken in moderation
it serves to nourish the body, but when taken in
excess it works to the detriment of the body and even
provokes vomiting. Or, again, a man who uses his
seed properly and chastely in the marital act generates
offspring, while he who masturbates accomplishes
nothing good and only befouls his body. So a
preacher who abuses words interferes with what is
already planted in the hearts of his hearers, what he
should be helping to grow. For this reason, if the
preacher has great fervor of spirit and has mastered
all his material, then he can add the possibility of
eloquence and style to the essentials, his own
virtues. Let him think of those who must listen in
silence to pompous inanities, and he will realize that
it is much better for them to hear a few things well-
presented than a great many things from which they
will retain almost nothing. Then he will not delay
making an end to one sermon so that, when he
preaches another his audience will be eager rather
than resentful.][70]

Certainly it is easy to recognize in Guibert's emphasis on memorable
brevity the impetus for the use of proverbs and *sententiae* that appears
in *The Morall Fabillis*. As was generally recognized in both the *ars
poetriae* and *ars dictaminis*, the use of proverbs provided a number of
rhetorical strengths.[71] Proverbs and *sententiae* provided a terse,
authoritative basis for beginning a discourse. Their compact statement
of a commonly-accepted moral perspective lent added authority to the
speaker or writer and could provide additional gravity to discourse at
any point while simultaneously providing a kernel for amplification. The
ars praedicandi, either directly or through other literary sources, would
have given the strongest theoretical and practical guidance for the use
of these devices in Henryson's verse.

    Henryson's use of proverbs and *sententiae* is integrated with his use
of allegory, a major and pervasive figure in his work directly related to
his use of metaphor and simile. The allegorical structure of the *Fabillis*
demonstrates Henryson's artistic sophistication and his attempts to reach
the largest possible audience. While allegory is treated in all three
schools of rhetoric, Henryson's extensive attention to the figure, along

with the length and moral tenor of his uses of it, suggests a distinct debt to the art of preaching.

Allegory is a figure innate in exegetical thinking. Indeed the possibility of using one thing to stand for another (based in general on St. Augustine's theory of signs[72]) is essential to any system of multiple interpretation. Owst suggests that the origins of medieval allegory are to be found in the fourfold approach to interpretation:

> It will be already clear that one favourite device of this exposition was to select some particular object or objects of the Scripture narrative, and to concentrate on their allegoric significance, irrespective of the part which they play in their particular episode.[73]

Owst's thesis suggests that allegory is derived by focusing the exegetical pattern of thought on a single object such as a ship or castle. While Owst's approach helps to explain the origins of allegorical thinking, the figure had become considerably more complex in the later Middle Ages. Reflecting both the more complicated devices of classical allegories and a highly structured code of Christian symbols, allegory became a central literary technique in exegetical thinking. W.T.H. Jackson takes special note of the Christian nature of medieval allegory:

> It may easily be argued that medieval writers allegorized freely and that they constantly interpreted anecdotes from the classics and even works of doubtful morality as parables of Christian revelation. No reader of the *Legenda aurea* or the *Gesta Romanorum* would deny the charge, but one important factor must not be overlooked. The interpretation was always within the framework of Christian revelation. The theologically acceptable reading of the Old Testament as a foreshadowing of the New, the acceptance of certain incidents, for example, Daniel in the lion's den, as foreshadowing Christ's descent into Hell, meant that by extension secular material could also be interpreted as reflecting God's purpose. Since all human acts and all events in

some way reflect the divine will, they can be interpreted as referring to Christian revelation.[74]

Jackson's focus on the Christian framework helps to explain the ethical structure of Henryson's verse. It sheds light on value structures of the *Orpheus* and the *Testament,* in particular, where Henryson has merged Christian and classical elements of plot, setting, characterization and theme. In similar fashion, it explains the structure of "The Garmont of Gud Ladeis," in which Henryson uses women's apparel as an allegorical basis for explaining female virtue. Jackson's later reference to the literary genre of allegory[75] helps in understanding Henryson's use of the beast fable and the *exemplum.* Rosemond Tuve has developed theories of medieval allegory which also relate directly to the metaphorical structure of the beast fable. Tuve especially comments on the "double vision" implicit in the beast fable:

> We are expected to be sufficiently aware of how fables work—and sufficiently alert—to see the "moral" double meaning almost as soon as we embark on the description or tale, the later outright statement of moral point being deliberately heavy-footed. Thus our enjoyment of the doubleness involves tiny details and is subtler. It is typical that the near-irony does not corrode the serious sense of the "moral" ("extended signification" would be more precise), and we catch this habit if we read at length. We, like earlier men, take amusement from the figurative sense long before its statement, and from the fact that fantasy is likely to be more striking in the literal story.[76]

Tuve's remarks have pointed implications for Henryson's use of personification in the beast fable, but they also illustrate the need to work with a double semantic framework, which is an essential part of the allegorical and exegetical habit of mind.[77] For the most part, Henryson's repertory of allegorical images is very traditional, occasionally interspersed with contemporaneous or perhaps ironic references, such as that to Cresseid's beaver hat. Clearly, every animal in *The Morall Fabillis* has an allegorical significance (an essential part of the artistic illusion of the beast fable), and the poet makes a point of explaining that significance in his *moralitates.* The double semantic framework of the fables is generally easily comprehensible and unobtrusive, as in the use of predators as officers of the court in "The Tale of the Sheep and the Dog." It is drawn to the reader's attention when the occasional disconformity or intrusion presents itself in the tales. In "The Cock and the Jasp," for instance, the modern reader with no knowledge of the *ars praedicandi* will be shocked into an awareness of incongruity by the perceived disconformity between the cock's apparent good sense in the tale and his treatment in the *moralitas*. Similar awareness can be produced by conflicts in the goals of a given fable. In "The Lion and the Mouse" the mouse's dual forms of execution make the conscientious reader simultaneously aware of the political allegory (the mouse is to be taken to the gallows) and the real role of beasts in the state of nature (the mouse is to be eaten). In similar fashion, perspicacious readers of the fifteenth century might have been aware that Cresseid's beaver hat was not just a symbol of her own vainglory but also a possible jab at a Scottish monarch. Usually, however, the sense and the symbol are appropriately integrated as in the "Abbey Walk" which represents aspects of the contemplative life and the "Bludy Serk," an object that represents Christ's love and mercy.[78]

Henryson's use of allegory is directly related to his use of personification, another useful element for the medieval preacher, which becomes essential for the creation of the beast fable. The tradition of personification of animals has a lengthy history. Indeed, some of the earliest and most primitive tales reflect the use of personified creatures to teach a moral lesson. The origins of the beast fable are impossible to determine, but some obvious factors involve the proximity of human beings to animals in early societies, the religious significance of certain animals in early (and even modern) societies, the artistic "concreteness" of the form, and the use of animals to "objectify" and universalize moral lessons in a non-threatening context.[79] Like many of the other figures of the *ars praedicandi*, personification was often used in a context of panegyric discourse to teach a lesson. The most frequently used *topos* was that of praise or blame, and, in the beast fable, narrative irony was often used to provide the ultimate moral judgment on the animal character. The following references to the allegorical significance of the boar from "Septuagesima Sunday" illustrate typical homiletic approaches:

> To þis boor may mannes flesch wel be likened,
> for þre propurtees þat longen to þe boor whiche moun

> be likned to þre synnes þat comen of þe flesch: first,
> a boor smyteþ sore wiþ his tusckis þat stonden in his
> mouþe; þe seconde is þat he wole gladli reeste him in
> foule slowis, or mury placis; þe₃ is þat he haþ a foule
> stynkynge sauur where he goþ. And bi þese moun be
> vndirstonde glotenye, sleuþe, and stynkynge lecherie.⁸⁰

The preacher then goes on to expand on each characteristic at length, relating it to human nature. John B. Friedman has shown how important the bestiary was to the art of preaching in his assessment of the *Liber de moralitatibus*.⁸¹ Douglas Gray has especially emphasized Henryson's approaches to allegory and their concomitant relationship with the beast fable.⁸² The form was a staple in both preaching and ecclesiastical art, influencing illumination and even architecture.⁸³

For the most part, Henryson tends to rely on traditional characteristics derived from bestiaries and earlier fable traditions in his use of this figure. In addition to MacDonald and Jamieson, David Crowne and Marianne Powell have also given attention to Henryson's sources, demonstrating the uses he might have made of the *Fabulae* of Gualterus Anglicus, the fables of Odo of Cheriton, the *Isopet*, and Caxton, among others.⁸⁴ Gray has evaluated Henryson's beasts in the context of the broader tradition of world fables, showing he incorporates the broadest traditional elements of the beast fable in his poems.⁸⁵ Henryson's traditionalism is evident in the personification of his animal villains. Henryson's wolf is often a predator intent only on satisfying his voracious appetite, as in "The Tale of the Wolf and the Lamb," where he victimizes the lamb by claiming satisfaction for an old grudge. Meeting the lamb by a stream, he accuses the hapless creature of unwonted pride in "befouling" the stream with his "foul slobberings." When the lamb attempts to show proper contrition, the wolf dismisses these reasonable arguments and simply invokes his strength as a reason to eat him anyway. The fable concludes with a gross injustice:

> 'Ha,' quod the volff, 'thou wald intruse ressoun
> Quhair wrang and reif suld duell in propertie.
> That is ane poynt and part of fals tressoun,
> For to gar reuth remane with crueltie.
> Be Goddis woundis, fals tratour, thow sall de

> For thy trespas, and for thy fatheris als.'
> With that anone he hint him be the hals.
>
> (ll. 2693-99)

This depiction of the wolf is consistent with his portrayal in "The Tale of the Sheep and the Dog" as a "fraudfull judge." In similar fashion Henryson's Lowrence the fox is built on the traditional craftiness and guile associated with foxes in the beast fable tradition. In Henryson's "Tale of Schir Chantecleir and the Fox" Lowrence relies on his wits and treachery to attempt to make a meal of the vain cock. His conduct in "The Trial of the Fox" is similar to that in "The Fox, The Wolf and the Cadger," as he uses his cunning to outwit the wolf and make him the object of the trick and physical abuse in both instances.

Henryson's animal heroes also share traditional characteristics. In "The Tale of the Two Mice," the uponland mouse seems to share the candor and honesty often found in personifications of the simple creature. His sheep, for the most part representatives of the lower classes, are likewise often trusting and naive, usually coupling such characteristics with honesty, straightforwardness, and religious dedication. The portrayal in "The Sheep and the Dog" is representative in its depiction of the sheep as a "selie" creature caught up in the intricacies of the law. "The Tale of the Wolf and the Lamb" also reinforces this traditional characterization, as the lamb operates on basic principles of honesty, humility, and courtesy, but still pays with his life for his unfortunate dealings with the rapacious wolf. Other examples abound in *The Morall Fabillis*, and they generally confirm this traditional basis for the depiction of Henryson's animal protagonists.

However, it would be a mistake to think that Henryson's use of personification is limited strictly to traditional characterization. First, it is important to acknowledge the possible occasional "slip" (or shrewd rhetorical trick) illustrated by "The Tale of the Lion and the Mouse," when the "maister mouse" ignores that fact that he has been sentenced to hang and makes a plea to the lion not to eat him. More significant by far are those instances where Henryson has used sources with non-traditional characteristics of personification or where he has apparently introduced non-typical characteristics himself. One major example is found in his portrayal of the wolf. The wolf is generally typified more in the fashion Henryson depicts in "The Tale of the Wolf and the Lamb," as a predator largely in control of his environment. However, at least two of the fables, "The Trial of the Fox" and "The

Fox, the Wolf, and the Cadger" Henryson has chosen to make him a victim of the fox's treachery. There is clearly precedent for this depiction of the wolf,[86] but Henryson's use of it in two fables shows an interest in going beyond the traditional characterization of the beast fable. In the portrayal of the wether in "The Tale of the Wolf and the Wether," Henryson has depicted one of his animal heroes in a less than favorable light, even ironically citing the proverb about the lack of thinking power sheep have in the process: "Quha sayis ane scheip is daft, they lieit of it" (1. 2492). For his presumption and lack of wisdom (even in a noble cause—to protect the flock) the wether pays the ultimate penalty and is criticized as a bad example in Henryson's *moralitas*. Once again, Henryson is not the innovator of this type of personification,[87] but his use of this less traditional characterization indicates the eclecticism of his use of the figure. His "localization" of his animal characters is another interesting aspect of his use of this device. As previously noted, critics have long observed that both the burgess mouse and the uponland mouse are specifically Scottish in their portrayal, evidenced by elements ranging from the uponland mouse's possible status as an outlaw to the fare which they eat. Political fables such as "The Lion and the Mouse" may also share Scottish settings and reflect Scottish social life. Similar arguments have been made about animal characters in "The Wolf and the Lamb," "The Trial of the Fox," and "The Sheep and the Dog."[88] In "The Trial of the Fox" (ll. 873–921), for instance, the court of animals constitutes a veritable theological bestiary, with special reference to Scotland.[89] Henryson's animal courtiers include three haughty leopards bearing Noble's crown, along with a mixture of mythological and real beasts. The minotaur and werewolf attend as well as the elephant, panther, bull, and greyhound. All ranks of the animal kingdom are present. These creatures are standard protagonists in the beast fables used by medieval preachers and clerics to instill a sense of moral responsibility, with traditional symbolism in medieval bestiaries.[90] Henryson carefully chose them to reflect on life at the Scottish court, as well as certain kinds of general moral virtues. Henryson's adaptation of these traditional beasts to the Scottish social structure and geography is yet another mark of his ability to transcend tradition. It also illustrates Henryson's use of the realism of the *ars dictaminis* and the *ars praedicandi*. This ability to invest moral lessons with "a local habitation and a name" was an important element of the art of preaching. Henryson demonstrates his ability to bring such realistic detail to bear not only in the *Fabillis* but also in *The*

Testament of Cresseid. Henryson's interest in transcending stereotypes in characterization and providing specifically Scottish details about his beasts illustrates how he moved beyond traditional elements of personification in his use of this figure.

Henryson's use of the beast fable reflects interests similar to those in his use of the *exemplum*. As noted above, the basic purposes of the *exemplum* and the beast fable were the same.[91] While the beast fable featured animal characters and was thereby bound to use personification, the *exemplum* dealt with human characters for the same purposes, illustrating some vice or virtue with the goal of objectifying moral lessons and moving the reader or auditor to moral conduct. Joseph A. Mosher and John D. Lyons have explored in detail the nature and techniques of the *exemplum*, along with a study of sources.[92] As in the case of the beast fable, the *exemplum* must be considered as a type of panegyric discourse, relying on the *topos* of praise or blame of its human subject to make a moral point. The *exemplum* was also a device of amplification, as the following definition and rhetorical advice from Robert of Basevorn illustrate:

> Alius est modus terrere eos aliqua [*fol.* 45vb] narratione vel exemplo terribili, quemadmodum Jacobus de Vitriaco narrat de quodam qui nunquam sponte voluit audire verbum Dei, tandem cum mortuus esset et delatus ad ecclesiam, et sacerdos, astante paroechia, incepisset commendationem quae super corpora de functorum dici solet, imago Christi stans inter chorum et ecclesiam avulsit et abstraxit manus suas proprias a clavis eas configentibus et a ligno cui infigebantur, et obturavit aures suas, quasi innuens nolle deprecationem pro eo audire qui ipsum quondam in suis praedicatoribus audire contemnebat.
>
> Similiter, ad idem spectant diversae narrationes quae docent quomodo Christus apparuit quibusdam induratis, projiciens palmam plenam sanguine accepto de latere ejus, dicens : Hic sanguis quem induratus contemnis testimonium perhibebit contra te in die judicii. Qui cum post aliquantulum vixerunt, copertum est frequenter quod nulla arte ablui potuit, sed cum illo sunt sepulti Aliqui poenituerunt et confessi sunt, et tunc satis faciliter quasi evanuit.

Hoc secundum ego ipse inveni de quadam muliere
flagitiosa et ad omnes sermones indurata, cui apparens
Christus accepit manum mulieris et intuilit vulneri
lateris ejus dicens, sicut ipsa dixit: Sanguis quem
abjicis tibi adhaerebit in malum, nisi te correxeris.
Hoc plane compertum est quod confessa est et adhuc
adhaesit nec ablui potuit, quoquomodo tandem
confitebatur unum magnum occultum, et statim post
quasi disparuit. Talia terribilia multum valent in
principio.

[Another way is to frighten them by some
terrifying tale or example, in the way that Jacques de
Vitry talks about some one who never willingly
wanted to hear the word of God; finally when he died
and was brought to the church, and the priest in the
presence of the parish began the eulogy which is wont
to be spoken over the body of the dead, the image of
Christ standing between the choir and the church tore
away and pulled His hands from the nails piercing
them and from the wood to which they were fixed,
and plugged His ears, as if to intimate that He did not
wish to hear the prayer from him who once spurned
to listen to Him in His preachers.

Likewise, pertinent to the same topic are the
different stories which teach how Christ appeared to
some hardened sinners, extending His palm full of
blood taken from His side, saying: This blood which
you so obdurately contemn will bear witness against
you on the day of judgment. After they lived awhile
it was frequently disclosed that the blood could not be
washed away and they were buried with it. Some
repented and confessed and then easily enough, as it
were, it disappeared.

This second example I myself have come upon,
in connection with an infamous woman hardened to
all sermons. Christ appeared to her and took the
woman's hand, putting it into the wound in His side,

saying, as she herself has said: the blood which you
reject will adhere to you for evil, unless you correct
yourself. It is well known that she confessed; still it
adhered to her and could not be washed away till
finally in some way she confessed a great hidden sin
and immediately after that it disappeared. Such
terrifying stories have great value in the beginning of
a sermon.][93]

As a narrative figure, the *exemplum* had many strengths. Used as a
device of amplification, it could help to arouse interest in audiences
unprepared for more refined theological arguments. The incorporation
of vivid or grisly details into *exempla* sometimes bordered on the lurid.
The tales could not only point audiences along with paths of virtue but
could also permit a type of cathartic ("There, but for the grace of
God . . .") release. However, the *exemplum* suffered a fate common to
other popular rhetorical techniques. It was overused, particularly by less
skillful preachers. That its overuse did not receive uncritical acceptance
is illustrated by Humbert of Romans in his *Treatise on Preaching*. He
bitterly attacked preachers who extended their sermons interminably,
loading detail after detail in their texts.[94] Yet by the later Middle Ages,
the *exemplum* could clearly be considered a more independent rhetorical
device than its initial use for amplification of sermons would
suggest. Boccaccio, Chaucer, and Dante all found uses for this figure
which extend its rhetorical significance. Henryson's best extended
exempla are *The Testament of Cresseid* and *Orpheus.*

The *Testament* has already been reviewed in terms of its possible
interpretations through exegetical techniques, but to understand its
nature as an *exemplum*, a more comprehensive overview is necessary.

Henryson's *Testament of Cresseid* is a dramatically powerful
exemplum, illustrating the fate of an unfortunate person, no matter
whether one believes the tale ends pessimistically or optimistically.[95]
Henryson's aesthetic sophistication in the narrative itself results in well-
rounded and multi-dimensional characters whose appeal is timeless. He
has further constructed a plot that, while relying for its inspiration on
Chaucer's *Troilus and Criseyde*, is a complete and integral unit in its
own right. The poem illustrates Henryson's best use of rhetorical
traditions. Using the overall framework of the *exemplum*, he has
incorporated the diction and *topoi* of the *ars praedicandi* along with

devices and techniques from other rhetorical schools. The result is a
compelling tale of transgression, forgiveness, and self-realization.

Henryson's overall theme—the transitory nature of the honors and
privileges of this life—is a central *topos* of the *ars praedicandi*. Yet,
even in the context of this harsh and generally pessimistic *topos*, he also
shows a sympathy for Cresseid which has been the subject of critical
controversy.[96] Periodically, Henryson introduces brief, obvious laments
about Cresseid's situation. One of the earliest examples appears in an
apostrophe:

> O fair Creisseid, the flour and A per se
> Of Troy and Grece, how was thow fortunait
> To change in filth all thy feminitie,
> And be with fleschelie lust sa maculait,
> And go amang the Greikis air and lait,
> Sa giglotlike takand thy foull plesance!
> I haue pietie thow suld fall sic mischance!
>
> (ll. 78–84)

Geoffrey of Vinsauf would not have been Henryson's only source for
the use of this device, for such apostrophes and direct address were also
techniques well established in the *ars praedicandi*.[97] The goal was to
inspire either fear or reflection in the congregation. Henryson's
conclusion might suggest that he uses the device to arouse fear in the
"worthie wemen" who should learn from Cresseid's plight. In that sense
he establishes a rhetorical stance with parallels to the rhetorical occasion
of preaching: The preacher (Henryson) attempts to lead his congregation
(the "worthie wemen") to the good life through an *exemplum* (the tale
of Cresseid). Yet, it is part of Henryson's genius that he did not permit
himself to be limited by the parameters of this rhetorical
occasion. Given the broader meanings and audiences of this poem,
Henryson has used the figure of the lament–apostrophe in other
ways. Besides inspiring fear in the "worthie wemen," it also causes the
audience to reflect on his general theme. Moreover, it heightens the
drama and provides Henryson an opportunity to develop the character
of his narrative *persona*. In this respect, as in many others, Henryson
was able to expand the uses of the rhetoric of preaching.

In thematic terms, the delineation of Cresseid's disease illustrates
a kind of "divine justice," a central concern of all *exempla*. The cruel
effects of that justice are no where more evident than in the final
sentence which the divine court pronounces on Cresseid:

Than Cynthia, quhen Saturne past away,
Out of hir sait discendit doun belyue,
And red ane bill on Cresseid quhair scho lay,
Contening this sentence diffinityue:
'Fra heit of bodie here I the depryue,
And to thy seiknes sall be na recure
Bot in dolour thy dayis to indure.

'Thy cristall ene mingit with blude I mak,
Thy voice sa cleir vnplesand hoir and hace,
Thy lustie lyre ouirspred with spottis blak,
And lumpis haw appeirand in thy face:
Quhair thow cummis, ilk man sall fle the place.
This sall thow go begging fra hous to hous
With cop and clapper lyke ane lazarous.'

(ll. 330–43)

This judgment is appropriately formulated in the *topoi* Henryson has
employed from the rhetoric of preaching. The penalty becomes even
more memorable through Henryson's use of vivid details. As earlier
noted, Simpson diagnosed Cresseid's disease as elephantiasis leprosy,
and Saul N. Brody has shown that Henryson has relied upon a
demonstrable convention in matching this disease to the sexual nature
of Cresseid's sin.[98] While syphilis was very likely not known at the time
of Henryson's writing, leprosy was considered to be a type of venereal
disorder, a result of promiscuity.

The characterization of the narrator, in his resignation regarding his
state in life, also shows a proper Christian humility and wisdom. Even
though he has previously been a follower of Venus, he does not rage
against the impotence brought on by old age and he does not offend the
physical nature of life by refusing to accept his condition.[99] His
understanding and acceptance of life's changes is an example of the
wisdom preachers sought to instill in their congregations. There are
many other implications for characterization based on Christian *topoi*.
For instance Troilus himself (revived from the dead) obviously
participates in an *exemplum* of proper *caritas* when he gives Cresseid
money. First, in even remembering Cresseid and, secondly, in giving the
"anonymous" leper girl a handsome reward in her memory, Troilus
shows himself capable of forgiveness and general Christian charity. His
example too reflects a major goal of pulpit rhetoric.

There is evidence to indicate that even the parliament of the gods
in this poem may have Christian roots. Such use of pagan gods was
already sanctioned for Christian purposes in medieval sermon
rhetoric.[100] Dating back to Fulgentius, there was a lengthy tradition of
interpreting Greek and Roman myth as a reflection of Christianity. This
brief passage from Theodulph, Bishop of Orleans, illustrates the
attitudes of medieval clergymen towards the use of pagan figures in
their sermons. With regard to Ovid, earlier one of the most questionable
sources for sermons, Theodulph states:

> *Falsa poetarum stilus affert, vera sophorum*
> *Falsa horum in verum vertere saepe solent ...*
>
> [. . . Even though there is much that is frivolous
> Even more truth lies under a false covering.][101]

The rhetorical theorists of the *ars praedicandi* could hardly be
insensitive to the potential value of pagan figures and motifs. In fact,
the successful blending of such pagan figures into Christian themes has
many of its original roots in this particular branch of rhetoric. Insofar
as the pagan gods represent the manifestation of universal forces,
Cresseid's argument to the gods that they have cheated her may be
considered a blasphemy of the Christian God. Her questions and
countercharges may be viewed by the conservative medieval mind as an
attempt to usurp divine providence and displace it with human wisdom,
an issue that Henryson has also taken up in the fables.[102] Closely related
to this philosophical theme, however, is the developing secular and
theological emphasis on taking personal responsibility for one's
fate. This theme was seldom used earlier in the *ars praedicandi* because
of its theological incompatibility with the notions of divine omnipotence
and omniscience. Henryson, however, has made it a central focus of the
poem. On the one hand, he agrees with medieval conservatives that it
is important and unprofitable to challenge the workings of
Providence. On the other, he asserts the need for individuals to use
intelligence and forethought in planning their own lives (within the
constraints of universal order) and to accept responsibility for the
result. While the parliament of the gods illustrates his perspective on the
broader forces of the universe, his emphasis on individual responsibility
is illustrated in the pivotal scene where Cresseid finally understands her
own critical role in her tragedy:

> Quha findis treuth, lat him his lady ruse;
> Nane but my self as now I will accuse. (ll. 573–74)

Cresseid's mature understanding of her life in these lines sharply contrasts with her earlier immaturity in blaming the gods. Henryson masterfully blends these contrasting notions about the course of human fate into a unified *exemplum* reinforcing both traditional Christian concepts about the nature of the universe and the emerging Renaissance emphasis on the individual. Not only does he provide a dramatic lesson on questions involving God's foreknowledge and human free will, but he also shows how the basic techniques of the *ars praedicandi* can be successfully adapted to new themes and literary tastes.

The *ars praedicandi* also sheds light on one of the *cruces* of the poem. A great deal has been made of Troilus's "indirect recognition" of Cresseid in lines 505–11 of the poem. As noted in chapter three, Stearns has argued that Henryson uses principles of Aristotelian psychology in this scene, and, in general, his argument is sound.[103] Yet, it may well be that one of the basic principles of Patristic exegesis is also involved here as it was in the preacher's interpretation of *exempla*. The lines

> The idole of ane thing in cace may be
> Sa deip imprentit in the fantasy
> That it deludis the wittis outwardly. . . .
>
> (ll. 509–11)

parallel not only Aristotelian psychology but also one of the basic principles of Patristic interpretation and sermon rhetoric.[104] Exegetical principles were used both inductively and deductively, as preachers first looked at contemporary and biblical events to draw a general moral principle which would be useful to their congregations or, secondly, applied the general principle to some specific event. Henryson's lines reflect the deductive approach, providing a theoretical basis for interpretation of the events of the narrative. The pattern is common in medieval sermons, where the initial scriptural quotation or citation of an *auctoritas* might provide a theological principle to be illustrated by *exempla* in the body of the sermon. It would be imprudent to argue that this influence is the sole basis for Henryson's classic recognition scene. Nonetheless, given the significance of the other elements of the *ars praedicandi* and the *exemplum* in his work, it was directly or indirectly at least one source of his thinking on this central scene in the poem.

Henryson's *Orpheus* shows the same kind of rhetorical focus. I have contended that the *Orpheus* is likely a relatively youthful work, in part because of its more inflated style, its closer reliance on its source, and the somewhat forced tone of the *moralitas*, which lacks the more intriguing ambiguity to be found in *The Testament*.[105] Nonetheless, it illustrates the same general moral intent, adapting a classical legend to the purposes of preaching a moral lesson. Henryson would likely have been aware of the legend of Orpheus from a variety of sources. John Block Friedman has shown that the Orpheus tale was widely disseminated and variously treated in the medieval period.[106] Henryson was working with the commentary of Nicholas Trivet in his interpretation of the tale. The assessment of Henryson's efforts has certainly spanned the critical spectrum. Friedman says that the poem is "one of the most charming and memorable portraits of Orpheus to come out of the romance tradition."[107] Maurice Lindsay, on the other hand, says "Henryson's version of the Orpheus is so far inferior to the Middle English 'Sir Orpheo' that it has little to commend it."[108] There has also been discussion of the extent to which Henryson simply used the tale as an interesting story in its own right to capture the reader's attention, employed the romance elements which had developed around it, or wished to use it in terms of traditional *exempla*.[109] Certainly there can be no doubt, at least in part because of his *moralitas*, that he was working with the tale in the *exemplum* tradition.

The basic plot is quite familiar. Orpheus' descent into Hades to rescue Eurydice and his ultimate failure have had a continuing appeal. Trivet invested the tale with his own allegory in order to provide the moral lesson which Henryson seems to reinforce. Trivet calls Orpheus "pars intellectiua instructa sapientia et elloquentia."[110] He sees Eurydice as passion, willing to be governed by reason. Henryson virtually paraphrases Trivet in calling Orpheus "the pairte intelletyfe/ Off manis saule and undirstanding fre,/ And seperat fra sensualitie" (ll. 428–30). Of Eurydice, he says she is

> . . . oure affection
> Be fantasy oft movit vp and doun:
> Quhile to reson it castis the delyte,
> Quhile to the flesch settis the appetite.
>
> (ll. 431–34)

If one accepts these elements at face value, it is possible to develop a straightforward, even if occasionally bewildering, interpretation of the poem, but in Henryson's hands the tale either develops more ambiguity than this interpretation would suggest or somehow becomes tangled as he attempts to reconcile his classical *matière* with the *sens* of the *exemplum*.

To mention only a few of the critical *cruces* which have puzzled readers, one might cite the introduction of romance elements into the tale, and the attempted rape by Aristaeus. MacQueen is particularly intrigued by the romance elements early in the poem[111]—he notes that Eurydice strolls in a typically romance setting:

> . . . Erudices the quene,
> Quhilk walkit furth in till a Maii mornyng,
> Bot with a madin, in a medowe grene,
> To take the dewe and se the flouris spring. . . .
> (ll. 92–95)

In addition, Kenneth Gros Louis comments on the romance origins of Orpheus' complaint after he has lost his beloved for the second time.[112] He finds the basic elements of the following lines particularly suggestive:

> Quhat art thou lufe? How sall I the dyffyne?
> Bitter and suete, cruel and merciable;
> Plesand to sum, til othir playnt and pyne;
> To sum constant, till othir variabil;
> Hard is thy law, thi bandis vnbrekable . . .
> (ll. 401–05)

Gros Louis believes that these lines also reflect the romance tradition in Henryson's use of the legend. While acknowledging these romance borrowings, Friedman and MacQueen both comment on Henryson's debt to Trivet and the *exemplum* tradition.[113] MacQueen also emphasizes the possibly Neoplatonic implications of Henryson's numerology in the poem. Friedman suggests that the basic lesson of this *exemplum* might fall into the *de cassibus* tradition, strongly emphasizing the political allegory of the tale. Another aspect of the poem which suggests a closer connection with the tradition of "learned literature" rather than romance is the encyclopedic aspect of the work. The famous digression on music

and the numerous individual tales (such as that of Tantalus) which
interrupt the main plot line suggest more association with Isidore of
Seville and the encyclopedic tradition than any other work in the
Henryson canon except *The Morall Fabillis*.[114] The attempted rape of
Eurydice by Aristaeus has engendered a similar variety of
interpretations. MacQueen contends that the episode is a "startling" one,
not in harmony with the major theme of the tale.[115] On the other hand,
Gray accepts Henryson's depiction as a part of the classical tradition.[116]
Trivet's notion, which Henryson borrowed, that Aristaeus represents
"gud vertew," is a perspective very hard for some modern readers to
digest. These critical problems represent only a few of the questions
raised which could have implications for Henryson's attempts to
illustrate the path to virtue in this tale.

The *moralitas* and Henryson's source unequivocally place the poem
in the *exemplum* tradition. Yet, just as in *The Testament of Cresseid*,
Henryson did not feel himself bound to follow slavishly only the
techniques of that tradition. He likely would have felt no constraints
about introducing romance settings. The rhetoric of courtly love would
also have appeared readily accessible since it had infused and been
influenced by the rhetoric of the pulpit for many decades. Henryson's
familiarity with the *de cassibus* tradition is well attested by his other
verse. As illustrated by the *Testament*, Henryson at his best can readily
adapt and smoothly incorporate new ideas and concepts into a
traditional rhetorical setting. The *Orpheus* is less successful because the
adaptions seem forced and the integration of elements is incomplete.
Its stylistic inconsistencies also reflect the struggle to achieve a mature
artistic vision and voice. Even if it is not nearly so polished as the
Testament, the poem still presents a fascinating study of a young poet's
effort to expand the boundaries of a traditional rhetorical form.

In both the *Testament* and the *Orpheus*, Henryson's use of the
exemplum demonstrates the same sort of eclecticism illustrated by his
use of personification in *The Morall Fabillis*. His conclusion to *The
Testament of Cresseid* states that he wishes to provide moral instruction,
an object lesson in immaturity and wantonness. So, too, in the *Orpheus*,
Henryson attempts to show the victories and failures of intellect and
passion. Yet, in part because of the sources he used, the intellectual
climate in which he found himself, and his own abilities as a writer, he
found a need to expand the traditional uses of the *exemplum* to fit his
own goals.

HENRYSON AND THE PRINCIPLES OF *DIVISIO* IN THE *ARS PRAEDICANDI*

In addition to Henryson's use of the *ars praedicandi* in the areas of invention, diction, and figures, Henryson owes this rhetorical tradition a debt in the area of arrangement. As Murphy has shown, attention to *divisio* and the development of formulaic patterns for sermons were an inextricable part of the *ars praedicandi* from its inception,[117] even though an occasional maverick such as Thomas Waleys would sometimes challenge the approach to structure.[118] Between 1200 and 1220, the development of the *ars praedicandi* was in large part reflected in formulaic structural principles generally appropriate to deliberative oratory.[119] Alain de Lille, in his *De arte praedicatoria*, gives special attention to the beginnings of the sermon, even prior to 1200. His emphasis on the use of Scripture at the outset of preaching as a means of establishing authority and gaining audience attention is closely related to Henryson's use of allusive introductions and his citation of secular *auctoritates* such as Chaucer and Aesop.[120] After 1200, however, more analytic attention was given to homiletic structure. In *De modo praedicandi*, Alexander of Ashby places a great deal of emphasis on audience appeal, stating that an audience should be rendered "dociles, benivoles, et attentos"[121] in the opening of a sermon. He also takes for granted that there is a standard format for the presentation of a sermon. His basic formula is in certain ways traditional: a four-part plan involving an introduction, statement, proof and conclusion. What is unusual in terms of classical models is his assertion that each "membrum" or substatement should be followed immediately by a proof. Whereas traditional classical rhetoric had generally maintained that the proof is a completely separate part of discourse, not to be mixed with individual statements or substatements, Alexander seems clearly to advocate a mixed format in which each statement would be followed by a proof. Murphy suggests that he might have derived this idea from the *Rhetorica ad Herennium*, where the suggestion is made that "each argument should be regarded as a mini-speech with its own self-contained plan of arrangement."[122] No matter what Alexander's source, his precept is evident in Henryson's organizational pattern. The less artificially-structured nature of Alexander's organizational principles for statement and proof lends itself perfectly to the necessities of dialogue and artistic variation. In most of

Henryson's dialogues, in fact, the pattern of immediate proof of a statement is employed. The discussion between the wolf and the lamb has already been explained in this regard. The wolf makes a statement (about, for instance, the lamb's lack of recognition of his social station) with whatever proof he deems appropriate, and the lamb either makes his own statement with proof about his actions or rebuts item-by-item.

The rebuttal is yet another mixture of classical elements into "mini" arguments, since the refutation was generally considered a separate part of discourse in earlier rhetorical traditions. One of Henryson's shorter poems uses the same structure in a more directly theological context. "The Abbey Walk" demonstrates as well his choice of a variation on a common *topos*—the *memento mori* motif—which he also employs in "The Ressoning betuix Aige and Yowth," and "The Ressoning betuix Deth and Man." The homiletic values of this theme are clear, since it reminds humans of their mortality, the importance of God's grace, and the transitory nature of life. Henryson uses the truncated form of argument advocated by Alexander in treating this common theme in "The Abbey Walk." The basic argument of this poem is advanced in stanza six in which Henryson expounds upon the divinely-ordained nature of change:

> 'This changeing and grit variance
> Of erdly staitis vp and doun
> Cwmis nocht throw casualtie and chance,
> As sum men sayis, withowt ressoun,
> Bot be the grit prouisioun
> Of God aboif that rewill the sall:
>
> Thairfoir evir thow mak the boun
> To obey and thank thy God of all.
>
> (ll. 41–48)

The theme is reinforced by images typical of the *ars praedicandi*. The "grit variance" of a life in which an individual's fortune may move "vp and doun" is explained by the "grit prouisioun/of God aboif." This climactic statement of the theme is found in the penultimate stanza of the poem but is a result of the dramatic interplay of arguments in the previous five stanzas. After Henryson's introductory stanza, which provides the setting, he introduces several substatements, each accompanied with its own type of proof. One of the best examples is found in the sequence beginning with stanza two, where he uses analogy to explain why worldly delights will not endure:

> 'Thy kindome and thy grit empyre,
> Thy ryeltie nor rich array,
> Sall nocht indure at thi desyre,
> Bot as the wind will wend away;
> Thy gold and all thi gudis gay,
> Quhen fortoun list, will fra the fall:
> Sen thow sic sampillis seyis ilk day,
> Obey and thank thi God of all. (ll. 9–16)

In stanza three, he uses an appeal to authority as a means of proving his statement in stanza two and providing a transition to his statement about how worldly woes will also not endure in stanza four:

> 'Iob was moist riche, in writ we find,
> Thobe moist full of cheretie—
> Iob wox peur and Thoby blynd,
> Baith temptit with aduersitie:
> Sen blindnes wes infirmitie,
> And povertie was naturall,
> Thairfoir in patience baith he and he
> Obeid and thankit God of all.

> 'Thocht thow be blind or haif ane halt,
> Or in thy face deformit ill,
> Sa it cum nocht throw thy defalt,
> Na man sowld the repreif by skill:
> Blame nocht thy lord, sa is his will,
> Spur nocht thy fute aganis the wall,
> Bot with meik hairt and prayar still
> Obey and thank thy God of all.

In its concise approach to the theme, this structure reflects Alexander's basic principles. Even in this brief poem, Henryson's "mini-argument" constitutes less than one half of the work, and only one aspect of his general argument (expanded through the refrain, "Obey and thank thy God of all"). The dramatic potential of this structure of argument offers a flexibility essential to the poet.

Another treatise on organization which might have had general implications for Henryson is Thomas Chobham's *Summa de arte praedicandi* (1200–1215). Perhaps of greatest interest is Chobham's comparison between homiletics and the works of the poets and the arts of the orator. Making a powerful plea for the use of "pagan" rhetorical arts (in the tradition of St. Augustine), he also observes that poets organize their discourse into three parts, proposition, invocation, and narration. In this respect he sees the poetic model closely resembling the model for the preacher who invokes a theme, prays for God's help in explaining it, and then enters his exposition of the theme (instead of narrating a sequence of events). Having made these points, he then describes a six-part pattern of discourse.

1. Opening prayer for divine aid
2. Protheme (antetheme), or introduction of theme
3. Theme, or statement of a Scriptural quotation
4. Division, or statement of parts of the theme
5. Development (prosecutio) of the members named in the division
6. Conclusion (not an integral part of the sermon)[123]

Chobham's organizational pattern is representative of the *ars praedicandi* but, as Franco Morenzoni notes, it is also designed to permit exploration of "les multiples possibilités" of the techniques of the rhetoric of preaching.[124] As will be demonstrated, elements of this rhetorical pattern and others appear in Henryson's "Preaching of the Swallow."

Robert of Basevorn also outlined essential elements a sermon should contain. While the list has already been quoted, it is useful to cite it again here:

> Ad propositum igitur descendendum est, ut de ornamentis quae in sermonibus exercentur a quibusdam curiosis dicatur. Sciendum igitur quod in sermonibus curiosissimis viginti duo maxime observantur, quae sunt : thematis inventio, auditus allectio, oratio, introductio, divisio, partium declaratio, partium confirmatio, dilatatio, digressio, quae magis proprie posset vocari transitus, correspondentia, correspondentiae congruentia, circulatio, convolutio, unitio, clausio, coloratio, vocis discretio, gestus

convenientia, opportuna jocatio, allusio, inculcatio, rei dicendae ponderatio. Horum prima quindecim locis suis semel ponuntur, vel saltem in paucis locis; residua tria in multis locis, et communiter allusio et inculcatio in omni fere loco poni possunt. Quod post haec sequitur, jocatio, in paucissimis locis et temperatissime poni debet. Sed ultimum semper et in omni loco servandum est.

[We must come now to our proposal to discuss the ornamentation which is used in sermons by certain of the careful craftsmen. It must be realized that in the most carefully contrived sermons twenty-two ornaments are especially employed. These are Invention of the Theme, Winning-over of the Audience, Prayer, Introduction, Division, Statement of the Parts, Proof of the Parts, Amplification, Digression, which is properly called 'Transition,' Correspondence, Agreement of Correspondence, Circuitous Development, Convolution, Unification, Conclusion, Coloration, Modulation of Voice, Appropriate Gesture, Timely Humor, Allusion, Firm Impression, Weighing of Subject Matter. The first fifteen of these are inserted into their proper places once, or at any rate into a few places; the remaining three, and generally Allusion and Firm Impression, can be placed almost anywhere.][125]

While some of these elements clearly relate to invention, style, or even delivery, several of them relate to organization. Basevorn's special attention to the introduction, division, statement of parts, proof of parts, firm impression, and weighing of the subject matter all establish important aspects of division (largely in Ciceronian terms) which require attention on the part of the homilist. There is an obvious interdependence on the other aspects of discourse. Henryson clearly knew the complex nature of homiletic organization, as illustrated by the work of Chobham and Basevorn, and employed many of these elements in his *Morall Fabillis*, particularly in his most directly homiletic fable.

Possibly one of the best illustrations of Henryson's use of the beast fable in direct conjunction with the organizational devices of the art of

preaching is to be found in "The Preaching of the Swallow." In this tale,
Henryson also integrated his organizational devices with the major
rhetorical figures of the *ars praedicandi* in the context of exegetical
thinking. This fable, as its name might suggest, is a direct illustration
of "Aesop's" interest in encouraging creatures to eschew the bad and
follow the good. One of the most beautiful and self-consciously
rhetorical tales in the Henryson canon, this poem deals with standard
topoi of medieval sermons from its beginning, which employs both
typical language and *topoi* of the *ars praedicandi*. The first few lines
are significant:

> The hie prudence and wirking meruelous,
> The profound wit off God omnipotent,
> Is sa perfyte and sa ingenious,
> Excellent far all mannis iugement;
> For quhy to him all thing is ay present,
> Rycht as it is or ony tyme sall be,
> Befoir the sicht off his diuinitie.

(ll. 1622–28)

Such emphasis upon the omnipotence of God and the inability of man
to understand God's ways is common in the introduction of the
medieval sermon.[126] In line with Chobham's notion of an opening prayer
for divine aid, it certainly functions as a kind of invocation, which
Chobham compares in poetry to the opening prayer of the preacher. It
might be added, parenthetically, that the "new" nature of Henryson's
theology is illustrated by a subsequent passage:

> ȝyt neuertheles we may haif knawlegeing
> Off God almychtie be his creatouris,
> That he is gude, fair, wyis, and bening.
> Exempill takis be thir iolie flouris,
> Rycht sweit off smell and plesant off colouris,
> Sum grene, sum blew, sum purpour, quhyte, and reid,
> Thus distribute be gift off his Godheid.

(ll. 1650–56)

The notion that we know God through nature is often considered to be
a key aspect of the philosophy and religion of the Renaissance.[127] It is
also an important aspect of the philosophy of the Middle Ages. In this

aspect of his theology, Henryson is not an innovator, but a transitional figure. Insofar as he feels the need to use this tale and others as a defense of the theological "usefulness" of the beast fable tradition, these lines may incorporate aspects of Chobham's Protheme.

As Henryson proceeds into the prologue of the swallow's sermon, he uses another standard *topos* from theology. He attempts to give an overview of the world, discussing the various types of creatures and the passing of the seasons, while providing a microcosmic view of the life of man. This *topos* was a standard approach in what Chobham calls the Protheme or part of what Robert of Basevorn labels the Antetheme. Henryson's verse is more beautiful than standard sermons, but his debt to the *ars praedicandi* is demonstrated by the numerous examples of this *topos* which are found in sermon collections such as the *Summa praedicantium*. The function of this overview of the cosmos and mankind has been disputed, along with the importance of its setting in the prologue and the narrative tone and persona.[128] The lines could indeed serve a variety of functions, illustrating Henryson's most beatific vision of the world, his genuine sense of *caritas*, or his optimistic vision of a rational universe. In the context of exegetical interpretation there is no reason to argue that only one theme has exclusive domain in this section of the poem. The principles of *divisio* of pulpit rhetoric would provide the preacher considerable latitude in this portion of his sermon, and a beautiful sermon is precisely what Henryson is molding.

When Henryson finally arrives at the fable itself and moves into the swallow's sermon, his use of homiletic rhetoric changes abruptly. As the swallow progresses from one section of her homily to another, she becomes more impassioned. She first attempts to woo her audience through reason and good will:

> 'Se ȝe ȝone churll', quod scho, 'beȝond ȝone pleuch
> Fast sawand hemp—lo se!—and linget seid?
> ȝone lint will grow in lytill tyme in deid,
> And thairoff will ȝone churll his nettis mak,
> Vnder the quhilk he thinkis vs to tak.
>
> 'Thairfoir I reid we pas quhen he is gone
> At euin, and with our naillis scharp and small
> Out off the eirth scraip we ȝone seid anone
> And eit it vp, for giff it growis we sall
> Haue cause to weip heirefter ane and all.

Se we remeid thairfoir furth—with, instante,
Nam leuius laedit quicquid praeuidimus ante.

'For clerkis sayis it is nocht sufficient
To considder that is befoir thyne ee;
Bot prudence is ane inwart argument
That garris ane man prouyde befoir and se
Quhat gude, quhat euill, is liklie for to be
Off euerilk thingis at the fynall end,
And swa fra perrell ethar him defend.'

(ll. 1743–61)

In these lines, the swallow's first address, her tone is moderate and her *topos* is generally of the "past fact-future fact" variety. The thrust of her effort is to persuade the other birds that they should follow her projected course of action based on her reasoning and their own self-interest. This certainly parallels the second element in Basevorn's formula, Winning Over the Audience, related to types of appropriate appeal. More pointedly, perhaps, the swallow states her Theme—the danger posed by hemp which the churl has sown. Her initial remarks also constitute her Division, briefly stating her theme, developing her argument, and previewing her conclusion which is, at this point, a fervent but gentle admonition. However, her tone changes abruptly in line 1790:

'O blind birdis, and full off negligence,
Vnmyndfull off ₃our awin prosperitie,
Lift up ₃our sicht and tak gude aduertence,
Luke to the lint that growis on ₃one le!
₃one is the thing I bad, forsuith, that we,
Quhill it wes seid, suld rute furth off the eird:
Now is it lint; now is it hie on breird.

'Go ₃it, quhill it is tender, ₃oung, and small,
And pull it vp, let it na mair incres!
My flesche growis, my bodie quaikis all,
Think and on it I may not sleip in peis!'

(ll. 1790–1800)

She has now moved to the "Proof of Parts," attempting to show the congregation vividly what the results will be of their inaction. Instead of using the softer and more scholarly *topoi* of his prologue to the sermon, Henryson has now shifted to the "fire and brimstone" *topoi* of the outraged preacher.[129] The introduction of the second address itself, "Oh blind birdis," sets the tone for the exhortation to follow. She chastises the creatures for their negligence and argues that they are not mindful of their "awin prosperitie," using the term to encompass both spiritual and physical welfare. In similar fashion, lines 1790–96 of the sermon rely on *topoi* intended to shame the creatures addressed and to insure their attention for the admonitions to follow. The first admonition ("Lift up ₃our sicht") argues for the kind of self-examination typically exhorted in medieval sermons. The admonition at the beginning of the second stanza caps the unit that, in its entire organization and use of *topoi*, reflects the influence of harsher rhetoric of the *ars praedicandi*. A fruitful point of comparison is "Septuagesima Sunday," citing Chrysostom, which uses a similar tone of admonition in encouraging men to avoid evil:

> 'Synful men,' seiþ Crisostom, 'beþ not idel, but ded; but he is idel þat wircheþ not þe werk of God. 3ef þou take [a]wei oþer mennes godes, þere þou art not idel, but ded; but ₃ed þou take not awei oþer mennes goodes, and naþeles / þou ₃euest not of þi godes to vnmi₃ti men, þan ou art idel. Wole þou not be idel? Take þou not awei oþer mennes godes, and of þyne owne ₃eue to pore men, and þenne þou worchest in þe vine₃erd of God þe vine of mercy.

> '3ef þou art drunke and art in delicis, þou art not idel, but þou art ded, as þe apostle seiþ; but ₃ef þou mesurabli <etist> and drynkist, þou synnest not, for þou etist not euele; naþeles, þou art idel, for þou worchest not þe vertu of fastynge (þat is, almes). Wolt þou not þerfore be idel? Faste, and þat þou schuldest ete on þe dai, ₃eue it be [be] vnmy₃te man, and þou hast itiled þe vine of fastynge.[130]

The sermon continues at length in chastising mankind for a variety of sins while continuing to sustain the same kind of harsh rhetoric to which the swallow turns. The assumption shared by both the swallow and the preacher is that the time for reasonable argument is past. The danger is so immediate and the time for action so limited that both must resort to direct exhortations and threats to make their points.

Henryson then turns to another approach typically used by medieval preachers. In lines 1799–1800 the swallow attempts to instill fear in her congregation, clearly a device in keeping with the rest of the tone set in the passage. Henryson, however, has added an interesting twist. Whereas ordinarily the medieval preacher would have tried to instill such fear by describing the terrors of Hell, the perils of the world, or the punishment for an unjust life, Henryson's swallow attempts to instill fear by using her ethical appeal and relating her own fear. Such a personal tone may, once again, reflect what has been called "the growth of a personal voice"[131] in Renaissance rhetoric. Henryson's decision to have the swallow employ such an individualized ethical appeal adds considerably to the interest of the poem. This same personal tone continues after the swallow's sermon has been interrupted by the other birds who believe her concerns are groundless. In response to the crying of the birds who bid her cease, she responds:

> 'Weill,' quod the swallow, 'freindes, hardlilie beid;
> Do as ȝe will, bot certane, sair I dreid
> Heirefter ȝe sall find als sour as sweit,
> Quhen ȝe ar speldit on ȝone carlis speit.
>
> 'The awner off ȝone lint ane fouler is,
> Richt cautelous–and full off subteltie;
> His pray full sendill tymis will he mis
> Bot giff we birdis all the warrer be.
> Full mony off our kin he hes gart de,
> And thocht it bot ane sport to spill thair blude;
> God keip me fra him, and the halie rude.'
>
> (ll. 1807–17)

Of particular interest in this passage is the description of the adversary, which is also an essential part of the "Proof." The phrase "Richt cautelous and full off subteltie" is the kind of description, as Henryson himself later states, that would apply directly to Satan. Other aspects of the description, especially the farmer's efforts to "snare" the birds, are also well-known parallels to *topoi* and descriptions found in medieval sermon rhetoric. The devil typically attempted to "ensnare" human souls through a variety of "devices" appealing to human appetites for wealth, fashion or food. In the course of the narrative, the birds are indeed ensnared and the swallow concludes her sermon after their fate is sealed:

'Into that calf scraip quhill ₃our naillis bleid—
Thair is na corne, ₃e laubour all in vane.
Trow ₃e ₃one churll for pietie will ₃ow feid?
Na, na, he hes it heir layit for ane trane.
Remoue, I reid, or ellis ₃e will be slane;
His nettis he hes set full priuely,
Reddie to draw; in tyme be war for thy!

'Grit fule is he that puttis in dangeir
His lyfe, his honour, for ane thing off nocht.
Grit fule is he that will not glaidlie heir
Counsall in tyme, quhill it auaill him mocht.
Grit fule is he that hes na thing in thocht
Bot thing present, and efter quhat may fall
Nor off the end hes na memoriall.'

(ll. 1853–66)

In this instance, the swallow relies on the familiar preacher's *exemplum*, to make a "Firm Impression" and to weigh her subject matter. In point of fact, the congregation itself through wrong action has turned out to be the horrible example to which this preacher—swallow will refer. In Chobham's terms, this is the best possible Development for the Conclusion Henryson draws.

In these lines, Henryson has made a major narrative shift. Obviously the swallow's advice is intended as direct discourse to the reader, rather than dramatic discourse with the birds themselves, as in the prologue. If Henryson had been unsuccessful in shifting his tone and the reader's attention in that regard, the admonitions of the swallow would seem to be extremely cruel, perhaps gloating over the fate of those who would not head good advice. Yet no critic has ever suggested that cruelty is the swallow's motive.[132] Of particular importance in redirecting the reader's attention are the abstract comments about the nature of foolhardiness (as illustrated by the congregation of birds) to be found in lines 1860-66. This same sort of advice to the reader also appears in lines 1881–87 after the birds have been killed:

> And quhen the swallow saw that thay wer deid,
> 'Lo,' quod scho, 'thus it happinnis mony syis
> On thame that will not tak counsall nor reid
> Off prudent men or clerkis that ar wyis.
> This grit perrell I tauld thame mair than thryis;
> Now ar thay deid, and wo is me thairfoir!'
> Scho tuke hir flicht, bot I hir saw no moir.
>
> (ll. 1881–87)

Thus, "The Preaching of the Swallow," using the action of the narrative as an *exemplum*, is in reality a completely developed sermon, preached at two levels. Henryson uses homiletic principles of *divisio* for the general framework of the whole tale, a type of artistic illusion in which the reader is clearly "the congregation" and Henryson is the preacher. At another level of illusion, the swallow preaches to her congregation of birds, who are too shortsighted to heed her device. She too uses the principles of homiletic *divisio* for her sermon–within–a–sermon. The bridge between the two structures is established by the swallow's direct address to the reader, which both reinforces the terrible example provided by the birds of this tale and unites the voice of the narrator with her own. The thrust of the sermon is gradually and progressively redirected from the birds whom the swallow tries to help to the reader whom Henryson believed to be in need of general moral advice. This tale, generally acknowledged to be one of the most beautiful and effective of the entire group of moral fables, or all of Middle Scots literature for that matter, shows how Henryson could adapt elements of invention, organization, and style from the *ars praedicandi* into a fable that transcends the usual limitations of the rhetoric he employed.

HENRYSON'S AUTHORIAL VOICE

"The Preaching of the Swallow" raises central issues regarding Henryson's use of an authorial voice. While an author's rhetorical stance was the ultimate concern of all medieval rhetorical schools (even if that concern was often not specifically treated), its development in the *ars praedicandi* illustrates an especially interesting evolution in the use of the appeal to authority and the emergence of artistic *personae* in the Middle Ages. Many of the issues are tied to how a writer uses authority and, especially in Henryson's case, allusion. The extent to which a writer felt free to manipulate authorities or ignore them entirely had a strong role in determining authorial independence. Henryson's apparent deference to Aesop and Chaucer makes his authorial role a critical question in *The Morall Fabillis* and *The Testament of Cresseid*. Through a careful study of both religious and secular literature in the Middle Ages, A.J. Minnis has focused on the four major functions of medieval authorship, demonstrating how medieval authors might use the roles of *scriptor*, *commentator*, *compilator*, and *auctor* as a framework for approaching the writing task.[133] The interplay of these roles, based in large part on the clearly defined roles of writers treating scriptural subjects, had implications for Chaucer and Gower, as well as Henryson.[134] Minnis' concepts of these roles has already been described. Henryson plays on the interaction of these authorial roles in his most important works.

One of the most widely discussed aspects of Henryson's authorial *persona* is his self-presentation in *The Testament of Cresseid*. Henryson opens the poem with a portrait of the narrator in his study, perhaps an expression of his intention to provide a direct comparison and contrast between his narrator and Chaucer's. Henryson's narrator is indeed different from his Chaucerian precursor.[135] Henryson's narrator goes out of his way to comment that he has been a servant of Venus but his ardor has cooled because he is "ane man of age" (l. 29). His self-depiction echoes that of Boccaccio in *The Decameron*. Boccaccio's narrator too has been a servant of love, but his love also has cooled. Like Henryson's narrator, he is able to accept and even embrace the loss.[136] As Henryson's poem begins, his narrator has just been in the midst of a prayer to Venus but has retired to his study because of the cold. Having tended the fire and fortified his spirits with a drink, he picks up Chaucer's *Troilus* as comfort for his meditations. After having read Chaucer's poem, he comments:

> Quha wait gif all that Chauceir wrait was trew?
> Nor I wait nocht gif this narratioun
> Be authoreist, or fenȝeit of the new
> Be sum poeit, throw his inuentioun
> Maid to report the lamentatioun
> And wofull end of this lustie Creisseid,
> And quhat distres scho thoillit, and quhat deid.

> (ll. 61–70)

Payne observes that, in this prologue, the narrator establishes himself as
"our friendly, sophisticated, urbane host" who "prepares to tell as a
marvellous story."[137] After his preparations, the narrator then proceeds
to relate what "sum poeit" has written in "ane vther quair" about
Cresseid's subsequent history. In point of fact, it now appears certain
that there was no "vther quair" and that Henryson himself originated the
events outlined in his poem.[138] Why, then, use such a fictional source?
In part Henryson's prologue is much in keeping with the need to cite
an *auctoritas* which Th.-M. Charland described as a central part of the
ars praedicandi.[139] In homiletic rhetoric, the *auctoritas* cited was often
Scripture, or perhaps a secular proverb or scriptural commentator.
Establishing such an authority as the basis for one's discourse
established credibility in the minds of the audience and became a basis
for invention in the sermon.

Henryson has used both Chaucer and the "vther quair" for the same
purposes. While his *auctoritas* is neither scriptural nor classical, even
contemporaneous authors were accepted as *auctoritates* in the later
Middle Ages.[140] The "vther quair" also shares the literary purpose of
Chaucer's comments on the pilgrimage setting in *The Canterbury
Tales*. Chaucer assumes additional artistic freedom in asserting that the
reader should "blameth nat me" if he finds some of the tales
offensive. The use of a source, whether that source was real life (as
Chaucer contends) or another book (as Henryson states) seems to free
the artist from the responsibility for "offensive material" and allows him
to range into subjects for which he might be unwilling to take personal
responsibility. How much this fiction was necessary even for Chaucer
or in the fifteenth century is difficult to determine with complete
certainty. Did Henryson feel obligated to put a barrier between himself
and his audience to deflect any criticisms which would result from his
treatment of sexual wantonness and disease? Or did he simply use the
device as part of his traditional inheritance from Chaucer or the
Ricardian tradition as a rhetorical structure which both he and his
readers enjoyed and had come to expect? The nature of both
Chaucerian and Ricardian verse suggests the latter.[141] The relatively
well-attested use of this rhetorical device argues that it had become
established more as a literary convention than as a defense against
censure, at least by Henryson's day. Nonetheless, this citation of two
auctoritates at the beginning of his poem *apparently* relieves Henryson
of authorial responsibilities and defines his role as *scriptor* or
commentator. Which of the two roles Henryson intended his audience

to accept for artistic purposes is open to some debate. His blatant relinquishing of responsibility in the prologue may make him appear to be merely a *scriptor*. Yet that role is clearly at odds with other facets of the poem. If Henryson wished to establish himself merely as a *scriptor*, how could he expect his audience to react to the amount of attention given to his own authorial *persona* (at least 91 lines)? Even after his citation of his source, and his additional entry into the narrative, he incorporates an apostrophe to Cresseid which reflects the strong feelings of his narrator:

> O fair Creisseid, the flour and A per se
> Of Troy and Grece, how was thow fortunait
> To change in filth all thy feminitie,
> And be with fleschelie lust sa maculait,
> And go amang the Greikis air and lait,
> Sa giglotlike takand thy foull plesance!
> I haue pietie thow suld fall sic mischance!

> ₃it neuertheles, quhat euer men deme or say
> In scornefull langage of thy brukkilnes,
> I sall excuse als far furth as I may
> Thy womanheid, thy wisdome and fairnes,
> The quhilk fortoun hes put to sic distres
> As hir pleisit, and nathing throw the gilt
> Of the—throw wickit langage to be spilt! (ll. 78–91)

In particular the comment "I sall excuse als far furth as I may/ Thy womanheid, thy wisdome and fairnes" clearly suggests the latitude of a *commentator*, even within the fiction Henryson has established. It must therefore be concluded that either Henryson was establishing his role as a *commentator* or that he was playing on the ironic understanding of his audience or both. Evidence for Henryson's choice of *commentator* as his central role here is to be noted also in the conclusion of the poem:

> Now, worthie wemen, in this ballet schort,
> Maid for ₃our worschip and instructioun,
> Of cheritie, I monische and exhort,
> Ming not ₃our lufe with fals deceptioun:
> Beir in ₃our mynd this sore conclusioun

> Of fair Cresseid, as I haue said befoir.
> Sen scho is deid I speik of hir no moir. (ll. 610–16)

In these lines, Henryson moves beyond the role of *scriptor* to deliver the moral lesson of the tale personally.[142] Henryson was generally relying on the sophistication of his more astitute readers and their understanding of the convention he was using. Establishing the overall stance of a *commentator*, Henryson felt free to modify and expand his authorial voice to suit his subject matter and technique.

Henryson's authorial posturing has deceived editors and critics over the years. For about one hundred years, *The Testament* was generally known as Chaucer's, in good part because of its inclusion in the 1598 edition of Chaucer's works edited by Thynne. Even more recently, at least one critic has been led to argue that there really was "ane vther quair" which might have influenced Henryson.[143] The fact is, however, that no such source has been discovered. The work, at this point, must be assumed to be Henryson's original effort. Given the ironic interplay of authorial *personae* in which Chaucer, Gower, and others in the Ricardian tradition indulge, it hardly stretches credibility to argue that Henryson enjoyed the same authorial game, disguising his authorial efforts behind the masks of *scriptor* and *commentator*. There is evidence in *The Morall Fabillis* of his delight in shifting among these authorial roles established in the *ars praedicandi*.

In *The Morall Fabillis*, Henryson has once again disguised his own role in his artistry. He cites Aesop as his major *auctoritas*, as his prologue and introductions to the tales (outlined in chapter two) make evident. In his general prologue, he comments on his functions, most especially "To mak ane maner of translatioun—":

> Of this poete, my maisteris, with ₃our leif,
> Submitting me to ₃our correctioun,
> In mother toung, of Latyng, I wald preif
> To mak ane maner of translatioun—
> Nocht of my self, for vane presumptioun,
> Bot be requeist and precept of ane lord,
> Of quhome the name it neidis not record.
>
> In hamelie language and in termes rude
> Me neidis wryte, for quhy of eloquence
> Nor rethorike, I neuer vnderstude.

> Thairfoir meiklie I pray ȝour reuerence,
> Gif ȝe find ocht that throw my negligence
> Be deminute, or ȝit superfluous,
> Correct it at ȝour willis gratious.

(ll. 29–42)

In this instance, his poet is Aesop, not Chaucer. He is therefore using a more traditional classical source. His litotical comment that "rethorike, I neuer vnderstude" is as trustworthy as his comments on his authorial role.[144] As in the prologue of *The Testament of Cresseid*, he presents himself in a narrow role, apologizing for his limited abilities. He throws himself on the mercy of his audience, praying their "reuerence" for his work. He elaborates further this authorial *persona* in the prologue of "The Lion and the Mouse" when he meets Aesop and asks for his guidance. Henryson uses this conversation as a means of reinforcing his authorial mask while simultaneously distancing himself from his audience. The fiction, after all, is that Aesop is the author of the tale, not Henryson, and that it is in fact Aesop's choice to tell this tale at this particular point in *The Morall Fabillis*.

Yet, just as in *The Testament of Cresseid*, Henryson clearly brings the skill of the *auctor* to bear on fables in which he represents himself only as a translator. As Copeland has shown the role of translator generally implies a lower level of authorial responsibility, much akin to the *scriptor*.[145] Henryson tempers this impression of his role by noting that he is translating tales from one language to another and commenting that he lacks rhetorical skills. Insofar as the general prologue and the prologue to "The Lion and the Mouse" suggest that he is using his native tongue and adapting the fables to his native Scotland, they certainly indicate a role far expanded beyond that of *scriptor*. Henryson shows an intimate knowledge of rhetoric, and he engages in adaptation of the fables to his own Scottish settings while using native Scottish elements in the language of his retellings. Moreover, Henryson's known sources give the lie to his suggestion that he is either a translator or *compilator*. Both roles would allow him limited discretion in modifying his material. The role of *compilator*, the most natural for *The Morall Fabillis*, is one which Chaucer also uses to deny responsibility for the offensive nature of some of the tales, arguing that they are simply reported as the pilgrims told them. The study of Chaucer's known sources has shown how false and ironic that denial of authorial responsibility on his part really is.[146] The same is true of

Henryson. In addition, his reliance on such intrusive allusive references as "Esope, myne authour, makis mentioun . . ." (l. 162) are surely designed to remind the reader of his artistic fiction. As noted in chapter two, Henryson tends to favor this allusive type of introduction. If he were using one received source, his citation of *auctoritates* might be more convincing. Yet no matter how many times he uses phrases such as "Esope ane taill puttis in memorie" (l. 1146), his professed reliance on a single version of the fables is just as false as the notion that *The Canterbury Tales* were also received strictly from a real group of pilgrims.

The evidence suggests an authorial personality much more in control of his material than the term *scriptor, compilator*, or "translator" might suggest. Henryson borrowed widely in selecting the versions of "Esope" that he wished to record. While there is continuing reassessment of his debt to his sources, some precepts seem to have general support. First, it is quite clear that Henryson did not use a single source. Smith identified four sources: the Latin fables of Gualterus Anglicus, the *Fabules* of John Lydgate, Caxton's editions of the *Reynard* and *Aesop*, and Petrus Alfonsus' *Disciplina clericalis*. Diebler had earlier argued for a debt to the *Roman de Renart*, which MacQueen and Fox have accepted. Odo of Cheriton and Chaucer have also been added to the list of sources, and there have been suggestions of even additional authors Henryson might have used.[147] There are rather complex arguments regarding which sources Henryson might have consulted at a given time because of the relative impact on the chronology of the fables.[148] In any of the proposed chronological sequences, Henryson's use of his sources demonstrates latitude and originality which compare well with those of any other medieval author.

Henryson used extensive discretion in selecting how to treat the tales. "The Two Mice" and "Schir Chantecleir and the Fox," represent extremes in his use of sources. Yet, as also noted, they tend to reflect trends in Henryson's thinking. His use of Chaucer's "Nun's Priest's Tale" illustrates as much as his use of Odo of Cheriton's "Two Mice" his tendency to be selective in his use of sources and to borrow details or general themes which he might expand or contract as his own sense of the tale dictates. In Odo, he clearly found the "germ" of a story which he chose to amplify using virtually every rhetorical device that Geoffrey discusses. In Chaucer's tale he found sections which did not suit his purposes and which he pruned away. Yet he found other portions of the tale which, even in a limited context, he chose to amplify. His general treatment of sources is exemplified by the kinds of techniques used in these two tales—in fact, his originality in incorporating sources is what creates such vexing problems in trying to trace them. His creative latitude also reflects the continuing development of his authorial voice. As Minnis has observed, greater freedom in the treatment of the *auctoritates* is a hallmark of the rhetoric of the later Middle Ages.[149] Given the number of his sources in this work and his relatively free treatment of the sources he chose, there can be no doubts about Henryson's originality. He is in many ways a splendid example of Morse's argument that the late medieval author often establishes his authority with the audience by displacing a received "text" with a "pre-text." This "pre-text" frequently appears as a deferential attitude toward the audience, sometimes even establishing the fiction that the members of the audience are nobles and the poet is their "humble servant."[150] This deference would also result in the poet's diminution of his own artistic skills by professing a less creative role in the production of the poem. His literary disguises served his own purposes and suited the taste of his audience, but to the modern critical eye they cannot mask his genius.

CONCLUSIONS

Insofar as the *ars praedicandi* took as its goal the conversion and salvation of human souls, Henryson's use of it in his verse suggests that he saw it as the most serious and elevated of the rhetorical arts. Henryson's poetry shows evidence of the influence of this school at virtually every level. Yet in his hands the rhetoric of preaching does not seem stale and outmoded. He is attuned the central goals of the *ars praedicandi*, and he is inspired by its *topoi*. He uses the diction, figures, principles of *divisio*, and exegetical habits of thinking of the rhetoric of preaching throughout his verse. Moreover, his understanding of the various authorial roles which developed from the religious traditions behind the *ars praedicandi* is a source of delight and interest in his works.

Henryson's freshness in his use of every tradition that he approached is also remarkable. While he would have likely taught the elements of the *ars poetriae* and would have been familiar with the *ars dictaminis*, most scholars who approach his work would agree that his poems do not "smell of the lamp." His use of the *ars praedicandi* also shows such innovation. Henryson uses the techniques of the art of preaching but substantially modifies them through his use of the first person tone, his introduction of Aristotelian psychology, his extra attention to detail in characterization, and other devices. In part, John MacQueen is correct that in this sense Henryson's rhetoric suggests his movement towards Renaissance humanism.[151] Yet Roderick Lyall is also accurate in suggesting that the general framework of Henryson's work is medieval,[152] owing a considerable debt to the scholarly traditions of which he would have become aware in his academic training. More important, however, than classifying Henryson in any single camp is understanding the significance of his contribution to rhetoric in the fifteenth century. He generally did not become absorbed in the kind of wordplay that so entranced Dunbar and has subsequently become a barrier to many of Dunbar's potential readers. While Henryson's language seems simple, direct, and "artless," the very simplicity of his style is deceiving, involving as it does the use of complicated Latin roots and a thorough understanding of the *ars poetriae*. So too, the simplicity of his *topoi* and the other rhetorical devices that he borrowed from the *ars praedicandi* tend to make much of his art seem transparent. Yet the student of rhetoric will readily understand that Henryson's simplicity is, itself, a highly skilled art. His mastery of the *ars praedicandi* and ability to go beyond it, along with his willingness to experiment and develop his own "personal voice," would suggest that in his rhetoric Henryson incorporated the best of medieval traditions into fifteenth-century British literature.

Notes
Chapter IV

1. For examples of this approach, see Gray, *Robert Henryson* especially pp. 85–6, 136–37 and "'Th'Ende is Every Tales Strengthe': Henryson's *Fables*"; MacQueen, *Robert Henryson* especially, pp. 153–65; Kindrick, *Robert Henryson*, especially pp. 56–117; and Kindrick, "Henryson and the Rhetoricians: The *Ars praedicandi*," in *Scottish Language and Literature, Medieval and Renaissance*, ed., Dietrich Strauss and Horst W. Drescher (Frankfurt am Main, 1984), pp. 254–80.

2. Many of the issues have been summarized by Stephan Khinoy in "Tale-Moral Relationships in Henryson's *Moral Fables*," *Studies in Scottish Literature*, 17 (1982), pp. 99–115; particularly on the fables, see also George Clark, "Henryson and Aesop: The Fable Transformed," *English Literary History*, 43 (1976), 1–18; Denton Fox, "Henryson's Fables," *English Literary History*, 29 (1962), 337–56; I. W. A. Jamieson, "'To preue thare preching be a poesye' Some Thoughts on Henryson's Poetics," *Parergon*, 8 (1974), 24-36. Daniel M. Murtaugh, "Henryson's Animals," *Texas Studies in Language and Literature*, 14 (1972), 405–21, in addition to Gray, Kindrick, and MacQueen in their volumes entitled *Robert Henryson*. For special comment on the *Orpheus* and the *Testament* see Gray, *Robert Henryson*, pp. 162–240, and Kindrick, *Robert Henryson*, pp. 118–63; both of these critics evaluate arguments with regard to the application of exegetical analysis of the two poems. On "The Preaching of the Swallow," see in addition to the works cited above MacQueen, *Robert Henryson*, pp. 153–65; Gray, *Robert Henryson*, pp. 132–38; Kindrick, *Robert Henryson*, pp. 95–101; and J.A. Burrow, "Henryson: The Preaching of the Swallow," pp. 25–37.

3. A useful summary of the issues will be found in Dorothy Bethurum, ed. *Critical Approaches to Medieval Literature*, pp. 1–82. For a valuable approach to the issues in Chaucer, see Siegfried L. Wenzel, "Chaucer and the Language of Contemporary Preaching," *Studies in Philology*, 73 (1976), 138–61; see also Allen, pp. 3–28.

4.	Among the many excellent studies which could be cited, see Minnis, *Medieval Theory of Authorship*; Jean Longère, *La prédication medieval* (Paris, 1983); *De Ore Domini*, ed. Thomas L. Amos, Eugene A. Green, and Beverly Mayne Kienzle (Kalamazoo, 1989); and *Medieval Eloquence*, ed. Murphy. George Kennedy has explored some of the fundamental bases of the *ars praedicandi* in "An Introduction to the Rhetoric of the Gospels," *Rhetorica*, 1, no. 1 (1983), 17–31. For an interesting perspective on the "supernatural" powers of rhetoric, see John O. Ward, "Magic and Rhetoric From Antiquity to the Renaissance: Some Ruminations," *Rhetorica*, 6, no. 1 (1988) 57–118. See also James J. Murphy, *Medieval Rhetoric: A Select Bibliography*, especially pp. 135–56. Other studies are cited throughout this volume.

5.	*De doctrina christiana*, IV, ed. Green, 151, 153, pp. 165-66; translation from St. Augustine, *On Christian Doctrine*, trans. Robertson, pp. 164–65.

6.	See Harry Caplan, "Classical Rhetoric and the Mediaeval Theory of Preaching," *Classical Philology*, 28 (1933), 73–96. See also Murphy, *Rhetoric in the Middle Ages*, pp. 269–99.

7.	See Caplan, "Classical Rhetoric and the Mediaeval Theory of Preaching," pp. 73–77; Murphy, *Rhetoric in the Middle Ages*, p. 299. For a few examples of citation of Chrysostom, see Gloria Cigman, ed. *Lollard Sermons*, Early English Text Society, Original Series 294 (Oxford 1989), "Septuagesima Sunday," p. 82, and "Sexagesima Sunday," p. 95.

8.	Murphy, *Rhetoric in the Middle Ages*, pp. 282–83.

9.	See Kennedy, "An Introduction to the Rhetoric of the Gospels," pp. 17–31; and Murphy, *Rhetoric in the Middle Ages*, pp. 276–7.

10.	Owst, *Preaching in Medieval England*, pp. 244-45.

11.	John W. O'Malley, "Introduction: Medieval Preaching," in *De Ore Domini*, p. 10.

12. See R.E. Kaske, "Patristic Exegesis: The Defense" in Bethurum, pp. 27–60; Bright, 147; and also, of course, Robertson's *A Preface to Chaucer*.

13. Vickers, p. 244.

14. Robert O. Payne, "Chaucer's Realization of Himself as Rhetor," in Murphy, *Medieval Eloquence*, p. 274.

15. See Charland for an outstanding survey of materials detailing the development of the techniques of this school. See also Baldwin, *Medieval Rhetoric and Poetic*, pp. 228–57, and Murphy, *Rhetoric in the Middle Ages*, 269–355.

16. Owst, *Literature and Pulpit*, especially, pp. 149–56. See also Baldwin, *Medieval Rhetoric and Poetic*, pp. 235–36.

17. Owst, *Literature and Pulpit*, pp. 149–209.

18. *De doctrina christiana*, ed. Green, IV, 96; translation from *St. Augustine: On Education*, trans. George Howie (South Bend, 1969), p. 383.

19. For an example of the pervasive influence of such figures in Medieval thought, see Margaret Jennings "The *Ars componendi sermones* of Ranulph Higden," in Murphy, *Medieval Eloquence*, pp. 112–26.

20. Margaret Jennings, ed., *The Ars Componendi Sermones of Ranulph Higden* (Leiden, 1991), see especially pp. 3–4.

21. *Forma praedicandi*, p. 238; translation from "The Form of Preaching," p. 120.

22. See Owst, *Literature and Pulpit*, p. 12.

23. In addition to sources previously cited, see George D. Gopen, "The Essential Seriousness of Robert Henryson's *Moral Fables*: A Study in Structure," *Studies in Philology*, 82 (1985), 42–59.

24. For a synopsis, see Khinoy, especially pp. 110–12. See also Gray, *Robert Henryson*, pp. 31–161.

25. Khinoy, pp. 99–115. See also Kindrick, *Robert Henryson*, pp. 65–117.

26. Gray suggests that Henryson himself indicates that his *moralitates* contain only "*one* possible message" of a fable instead of "*the* message," "'The Ende is Every Tales Strengthe': Henryson's *Fables*," p. 249. However, Henryson's *moralitates* may contain either implicitly or explicitly more than just one level of interpretation. See also Gregory Kratzmann, "Henryson's *Fables*: 'the subtell dyte of poetry,'" *Studies in Scottish Literature*, 20 (1985), pp. 49–68 for comment on the importance of multiple levels of interpretation.

27. See, for instance, Caplan, "A Late Mediaeval Tractate on Preaching," in *Of Eloquence*, especially, pp. 45–48 in addition to "Classical Rhetoric and the Medieval Theory of Preaching," in the same volume, pp. 105–34; Owst, *Preaching in Medieval England: An Introduction to Sermon Manuscripts of the Period, c. 1350–1450* (Cambridge, 1926) and *Literature and Pulpit in Medieval England*, passim; and Minnis, *Medieval Theory of Authorship*, pp. 136–38 and 174–77.

28. Guibert, 25-6; translation from "The Way A Sermon Ought to be Given," pp. 170–71. Owst also cites Master Rypon of Durham who quotes the most traditional, widely-known summary of the four senses:

> Littera gesta docet; quid credas, allegoria;
> Moralis, quid agas; quo tendas, anagogia

See Owst, *Literature and Pulpit*, pp. 59–60.

29. Minnis, pp. 73–117.

30. *Forma praedicandi*, V, 242-43; translation in "The Form of Preaching," pp. 124–26.

31. Allen, p. 53.

32. Kindrick, *Robert Henryson* pp. 37–39.

33. Morse, p. 44.

34. MacQueen, *Robert Henryson*, p. 100.

35. Fox, "Henryson's Fables," 338–39; James Kinsley, *Scottish Poetry* (London, 1955), p. 18; Wittig, p. 40.

36. Gopen, "The Essential Seriousness of Robert Henryson's *Moral Fables*," pp. 46–47. Bishop, pp. 475–77.

37. Kindrick, *Robert Henryson*, pp. 69–72; see also Philippa M. Bright, "Henryson's Figurative Technique in *The Cock and the Jasp*," in *Words and Wordsmiths: A Volume for H. L. Rogers*, ed. Geraldine Barnes, John Gunn, Sonya Jensen, and Lee Jobling (Sydney, 1989), pp. 13–21.

38. This phrase is borrowed from MacQueen, *Robert Henryson*, p. 107.

39. "Sermon of Dead Men," in *Lollard Sermons*, ed. Cigman, p. 212.

40. *Ibid.*, p. 213.

41. For comment on possible political allegory in "The Wolf and the Wether," see MacQueen, *Robert Henryson*, pp. 184–85; Kindrick, *Robert Henryson*, pp. 113–17; and for general comment on the king's "favorites to whom the poem might refer, see Nicholson, pp. 501–04.

42. Owst, *Literature and Pulpit*, pp. 212–470.

43. Manuscript Add. 41321, fol. 19, as reprinted in Owst, *Literature and Pulpit*, p. 320.

44. Lyall, "Politics and Poetry in Fifteenth and Sixteenth Century Scotland," pp. 5–27.

45. Owst, *Literature and Pulpit*, pp. 46–47.

46. See Gray, *Robert Henryson*, pp. 207–08; McDiarmid, *Robert Henryson*, pp. 114–15; and Robert Henryson, *The Testament of Cresseid*, ed. Denton Fox, (London, 1968), pp. 57–59, for a sample of the perspectives on these lines.

47. Guibert, 25; translation from "The Way A Sermon Ought to be Given," p. 170.

48. E. M. W. Tillyard, "Henryson: *The Testament of Cresseid* 1470?," in *Five Poems 1470–1870* (London, 1948), pp. 5–29.

49. Spearing, p. 144; Moran, "*The Testament of Cresseid* and the *Book of Troylus*," especially pp. 23–24.

50. E. Duncan Aswell, "The Role of Fortune in *The Testament of Cresseid*," *Philological Quarterly*, 46 (1967), 485–86.

51. K. J. Harty, "Cresseid and Her Narrator: A Reading of Robert Henryson's *Testament of Cresseid*," *Studi Medievali*, 23 (1984), 753–65.

52. For a history of Cresseid's character, see Gretchen Mieszowski, "The Reputation of Criseyde: 1155–1500," *Transactions* of the Connecticut Academy of Arts and Sciences, 43 (1971), 71–153; for an interpretation of sexual attitudes in the poem see Nikki Stiller, "Robert Henryson's Cresseid and Sexual Backlash," *Literature and Psychology* 31 (1983), 88–95; see also Mari Ann Cullen, "Cresseid Excused: A Re-reading of Henryson's *Testament of Cresseid*," *Studies in Scottish Literature*, 20 (1985), pp. 137–59. For a summary of interpretations, see Kindrick, *Robert Henryson*, pp. 143–48.

53. Kindrick, *Robert Henryson*, pp. 147–48.

54. For additional comment, see Harry Caplan, "Rhetorical Invention in some Medieval Tractates on Preaching," *Speculum*, 2 (1927), 284–95.

55. On these two *topoi*, see Curtius, pp. 80–82.

56. Mueller, especially pp. 85–110.

57. *Forma praedicandi*, XIII, p. 248; translation from "The Form of Preaching," pp. 131–32.

58. Owst, *Literature and Pulpit*, pp. 6–7; Mueller, pp. 87–89.

59. See Murphy, *Rhetoric in the Middle Ages*, pp. 300–55; David L. D'Avray, *Preaching of the Friars: Sermons diffused from Paris before 1300* (Oxford, 1985); and Beryl Smalley, *English Friars and Antiquity in the Early Fourteenth Century* (New York, 1960), especially pp. 28–44.

60. Mueller, especially, pp. 111–32.

61. Owst, *Literature and Pulpit*, pp. 4–5.

62. Ellenberger, pp. 57–70.

63. Mueller, pp. 162–77.

64. See, for instance, Michael Spiller, "Poetry after the Union 1603–1660," in *The History of Scottish Literature I*, pp. 142–43; and, for an earlier perspective, G. Gregory Smith, ed., *Specimens of Middle Scots* (Edinburgh, 1902), pp. lx–lxv.

65. "Euanguelium vnius Martiris. Sermos," in *English Wycliffite Sermons*, 2, ed. Pamela Gradon (Oxford, 1988), pp. 23–24.

66. See Owst, *Literature and Pulpit*, pp. 375–404.

67. Owst, *Literature and Pulpit*, especially pp. 10–55.

68. This translation is from Owst, *Literature and Pulpit* p. 334. The original text is from John Bromyard, *Summa Praedicantium*, "Nobilitas" (Venice, 1586), 110a. For an interesting parallel in the use of such realistic detail for purposes of satire by an important medieval rhetorician, see Robert Levine, "Satiric Vulgarity in Guibert de Nogent's *Gesta Dei per Francos*," *Rhetorica*, 7, no. 3 (1989), 261–73.

69. MacDonald, "Chaucer's Influence on Henryson's Fables: The Use of Proverbs and *Sententiae*," pp. 21–27. See also B. J. Whiting,

"Proverbs and Proverbial Sayings from Scottish Writings before 1600," *Medieval Studies*," 11 (1949), 123–205, and 13 (1951), 87–164.

70. Guibert, 25; translation from "The Way A Sermon Ought to be Given," pp. 169–70.

71. Gallo, "The *Poetria nova* of Geoffrey of Vinsauf," pp. 76–77, and Jennings, "The *Ars componendi sermones* of Ranulph Higden," p. 121.

72. For a review of modern approaches to Augustine's concepts, see *On the Medieval Theory of Signs*, ed. Umberto Eco and Costantino Marmo (Amsterdam, 1989); *Sign; Sentence, Discourse*, ed. Wasserman and Roney; and a special issue of *Style*, 20 (1986) edited by Ruth Hamilton. See also Murphy, *Rhetoric in the Middle Ages*, pp. 287–92, and Judson B. Allen, *The Ethical Poetic of the Later Middle Ages* (Toronto, 1982).

73. Owst, *Literature and Pulpit*, p. 67.

74. W.T.H. Jackson, *The Challenge of the Medieval Text*, ed. Joan M. Ferrante and Robert W. Hanning (New York, 1985), p. 157.

75. *Ibid.*, p. 158.

76. Rosemond Tuve, *Allegorical Imagery* (Princeton, 1966), p. 11.

77. For additional comment on the classical basis of this pattern of thinking and its implications for Christian allegory, see Philip Rollinson, *Classical Theories of Allegory and Christian Culture* (Pittsburgh, 1981), especially pp. 29–86. See also James I. Wimsatt, *Allegory and Mirror* (New York, 1970), especially pp. 17–35, and D.W. Robertson, "The Allegorist and the Aesthetician," *Essays in Medieval Culture* (Princeton, 1980), pp. 85–101. For comment on a doctrine specific to the Middle Ages, see William Purcell, "*Transsumptio*: A Rhetorical Doctrine of the Thirteenth Century," *Rhetorica*, 5, no. 4 (1987), 369–410.

78. On "The Bludy Serk," see Edward C. Schweitzer, "The Allegory of Robert Henryson's 'The Bludy Serk,'" *Studies in Scottish Literature*, 15 (1980), pp. 165–74.

79. See Roy Willis, *Man and Beast* (London, 1974); B.E. Perry, "Fable," *Studium Generale*, 12 (1959), 17–37; Beryl Rowland, "The Arts of Memory and the Bestiary," in *Beasts and Birds of the Middle Ages*, ed. Willene B. Clark and Meradith McMunn (Philadelphia, 1989), pp. 12–25; Gray, *Robert Henryson*, pp. 31–69; and Evelyn S. Newlyn, "Robert Henryson and the Popular Fable Tradition in the Middle Ages," *Journal of Popular Culture*, 14 (1984), 108–18.

80. "Septuagesima Sunday," in *Lollard Sermons*, ed. Cigman, p. 90.

81. John B. Friedman, "Peacocks and Preachers: Analytic Technique in Marcus of Orvieto's *Liber de moralitatibus*, Vatican lat. MS 5935," in *Beasts and Birds of the Middle Ages*, ed. Clark and McMunn, pp. 179–96. See also George C. Bruce, "The Medieval Bestiaries and Their Influence on Ecclesiastical Decorative Art," *Journal of the British Archaeological Association* (December, 1919), 40–82.

82. Gray, *Robert Henryson*, pp. 31–69.

83. See Bruce, pp. 40-82.

84. See MacDonald, "Henryson and Chaucer: Cock and Fox"; Jamieson, "A Further Source for Henryson's 'Fabillis,'" "Henryson's 'Fabillis': An Essay Towards a Revaluation," "Henryson's *Taill of the Wolf and the Wedder*," and "The Minor Poems of Robert Henryson"; David Crowne, "A Date for the Composition of Henryson's Fables," *Journal of English and Germanic Philology*, 61 (1962), 583–90; and Powell, *Fabula Docet*. See also Diebler, *Henrisone's Fabeldichtungen* for a thorough earlier study.

85. Gray, *Robert Henryson*, especially pp. 62–69; see also John Black Friedman, "Henryson, The Friars, and the *Confessio Reynardi*," *Journal of English and Germanic Philology*, 66 (1967), especially 552–54, for a discussion of traditional characterizations of the fox.

86. See, for instance, Odo's "The Fox, the Wolf, and the Well-Bucket," in Jacobs, p. 89, as well as numerous examples from Caxton's *Reynard*, among others. T.H. White explains factors that contributed to problems in understanding the characterization of beasts in *The Bestiary* (New York, 1954), pp. 248–61. W.T.H. Jackson comments that the lack of consistency in personification is the result of the fact that animal kingdoms are run "by human methods," *The Literature of the Middle Ages* (New York, 1960), p. 339.

87. See Jamieson, "Henryson's *Taill of the Wolf and the Wedder*," pp. 251–52 for comment on Henryson's deletion of material in Caxton which was even more critical of the wether.

88. For comment see McDiarmid, *Robert Henryson*, pp. 62–87; and Stearns, *Robert Henryson*, pp. 14–47 and 106–29.

89. See MacQueen, *Robert Henryson*, pp. 149–51. For general comment on how bestiaries began to parody "human and not animal behavior" (p. 98), see Jeanette Beer, "Duel of Bestiaries," in *Beasts and Birds of the Middle Ages*, ed. Clark and McMunn, pp. 96–105.

90. See Baldwin, *Medieval Rhetoric and Poetic*, p. 236 and Owst, *Literature and Pulpit*, pp. 195–207.

91. Owst, *Literature and Pulpit*, pp. 149–56.

92. Joseph A. Mosher, *The Exemplum in the Early Religious and Didactic Literature of England* (New York, 1911); and John D. Lyons, *Exemplum* (Princeton, 1990).

93. Robert of Basevorn, pp. 146–47.

94. See Humbert of Romans, *A Treatise on Preaching* (Westminster, MD, 1951), pp. 33–34. See also Simon Tugwell, "Humbart of Romans's Material for Preachers," *De Ore Domini*, pp. 105–77.

95. See particularly Fox, ed. *The Testament of Cresseid*, p. 1, and Kindrick, *Robert Henryson*, pp. 118–19.

96. See Tillyard, pp. 27–29, and, for a brief history of this point of view, Fox, ed., *The Testament of Cresseid*, pp. 48–58 for two examples of this attitude.

97. See, for instance, Alberic of Monte Cassino, "Flowers of Rhetoric" in *Readings in Medieval Rhetoric*, p. 159.

98. See Simpson *passim*, and Brody, pp. 144–46. See also Kathryn Hume, "Leprosy or Syphilis in Henryson's *Testament of Cresseid*," *English Language Notes*, 6 (1969), 242–45.

99. See C. W. Jentoft, "Henryson as Authentic 'Chaucerian,'" pp. 95–96 and Kindrick, *Robert Henryson*, pp. 122–23.

100. See Owst, *Literature and Pulpit*, pp. 111–12 and Jean Seznec, *The Survival of the Pagan Gods*, trans., Barbara Sessions, (Princeton, 1972), pp. 84–147.

101. Trans., Sessions in Seznee, p. 91.

102. See Tillyard, "Henryson: *The Testament of Cresseid* 1470?," pp. 16–17; and Kindrick, *Robert Henryson* pp. 143–48.

103. Stearns, *Robert Henryson*, pp. 97–105; Kindrick, *Robert Henryson* pp. 140–41.

104. See Robertson, pp. 52–64 and Owst, *Literature and Pulpit*; note also Denton Fox's comment on the etymology of "idole," *The Testament of Cresseid*, p. 124.

105. Kindrick, *Robert Henryson*, pp. 159–63.

106. John Block Friedman, *Orpheus in the Middle Ages* (Cambridge, MA, 1970).

107. *Ibid.*, p. 196.

108. Maurice Lindsay, *History of Scottish Literature* (London, 1977), p. 44.

109.   For comment on some of these points of view, see Friedman, *Orpheus in the Middle Ages*, pp. 196–202; Carol Mills, "Romance Conventions of Robert Henryson's *Orpheus and Eurydice*," in *Bards and Makars*, pp. 52–60; and, for a summary, see Kindrick, *Robert Henryson*, pp. 151–53.

110.   Text from Fox, *Poems*, p. 385. Fox prints Trivet's entire commentary.

111.   MacQueen, *Robert Henryson*, p. 33; see also Mills, pp. 54–55.

112.   Kenneth R.R. Gros Louis, "Robert Henryson's Orpheus and Eurydice and the Orpheus Traditions of the Middle Ages," *Speculum*, 41 (1966), 653.

113.   Friedman, *Orpheus in the Middle Ages*, pp. 2, 207–08; MacQueen, "Neoplatonism and Orphism in Fifteenth-Century Scotland," especially p. 75.

114.   See Kindrick, *Robert Henryson*, pp. 155–58.

115.   MacQueen, *Robert Henryson*, p. 34.

116.   Gray, *Robert Henryson*, pp. 221–22.

117.   Murphy, *Rhetoric in the Middle Ages*, especially pp. 305–44.

118.   See Waleys, *De modo componendi sermones* in Charland, especially II-V; pp. 341–68.

119.   For an analysis of the importance of each part of discourse, see Charland, pp. 107–226.

120.   Minnis, especially, pp. 15–39.

121.   Murphy, *Rhetoric in the Middle Ages*, p. 312.

122.   *Ibid.*, p. 316.

123. *Ibid.*, p. 325; for the original text see Thomas Chobham, *Summa de arte praedicandi*, ed. Franco Morenzani (Brussels, 1988), pp. 262–68.

124. Chobham, p. LXI.

125. *Forma praedicandi*, XIV, p. 249; translation from "The Form of Preaching," pp. 132–33.

126. Owst, pp. 56–109. See also Dietrich Strauss, "The Opening Lines of *The Testament of Cresseid* Reconsidered," *Proceedings of the Third International Conference on Scottish Language and Literature*, pp. 301–14.

127. The assertion is easily refuted by a review of medieval attitudes, but it persists as described in Basil Willey, *The Seventeenth Century Background* (New York, 1934; rpt. 1953), pp. 32–48.

128. See Gray, *Robert Henryson*, pp. 162–76; for a summary, see Kindrick, *Robert Henryson* pp. 120–26.

129. *Forma praedicandi*, XXIV, p. 261; translation in "The Form of Preaching," pp. 146–47.

130. "Septuagesima Sunday," in *Lollard Sermons*, ed. Cigman, p. 82.

131. For special comment on this development, see Judith H. Anderson, *The Growth of a Personal Voice* (New Haven, 1976), especially pp. 198–203. Yet also see Owst, *Literature and Pulpit*, pp. 169–70, for comment on the traditional use of this technique in medieval sermons.

132. See J.A. Burrow, "Henryson: *The Preaching of the Swallow*," pp. 25–37, and Kindrick, *Robert Henryson*, pp. 95–101.

133. Minnis, especially pp. 94–95.

134. *Ibid.*, pp. 160–210.

135.   For a summary of points of comparison, see Robert O. Payne, "Late Medieval Images and Self-Images of the Poet: Chaucer, Gower, Lydgate, Henryson, Dunbar," in *Vernacular Poetics in the Middle Ages*, ed. Lois Ebin (Kalamazoo, 1984), pp. 249–55 and 258–61.

136.   Giovanni Boccaccio, *The Decameron*, trans. G. H. McWilliam (Baltimore, 1972), p. 45.

137.   Payne, "Late Medieval Images and Self-Images of the Poet," p. 259.

138.   See Sydney J. Harth, "Convention and Creation in the Poetry of Robert Henryson," (Diss., University of Chicago, 1962), pp. 9–24. However for comment that the "uther quair" might have been merely the fifth book of Chaucer's *Troilus,* see Fox, *Poems*, p. 343.

139.   Charland, p. 166; see also Minnis, pp. 15–39.

140.   Minnis, pp. 98–112; see also Minnis, Scott, and Wallace, pp. 205–207.

141.   See Curtius, pp. 83–85, and, for more specific comment on Henryson, *The Testament of Cresseid*, ed. Fox, pp. 21–23.

142.   On Henryson's "double perspective" in this poem and his use of the narrator, see Alicia K. Nitecki, "Fenzeit of the New : Authority in *The Testament of Cresseid*," *Journal of Narrative Technique*, 15 (1986), 120–32.

143.   Eleanor R. Long, "Robert Henryson's 'Uther Quair,'" *Comitatus*, 3 (1972), 97–101. See also Anna Torti, "From 'History' to 'Tragedy': The Story of Troilus and Criseyde in Lydgate's *Troy Book* and Henryson's *Testament of Cresseid*," *The European Tragedy of Troilus*, ed. Piero Boitani (Oxford, 1989), pp. 171–97.

144.   For useful comments, see Curtius, pp. 83–85 and Fox, *Poems*, p. 191.

145.   Copeland, pp. 42–55; see also Morse, pp. 179–230.

146.   See *Sources and Analogues of Chaucer's Canterbury Tales*, ed. W.F. Bryan and Germaine Dempster (Chicago, 1941), and, for a more recent treatment, Robert P. Miller, ed., *Chaucer: Sources and Backgrounds* (New York, 1977).

147.   Smith, ed., *Poems*, I, pp. xxx–xliv; Diebler, *Henrisone's Fabeldichtungen*; and works cited by Crowne, MacDonald, Jamieson, and Powell.

148.   See Crowne, 583–90; MacQueen, *Robert Henryson*, pp. 208–21; and Fox, *Poems*, pp. xli–l. For a summary of the issues, see Kindrick, *Robert Henryson*, pp. 59–65.

149.   Minnis, *Medieval Theory of Authorship*, pp. 98–112.

150.   Morse, pp. 231–48. For an example of how Andrew of Wyntoun used this same technique, see R. James Goldstein, "'For he wald vsurpe na fame': Andrew of Wyntoun's Use of the Modesty *Topos* and Literary Culture in Early Fifteenth-Century Scotland," *Scottish Literary Journal*, 14 (1987), 5–18.

151.   MacQueen, *Robert Henryson*, pp. 22–23.

152.   Roderick J. Lyall, "Did Poliziano Influence Henryson's *Orpheus and Erudices?*" *Forum for Modern Language Studies*, 15 (1979), 220–21.

Henryson, Quintilian, and the Renaissance

While periodic concepts such as "Renaissance" and "medieval" are inadequate to reflect the rich texture of rhetorical studies and verse in the fifteenth century, they are useful tools in evaluating Henryson's role as a transitional figure. Henryson's rhetoric clearly shows that he is a child of the Middle Ages. His reliance on the *ars poetriae*, the *ars dictaminis*, and the *ars praedicandi* demonstrates his debt to medieval patterns of organizing his language and subject matter. Yet MacQueen is also accurate in pointing out that he has a debt to the Renaissance[1]. His notion of Cresseid's redemption, to cite only one example, shows how he incorporates Renaissance concepts of sin and personal responsibility. His interest in aureation, limited though it is, reflects both the pulpit tradition in the Scottish Middle Ages and the developing sense of wordplay in the Renaissance.

Henryson's eclectic selection from a wide range of rhetorical techniques and ideas makes his verse an excellent "bridge" between the two periods in Scotland. On the one hand, he incorporates medieval ideas in ways not likely envisioned by the originators of the traditions on which he draws. His work demonstrates his ability to blend the *ars poetriae, ars dictaminis*, and *ars praedicandi* into a comprehensive approach to rhetorical situations. Especially as demonstrated in *The Morall Fabillis*, his use of the techniques from medieval rhetorical traditions eliminates pedantic tone and approach. On the other hand, it may also be possible to show the influence on his work of a major revival of interest in Quintilian during the Renaissance. Henryson could not have derived his entire knowledge of rhetoric from Quintilian. Both his social and educational background would have subjected him to the influences of medieval rhetorical traditions. Yet given his likely education and social background, it is certainly possible that he was exposed to the complete text of Quintilian as rediscovered in 1416. There may be in Henryson's verse both avenues of influence and basic use of the rhetorical principles of Quintilian's *Institutio oratoria*.

Dating the beginnings of the Renaissance in Scotland is problematic.[2] The revival of Quintilian's influence is one significant benchmark. In the earlier Middle Ages, the work seems to have had considerable impact. St. Jerome considers Quintilian "flumen Tullianem eloquentiae" and his work shows the effects of his use of Quintilian's ideas about education.[3] While Quintilian's influence persisted through the ninth century, there appears to be a lacuna in his impact during the tenth and eleventh centuries. Unfortunately, what finally reappeared was a highly edited version of the *Institutio oratoria*. Two versions circulated and both omitted vital sections of Quintilian's rhetorical theory. The first two books, dealing with Quintilian's ideas about pedagogy (including his position that Aesop's fables should be an early subject of study) survived generally as written. The sections lost were those where Quintilian provides detailed information on organization and style.

The losses are all the more remarkable because of Quintilian's pronounced morality. His notion of the rhetor as "vir bono docendi perito" provides an excellent basis for bridging pre-Augustinian distaste for all things pagan (including rhetoric) and Augustine's argument that clergy should use all means available to save souls, even though Augustine did not believe that there was an essential relationship between the moral qualities of the orator and the effectiveness of the discourse. With the survival of Quintilian's first two books some of the major influences of importance to Henryson's profession and art were in circulation even prior to Bracciolini's rediscovery of the complete manuscript. The moral emphasis of the first two books along with their approach to pedagogy might well have suited clerical purposes better than Quintilian's detailed study of rhetorical structure. Yet his practical and specific studies of rhetoric would also have suited the needs of the *ars praedicandi*, as well as the *ars dictaminis* and *ars notaria*. Quintilian's influence is attested throughout the period by other writers from Wibald de Corvey (first half of the twelfth century) to Alexander Neckham (early fifteenth century). The renaissance of the twelfth century provided a major impetus to the study of Quintilian. His influence in Chartres and Bec is well attested.[4] John of Salisbury notes that Baldwin gave Quintilian his closest attention in his *Liber de dictaminis*, and John's own writings reflect both theoretical and direct verbal influence of Quintilian's works. There are also direct parallels in the goals of education between John's *Metalogicon* and the first two books of Quintilian's *Institutio oratoria*. John makes the following comments about the education of the orator:

> Qui ergo ad philosophiam aspirat, apprehendat
> lectionem, doctrinam, et meditationem, cum exercitio

boni operis, nequando irasatur Dominus, et quod uidebatur habere, auferatur ab eo. Sed quia legendi uerbum equiuocum est, tam ad docentis et discentis exercitium quam ad occupationem per se scrutantis scripturas; alterum, id est quod inter doctorem et discipulum communicatur, (ut uerbo utamur Quintiliani) dicatur prelectio, alterum quod ad scrutinium meditantis accedit, lectio simpliciter appeletur Erbo, ab auctoritate eiusdem Quintiliani, in prelegendo gramaticus et illa quidem minora prestare debebit, ut partes orationis reddi sibi soluto uersu desideret, et pedum proprietates que debent in carminibus note esse. Deprehendat que barbara, que impropria aut alias contra legem loquendi composita.

One who aspires to become a philosopher should therefore apply himself to reading, learning, and meditation, as well as the performance of good works, lest the Lord become angry and take away what he seems to possess. The word "reading" is equivocal. It may refer either to the activity of teaching and being taught, or to the occupation of studying written things by oneself. Consequently the former, the intercommunication between teacher and learner, may be termed (to use Quintilian's term) the "lecture" (prelectio); the latter, or the scrutiny by the student, the "reading" (lectio), simply so called. On the authority of the same Quintilian, "the teacher of grammar should, in lecturing, take care of such details as to have his students analyze verses into their parts of speech, and point out the nature of the metrical feet which are to be noted in poems. He should, moreover, indicate and condemn whatever is barbarous, incongruous, or otherwise against the rules of composition."][5]

The impact of Quintilian seems equally clear in John's subsequent comment that "Illa autem que ceteris philosophie partibus preminet, Ethicam dico,. . ." [of all branches of learning, that which confers the greatest beauty is Ethics].[6] Yet the *Metalogicon* itself may explain part of the reason for Quintilian's subsequent lack of attention during the later thirteenth century and the fourteenth century. The length of Quintilian's complete work, in comparison with other available texts, might have been a significant problem. The advantage of Cicero's shorter text would have been obvious to teachers as well as those interested in a quick and practical approach to rhetorical arts.

The rediscovery of Quintilian's complete text of the *Institutio oratoria* by Poggio Bracciolini in 1416 marks the beginning of the Renaissance in rhetorical studies. The story itself contains a certain high drama. In the Autumn of 1416 Poggio visited St. Gall during a forced recess of the Council of Constance. In search of manuscripts, his hopes were dashed initially by the lack of literary and humanistic interest on the part of the monks. Yet he made a remarkable discovery, a complete manuscript of Quintilian's *Institutio oratoria*, in a most unlikely place. He revealed that it was found not in a library but at the bottom of a tower in a place suited to criminals.[7] Poggio immediately transcribed the manuscript, and news of its discovery spread rapidly as reflected in Aretino's letter to his friend Poggio while the latter was still engaged in study and transcription of the manuscript.[8]

There is adequate evidence to indicate that Henryson might have been exposed to Quintilian. First, if he was educated in Scotland, as Roderick Lyall contends,[9] the impact of Quintilian's rhetoric was transmitted to Scotland in the fifteenth century by at least one major Italian humanist, Aeneas Sylvius Piccolomini. Colson observes that his letter to the king of Bohemia (ca. 1450) is "full of Quintilian."[10] Colson then demonstrates how Aeneas Sylvius borrows directly from Quintilian most specifically in his ideas about education. As a papal legate, before he became Pope Pius II, Aeneas Sylvius visited Scotland during the reign of James I. His mission remains uncertain--he was either interested in making a peace between James and one of his bishops or he was intent on gaining James' enmity against the English.[11] It is clear from his commentaries on Scotland that he had wide access to the country. The direct degree of his influence is of course impossible to trace. Yet, in part because his mission placed him in direct touch with the king, he was likely introduced to the important politicians and intellectuals in the country. If he did not provide personally for the interest in Quintilian in Scotland, he could certainly have alerted the Scottish learned classes to the interest on the continent.

Other sources of influence on Henryson are also possible. The interaction between Scotland and the continent in the fifteenth century

would have provided early access to the developing Renaissance culture
of Italy and France. MacQueen has already shown how Henryson's
verse might show the impact of the Italian Quattrocento, especially in
the *Orpheus*.[12] Henryson's opportunities to become familiar with
Quintilian would have been especially numerous if he were educated in
Italy, as Jack believes.[13] There is evidence that, after 1416, the complete
text of Quintilian was rapidly promulgated in Italy. Poggio's discovery
was immediately communicated to Brunetto Latini, who considered it
a major scholarly event. Lorenzo Valla confesses that he almost knew
Quintilian by heart by 1457, and Seigel contends that Valla used him
to "carry out oratory's revenge on philosophy."[14] Valla, in fact, might
have been a major factor in the transmission of Quintilian to Scotland,
since his works are attested in Aberdeen University Ms. 222 which was
owned by Bishop William Elphinstone. Colson comments on how the
spread of Quintilian resulted in Platina's eulogy to Vittorino de Feltre
as a "Quintilian *redivivus*."[15] Scaglione observes that the humanists
"produced a plethora of rhetorical manuals" which rely on Quintilian,
Cicero, and Hermogenes.[16] The immediate impact of Quintilian's text
has been chronicled by Kennedy and Murphy in addition to Colson.[17]
Given the extensive interaction between Scotland and Italy, it would
hardly be surprising if Henryson had access to Quintilian's ideas
through direct interaction with continental scholars, in addition to any
influence exercised by Aeneas Sylvius. There is further evidence of
potential sources of contact in the widespread acceptance of Quintilian's
ideas about education.

Henryson's career as a schoolmaster might have provided another
opportunity for him to have been swept up in the general enthusiasm[18]
about Quintilian's work. In addition to the impact the rediscovery of his
text had on rhetoric, it also had a pronounced effect on educational
treatises. Even the mutilated text of Quintilian contained a significant
portion of his comments on the education of the citizen-orator. The texts
that circulated in the thirteenth and fourteenth centuries contained a
version of the first two books, which outline how Quintilian organizes
the early education of the potential orator.[19] The regimen he establishes
is a rigorous one. His curriculum includes not only literature and
grammar but also music, geometry, and acting, and he even shows a
tolerance for gymnastics. He has very specific advice on classroom
techniques and establishes a comprehensive goal for the preparation of
the citizen orator. Basing his argument on the assumption that rhetoric
is possibly the most comprehensive art of all, he asserts that:

. . . mores ante omnia oratori studiis erunt
excolendi atque omnis honesti iustique disciplina
pertractanda, sine qua nemo nec vir bonus esse nec
dicendi peritus potest. Nisi forte accedemus iis, qui
natura constare mores et nihil adiuvari disciplina
putant. . . . Ad illud sequens praevertar, ne dicendi
quidem satis peritum fore, qui non et naturae vim
omnem penitus perspexerit et mores praeceptis ac
ratione formarit.

[The orator must above all things devote his
attention to the formation of moral character and must
acquire a complete knowledge of all that is just and
honourable. For without this knowledge no one can be
either a good man or skilled in speaking, unless
indeed we agree with those who regard morality
as intuitive and as owing nothing to instruction
. . . . I will proceed to my next point, that no one will
achieve sufficent skill even in speaking, unless he
makes a thorough study of all the workings of nature
and forms his character on the precepts of philosophy
and the dictates of reason.][20]

Such comments on education are central to the work. Colson suggests
that "in Quintilian's own view, the strictly educational part [of the
Institutio] is subordinate."[21] In one sense, his assertion is correct, for the
Institutio is a comprehensive rhetoric which had an extensive impact on
rhetorical studies. However, Quintilian himself made a point of
emphasizing his pedagogical contribution. In fact, he asserts it is his
major goal:

In ceteris enim admiscere temptavimus aliquid
nitoris, non iactandi ingenii gratia (namque in id eligi
materia poterat uberior), sed ut hoc ipso adliceremus
magis iuventutem ad cognitionem eorum, quae
necessaria studiis arbitrabamur, si ducti iucunditate
aliqua lectionis libentius discerent ea,. . . .

[I have attempted to introduce a certain amount of
ornateness, not, I may say, to advertise my style (if I

had wished to do that, I could have chosen a more
fertile theme), but in order that I might thus do
something to lure our young men to make themselves
acquainted with those principles which I regarded as
necessary to the study of rhetoric: for I hoped that by
giving them something which was not unpleasant to
read I might induce a greater readiness to learn those
rules . . . .]

(III, i, 3)

He further states that he will not omit anything with pedagogical value
for fear that students will complain (II, x, 15). Other references to
education appear throughout the *Institutio oratoria,* as for instance in
Book III when he advises reading history as well as rhetoric and
comments to his younger readers that his admonitions are directed
specifically to them (III, viii, 70) and in Book VII where he comments
on "adolescentibus meis (meos enim semper adolescentes putabo)" [my
young students (and I call them mine, because the young student is
always dear to me] (VII, iii, 30). In addition to his continuing comments
to Marcellus Victorius about the education of his child and Quintilian's
own child, his mention at the beginning of Book IV of the fact that he
has been charged with the education of the child of Domitianus
Augustus and his lament over the death of his son at the beginning of
Book VI also demonstrate his commitment to nurturing the young. As
Preminger, Hardison, and Kerrane observe, all of his judgments on
literature in Book X are tempered by the value of a given work for
instruction.[22] His persistent emphasis on pedagogy reappears throughout
the work, culminating in Book X with additional comments on writing
and meditation.

Certainly his ideas with regard to education were given general
credibility in the Middle Ages. Particularly in the fifteenth century,
Colson records a number of treatises on education in Italy which could
have had an impact on Henryson in his role as a schoolmaster.[23] In
addition to Aeneas Sylvius, Colson notes that Guarino's *De ordine
docendi et studendi* adapts the methodology and organization of
Quintilian's work. The work was written about 1458 and reflects
traditions of Italian pedagogy for some years before its composition.
The *Vita civile* of Matteo Palmieri (ca. 1440) demonstrates Quintilian's
influence on the development of the citizen-orator. Henryson's wide
reading in other fields would suggest that he might well have absorbed

some of the ideas of Quintilian through these or similar sources. Moreover, his professional and literary interest in teaching moral lessons would have made these works doubly attractive.

If Henryson were influenced by the interest in Quintilian which occurred in the last eight decades of the fifteenth century, specifically what areas of contact are there between his verse and the *Institutio oratoria*? There are some areas of Quintilian's study of rhetoric that are so comprehensive as to offer little by way of specific discernible influence or even specific analogy with Henryson's verse. As Vickers observes about Quintilian, "the range of his work is so all-embracing that we find here almost everything we need to know."[24] Such is the case with three of the five major parts of rhetoric. Quintilian's approach to style, memory, and delivery, tantalizing though they may be, are so thorough and encyclopedic that they encompass all of Henryson's interests and more. In addition, there is the added problem of attempting to trace the influence of statements on memory and delivery without external evidence or a concrete statement of rhetorical principles from Henryson himself. For instance, Mary Carruthers has recently demonstrated the importance of Quintilian to the study of memory in the Middle Ages. Her methodology is based on written testimony from medieval writers or external accounts of their lives (as in the case of St. Thomas).[25] Without such documentation, it is virtually impossible to determine any writer's approach to this area of rhetorical study. Quintilian even notes problems about the legitimacy of memory and delivery in the overall structure of rhetorical studies, while simultaneously asserting their importance:

> Nec audiendi quidam, quorum est Albutius, qui tris modo primas esse partes volunt, quoniam memoria atque actio natura non arte contingant (quarum nos praecepta suo loco dabimus). . . .

> [Those (and Albutius is among them), who maintain that there are only three departments on the ground that memory and delivery (for which I shall give instructions in their proper place) are given us by nature not by art, may be disregarded. . . .]
>   (III, iii, 4)

Quintilian's advice to read widely in order to enhance memory certainly appears to be advice that Henryson accepted. His remarks on delivery provide additional valuable emphasis on audience appeal, associating particular gestures with impersonation and with their effect on the audience. No matter how much Quintilian's comments may coincide with Henryson's personality (as we know it) or his verse, the breadth of Quintilian's approaches would limit possible evaluations of influence in these two fields.

Because of the comprehensive nature of Quintilian's study of style, there is also little evidence of any specific influence in this area. His approach to style shows a great deal of audience sensitivity, constantly keeping the effect on the audience in the mind of the orator. He also outlines the major types of style which were later discussed by John of Garland and Geoffrey of Vinsauf, similarly pointing out that each type of style demands its appropriate subject matter (XI, i, 2-4). His catalogue of figures is relatively complete, and his definitions of essential figures such as the *exemplum* and personification would certainly fit Henryson's uses of them, as would his approach to allegory:

> Allegoria, quam inversionem interpretanur, aut aliud verbis aliud sensu ostendit aut etiam interim contrarium. . . . ex arcessitis verbis venit et intellectus ex propriis. Illud vero longe speciosissimum genus orationis, in quo trium permixta est gratia, similitudinis, allegoriae. . . .

> [*Allegory*, which is translated in Latin by *inversio*, either presents one thing in words and another in meaning, or else something absolutely opposed to the meaning of the words. . . . the ornamental element is provided by the metaphorical words and the meaning is indicated by those which are used literally. But far the most ornamental effect is produced by the artistic admixture of simile, metaphor and allegory. . . .]
> (VIII, vi, 44 and 48-49)

Quintilian expands this definition at length in Book VIII, vi, 44ff. He also notes the values of amplification and diminution, providing an ample and harmonious supplement to Geoffrey's statements on the

subject (III, 263-301). Quintilian's approach to style is so thorough and
so broad that it would be difficult to point out specific influences on
Henryson. Perhaps, however, the comprehensive nature of Quintilian's
approach would suggest his potential value for the poet.

Other areas of the *Institutio* are more fertile. A complete study of
reflexes of Quintilian's *Institutio oratoria* in Henryson's verse would
require another volume, but a few examples should make the point that
significant analogies exist. In addition to his interest in Quintilian's
doctrines on education, Henryson might have been influenced by
Quintilian's notions of invention, and organization. He would also have
had to wrestle with Quintilian's concept of the essential morality of the
orator. The latter issue may deserve consideration first because of its
primacy in the nature of Quintilian's rhetoric. He boldly asserts that
"neque enim esse oratorem nisi bonum virum iudico..." [no one can be
a true orator unless he is also a good man . . .] adding perhaps
somewhat preciously, "et fieri etiamsi potest nolo" [and, even if he
could be, I would not have it so] (I, ii, 3), a perspective he reinforces
in his comments in Book XII, i. Leaving apart for the moment
Quintilian's narrowly stipulative definition, his approach to the
relationship between oratory and morality apparently stands in contrast
to Augustine's. The Augustinian attitude toward rhetoric indicates that
even a moral reprobate can be successful if the ultimate result of his
discourse is the salvation of the auditor. Quintilian attacks this argument
head on, observing that it was common in his times:

> Ante omnia, quid sit rhetorice. Quae finitur
> quidem varie, sed quaestionem habet duplicem, aut
> enim de qualitate ipsius rei aut de comprehensione
> verborum dissensio est. Prima atque praecipua
> opinionum circa hoc differentia, quod alii malos
> quoque viros posse oratores dici putant; alii, quorum
> nos sententiae accedimus, nomen hoc artemque, de
> qua loguimur, bonis demum tribui volunt. Eorum
> autem, qui dicendi facultatem a maiore ac magis
> expetenda vitae laude secernunt, quidam rhetoricen
> vim tantum, quidam scientiam sed non virtutem,
> quidam usum, quidam artem quidem sed a scientia et
> virtute diiunctam, quidam etiam pravitatem quandam
> artis, id est *kakotexvíav*, nominaverunt. Hi fere aut in
> persuadendo aut in dicendo apte ad persuadendum
> positum orandi munus sunt arbitrati. Id enim fieri

potest ab eo quoque, qui vir bonus non sit. Est igitur
frequentissimus finis, rhetoricen esse vim persuadendi.

[The first question which confronts us is "What is
rhetoric?" Many definitions have been given; but the
problem is really twofold. For the dispute turns either
on the quality of the thing itself or on the meaning of
the words in which it is defined. The first and chief
disagreement on the subject is found in the fact that
some think that even bad men may be called orators,
while others, of whom I am one, restrict the name of
orator and the art itself to those who are good. Of
those who divorce eloquence from that yet fairer and
more desirable title to renown, a virtuous life, some
call rhetoric merely a power, some a science, but not
a virtue, some a practice, some an art, though they
will not allow the art to have anything in common
with science or virtue, while some again call it a
perversion of art or kakotexvia. These persons have as
a rule held that the task of oratory lies in persuasion
or speaking in a persuasive manner: for this is within
the power of a bad man no less than a good. Hence
we get the common definition of rhetoric as the
power of persuading.]

(II, xv, 1-3)

That ancient orators also subsumed this argument should hardly be
surprising, considering the other arguments against the art of rhetoric
that both Cicero and Quintilian felt obliged to refute. Among them were
the notions that rhetoric is not an art because it has no subject matter,
that rhetoricians were not taught but born, and that there were no
established goals for rhetoric.[26]

Henryson and Chaucer shared approaches in untangling the knotty
question of the speaker's integrity and trying to reconcile Augustine's
realism with Quintilian's ideals. Chaucer's "Pardoner's Tale" vividly
illustrates one solution to the problem. No matter what one may think
of the pardoner as a character, there is no doubt that the tale he tells is
a perfect *exemplum*,[27] illustrating perhaps ideally Quintilian's notion that
rhetoric is "action." Yet Chaucer's Pardoner is hardly successful as
dramatically attested by the epilogue of his tale. In the broader context

of the pilgrimage, he is revealed for the scoundrel he is. Henryson's reaction to this rhetorical dilemma shows the same dual approach to the dramatic context. On the one hand, few of his characters ultimately seem to be effective rhetoricians if they are not morally good creatures. The judgment about rhetorical effectiveness depends as much on the assessment of the audience as does the evaluation of Chaucer's "Pardoner's Tale." On the other hand, Henryson does indeed have characters of questionable moral character who are effective rhetoricians within the narrative framework of a given poem. Perhaps the outstanding example is his fox in *The Morall Fabillis*. Lowrence is able to convince his stronger colleague, the wolf, to folly in a variety of fables. In the sense that he is able to convince the wolf to descend into a well or examine a mare's hoof for a non-existent respite, he is effective in achieving his desired ends in the context of his tales. Yet, his speeches are not effective with the reader of the tales. Henryson establishes enough signals in his moral and narrative framework to alert the reader that sophistry is afoot. Lowrence is hardly an admirable character, and his arguments are acceptable, for the most part, only because he works his wiles on the wolf, a figure who inspires no sympathy. "The Trial of the Fox" illustrates vividly the unsavory fate that befalls such tricksters.

Other characters cut from the same mold are the cock in "The Cock and the Jasp" and the frog in "The Paddock and the Mouse." The essential problem about the untrustworthiness of the cock's evaluation of the jewel he discovers has previously been outlined. While the cock's feeling that the jewel is unsuitable to his needs reflects a lack of broader understanding of the essentials of life, Henryson's comment on his point of view in the *moralitas* is indeed jolting to many modern readers. The same rhetorical issue reappears in "The Paddock and the Mouse." Attacking the superficial nature of "appearance," the Paddock's invitation to the mouse to ride across the stream on his back is a similarly defective kind of rhetoric:

> 'With my twa feit,' quod scho, 'lukkin and braid,
> In steid off airis, I row the streme full styll,
> And thocht the brym be perrillous to waid,
> Baith to and fra I swyme at my awin will.
> I may not droun, for quhy my oppin gill
> Deuoidis ay the watter I resaiff:
> Thairfoir to droun, forsuith, na dreid I haif.'

....
For fair thingis oftymis ar fundin faikin;
The blaberyis, thocht thay be sad off hew,
Ar gadderit vp quhen primeros is forsakin;
The face may faill to be the hartis takin;
Thairfoir I find this scripture in all place:
'Thow suld not iuge ane man efter his face.'

'Thocht I vnhailsum be to luke vpon,
I haue na wyt; quhy suld I lakkit be?
Wer I als fair as iolie Absolon,
I am no causer off that
This difference in forme and qualitie
Almychtie God hes causit dame Nature
To prent and sent in euerilk creature.'

                                (ll. 2812-18, 2834-46)

The frog has no intention of delivering the mouse to the other side, and careful analysis of his arguments in the context of medieval ideas will make his intention clear. However, his arguments are effective with the foolish mouse in the context of the fable. Both the cock and frog are hardly landable creatures: one is ignorant and the other malicious. Yet, in one sense these characters and others succeed as orators. They show that Henryson accepted the Augustinian thesis that even ethically unacceptable creatures could be effective rhetoricians in a limited context. The fox does indeed persuade the wolf to take foolish chances. The cock seems to persuade certain audiences to accept his perspective on the value of the jewel until Henryson intrudes on his rhetoric to point the way to salvation in the *moralitas*. The frog persuades the mouse to accept his crafty (but illogical and self-destructive) offer to ferry the mouse across the stream.[28] From one viewpoint all of these characters have been effective in their pleas. Some critics of *The Testament of Cresseid* would also contend that the appealing nature of her lament and challenge to the gods might show how yet another "unredeemed" character can exploit the emotions of the audience.[29]

However, the ultimate success of these characters depends on Henryson's sense of audience reaction and his control of his narrative framework. Even if they are successful within the closed world of their fables, the fox and the frog are not admirable characters from the reader's perspective. The situation with regard to Cresseid and the cock is less certain. In Cresseid's case, the ultimate judgment is less harsh. She is an evolving character, and her attack on the gods in lines 125-40 is misguided, reflecting an immature approach to life. Yet Henryson clearly intends that her misguided efforts be finally understood by the reader for what they are, steps in the development of her maturity. After line 574, she has gained new wisdom, and her final lament is to be trusted as a genuine expression of her feelings and a statement of the major themes of the poem. As noted in Chapter Four, the cock is a sincere but untrustworthy source for his audience. Henryson has included a number of signals of the cock's false pride to alert the reader that his comments are not to be trusted. For the reader who heeds those foreshadowings, the *moralitas* of the tale does not come as a surprise.

For dramatic purposes, Henryson does accept Augustine's premise that a bad person can be an effective orator, but he seems to find an accommodation with Quintilian's perspective as well. Quintilian's definition, after all, is clearly personally stipulative. Indeed even his over-insistence on his own point of view may suggest that Quintilian himself realized that it did not completely reflect reality. In the *Institutio* there are even stronger indications that Quintilian realized that his ideal did not always obtain in the imperfect world in which oratory was exercised. He is well aware of the need for audience analysis and the need to use subtlety and diplomacy (perhaps even bordering on mendacity) to achieve the desired ends. He observes, for instance:

> Et honesta quidem honestis suadere facillimum est; si vero apud turpes recta obtinere conabimur, ne videamur exprobrare diversam vitae sectam, cavendum. Et animus deliberantis non ipsa honesti natura, quam ille non respicit, permovendus, sed laude, vulgi opinione, et si parum proficiet haec vanitas, secutura ex his utilitate, aliquanto vero magis obiiciendo aliquos, si divesa fecerint, metus.

> [It is an easy task to recommend an honourable course to honourable men, but if we are attempting to keep men of bad character to the paths of virtue, we must take care not to seem to upbraid a way of life unlike our own. The minds of such an audience are not to be moved by discoursing on the nature of

virtue, which they ignore, but by praise, by appeals to popular opinion, and if such vanities are of no avail, by demonstration of the true advantage that will accrue from such a policy, or more effectively perhaps by pointing out the appalling consequences that will follow the opposite policy.]

(III, viii, 38-40)

Quintilian's argument provides a basis for briefly discussing the types of appeal that may be used depending on the nature of the audience. While he continues to insist on the importance of ethics in using these appeals, he recognizes the need to use devices which may be based on less than completely honest or ethical approaches, commenting that sometimes it is even necessary to deceive the judge "et variis artibus subeundus" (IV, v. 5). He extends this argument considerably in Book XII, where he considers the plight of a lawyer who has been assigned to defend a person who is guilty as charged:

Pertractare enim, quomodo aut pro falsis aut etiam pro iniustis aliquando dicatur, non est inutile, vel propter hoc solum, ut ea facilius et deprehendamus et refellamus; quemadmodum remedia melius adhibebit, cui nota quae nocent fuerint.

[For it is by no means useless to consider how at times we should speak in defence of falsehood or even of injustice, if only for this reason, that such an investigation will enable us to detect and defeat them with the greater ease, just as the physician who has a thorough knowledge of all that can injure the health will be all the more skillful in the prescription of remedies.]

(XII, i, 34)

Moreover, in his discussion of proof in Book V, vii, he gives advice on questioning witnesses which generally relates to effective rhetoric instead of ethical rhetoric or the search for truth. George Kennedy takes special note of the moral dilemmas of Quintilian's approach to oratory, comparing his work with that of Cicero and noting particular social conditions which formed his views.[30] Kennedy helps to explain some of

the apparent contradictions between Quintilian's precepts and his
practical advice, emphasizing his realism in approaching political
oratory. Some of the contradictory or "realistic" elements of Quintilian's
work caused Voltaire to describe the *Institutio* as a work on "Lying as
a Fine Art for those fully conscious of their own rectitude."[31] This kind
of understanding of the *realpolitik* of oratory would have provided
adequate latitude for Henryson's narrative needs. Like Chaucer,
Henryson could not ignore the fact that demagogues and charlatans were
often effective orators, at least for a limited audience and a limited
period of time. But, like Quintilian, he believed that no evil person
would ultimately prevail through false rhetoric, as reflected by his
narrative ironies (in the case of the fox, the paddock, and the cock) and
his sense of character evolution (Cresseid). Through the subtleties of his
art, he ensured that the audience was alerted to the character of his
speakers. His characters, like Chaucer's Pardoner, may be effective in
a narrow context, but once the context expands, their moral deficiencies
become apparent. In summary, while Henryson accepts Augustinian
realism about the ethics of rhetoric, the moral nature of his art requires
that he encourage his audience to agree with Quintilian in the longer
perspective.

Henryson could have learned much from Quintilian's approaches
to invention. As noted above, Quintilian provides a basis for audience
analysis which would have dovetailed neatly with what Henryson would
have learned from the medieval arts of rhetoric. Book XI, on delivery,
gives special attention to the impression certain gestures and
mannerisms will have on an audience. Quintilian focuses on matching
voice and gesture to subject, making some general assumptions about
how certain factors will uniformly affect audiences. In Book III, he
comments quite specifically on the need for audience analysis and
ethical appeal. Throughout his section on *divisio* (Books IV-VII), he
comments on the importance of making the proper impression on the
audience in every part of discourse. He observes, for instance, in
discussing the *exordium* that it is vitally important to make the judge
sufficiently docile to receive instructions (IV, i, 34) and he makes a
special point of the impact of the conclusion on the audience:

> Est igitur utrisque commune, conciliare sibi,
> avertere ab adversario iudicem, concitare adfectus et
> componere. Et brevissimum quidem hoc praeceptum
> dari utrique parti potest, ut totas causae suae vires

orator ponat ante oculos; et cum viderit, quid
invidiosum, favorabile, invisum, miserabile aut sit in
rebus aut videri possit, ea dicat, quibus, si iudex esset,
ipse maxime moveretur.

[On the other hand in the peroration we have to
consider what the feelings of the judge will be when
he retires to consider his verdict, for we shall have no
further opportunity to say anything and cannot any
longer reserve arguments to be produced later. It is
therefore the duty of both parties to seek to win the
judge's goodwill and to divert it from their opponent,
as also to excite or assuage his emotions. And the
following brief rule may be laid down for the
observation of both parties, that the orator should
display the full strength of his case before the eyes of
the judge, and, when he has made up his mind what
points in his case actually deserve or may seem to
deserve to excite envy, goodwill, dislike or pity,
should dwell on those points by which he himself
would be most moved were he trying the case.]
(VI, i, 10-11)

These kinds of comments also inform Quintilian's views on style in
Book XII. His analysis would have provided a comprehensive overview
of the questions which medieval rhetoricians also considered.
Especially in Henryson's use of the *ars dictaminis* and the *ars notaria*,
Quintilian's notions of audience analysis would have served the Scottish
poet well.

Quintilian's inventory of *topoi* would also have provided Henryson
with the tools that he needed in his rhetoric. Particularly in Henryson's
use of the deliberative and forensic rhetoric of the *ars dictaminis* and
the *ars notaria*, Henryson employs virtually all of Quintilian's
techniques. Specific parallels might derive from Henryson's interest in
legal rhetoric, which would have been another reason for him to have
studied Quintilian. Among other *topoi*, Quintilian gives special attention
to comparison, definition, contradiction, the greater and the lesser,
consequence, and expediency, along with past fact-future fact.
Comparison is a basic *topos* of political fables such as "The Two Mice"
and "The Wolf and the Lamb." Definition is the basic *topos* of, among

other poems, "The Garmont of Gud Ladeis," in which Henryson
attempts to define feminine virtue. Contradiction forms the basis for a
number of poems, including "The Tale of the Cock and the Jasp," and
all of his debate poems. The *topos* of the greater and the lesser plays a
central role in the *Orpheus* and "The Tale of the Wolf and the Wether,"
among others. Consequence is certainly a basic *topos* of all the fables
and *The Testament of Cresseid*. Expediency is a central *topos* of "The
Paddock and the Mouse."

Quintilian's use of these *topoi* in legal arguments would also have
been of value to Henryson. Some points of reference are found in "The
Tale of the Sheep and the Dog," which illustrates Henryson at his most
legalistic, and *The Testament of Cresseid*, which illustrates Henryson's
use of an interesting twist on one of Quintilian's legal *topoi*. Henryson
makes particular use of contradiction and past fact-future fact in "The
Tale of the Sheep and the Dog." The basic point of contention is
whether in fact the sheep did indeed receive "certaine breid" from the
dog. The dog's basic contention is that he did, while the sheep flatly
contradicts the dog's assertion. This kind of flat "yes/no" assertion is
treated in great detail in Quintilian's legal *topoi*, and Henryson has used
it to good effect in a combination of common legal *topoi*. Also of
special interest in Quintilian's analysis of the *topoi* is his discussion of
the *topos* of "competence" in legal rhetoric:

> Nec ignoro fuisse quosdam, qui translationem in
> rationali quoque genere ponerent hoc modo, *hominem
> occidi, iussus ab imperature. Dona templi cogenti
> tyranno dide. Deserui tempestatibus, fluminibus,
> valetudine impeditus.* Id est, non per me stetit, sed per
> illud.

> [I am aware that there have been some who
> placed *competence* among *rational bases*, using as
> illustrations cases such as, "I killed a man under
> orders from my general," "I gave the votive offerings
> in a temple to a tyrant under compulsion," "I deserted
> owing to the fact that storms or floods or ill health
> prevented me from rejoining." That is to say it was
> not due to me, but some external cause.]

> (III, vi 78)

This particular *topos* appears in an unlikely setting in Henryson's poetry. It is the impetus to Cresseid's trial by the parliament of the gods. In lamenting her case immediately after her return from the Greek court, she attempts to excuse her actions:

> And on hir kneis bair fell doun in hy;
> opon Venus and Cupide angerly
> Scho cryit out, and said on this same wyse,
> 'Allace, that euer I maid ʒow sacrifice!
>
> ʒe gaue me anis ane deuine responsaill
> That I suld be the flour of luif in Troy;
> Now an I maid ane vnworthie outwaill,
> And all in cair translatit is my ioy.
> Quha sall me gyde? Quha sall me now conuoy,
> Sen I fra Diomeid and nobill Troylus
> Am clene excludit, as abiect odious?
>
> 'O fals Cupide, is nane to wyte bot thow
> And thy mother, of lufe the blind goddes!
> ʒe causit me alwayis vnderstand and trow
> The seid of lufe was sawin in my face,
> And ay grew grene throw ʒour supplie and grace.
> Bot now, allace, that seid with froist is slane,
> And I fra luifferis left, and all forlane.'
>
> (ll. 123-40)

Cresseid's attack on the gods is based on her belief that she was acting with their approval. After all, Venus and Cupid led her to understand that she was to be "the flour of luif in Troy." If she has erred, the fault is not hers but theirs. Ironically, her anger in her plea of "competence" regarding her own fate sparks the trial which results in her punishment through leprosy. An Edwin D. Craun has observed, "she is so threatened by the loss of the life she has known and so mistrustful of her 'awin gods' that she commits an irreparable act of injustice which condemns her to a leper's fetid life."[32] Henryson's use of this kind of *topos* to instigate a trial setting is directly parallel to the *topos* as Quintilian describes it.

A final example of Quintilian's approaches to invention which could have been useful to Henryson also involves legal rhetoric. In

Book III, Quintilian enters into his discussion of legal bases a particular distinction which Henryson found useful in conjunction with the *ars notaria*:

> Cadent ergo in unam controversiam vel specialiter duo legitimi status scripti et voluntatis et syllogismos et praeterea finitio, vel tres illi, qui natura soli sunt, coniectura in scripto et voluntate, qualitas in syllogismo, et, quae per se est aperta, finitio.

> [Thus in one case we shall have either two special *legal bases*, namely the *letter of the law* and *intention*, with the *syllogism* and also *definition*, or those three which are really the only *bases* strictly so called, *conjecture* as regards the *letter of the law* and *intention*, *quality* in the *syllogism*, and *definition*, which needs no explanation.]

(III, vi, 103)

Quintilian considers this point of law sufficiently important to comment on it throughout the *Institutio oratoria*, and he devotes a whole chapter to it in Book VII, where he defines the problem in greater detail. While this distinction plays a role in the scriptural concept of law, Quintilian's discussion of specific examples would have been doubly valuable to Henryson.

Henryson makes use of this definitional theme in a variety of the fables. In "The Wolf and the Lamb," for instance, it is the basis for the lamb's appeal for due process (ll. 2678-92). The wolf, as previously noted, ignores the appeal and proceeds to devour the lamb. In particular, it also appears as the central *topos* for "The Tale of the Fox, the Wolf, and the Husbandman." In this fable, a farmer having trouble with his oxen in the field shouts in anger to his team, "The volff . . . mot haue ȝou all at anis!" (l. 2344). The wolf overhears this angry oath and, biding his time, plans to pursue his gift. In the meantime, the oxen begin to work more cooperatively, and the farmer makes good progress. On his way home, he is stopped by the wolf, demanding his team of oxen (as technically deeded to him by the letter of the law) from the farmer. The farmer appeals to the spirit of the law (fairness) in a reverse "consumer's rights" argument and, like the lamb, makes an appeal to due process:

> 'Schir,' quod the husband, 'ane man may say in greif,
> And syne ganesay fra he auise and se.
> I hecht to steill; am I thairfoir ane theif?
> God forbid, schir, all hechtis suld haldin be.
> Gaif I my hand or oblissing,' quod he,
> 'Or haue ȝe witnes or writ for to schau?
> Schir, reif me not, bot go and seik the lau.'
>
> (ll. 2273-79)

The farmer pleads excess emotion as a motivation for his comments and argues that a person may legitimately "ganesay" under such circumstances. He also makes his own appeal to the letter of the law, asking if the wolf has a witness. His concluding exhortation to the wolf will have ironic consequences. The wolf continues to insist on the letter of the law. He couches his argument in terms of the spirit of the law, even quoting a proverb:

> 'Carll,' quod the volff, 'ane lord, and he be leill,
> That schrinkis for schame, or doutis to be repruuit--
> His sau is ay als sickker as his seill.
> Fy on the leid that is not leill and lufit!
> Thy argument is fals, and eik contrufit,
> For it is said in prouerb: "But lawte
> All vther vertewis ar nocht worth ane fle."'
>
> (ll. 2280-86)

The wolf challenges the farmer's very integrity by questioning whether he is "a man of his word." The farmer's response continues to make an appeal to the spirit of the law, also making an appeal in matters of procedure by reiterating his call for a witness.

> 'Schir,' said the husband, 'remember of this
> thing: Ane leill man is not tane at halff ane taill.
> I may say and ganesay; I am na king.
> Quhair is ȝour witnes that hard I hecht thame haill?'
>
> (ll. 2287-90)

His comment "I am na king" may be an ironic comment on how class differences also make a difference in the application of the law. In response to the farmer's request for a witness, the wolf produces the fox, but, with the agreement of the farmer, the fox offers himself as a judge to give "sentence finall" (1. 2302). He then approaches the farmer about a bribe, commenting ironically on the legal system and the wolf's stinginess. Once assured of a bribe of six or seven hens, he then proceeds to trick the wolf into believing that his claim will be compensated by a large cheese, which is actually the reflection of moon in the bottom of a well. Offering to go down himself to retrieve the cheese, the fox persuades the wolf to descend into the well in pursuit of his "compensation." The tale ends with the wolf in water up to his waist in the bottom of the well and with a sense that the spirit of justice and the law are well-served. The tale is not an outstanding example of Henryson's use of the *ars notaria* (particularly when compared with "The Sheep and the Dog"), but its narrative structure is organized at least in part around the question of the letter versus the spirit of the law, as Quintilian describes it. If indeed Henryson were introduced to Quintilian as a young notarial student, these particular *topoi* would have offered fertile ground for his imagination.

Other *topoi* could be adduced throughout Henryson's work. Given his use of figures such as the *exemplum*, the beast fable, and personification, which all are used in basically panegyric discourse, he would have found Quintilian's remarks on the *topos* of "praise and blame" to be of particular value:

> Ut desiderat autem laus, quae negotiis adhibetur, probationem, sic etiam illa, quae ostentationi componitur, habet interim aliquam speciem probationis. . . . Quae materia praecipue quidem in deos et homines cadit, est tamen et aliorum animalium, etiam carentium anima.

> However, just as panegyric applied to practical matters requires proof, so too a certain semblance of proof is at time required by speeches composed entirely for display. . . . This form of oratory is directed in the main to the praise of gods and men, but may occasionally be applied to the praise of animals or even of inanimate objects.
>
> (III, vii, 4 and 6)

Henryson's doctrinal bent is such that he was doubtless influenced by the *ars praedicandi*, but Quintilian's comprehensive description of this *topos* would have provided a basis for Henryson's use of it in *The Testament of Cresseid* and the *Orpheus*, as well as *The Morall Fabillis*. Quintilian's observation that the *topos* of praise and blame may be applied to animals and even inanimate objects would certainly have extended it sufficiently broadly to make provision for the figures of the *ars praedicandi*. He extends the value of this *topos* in his discussion of simile, example, and analogy, key elements of the art of preaching, in his comments on the proof (V, xi, 5-44).

Henryson could have learned some basic elements of *divisio* from Quintilian's *Institutio*. In this area, there are fewer specific parallels in part because of Quintilian's argumentative and expository framework, but nonetheless Henryson might have made good use of reading Quintilian, especially in some of his poems which rely heavily on dictaminal and notarial rhetoric. Kennedy observes that Quintilian's view of arrangement "leads him into some repetition and confusion."[33] There is repetition in Quintilian's insistence on his pedagogical goals, his emphasis on drama and audience sensitivity, and even his approach to individual parts of rhetoric, but Quintilian's exhaustive review of the subject would certainly have made him useful for the student of legal rhetoric or the poet. Illustration of a few potential areas of influence may help to demonstrate how Henryson could have incorporated Quintilian's approach to organization in his poems. In his approach to the *exordium*, Quintilian shows his sensitivity to the fine arts, noting that the beginning of discourse has a great deal in common with an introductory piece of music designed "to win the favour of the audience" (IV, i, 1-3). This emphasis on audience appeal continues throughout his discussion of the principles of organization. He often couches his remarks in terms of the disposition of the "judge" but the term is also extended to juries, and he shows interest in this type of audience analysis in every part of discourse. He emphasizes how important it is to render the audience "benevolum, attentum, docilem" (IV, i, 5). Quintilian's language might be compared with that of Alexander of Ashby who comments in his *De modo praedicandi* on the need to render the audience "dociles, benivoles, et attentos."[34] There is also a parallel with Robert of Basevorn in Quintilian's emphasis on winning good-will. Quintilian comments on the importance of winning over the audience as an initial task in the oratorical process:

Causa principii nulla alia est, quam ut auditorem,
quo sit nobis in ceteris partibus accommodatior,
praeparemus. Id fieri tribus maxime rebus inter
auctores plurimos constat, si benevolum, attentum,
docilem facerimus, non quia esta non per totam
actionem sint custodienda, sed quia initiis praecipue
necessaria, per quae in animum iudicis, ut procedere
ultra possimus, admittimur.

[The sole purpose of the exordium is to prepare
our audience in such a way that they will be disposed
to lend a ready ear to the rest of our speech. The
majority of authors agree that this is best effected in
three ways, by making the audience well-disposed,
attentive and ready to receive instruction. I need
hardly say that these aims have to be kept in view
throughout the whole speech, but they are especially
necessary at the commencement, when we gain
admission to the mind of the judge in order to
penetrate still further.]

(IV, i, 5)

Quintilian even notes that there are certain "tricks" for gaining good-will
(IV, i, 33), illustrating them in detail for the potential orator. While he
does not suggest that it is a separate section of discourse as Robert
does, he demonstrates its importance for the exordium in a way that
would have coincided well with Henryson's training in the *ars
praedicandi.*

Quintilian maintains an emphasis on audience appeal in all parts of
discourse. He also emphasizes another element which would have been
of interest to the creative artist--impersonation. He first treats
impersonation under invention, commenting:

Ideoque longe mihi difficillimae videntur
prosopopoeiae, in quibus ad reliquum suasoriae
laborem accedit etiam personae difficultas. Namque
idem illud aliter Caesar, aliter Cicero, aliter Cato
suadere debebit. Utilissima vero haec exercitatio, vel
quod duplicis est operis, vel quod poetis quoque aut

historiarum futuris scriptoribus plurimum confert
Verum et oratoribus necessaria.

[Consequently I regard *impersonation* as the most
difficult of tasks, imposed as it is in addition to the
other work involved by a deliberative theme. For the
same speaker has on one occasion to impersonate
Caesar, on another Cicero or Cato. But it is a most
useful exercise because it demands a double effort
and is also of the greatest use to future poets and
historians, while for orators of course it is absolutely
necessary.]

(III, viii, 49)

He continues to treat impersonation under arrangement, observing, for
instance, about the statement of fact:

Credibilis autem erit narratio ante omnia, si prius
consuluerimus nostrum animum, ne quid naturae
dicamus adversum, deinde si causas ac rationes factis
praeposuerimus, non omnibus sed de quibus quaeritur,
si personas convenientes iis, quae facta credi volemus.
. . . Est autem quidam et ductus rei credibilis, qualis
in comoediis etiam et in mimis.

[The *statement of fact* will be credible, if in the
first place we take care to say nothing contrary to
nature, secondly if we assign reasons and motives for
the facts on which the inquiry turns (it is unnecessary
to do so with the subsidiary facts as well), and if we
make the characters of the actors in keeping with the
facts we desire to be believed. . . . It is also possible
to treat the subject in such a way as to give it an air
of credibility, as is done in comedy and farce.]

(IV, ii, 52-53)

Given traditional wisdom that the statement of fact can be a dangerous
place for any intrusions on objectivity, Quintilian's emphasis on the
value of impersonation seems all the more remarkable. This attention to
the dramatic nature of rhetoric continues throughout his analysis of

divisio. He even takes special note of the importance of impersonation
in developing the emotional appeal in the peroration (VI, i, 25-26). His
perspective is based on a more general approach to the dramatic nature
of pleading. His remarks would certainly have been attractive to the
burgeoning poet, even though they may bring into doubt how much
sincerity is to be expected of the *vir bono* who is the proper orator:

> Declamaturus autem maxime positas in adfectibus
> causas propriis personis debet induere. Hi sunt enim,
> qui mandari non possunt, nec eadem vi profertur
> alieni animi qua sui motus.

> [When we are going to deliver a declamation on
> a theme that turns largely on its emotional features,
> we must give it a dramatic character suited to the
> persons concerned. For emotions are not transferable
> at will, nor can we give the same forcible expression
> to another man's emotions that we should give to our
> own.]
>
> (IV, i, 47)

All of these comments reflect not only an acceptance of creativity in
characterization, but actually provide helpful advice to the poet as well
as the lawyer.[35] Henryson is certainly able to create and empathize with
a variety of characters—a "fallen woman," the father of music, a variety
of scoundrels including his fox and wolf, and heroes derived from the
lowest as well as the highest classes of society. Quintilian's continued
emphasis on these dramatic elements throughout his approach to
organization demonstrates how much importance he feels impersonation
merits even in the courts of law.

Quintilian's remarks on logic have a special relevance for
Henryson's use of argument in his dramatic settings. In Book IV he
suggests a structure for the proof based on mini-arguments similar to
those espoused by Alexander of Ashby and the *Rhetorica ad
Herrenium*:

> Quae vero turba valebunt, diducenda erunt, ut,
> quod paulo ante dixi: *Heres eras et pauper et magna
> pecunia appellabaris a creditoribus et offenderas et
> mutaturum tabulas testamenti sciebas.*

[On the other hand those arguments which rely on their cumulative force must be analyzed individually, as for example in the case which I cited above: 'You were the heir, you were poor and were summoned by your creditors for a large sum: you had offended him and knew that he intended to change his will.']

(V, xiii, 12-13)

Quintilian's recognition of the force of such individual arguments is likely related to his approach to impersonation and sensitivity to human speech. In Book VI, commenting on debate, he further reinforces the notion that arguments and refutations must be arranged to meet the demands of personality and circumstance (VI, iv, 2). He eschews absolute rules, asserting that circumstances vary too much to make them useful. He argues that the basic criterion for argument is common sense, which "cannot be taught." Quintilian's general flexibility in *divisio* is fully revealed in Book VII, x, where he explains his own method of approaching a case. While his remarks have implications extending beyond the proof and refutation, they illustrate the full impact of personality and circumstance in thinking about organization:

Illa enim potentissima est, quaeque vere dicitur oeconomica totius causae dispositio, quae nullo modo constitui nisi velut in re praesente potest: ubi adsumendum prooemium, ubi omittendum, ubi utendum expositione continua, ubi partita, ubi ab initiis incipiendum, ubi more Homerico e mediis vel ultimis, ubi omnino non expondendum, quando a nostris, quando ab adversariorum propositionibus incipiamus, quando a firmissimis probationibus, quando a levioribus; qua in causa praeponendae prooemiis quaestiones, qua praeparatione praemuniendae, quid iudicis animus accipere possit statim dictum, quo paulatim deducendus, singulis an universis opponenda refutatio, reservandi perorationi an per totam actionem diffundeni adfectus, de iure prius an de aequitate dicendum, anteacta crimina an de quibus iudicium est prius obiicere vel diluere conveniat; si multiplices causae erunt, quis ordo

faciendus, quae testimonia tabulaeve cuiusque generis
in actione recitandae, quae reservandae.

[For the most effective, and what is justly styled
most *economical* arrangement of a case as a whole, is
that which cannot be determined except when we
have the specific facts before us. It consists in the
power to determine when the *exordium* is necessary
and when it should be omitted; when we should make
our statement of facts continuous, and when we
should subdivide it; when we should begin at the very
beginning, when, like Homer, start at the middle or
the end; when we should omit the statement of facts
altogether; when we should begin by dealing with the
arguments advanced by our opponents, and when with
our own; when we should place the strongest proofs
first and when the weakest; in what cases we should
prefix *questions* to the *exordium*, and what
preparation is necessary to pave the way for these
questions; what arguments the judge will accept at
once, and to what he requires to be led by degrees;
whether we should refute our opponent's arguments
as a whole or in detail; whether we should reserve
emotional appeals for the peroration or distribute them
throughout the whole speech; whether we should first
advance (or refute) charges as to past offences or the
charges connected with the actual trial; or, again, if
the case is complicated, what order we should adopt,
what evidence or documents of any kind should be
read out in the course of our speech, and what
reserved for a later stage.]

(VII, x, 11-13)

These remarks on the proof and refutation would provide reinforcement
for Henryson's dramatic structuring of arguments as previously
outlined. Such structuring is an important principle of artistic realism,
reflecting ordinary human discourse outside the strictly formal settings
of law courts or debates. Henryson might have learned it from a number
of sources, including his reading of Chaucer or other poetic sources.

Yet Quintilian offers a classical source current in Henryson's time from which the principle could have been derived.

In a general way, Quintilian's rhetoric also makes provision for Henryson's use of the *moralitas*. In commenting on types of emotional appeals in the peroration, he observes the basic distinction between *ethos* and *pathos*:

> Horum autem, sicut antiquitus traditum accepimus, duae sunt species: alteram Graeci πάθος vocant, quod nos vertentes recte ac proprie adfectum dicimus, alteram ἦθος, cuius nomine, ut ego quidem sentio, caret sermo Romanus; mores appellantur, atque inde pars quoque illa philosophia ἠθική moralis est dicta. Sed ipsam rei naturam spectanti mihi non tam mores significari videntur quam morum quaedam proprietas; nam ipsis quidem omnis habitus mentis continetur. Cautiores voluntatem complecti quam nomina interpretari maluerunt. Adfectus igitur πάθος consitatos, ἦθος mites atque compositos esse dixerunt; in altero vehementer commotos, in altero lenes; denique hos imperare, illos persuadere; hos ad perturbationem, illos ad benivolentiam praevalere]. . . . . Nam cum ex illo ethico loco nihil non ab oratore tractetur, quidquid de honestis et utilibus, denique faciendis et non faciendis dicitur, *ethos* vocari potest. . . . *Ethos*, quod intelligimus quodque a dicentibus desideramus, id erit, quod ante omnia bonitate commendabitur,. . . .
>
> [Emotions however, as we learn from ancient authorities, fall into two classes; the one is called *pathos* by the Greeks and is rightly and correctly expressed in Latin by *adfectus* (emotion): the other is called *ethos*, a word for which in my opinion Latin has no equivalent: it is however rendered by *mores* (morals) and consequently the branch of philosophy known as ethics is styled moral philosophy by us. But close consideration of the nature of the subject leads me to think that in this connexion it is not so much morals in general that is meant as certain peculiar

aspects; for the term *morals* includes every attitude
of the mind. The more cautious writers have preferred
to give the sense of the term rather than to translate
it into Latin. They therefore explain *pathos* as
describing the more violent emotions and *ethos* as
designating those which are calm and gentle: in the
one case the passions are violent, in the other
subdued, the former command and disturb, the latter
persuade and induce a feeling of goodwill. . . . For as
everything treated by the orator may be regarded from
the ethical standpoint, we may apply the word *ethos*
whenever he speaks of what is honourable and
expedient or of what ought or ought not to be
done . . . . The *ethos* which I have in my mind and
which I desiderate in an orator is commended to our
approval by goodness more than aught else . . . .]
(VI, ii, 8-9, 11, 13)

Quintilian's broad notion of *ethos* in the emotional appeal includes the
general goals of Henryson's *moralitates*. As Henryson himself observes,
the goal of the fables in particular is to be "full of prudence and
moralitie" (1. 1381). Even within the context of legal pleading,
Quintilian certainly sees a vital role for this kind of peroration in stating
"what ought or ought not to be done." Of exceptional interest is
Quintilian's recognition of the proper use of irony in the *ethos* of the
peroration:

Verum aliquanto magis propria fuit virtus
simulationis, satisfaciendi rogandi εἰρωνεία, quae
diversum ei quod dicit intellectum petit.

[More closely dependent on *ethos* are the skilful
exercise of feigned emotion or the employment of
irony in making apologies or asking questions, irony
being the term which is applied to words which mean
something other than they seem to express.]
(VI, ii, 15)

Quintilian's remarks reflect the multiple uses of irony which Henryson
employed in his *moralitates*. There has been extensive critical comment
on Henryson's ironic *moralitates*, as to be found in "The Cock and the

Jasp," "The Paddock and the Mouse," *The Testament of Cresseid*, and even *Orpheus*.[36] In part some of the questions about Henryson's ironic use of the *moralitas* could reflect a lack of understanding of his goals or foreshadowing. However, it must be acknowledged that Henryson's *moralitates* strike some readers as artificial or, at the least, non-traditional. Perhaps some of the critical problems associated with his use of the *ars praedicandi* in this regard may be better understood in terms of Quintilian's reflections on the potential for ironic uses of *ethos* in the peroration. The implications for political irony in tales such as "The Lion and the Mouse" and "The Wolf and the Wether" are particularly rich, providing an opportunity for fruitful union with the political interests of the *ars dictaminis* and the exegetical tradition of the *ars praedicandi*. While the distinction is not new to Quintilian, his broad views would have encouraged Henryson's adaptation of his legal rhetoric to a poetic setting.

In addition to his remarks on audience appeal, impersonation, and judicial procedures, Quintilian's flexibility in his approach to organization demands further comment. He is always aware that circumstances, ethical appeal, emotions, and personality all play a role in determining how a piece of oratory should be organized. One of his favorite expressions with regard to organization is "let not superstition determine what you must do." Quintilian does not let "superstition" or respect of ancient standards alone determine how a document is to be organized. Instead he emphasizes the flexibility of the parts of discourse, using the basic framework of circumstance and personality as a determinant of organization and type of appeal. To cite only one example of his sense of the variables that must be taken into account in organization, his remarks on "accidents of persons" in Book V will provide some insight into his awareness of human foibles which have made his work a fertile source for poets:

> Personis autem non quidquid accidit exsequendum mihi est, ut plerique fecerunt, sed unde argumenta sumi possunt. Ea porro sunt, genus, nam similes parentibus ac maioribus suis plerumque creduntur, et nonnunquam ad honeste turpiterque vivendum inde causae fluunt; natio, nam et gentibus proprii mores sunt, nec idem in barbaro, Romano, Graeco probabile est; patria, quia similiter etiam civitatum leges, instituta, opiniones habent differentiam; sexus, ut

latrocinium facilius in viro, veneficium in femina
credas; aetas, quia aliud aliis annis magis conventi;
educatio et disciplina, quoniam refert, a quibus et quo
quisque modo sit institutus; habitus corporis, ducitur
enim frequenter in argumentum species libidinis,
robur petulantiae, his contraria in diversum; fortuna,
neque enim idem credible est in divite ac paupere,
propinquis amicis clientibus abundante et his omnibus
desituto; condicionis etiam distantia, nam clarus an
obscurus, magistratus an privatus, pater an filius, civis
an peregrinus, liber an servus, maritus an caelebs,
parens liberorum an orbus sit. . . .

[I have no intention of tracing all the accidents of
persons, as many have done, but shall confine myself
to those from which arguments may be drawn. Such
are birth, for persons are generally regarded as having
some resemblance to their parents and ancestors, a
resemblance which sometimes leads to their living
disgracefully or honourably, as the case may be; then
there is nationality, for races have their own character,
and the same action is not probable in the case of a
barbarian, a Roman and a Greek; country is another,
for there is a like diversity in the laws, institutions
and opinions of different states; sex, since for
example man is more likely to commit a robbery, a
woman to poison; age, since different actions suit
different ages; education and training, since it makes
a great difference who were the instructors and what
the method of instruction in each individual case;
bodily constitution, for beauty is often introduced as
an argument for lust, strength as an argument for
insolence, and their opposites for opposite conduct;
fortune, since the same acts are not to be expected
from rich and poor, or from one who is surrounded
by troops of relations, friends or clients and one who
lacks all these advantages; condition, too, is
important, for it makes a great difference whether a
man be famous or obscure, a magistrate or a private
individual, a father or a son, a citizen or a foreigner,

> a free man or a slave, married or unmarried, a father
> or childless.
>
> (V, x, 23-27)

His attitude is summarized by his admonition that "omnia potius a causa quam ab oratore profecta credantur" [everything must seem to spring from the case itself rather than the art of the orator] (IV, ii, 126). Quintilian's attention to flexibility in organization and his emphasis on the importance of circumstances and persons in rhetoric would appeal to poet, as well as the notary and schoolmaster. These two elements are also supported by Quintilian's emphasis on the *narratio*. John D. O'Banion has demonstrated how central this part of discourse is to Quintilian's notion of argument.[37] The fact that the *narratio* is clearly dependent on powers of vivid, realistic description would have made this aspect of Quintilian's approach to *divisio* of interest to a poet influenced by major trends of literary realism from the South. This organizational flexibility, sensitivity to audience, and sense of dramatic style would have helped Henryson as he attempted to integrate the major medieval approaches to rhetoric and to forge his own rhetorical techniques.

The most powerful evidence that Henryson read Quintilian is circumstantial. Most of the parallels that suggest a relationship involve Quintilian's definition of rhetoric and the character of the orator, invention, and organization. The major revival of interest in Quintilian that occurred just before Henryson's birth, Quintilian's emphasis on legal rhetoric (an interest clearly reflected in Henryson and likely associated with his profession as a notary), and the likelihood that Henryson would have had access to the doctrines of the *Institutio oratoria* through the impact of the rediscovery on either Scotland or Italy all suggest that Henryson might well have read Quintilian. In addition, specific analogies between Henryson's poetry and the *Institutio*, such as those outlined above, reinforce the arguments for potential influence. Even from the examples adduced here, it is obvious that the subject deserves additional attention.

If Henryson did know Quintilian, his use of the *Institutio oratoria* provides even further insight into his creative genius. His ability to weave the three major traditions of rhetoric into a comprehensive poetic demonstrates his refined eclecticism in his artistic craft. His additional use of Quintilian would represent an extension of that eclecticism and further reinforce his position as one of the most profound and satisfying poetic voices of the fifteenth century.

Notes
Chapter V

1. MacQueen, *Robert Henryson*, pp. 22–23. On the "transitional" nature of Henryson's verse and his debt to the Renaissance, see Evelyn S. Newlyn, "Humanism and Theodicy: Oppositions in the Poetry of Robert Henryson," *Proceedings of the Third International Conference on Scottish Language and Literature*, pp. 251–58. For some perspectives on the fifteenth century as an age of transition and a context for evaluating Henryson's work, see Paul O. Kristeller, *Renaissance Thought and Its Sources*, ed. Michael Mooney (New York, 1979); and John F. Tinkler, "Renaissance Humanism and the *genera eloquentiae*," *Rhetorica* 5, no. 3 (1987), 279–309.

2. See Wittig, *The Scottish Tradition in Literature*, p. 77 and Roderick Watson, *The Literature of Scotland* (New York, 1985), pp. 71–72.

3. *Institutionis oratoriae*, ed Colson, pp. xliv–xlv.

4. *Ibid.*, pp. l–li.

5. *Metalogicon*, ed. Webb, I, xxiv; trans. McGarry, pp. 65-66.

6. *Ibid.*, I, xxiv; McGarry, p. 67.

7. See *Pogii epistolae*, ed. T. de Tonellis (Turin, 1963), I, pp. 5–29.

8. See William Shepherd, *The Life of Poggio Bracciolini* (Liverpool, 1837), pp. 95-96.

9. Lyall, "Glasgow's First Poet: In Search of Robert Henryson," 13–16.

10. Colson, ed., *Institutionis oratoriae*, p. lxvii. See also *Selected Letters of Aeneas Silvius Piccolomini*, trans., Albert R. Baca (Northridge, CA, 1969), especially pp. 9, 33, and 48.

11. P. Hume Brown, ed. *Early Travellers in Scotland* (Edinburgh, 1891), p. 24.

12. MacQueen, "Neoplatonism and Orphism in Fifteenth-Century Scotland," pp. 69–89.

13. Jack, pp. 8–9.

14. Seigel, p. 143; on Valla's assertion about memorizing Quintilian, see Colson, ed., *Institutionis oratoriae*, p. lxiv and Seigel, p. 161.

15. Colson, ed., *Institutionis oratoriae*, p. lxvi.

16. Scaglione, p. 140.

17. See Colson, ed., *Institutionis oratoriae*, pp. lxiv–lxxxix; George Kennedy, *Classical Rhetoric and Its Christian and Secular Traditions from Ancient to Modern Times*, p. 199; Murphy, *Rhetoric in the Middle Ages*, pp. 357–63; and Vickers, pp. 254–57.

18. Colson, ed., *Institutionis oratoriae*, p. lxvi.

19. For comment on the text, see Colson, pp. lx–lxiii, and Murphy, *Rhetoric in the Middle Ages*, pp. 359–63.

20. *Institutio oratoria*, XII, ii, 1–4, Butler edition, IV, p. 383. This edition has been chosen for reasons already explained in note four of Chapter Two. Hereafter passages from Quintilian will be identified in the traditional fashion by providing book, chapter, and section numbers after the quotation.

21. Colson, ed., *Institutionis oratoriae*, p. xxv.

22. Alex Preminger, O.B. Hardison, and Kevin Kerrane, eds. *Classical and Medieval Literary Criticism* (New York, 1974), pp. 178-79.

23. Colson, ed., *Institutionis oratoriae*, pp. lxv–lxix.

24. Vickers, p. 41.

25. Carruthers, see especially pp. 16–45.

26. See Quintilian, II, xv, and Watson, trans. and ed., *Cicero on Oratory and Orators*, especially Book I, pp. 5–82.

27. For recent examples of the critical concerns involving the contrast between the character of the Pardoner and the nature of his tale, see Donald R. Howard, *The Idea of the Canterbury Tales* (Berkeley, 1976), pp. 333–87; and Warren Ginsberg, "Preaching and Avarice in the Pardoner's Tale," *Mediaevalia*, 2 (1976), 77-99.

28. See Elizabeth Jackson, "Henryson's Fable *The Paddock and the Mouse* as Wisdom Literature," *Unisa English Studies*, 21 (1983), 1–5.

29. See especially Aswell, "The Role of Fortune in The Testament of Cresseid," pp. 471–87; and Lindsay, pp. 43–44.

30. George Kennedy, *Quintilian* (New York, 1969), pp. 125–32.

31. Cited by Colson, ed., *Institutionis oratoriae*, p. xxviii.

32. Edwin D. Craun, "Blaspheming Her 'Awin God': Cresseid's 'Lamentatioun' in Henryson's *Testament*," *Studies in Philology*, 82 (1985), 41.

33. Kennedy, p. 77.

34. Cited by Murphy, *Rhetoric in the Middle Ages*, p. 312.

35. To cite only one other example, VI, ii, 29–36.

36. For only a few of the commentaries, see Khinoy, "Tale-Moral Relationships in Henryson's Moral Fables," pp. 99–115; Clark, "Henryson and Aesop," pp. 1–18; MacQueen, *Robert Henryson*, pp. 94–188; Gray, *Robert Henryson*, pp. 70–159; Kindrick, *Robert Henryson*, pp. 57–117; and Benson, pp. 215–35.

37. John D. O'Banion, "Narration and Argumentation: Quintilian on *Narratio* as the Heart of Rhetorical Thinking," *Rhetorica*, 5 no. 4 (1987), 325–51.

WORKS CITED

Aegidius de Fuscarariis. *Der Ordo Iudicarius des Aegidius de Fuscarariis*. Ed. Ludwig Wahrmund. Innsbruck, 1916.

Aitken, Adam J., Matthew P. McDiarmid, and Derick S. Thompson. *Bards and Makars*. Glasgow, 1977.

Alberic of Montecassino. *Flores rhetorici*. Ed. D. M. Inguanez and E. H. M. Willard. Monte Cassino, 1938.

Aldis, Harry G. *A List of Books Printed in Scotland before 1700*. Edinburgh, 1904.

Allen, Judson B. *The Ethical Poetic of the Later Middle Ages*. Toronto, 1962.

_____. *The Friar as Critic*. Nashville, 1971.

_____. "Hermann the German's Averroistic Aristotle and Medieval Poetic Theory." *Mosaic*, 9 (1976): 67-81.

Amos, Thomas L., Eugene A. Green, and Beverly Mayne Kienzle, eds. *De Ore Domine*. Kalamazoo, 1989.

Anderson, Judith H. *The Growth of a Personal Voice*. New Haven, 1976.

Aristotle. *The "Art" of Rhetoric*. Trans. John Henry Freese. Cambridge, MA, 1926.

Aswell, E. Duncan. "The Role of Fortune in *The Testament of Cresseid*." *Philological Quarterly*, 46 (1967): 471-87.

Atkins, J. W. H. *English Literary Criticism: The Medieval Phase*. Cambridge, 1934.

Auerbach, Erich. *Literary Language and Its Public in Late Latin Antiquity and in the Middle Ages*. Trans. Ralph Manheim. New York, 1965.

Augustine, S. Aurelius. *Concerning the Teacher and On the Immortality of the Soul*. Trans. George G. Leckie. New York, 1938.

_____. *De doctrina christina*. Ed. William M. Green. Vienna, 1963.

_____. *Of Christian Doctrine*. Trans. D. W. Robertson, Jr. New York, 1958.

Bagni, Paolo. "Grammatica e Retorica nella Cultura Medievale." *Rhetorica*, 2, no. 3 (1984): 267-80.

Baldwin, Charles Sears. *Medieval Rhetoric and Poetic*. New York, 1928.

_____. *Renaissance Literary Theory and Practice*. Ed. D. L. Clark. New York, 1939.

Baltzell, Jane. "Rhetorical Amplification and Abbreviation in the Structure of Medieval Narrative." *Pacific Coast Philology*, 2 (1966): 32-38.

Barilli, Renato. *Rhetoric*. Trans. Guiliana Menozzi. Minneapolis, 1989.

Barraclough, Geoffrey. *Public Notaries and the Papal Curia*. London, 1934.

Bethurum, Dorothy, ed. *Critical Approaches to Medieval Literature*. New York, 1960.

Bishop, Ian. "Lapidary Formulas as Topics of Invention – From Thomas of Hales to Henryson." *Review of English Studies*, 37 (1986): 469-77.

Blanchot, Jean-Jacques and Claude Graf., eds. *Actes du 2ᵉ Colloque de Langue et de Litterature Ecossaises*. Strasbourg, 1979.

Boccaccio, Giovanni. *The Decameron.* Trans. G. H. McWilliam. Baltimore, 1972.

Boitani, Piero and Jill Mann, eds. *The Cambridge Chaucer Companion.* Cambridge, 1986.

Bone, Gavin. "The Source of Henryson's 'Fox, Wolf, and Cadger,'" *Review of English Studies,* 10 (1934): 319-20.

Bracciolini, Poggio. *Pogii epistolae.* Ed. T. de Torellis. Turin, 1963.

Brewer, Derek, ed. *Geoffrey Chaucer.* Athens, Ohio, 1975.

Bright, Philippa M. "Medieval Concepts of the *figure* and Henryson's Figurative Technique in *The Fables,*" *Studies in Scottish Literature,* 25 (1990): 134-53.

_____. "Henryson's Figurative Technique in *The Cock and the Jasp.*" In *Words and Wordsmiths: A Volume for H. L. Rogers.* Ed. Geraldine Barnes, John Gunn, Sonya Jensen, and Lee Jobling. Sydney, 1989. Pp. 13-21.

Brody, Saul N. *The Disease of the Soul: Leprosy in Medieval Literature.* Ithaca, 1974.

Bromyard, John. *Summa Praedicantium.* Venice, 1586.

Brown, Jennifer M., ed. *Scottish Society in the Fifteenth Century.* London, 1977.

Brown, P. Hume, ed. *Early Travellers in Scotland.* Edinburgh, 1891.

Bruce, George C. "The Medieval Bestiaries and Their Influence on Ecclesiastical Decorative Art." *Journal of the British Archaeological Association* (December, 1919): 40-82.

Bryan, W. F. and Germaine Dempster, eds. *Sources and Analogues of Chaucer's Canterbury Tales.* Chicago, 1941.

Burnley, J. D. "Sources of Standardization in Later Middle English." In *Standardizing English*. Ed. Joseph B. Trahern. Knoxville, 1989. Pp. 23-41.

Burrow, J. A. "Henryson: *The Preaching of the Swallow*." *Essays in Criticism*, 25 (1975): 25-37.

_____. *Ricardian Poetry*. New Haven, 1971.

Camargo, Martin. *Ars Dictaminis, Ars Dictandi*. Turnhout, 1991.

_____. "Toward A Comprehensive Art of Written Discourse: Geoffrey of Vinsauf and the *Ars Dictaminis*." *Rhetorica*, 6, no. 2 (1988): 167-94.

Caplan, Harry. "Classical Rhetoric and the Mediaeval Theory of Preaching." *Classical Philology*, 28 (1933): 73-96.

_____. "The Decay of Eloquence at Rome in the First Century." In *Studies in Speech and Drama in Honor of Alexander M. Drummond*. Ed. Herbert A. Wichelns. Ithaca, 1944. Pp. 295-325.

_____. "The Four Senses of Scriptural Interpretation and the Medieval Theory of Preaching." *Speculum*, 4 (1929): 282-90.

_____. "Rhetorical Invention in Some Medieval Tractates on Preaching." *Speculum*, 2 (1927): 284-95.

Carruthers, Mary. *The Book of Memory*. Cambridge, 1990.

Cassiodorus, Senator. *The Letters of Cassiodorus*. Trans. Thomas Hodgkin. London, 1886.

_____. *Variae*. Ed. T. Mommsen. Monumenta Germaniae Historica, Auctorum Antiquissimorum, XII. Berlin, 1894.

Caterina de Siena, S. *Epistole*. Ed. P. Federico Burlamacchi. Milan, 1842.

Charland, Th-M. *Artes Praedicandi*. Paris, 1936.

Works Cited   315

Chaucer, Geoffrey. *The Works of Geoffrey Chaucer.* Ed. F. N. Robinson. Boston, 1957.

Chobham, Thomas. *Summa de arte praedicandi.* Ed. Franco Morenzani. Brussels, 1988.

Cicero, Marcus Tullius. *Cicero on Oratory and Orators.* Trans. John Selby Watson. Carbondale, 1986.

Cigman, Gloria, ed. *Lollard Sermons.* EETS, o.s. 294, Oxford, 1989.

Clark, George. "Henryson and Aesop: The Fable Transformed." *English Literary History*, 43 (1976): 1-18.

Clark, Willene B. and Meradith McMunn, eds. *Beasts and Birds of the Middle Ages.* Philadelphia, 1989.

Cobham, A. B. *The Medieval Universities.* London, 1970.

Coleman, Janet. *Medieval Readers and Writers 1350-1400.* New York, 1981.

Conley, Thomas M. *Rhetoric in the European Tradition.* New York, 1990.

Constable, Giles. *Letters and Letter-Collections.* Louvain, 1976.

———. "The Structure of Medieval Society According to the *Dictatores* of the Twelfth Century." In *Law, Church and Society.* Ed. Kenneth Pennington and Robert Somerville. Philadelphia, 1977. Pp. 253-67.

Copeland, Rita. *Rhetoric, Hermeneutics, and Translation in the Middle Ages.* Cambridge, 1991.

Courtenay, William J. *Schools and Scholars in Fourteenth-Century England.* Princeton, 1987.

Craun, Edwin D. "Blaspheming Her 'Awin God': Cresseid's 'Lament-acioun' in Henryson's *Testament*." *Studies in Philology*, 82 (1985): 25-41.

Crow, Martin, M., and Clair C. Olson, eds. *Chaucer Life Records*. Oxford, 1966.

Crowne, David. "A Date for the Composition of Henryson's Fables." *Journal of English and Germanic Philology*, 61 (1962): 583-90.

Cullen, Mari Ann. "Cresseid Excused: A Re-reading of Henryson's *Testament of Cresseid*." *Studies in Scottish Literature*, 20 (1985): 137-59.

Curtius, Ernst R. *European Literature and the Latin Middle Ages*. Trans. Willard R. Trask. New York, 1953.

D'Avray, David L. *Preaching of the Friars: Sermons diffused from Paris before 1300*. Oxford, 1985.

Delisle, Leopold. "Notice sur une 'summa dictaminis' jadis conservé a Beauvais." *Notices et extraits*, 36 (1899): 171-205.

Denholm-Young, Noel. "Cursus in England." In *Collected Papers of N. Denholm-Young*. Cardiff, 1969. Pp. 42-73.

Dibben, L. B. "Secretaries in the Thirteenth and Fourteenth Centuries." *English Historical Review*, 25 (1910): 430-44.

Dickinson, W. Croft, and Archibald A. M. Duncan. *Scotland from the Earliest Times to 1603*. Oxford, 1977.

Diebler, A. R. *Henrison's Fabeldichtungen*. Halle, 1885.

Doe, Norman. *Fundamental Authority in Late Medieval English Law*. Cambridge, 1990.

Donaldson, Gordon, ed. *Scottish Historical Documents*. New York, 1970.

Eberhard. *The Laborintus of Eberhard.* Trans. Evelyn Carson. Unpublished thesis: Cornell University, 1930.

Eco, Umberto. *Art and Beauty in the Middle Ages.* Trans. Hugh Bredin. New Haven, 1986.

Eco, Umberto and Constantio Marmo, eds. *On the Medieval Theory of Signs.* Amsterdam, 1989.

Ellenberger, Bengt. *The Latin Element in the Vocabulary of the Earlier Makars: Henryson and Dunbar.* Lund, 1977.

Erdmann, Carl, ed. *Die Briefe Heinrichs IV.* Leipzig, 1937.

Faral, Edmond, ed. *Les arts poetiques du XIIe et du XIIIe siècle.* Paris, 1923.

Fisher, John Hurt, with Malcolm Richardson and Jane L. Fisher. *An Anthology of Chancery English.* Knoxville, 1984.

_____. "European Chancelleries and the Rise of Standard Languages." *Proceedings of the Illinois Medieval Association,* 3 (1986): 1-33.

Fox, Denton. "Henryson and Caxton." *Journal of English and Germanic Philology,* 67 (1968): 586-93.

_____. "Henryson's Fables." *English Literary History,* 29 (1962): 337-56.

_____. "Henryson's 'Sum Practysis of Medecyne.'" *Studies in Philology,* 69 (1972): 453-60.

Friedman, John B. "Henryson, The Friars, and the *Confessio Reynardi.*" *Journal of English and Germanic Philology,* 66 (1967): 550-61.

_____. "Henryson's *Testament of Cresseid* and the *Judicio Solis in Conviviis Saturni* of Simon of Cavin." *Modern Philology,* 83 (1985): 12-21.

_____. *Orpheus in the Middle Ages.* Cambridge, MA, 1970.

Gallo, Ernest. *The Poetria Nova and Its Sources In Early Rhetorical Doctrine*. The Hague, 1971.

Gehl, Paul F. "From Monastic Rhetoric to *Ars dictaminis*: Traditionalism and Innovation in the Schools of Twelfth-Century Italy." *American Benedictine Review*, 34 (1983): 33-47.

Geoffrey of Vinsauf. *Documentatum de modo et arte dictandi et versificandi*. Trans. Roger P. Parr. Milwaukee, 1968.

Ginsberg, Warren, "Preaching and Avarice in the Pardoner's Tale." *Medievalia*, 2 (1976): 77-99.

Giry, A. *Manuel de diplomatique*. Paris, 1925.

Goldstein, R. James. "'For he wald vsurpe na fame': Andrew of Wynton's Use of the Modesty *Topos* and Literary Culture in Early Fifteenth-Century Scotland." *Scottish Literary Journal*, 14 (1987): 5-18.

Gopen, George D. "The Essential Seriousness of Robert Henryson's *Moral Fables*: A Study in Structure." *Studies in Philology*, 82 (1985): 42-59.

Gradon, Pamela, ed. *English Wycliffite Sermons*. Oxford, 1988.

Gray, Douglas. *Robert Henryson*. Leiden, 1979.

Green, A. Wigfall. "Meter and Rhyme in Chaucer's *Anelida and Arcite*." *University of Mississippi Studies in English*, 2 (1961): 55-63.

Gregory, S. *De cura pastoralis*, Brussels, 1685.

_____. *Pastoral Rule*. New York, 1895.

Gros Louis, Kenneth R. R. "Robert Henryson's Orpheus and Eurydice in the Orpheus Traditions of the Middle Ages." *Speculum*, 41 (1966): 643-55.

Guibert of Nogent. "Liber quo ordine sermo fieri debeat." In *PL*, 156. Ed. J. P. Migne. Paris, 1853.

Halm, Carolus, ed. *Rhetores Latini Minores*. Leipzig, 1863.

Hamilton, Ruth, ed. *Style*, 20 (1986).

Harth, Sydney J. "Convention and Creation in the Poetry of Robert Henryson." Dissertation: University of Chicago, 1962.

Harty, K. J. "Cresseid and Her Narrator: A Reading of Robert Henryson's *Testament of Cresseid*." *Studi Medievali* 23 (1984): 753-65.

Haskins, Charles H. "The Early *Artes Dictandi* in Italy." *In Studies in Medieval Culture*. Oxford, 1929. Pp. 170-92.

Hawes, Stephen. *The Pastime of Pleasure*. London, 1865.

Henryson, Robert. *Moral Fables*. Trans. and Ed. George D. Gopen. Notre Dame, 1987.

_____. *The Poems and Fables of Robert Henryson*. Ed. David Laing. Edinburgh, 1865.

_____. *Poems and Fables of Robert Henryson*. Ed. H. Harvey Wood. Edinburgh, 1933: rev. 1958.

_____. *The Poems of Robert Henryson*. Ed. Denton Fox. Oxford, 1981.

_____. *The Poems of Robert Henryson*. Ed. G. Gregory Smith. STS, 64, 55, 58. Edinburgh: 1914, 1906, 1908.

_____. *Robert Henryson, Poems*. Ed. Charles Elliott. 2nd ed. Oxford, 1975.

_____. *The Testament of Cresseid*. Ed. Denton Fox. London, 1968.

Herrtage, Sidney J. H., ed. *The Taill of Rauf Coilyear*. EETS, e.s. 39. Oxford, 1882.

320   *Henryson and the Medieval Arts of Rhetoric*

Hervieux, Leopold, ed. *Les Fabulistes Latins*. Paris, 1896.

Higden, Ranulph. *The Ars Componendi Sermones of Ranulph Higden*. Ed. Margaret Jennings. Leiden, 1991.

Hornsby, Joseph Allen. *Chaucer and the Law*. Norman, 1988.

Howard, Donald R. *The Idea of the Canterbury Tales*. Berkeley, 1976.

Howell, Wilbur Samuel, trans. *The Rhetoric of Alcuin and Charlemagne*. Princeton, 1941.

Hugh of St. Victor. *Didascalicon*. Ed. C. H. Butimer. Washington, 1939.

_____. *Didascalison*. Trans. Jerome Taylor. New York, 1961.

Humbert of Romans. *A Treatise on Preaching*. Westminster, MD, 1951.

Hume, Kathryn. "Leprosy or Syphilis in Henryson's *Testament of Cresseid*." *English Language Notes*, 6 (1969): 242-45.

Jack, R. D. S. *The Italian Influence on Scottish Literature*. Edinburgh, 1972.

Jackson, Elizabeth. "Henryson's Fable *The Paddock and the Mouse* as Wisdom Literature." *Unisa English Studies*, 21 (1983): 1-5.

Jackson, W. T. H. *The Challenge of the Medieval Text*. Ed. Joan M. Ferrante and Robert W. Hanning. New York, 1985.

_____. *The Literature of the Middle Ages*. New York, 1960.

Jamieson, I. W. A. "A Further Source of Henryson's 'Fabillis.'" *Notes and Queries*, 14 (1967): 403-05.

_____. "Henryson's 'Fabillis': An Essay Towards a Revaluation." *Words: Wai-Te Atu Studies in Literature*, no. 2 (1966): 20-31.

_____. "Henryson's *Taill of the Wolf and the Wedder.*" *Studies in Scottish Literature*, 6 (1969): 248-57.

_____. "Some Attitudes to Poetry in Late Fifteenth-Century Scotland." *Studies in Scottish Literature*, 15 (1980): 28-42.

_____. "To preue thare preching be a poesye": Some Thoughts on Henryson's Poetics." *Parergon*, 8 (1974): 24-36.

Jentoft, C. W. "Henryson as Authentic 'Chaucerian': Narrator, Character, and Courtly Love in *The Testament of Cresseid.*" *Studies in Scottish Literature*, 10 (1972): 94-102.

John of Garland. *Parisiana Poetria of John of Garland.* Ed. Traugott Lawler. New Haven, 1974.

John of Salisbury. *Metalogicon.* Ed. Clemens C. I. Webb. Oxford, 1929.

_____. *The Metalogicon of John of Salisbury.* Trans. David D. McGarry. Berkeley, 1955.

John of Tilbury. "*Ars Notaria*: Tironische Noten und Stenographie im 12. Jahrhundert." Ed. Valentin Rose. *Hermes*, 8 (1874): 303-26.

Johnston, Mark D. "The Treatment of Speech in Medieval Ethical and Courtesy Literature." *Rhetorica*, 4, no. 1 (1986): 21-46.

Kantorowicz, Herman. *Studies in the Glossators of the Roman Laws.* Cambridge, 1938.

Kelly, Douglas. *The Arts of Poetry and Prose.* Turnhout, 1991.

_____. *Medieval Imagination: Rhetoric and the Poetry of Courtly Love.* Madison, 1978.

Kendall, Paul Murray. *The Yorkist Age.* New York, 1962.

Kennedy, George. *Classical Rhetoric and Its Christian and Secular Traditions from Ancient to Modern Times.* Chapel Hill, 1980.

_____. "An Introduction to the Rhetoric of the Gospels." *Rhetorica*, 1, no. 1 (1983): 17-31.

_____. *Quintilian*. New York, 1969.

Kern, Fritz. *Kingship and Law in the Middle Ages*. New York, 1970.

Khinoy, Stephan. "Tale-Moral Relationships in Henryson's *Moral Fables*." *Studies in Scottish Literature*, 17 (1982): 99-115.

Kindrick, Robert L. "Politics and Poetry at the Court of James III." *Studies in Scottish Literature*, 19 (1984): 40-55.

_____. *Robert Henryson*. Boston, 1979.

_____. "Robert Henryson and the *Ars dictaminis*." In *Bryght Lanternis*. Ed. J. Derrick McClure and Michael R. G. Spiller. Aberdeen, 1989. Pp. 150-61.

Kinghorn, A. M. "The Minor Poems of Robert Henryson." *Studies in Scottish Literature*, 3 (1965): 30-40.

Kinsley, James. *Scottish Poetry*. London, 1955.

Kirshner, Julius, and Karl F. Morrison, eds. *Readings in Western Civilization 4: Medieval Europe*. Chicago, 1986.

Kratzmann, Gregory. *Anglo-Scottish Literary Relations*. Cambridge, 1980.

_____. "Henryson's *Fables*: 'the subtell dyte of poetry.'" *Studies in Scottish Literature*, 20 (1985): 49-68.

Kristeller, Paul O. *Renaissance Thought and Its Sources*. Ed. Michael Mooney. New York, 1979.

Lacombe, George, ed. *Aristoteles Latinus II*. Cambridge, 1955.

Leach, A. F. *The Schools of Medieval England*. London, 1915.

Levine, Robert. "Satiric Vulgarity in Guibert de Nogent's *Gesta Dei per Francos*." *Rhetorica*, 7, no. 3 (1989): 261-73.

Lewry, P. Osmund. "Rhetoric at Paris and Oxford in the Mid-Thirteenth Century." *Rhetorica* 1, no. 1 (1983): 45-63.

Licitra, V. "Il mito di Alberico di Monte cassino iniziatore dell' *Ars dictaminis*." *Studi medievali*, 3a. ser. 18 (1977), fasc. 2: 609-27.

Lindsay, Maurice. *History of Scottish Literature*. London, 1977.

Long, Eleanor R. "Robert Henryson's 'Vther Quair.'" *Comitatus*, 3 (1972): 97-101.

Longére, Jean. *La prédication medieval*. Paris, 1983.

Lyall, Roderick J. "Did Poliziano Influence Henryson's *Orpheus and Erudices*?" *Forum for Modern Language Studies*, 15 (1979): 209-21.

_____. "Glasgow's First Poet: In Search of Robert Henryson." *College Courant*, 72 (1984): 13-16.

_____. "Henryson and Boccaccio." *Anglia*, 99 (1981): 38-59.

_____. "Politics and Poetry in Fifteenth and Sixteenth Century Scotland." *Scottish Literary Journal*, 3 (1976): 5-27.

Lyall, Roderick J. and Felicity Riddy, eds. *Proceedings of the Third International Conference on Scottish Language and Literature*. Stirling/Glasgow, 1981.

Lyons, John D. *Exemplum*. Princeton, 1990.

MacDonald, Donald. "Chaucer's Influence on Henryson's *Fables*: The Use of Proverbs and Sententiae." *Medium Aevum*, 39 (1970): 21-27.

_____. "Henryson and Chaucer: Cock and Fox." *Texas Studies in Language and Literature*, 8 (1966): 451-61.

_____. "Henryson and the *Thre Prestis of Peblis.*" *Neophilologus*, 51 (1967): 168-77.

_____. "Narrative Art in Henryson's *Fables.*" *Studies in Scottish Literature*, 3 (1965): 101-13.

Macdougall, Norman. *James III*. Edinburgh, 1982.

MacQueen, John. "Neoplatonism and Orphism in Fifteenth-Century Scotland." *Scottish Studies*, 20 (1976): 69-89.

_____. *Robert Henryson*. Oxford, 1967.

Manly, John M. "Chaucer and the Rhetoricians." *Proceedings of the British Academy*, 12 (1926): 95-113.

Marken, Ronald. "Chaucer and Henryson: A Comparison." *Discourse*, 7 (1964): 381-87.

Masui, Michio. *The Structure of Chaucer's Rime Words*. Tokyo, 1964.

Matthew of Vendôme. *The Art of Versification*. Trans. Aubrey E. Galyon. Ames, 1980.

Maxwell, David. *An Introduction to Scottish Legal History*, I Edinburgh, 1988.

McDiarmid, Matthew P. M. *Robert Henryson*. Edinburgh, 1981.

McKeon, Richard. "Rhetoric in the Middle Ages." *Speculum*, 17 (1942): 1-32.

Mezières, Phillippe de. *Letter to King Richard II*. Ed. and trans. G. W. Coopland. Liverpool, 1975.

Mieszowski, Gretchen. "The Reputation of Criseyde: 1155-1500." *Transactions* of the Connecticut Academy of Arts and Sciences, 43 (1971): 71-153.

Miller, Joseph M., Michael H. Prosser, and Thomas W. Benson. *Readings in Medieval Rhetoric*. Bloomington, 1973.

Miller, Robert P. ed. *Chaucer: Sources and Backgrounds*. New York, 1977.

Minnis, A. J., and A. B. Scott with David Wallace, eds. *Medieval Literary Theory*. Oxford, 1988.

Minnis, A. J. *Medieval Theory of Authorship*. Philadelphia 1984. Rev. ed, 1988.

Mommsen, T. E., and Karl Morrison, trans.; R. Benson ed. *Imperial Lives and Letters of the Eleventh Century*. New York, 1962.

Monfasani, John. *George of Trebizand*. Leiden, 1976.

Moran, Tatyana. "*The Testament of Cresseid* and the *Book of Troylus*." *Litera*, 6 (1959): 18-24.

Morse, Ruth. *Truth and Convention in the Middle Ages*. Cambridge, 1991.

Mosher, Joseph A. *The Exemplum in the Early Religious and Didactic Literature of England*. New York, 1911.

Mueller, Janel M. *The Native Tongue and the Word*. Chicago, 1984.

Murphy, Colette. "Henryson's Mice: Three Animals of Style." *Poetica*, 23 (1986): 53-73.

Murphy, James J. "The Earliest Teaching of Rhetoric at Oxford." *Speech Monographs*, 27 (1960): 345-47.

_____. "A Fifteenth-Century Treatise on Prose Style." *Newberry Library Bulletin*, 6, no. 7 (1966): 205-10.

_____., ed. *Medieval Eloquence*. Berkeley, 1978.

_____. *Medieval Rhetoric: A Select Bibliography*. 2nd Ed. Toronto, 1989.

_____. "A New Look at Chaucer and the Rhetoricians." *Review of English Studies*, 15 (1964): 1-20.

_____., ed. *Renaissance Eloquence*. Berkeley, 1983.

_____. "Rhetoric in Fourteenth-Century Oxford." *Medium Aevum*, 34 (1965): 1-20.

_____. *Rhetoric in the Middle Ages*. Berkeley, 1974.

_____. "Saint Augustine and the Debate about a Christian Rhetoric." *Quarterly Journal of Speech*, 46 (1960): 400-10.

_____., ed. *A Short History of Writing Instruction*. Davis, 1990.

_____., ed. *Three Medieval Rhetorical Arts*. Berkeley, 1971.

Murtaugh, Daniel M. "Henryson's Animals." *Texas Studies in Language and Literature*, 14 (1972): 405-21.

Newlyn, Evelyn S. "Robert Henryson and the Popular Fable Tradition in the Middle Ages." *Journal of Popular Culture*, 14 (1984): 108-18.

_____. "Tradition and Transformation in the Poetry of Robert Henryson." *Studies in Scottish Literature*, 18 (1983): 33-58.

Nicholson, Ranald. *Scotland: The Later Middle Ages*. New York, 1974.

Nitecki, Alicia K. "'Fenzeit of the New': Authority in the *Testament of Cresseid*." *Journal of Narrative Technique*, 15 (1986); 120-32.

O'Banion, John D. "Narration and Argumentation: Quintilian on *Narratio* as the Heart of Rhetorical Thinking." *Rhetorica*, 5, no. 4 (1987): 325-51.

Odo of Cheriton. *The Fables of Odo of Cheriton*. Trans. John C. Jacobs. Syracuse, 1985.

Ogle, Marburg B. "Some Aspects of Medieval Latin Style." *Speculum*, 1 (1926): 170-89.

Ong, Walter J. "Orality, Literacy, and Medieval Textualization." *New Literary History*, 15 (1984): 1-12.

Orlandelli, Gianfranco. "Genesi dell' 'Ars notarie' nel Secolo XIII:" *Studi Medievali*, 4 (1965), fasc. 2,: 329-66.

Owen, C. David. "O Moral Henryson." In *Fifteenth-Century Studies*. Ed. Robert F. Yeager. Hamden, CT, 1984. Pp. 215-35.

Owst, G. R. *Literature and Pulpit in Medieval England*. 2nd ed. Oxford, 1966.

_____. *Preaching in Medieval England: An Introduction to Sermon Manuscripts of the Period c. 1350-1450*. Cambridge, 1926.

Pantin, W. A., ed. "A Medieval Treatise on Letter-Writing with Examples from the Rylands Latin MS. 304." *Bulletin of the John Rylands Library*, 13 (1929): 326-82.

Parkes, Malcolm B. "The Literacy of the Laity." *In Literature and Western Civilization: The Medieval World*. Ed. David Daiches and Anthony Thorlby. London, 1973. Pp. 555-77.

Parks, Ward. "The Oral-Formulaic Theory in Middle English Studies." *Oral Tradition*, 1 (1986): 636-94.

Paton, Campbell H., ed. *An Introduction to Scottish Legal History*: Edinburgh, 1958.

Patterson, Annabel. *Fables of Power*. Durham and London, 1991.

Payne, Robert O. "Late Medieval Images and Self-Images of the Poet: Chaucer, Gower, Lydgate, Henryson, and Dunbar." In *Vernacular Poetics in the Middle Ages*. Ed. Lois Ebin. Kalamazoo, 1984. Pp. 249-61.

Perry, B. E. "Fable." *Studium Generale*, 12 (1959): 17-37.

Piccolomini, Aeneas Silvius. *Selected Letters of Aeneas Silvius Piccolomini*. Trans. Albert R. Baca. Northridge, CA, 1969.

Powell, Marianne. *Fabula Docet*. Odense, 1983.

Preminger, Alex, O. B. Hardison, and Kevin Kerrane, eds. *Classical and Medieval Literary Criticism*. New York, 1974.

Prill, Paul E. "Rhetoric and Poetics in the Early Middle Ages." *Rhetorica*, 5, no. 2 (1987): 129-47.

Procopius. *The Secret History*. Trans. G. A. Williamson. New York, 1966.

Purcell, William. "*Transsumptio*: A Rhetorical Doctrine of the Thirteenth Century." *Rhetorica*, 5, no. 4 (1987): 369-410.

Quintilian, Marcus Fabius. *The Institutio oratoria of Quintilian*. Trans. H. E. Butler. Cambridge, MA, 1930.

_____. *Institutionis oratoriae*. Ed. F. H. Colson. Cambridge, 1924.

_____. *On the Teaching of Speaking and Writing*. Ed. James J. Murphy. Carbondale, IL, 1987.

Radding, Charles M. *The Origins of Medieval Jurisprudence*. New Haven, 1988.

Rainerius of Perugia. *Ars notariae*. Ed. Ludwig Wahrmund. Innsbruck, 1917.

Ramson, W. S. "The Aureate Paradox." *Parergon*, n.s. 1 (1983): 93-104.

_____. "A Reading of Henryson's *Testament* or 'Quha falsit Cresseid?'" *Parergon*, 17 (1977): 25-35.

Rashdall, Hastings. *The Universities of Europe in the Middle Ages*. Ed. F. M. Powicke and A. B. Emden. London, 1936.

Richardson, Henry Gerald. "Business Training in Medieval Oxford." *American Historical Review*, 46 (1941): 259-80.

Richardson, Janette. *Blameth Nat Me: A Study of Imagery in Chaucer's Fabliaux*. The Hague, 1970.

Richardson, Malcolm. "The *Dictamen* and Its Influence on Fifteenth-Century Prose." *Rhetorica*, 2 no. 3 (1984): 207-26.

Ridley, Florence. "A Plea for the Middle Scots." In *The Learned and the Lewed*. Ed. Larry D. Benson. Cambridge, MA, 1974. Pp. 175-96.

Robertson, D. W. *Essays in Medieval Culture*. Princeton, 1980.

_____. *A Preface to Chaucer*. Princeton, 1962.

Robertson, Stuart. "Old English Verse in Chaucer." *Modern Language Notes*, 42 (1928): 234-36.

Robinson, Ian. *Chaucer and the English Tradition*. Cambridge, 1972.

Rockinger, Ludwig. *Briefsteller und formelbucher des eilften bis vierzehnten Jahrhunderts*. Munich, 1863. Rpt. New York, 1961.

Rollinson, Philip. *Classical Theories of Allegory and Christian Culture*. Pittsburgh, 1981.

Rosenthal, Joel T., ed. *Nobles and the Noble Life 1295-1500*. London, 1976.

Rowlands, Mary. "Robert Henryson and the Scottish Courts of Law." *Aberdeen University Review*, 39 (1962): 219-26.

Scaglione, Aldo. *The Classical Theory of Composition.* Chapel Hill, 1972.

Scheps, Walter. "Chaucer and the Middle Scots Poets." *Studies in Scottish Literature,* 22 (1987): 44-59.

Schoeck, Richard J. "On Rhetoric in Fourteenth-Century Oxford." *Medieval Studies,* 30 (1968): 214-25.

Schultz, James A. "Classical Rhetoric, Medieval Poetics, and the Medieval Vernacular Prologue." *Speculum,* 59 (1985): 1-15.

Schweitzer, Edward C. "The Allegory of Robert Henryson's 'The Bludy Serk.'" *Studies in Scottish Literature,* 15 (1980): 165-74.

Scotland, Parliament of. *The Lawes and Actes of Parliament.* Edinburgh, 1597.

Seagle, W. *The History of Law.* New York, 1946.

Seigel, Jerrold E. *Rhetoric and Philosophy in Renaissance Humanism.* Princeton, 1968.

Seznec, Jean. *The Survival of the Pagan Gods.* Trans. Barbara Sessions. Princeton, 1972.

Shepherd, William. *The Life of Poggio Bracciolini.* Liverpool, 1837.

Simpson, J. A. Y. "Antiquarian Notices of Leprosy and Leper Hospitals in Scotland and England." *Edinburgh Medical and Surgical Journal,* 56 (1841): 301-30; 57 (1842): 121-56, 294-429.

Smalley, Beryl. *English Friars and Antiquity in the Early Fourteenth Century.* New York, 1960.

Smith, G. Gregory. *Specimens of Middle Scots.* Edinburgh, 1902.

Smith, Roland M. "Three Notes on the Knight's Tale." *Modern Language Notes,* 51 (1936): 320-22.

Spearing, A. C. "*The Testament of Cresseid* and the High Concise Style." In *Criticism and Medieval Poetry*. London, 1964. Pp. 118-44.

Stearns, Marshall W. "Henryson and Chaucer." *Modern Language Quarterly*, 6 (1945): 271-84.

_____. *Robert Henryson*. New York, 1949.

Stiller, Nikki. "Robert Henryson's Cresseid and Sexual Backlash." *Literature and Psychology*, 31 (1983): 88-95.

Stones, E. L. G., ed. and trans. *Anglo-Scottish Relations*. Oxford, 1970.

Strauss, Dietrich and Horst W. Drescher, eds. *Scottish Language and Literature, Medieval and Renaissance*. Frankfurt am Main, 1984.

Stump, Eleonore. *Dialectic and Its Place in the Development of Medieval Logic*. Ithaca, 1989.

Swearingen, C. Jan. *Rhetoric and Irony*. New York, 1991.

Thatcher, Oliver and Edgar McNeal, eds. and trans. *A Source Book for Medieval History*. New York, 1965.

Tillyard, E. M. W. "Henryson: *The Testament of Cresseid*." In *Five Poems 1470?-1870*. London, 1948. Pp. 5-29.

Tinkler, John F. "Renaissance Humanism and the *genera eloquentiae*." *Rhetorica*, 5, no. 3 (1987): 279-309.

Torti, Anna. "From 'History' to 'Tragedy': The Story of Troilus and Criseyde in Lydgate's *Troy Book* and Henryson's *Testament of Cresseid*." In *The European Tragedy of Troilus*. Ed. Piero Boitani. Oxford, 1989. Pp. 171-97.

Tout, T. F. "Literature and Learning in the English Civil Service in the Fourteenth Century." *Speculum*, 4 (1929): 365-89.

Toynbee, Paget. "The Bearing of the *Cursus* on the text of Dante's *De vulgari eloquentia.*" *Proceedings of the British Academy*, 10 (1923): 359-77.

Trimpi, Wesley. "The Quality of Fiction: The Rhetorical Transmission of Literary Theory," *Traditio*, 30 (1974): 1-118.

Tuve, Rosemond. *Allegorical Imagery*. Princeton, 1966.

Vickers, Brian. *In Defense of Rhetoric*. Oxford, 1988.

Waddell, Helm. *The Wandering Scholars*. New York, 1961.

Wagner, David, ed. *The Seven Liberal Arts in the Middle Ages*. Bloomington, 1983.

Waldron, Ronald A. "Oral-Formulaic Technique and Middle English Alliterative Poetry." *Speculum*, 32 (1957): 792-804.

Wallace, William A. "Aristotelian Science and Rhetoric in Transition: The Middle Ages and the Renaissance." *Rhetorica*, 7, no. 1 (1989): 7-21.

Ward, John O. "Magic and Rhetoric From Antiquity to the Renaissance: Some Ruminations." *Rhetorica*, 6, no. 1 (1988): 57-118.

Wasserman, Julian N. and Lois Roney, eds. *Sign, Sentence, Discourse*. Ithaca, 1989.

Watson, Roderick. *The Literature of Scotland*. New York, 1985.

Wenzel, Siegfried L. "Chaucer and the Language of Contemporary Preaching." *Studies in Philology*, 73 (1976): 138-61.

White, James Boyd. *Heracles' Bow: Essays on Rhetoric and the Poetrics of the Law*. Madison, WI, 1985.

White, T. H. *The Bestiary*. New York, 1954.

Whiting, B. J. "Proverbs and Proverbial Sayings from Scottish Writings before 1600." *Medieval Studies*, 11 (1949): 123-205; 13 (1951): 87-164.

Wieruszowski, Helene. "*Ars dictaminis* in the Time of Dante." *Medievalia et Humanistica*, 1 (1943): 95-108.

Willey, Basil. *The Seventeenth Century Background*. New York, 1934; rpt. 1953.

Willis, Roy. *Man and Beast*. London, 1974.

Wimsatt, James I. *Allegory and Mirror*. New York, 1970.

Witt, Ronald. "On Bene of Florence's Conception of the French and Roman *Cursus*." *Rhetorica*, 3, no. 2 (1985): 77-98.

Wittig, Kurt. *The Scottish Tradition in Literature*. Edinburgh, 1958.

Wood, H. Harvey. "Robert Henryson." In *Edinburgh Essays in English and Scots*. Ed. Adam J. Aitkin, Angus McIntosh, and Hermann Palsson. London, 1971. Pp. 177-209.

_____. "Robert Henryson." In *Two Scots Chaucerians*. London, 1967. Pp. 7-23.

Woods, Marjorie Curry, ed. and trans. *Early Commentary on the "Poetria Nova" of Geoffrey of Vinsauf*. New York, 1985.

Zeumer, Karl. *Formulae merowingici et Karolini aevi*. Monumenta Germaniae Historica, Legum V. Hanover, 1886.

INDEX